Table of Contents

P9-CQW-906

PART II Protecting Children's Rights

3 Children and the Civil Courts

4 Children and the Family Law

Child Protection and Canadian Law

A SERVICE PERSPECTIVE

Nora Rock, JD

2005
Emond Montgomery Publications
Toronto, Canada

Copyright © 2005 Emond Montgomery Publications Limited. All rights reserved. No part of this publication may be reproduced, stored in a retrieval system, or transmitted, in any form or by any means, photocopying, electronic, mechanical, recording, or otherwise, without the prior written permission of the copyright holder.

Printed in Canada.
Reprinted July 2011.

We acknowledge the financial support of the Government of Canada through the Canada Book Fund for our publishing activities.

The events and characters depicted in this book are fictitious. Any similarity to actual persons, living or dead, is purely coincidental.

Acquisitions editor
Peggy Buchan

Marketing manager
Christine Davidson

Director, sales and marketing, higher education
Kevin Smulan

Copy editor
Kate Hawkins

Production editor
Jim Lyons

Proofreader and indexer
David Handelsman

Cover designer
Susan Darrach, Darrach Design Inc.

Library and Archives Canada Cataloguing in Publication

Rock, Nora, 1968-
    Child protection and Canadian law : a service perspective / Nora Rock.

Includes index.
Includes text of Child and Family Services Act (Ontario).
ISBN 978-1-55239-124-2

    1. Children—Legal status, laws, etc.—Canada.   I. Ontario. Child and Family Services Act.   II. Title.

KE3515.R62 2005   344.7103'27   C2005-902642-1
KF3735.R62 2005

For my children, Jake and William

■PART III Protecting Children's Safety

7 Child Protection Under the Criminal Code

8 The Child and Family Services Act

9 Children in Residential Care

10 Special Issues

■APPENDIXES

Preface

Historically, the protection of children was a parental responsibility. Although the Canadian government has always made some provision for children in dire circumstances (usually orphans or the desperately poor), the emphasis in such cases was on Christian charity and the state's perceived duty to provide a minimum standard of living to children who would otherwise perish.

It was not until around the time of the Industrial Revolution, in Europe, that the notion of childhood as a vulnerable life stage began to emerge. Since that era, scientific research about childhood and the unique needs of children has influenced people's values with respect to how children ought to be treated.

Modern child development specialists can readily describe the physical, social, and learning environment that best supports healthy development. We now know that children need not only nutritious food and comfortable shelter, but also a plethora of other things: playtime, schooling, socialization, and affection, to name a few. Children need to interact not only with other children but also with adults; and the quality of these interactions can have a vital impact on their success as adults, and as parents in their own right. We know that children fare best when they are raised in a family-style rather than an institutional setting. We know that they need both close supervision and reasonable privacy, both clear limits and opportunities to learn from their own mistakes. And we know that individual children have individual needs.

We also know, as realists, that there is no such thing as a perfectly supportive environment. Canadian children are more likely than any other segment of the population to live in poverty: housing problems are a factor in 20 percent of residential placements. Children are raised by imperfect adults, many of whom are survivors of child abuse themselves, and many of whom suffer addictions, learning disabilities, mental illness, and personality disorders. Government resources available for improving the lot of children in need of protection are limited, and must be allocated according to greatest need.

This tension between the "ideal" child development environment and the challenges of the real world forms one-half of the backdrop for the work of Ontario's child protection workers. The other half is the legal framework that dictates how and when the government and its agents can (and often must) intervene to improve the lives of children whose environments have slipped too far below the standards acceptable in modern society. This book is designed to provide a thorough introduction to the legal context in which child protection workers must practice, without losing sight of the social context that makes up the other half of the picture. I hope that child protection workers will find it a useful reference as they work to support and protect our most precious social resource: children.

Nora Rock
April 2005

PART I

Introduction to Child Protection Law

1 Special Legal Status for Children and Youth

NOT JUST SHORT ADULTS

Society's view of children was once very different from what it is today. Most of us now understand childhood and adolescence to be life stages that are distinct from adulthood, and we generally accept the idea that children and youth are in need of special protection because they are more vulnerable than adults. However, these ideas have not always been considered self-evident. Like most other social concepts and values, they are the product of a slow evolution in thinking.

Until nearly the end of the 17th century, children moved straight from toddlerhood into adult society. Once a child was old enough to feed and dress herself, she was expected to begin contributing to the support and prosperity of the family and the community. Children as young as six or seven worked on farms, practised trades (sometimes as apprentices), and participated in commerce.

While people understood that a 7-year-old could, for example, carry less firewood in one load than a 27-year-old, society subjected them to the same general expectation: work as hard as you can for as long as it takes to get the job done. A child's work was not understood, as it often is today, as "doing her chores" or "helping his mom." Instead, the child was depended on as a full-status (if not always an equal) contributor to the family's survival.

Along with the early social integration of children went a related notion about competence. Because much of the work required to support a farming family was technically simple, children were able to master it before their physical and intellectual development was complete. And if the family were tradespeople — carpenters, for example — children were simply taught the trade in the same way an adult learner would be taught. A lack of proficiency in the early stages was attributed to inexperience, not to incomplete physical or intellectual development.

CHAPTER OBJECTIVES

After reading this chapter, you should be able to:

- Summarize the evolution of social and cultural views of childhood.

- Explain the concepts of age-based legal capacity, age of majority, and age-based lack of criminal responsibility.

- Explain the concepts of duty of care and fiduciary duty.

- List statutes and classes of legislation that grant protected status to, or impose special rules on, children and youth.

- Provide examples of the special treatment of children in the criminal law.

- Provide examples of statutes designed to protect the rights of children and youth.

Today, we realize that children must complete their development before they will be fully competent workers, and we adjust our expectations accordingly.

Around the turn of the 18th century, things began to change. New scholarly thinking and writing about psychosocial development introduced the idea that children and adolescents were less than full grown not only in the physical sense, but also in the emotional, intellectual, and moral senses. People began to understand that children behaved (or misbehaved) as they did not simply because of flaws in character, but also because their character and abilities were still developing.

The emergence of these ideas led to the increased segregation of children and adolescents on the one hand, and adults on the other. Upper-class children were kept in school longer than ever before. Working-class children, for the first time, were denied full access to jobs. This happened for three reasons. First, the technological leaps of the 18th century meant that many types of work were becoming more complicated, and longer and longer periods of apprenticeships were required to master the new skills and absorb the new knowledge. Second, as some kinds of work — such as manufacturing — became increasingly mechanized, the number of jobs decreased, and youth jobs were often eliminated first. Finally, as the dangers and health risks of factory and mining work began to become known, a social movement emerged with the goal of protecting children by limiting their access to dangerous work and long hours.

For the first time, working-class teenage children whose families could not afford schooling were shut out of the working world. Without a role to play in society, little to do, and no way to earn money, some of these children became involved in (usually petty) crime. With the rise of urban youth crime, the term "juvenile delinquent" was coined, and society began paying attention to the unique developmental stage that we now recognize as adolescence.

Over the course of the 18th and 19th centuries, society's perception of children and youth shifted. On the one hand, new ideas about child development led people to understand that the immaturity of children and youth made them vulnerable and worthy of protection. On the other, the new segregation of children from adults led to idleness and social problems, making people wary and mistrustful of "troublesome" teens.

■ SPECIAL STAGES, SPECIAL RULES

Before these shifts in the perception of childhood, the law typically applied to children and youth in the same ways it applied to adults. While a few legal rules — notably those relating to property ownership — suspended certain rights until adulthood, most laws designed to punish or protect the populace applied equally to children as to adults. The government held children of all ages responsible for the crimes they committed and provided children with the usual benefits of citizenship.

But as governments began to recognize the uniqueness of childhood and adolescence, things began to change. The idea of legal capacity evolved. **Legal capacity** is a concept that describes a person's ability to exercise legal rights and accept legal responsibilities. For example, in Canada today, a 12-year-old citizen lacks the legal capacity to vote, a legal right that other Canadian citizens enjoy. Historically, children were not the only group limited by the concept of legal capacity. Certain other categories of people were also excluded from the exercise of legal rights for various

legal capacity the ability of a person, based on his or her personal characteristics (for example, age of majority), to take actions with legal effects (for example, bring a lawsuit)

reasons. Women, for example, were often denied the right to own property and the right to vote in elections. People with cognitive deficits and those suffering from mental illness were judged incapable of making legal decisions for themselves. And children, once full participants in adult society, were deemed to lack legal capacity until they completed the physical, intellectual, emotional, and moral development that marked adulthood.

The notion that children and adults are different before the law endures today. While most governments have passed laws defining an **age of majority** — that is, an age at which children can exercise most legal rights — there are many exceptions that apply in different contexts. For example, while Ontario youth can vote from age 18 onward, they cannot buy alcohol until age 19. Three years earlier, however — at age 16 — they can choose to leave school, get a job, and marry with their parents' consent. The different ages at which various activities are permitted are to some degree historical, but in general they reflect society's ideas about the average maturation rates of children.

A principle closely related to legal capacity is **criminal responsibility**. As the **criminal law** has evolved, so too has the idea that not all people who commit criminal acts should bear the usual legal consequences of those acts. For example, the verdict of "not criminally responsible on account of mental disorder" is available in appropriate cases under section 672.34 of Canada's ***Criminal Code***. An appropriate case for such a verdict is one in which a person's exceptional mental state warrants absolution from criminal responsibility for otherwise criminal acts.

Eliminating criminal responsibility by establishing a mental disorder is a complicated legal affair. A much clearer bar to criminal responsibility is being underage. When it comes to crimes committed by children, section 13 of the *Criminal Code* succinctly provides:

> No person shall be convicted of an offence in respect of an act or omission on his part while that person was under the age of twelve years.

Twelve years is the age of criminal responsibility in Canada; however, youths aged 12 to 17 are treated differently from people aged 18 and over. Where a crime — as defined by the *Criminal Code* — is committed by a person aged 12 to 17, the prosecution of the matter is governed by the *Youth Criminal Justice Act*. This **statute**, enacted by the Parliament of Canada, creates a comprehensive system for the management of young offenders. The system that the Act establishes is discussed in chapter 6.

■ THE ROOTS OF LAW AS A TOOL FOR CHILD PROTECTION

As ideas about child development flourished and society began to view childhood as a vulnerable stage of life, people became increasingly interested in child protection.

Before the 18th century, protecting children was viewed as simply one facet of raising them and as being within the exclusive province of parents. While neglecting or harming children was often denounced as morally wrong, society generally gave parents broad authority over how children were provided for, supervised, and disciplined. In extreme cases of abusive treatment, a relative might intervene by taking a child into her own home, but the courts and the government were rarely involved.

age of majority the age at which a young person is given full adult rights or responsibilities with respect to a particular subject matter (the age varies depending on the subject matter)

criminal responsibility the condition of being liable to criminal sanctions because one has the capacity to understand the moral wrongness or illegality of one's actions

criminal law laws designed to prevent behaviour harmful to society by punishing those who demonstrate it and by deterring others who might contemplate it

Criminal Code the statute that describes the legislative component of Canada's criminal law

statute a written law passed by a parliament

CANADIAN LAW: UNDERSTANDING THE BIG PICTURE

Laws that touch on children's rights and the protection of children come from many different parts of the Canadian legal system: from the common law; from statutes passed by the federal, provincial, and municipal governments; and from regulations. The following is a guide to understanding how all of the various parts of Canada's system of laws fit together.

JUSTICE SYSTEM

The justice system is composed of law enforcement agencies, courts, and correctional facilities.

Law Enforcement Agencies

Some law enforcement agencies are controlled by the federal government (for example, the Royal Canadian Mounted Police [RCMP]); some are controlled by the provincial government (for example, the Ontario Provincial Police [OPP]); and some are controlled by regional or municipal governments (for example, the Durham (County) Regional Police). Not all three levels of government are involved in law enforcement in every part of the country. Certain types of laws are traditionally managed by particular levels of government. For example, drug and gun laws, which are created by the federal government, are often enforced by the RCMP. Traffic laws, which are created by the provincial government, tend to be enforced by provincial police forces.

Courts

The court system is made up of three general levels: provincial trial courts, including specialty courts, such as the Small Claims Court and Family Court; provincial courts of appeal; and the Supreme Court of Canada. (There is also a separate federal court system for dealing with some federal matters — for example, federal taxation.)

At the trial court level, criminal and non-criminal matters are typically dealt with in separate courts because the procedure is different.

Correctional Facilities

The third branch of the justice system is the corrections branch. Corrections facilities include penitentiaries, which are managed by the federal government, and provincial jails and prisons. In general, offenders who receive longer sentences because they have committed more serious crimes are sent to penitentiaries, while offenders who receive sentences of less than two years' duration serve their time in provincial facilities.

LEGAL SYSTEM

The justice system is the arena in which decision makers — judges and juries — enforce the laws that make up the legal system. The legal system operates on the basis of common law and statute law.

Common Law

The common law is a body of legal principles that has been established by judges through court decisions. It is also referred to as "case law." These decisions often deal with particular legal issues or subject areas that are not covered by statutes.

The common law has no single source or official code; it is an amalgamation of the written decisions of various judges over time. It has its own internal divisions — for example, tort law (the law of harms done by people to others) and contract law (the law of agreements made between people).

The common law "rules" that judges create in their decisions bind judges of subsequent cases through the principle of precedent. In the simplest terms, if a judge has created a common law rule that applies to a particular situation, another judge is not free to apply another rule to a substantially similar situation that arises in a future case.

Sometimes legislators incorporate common law precedents into statutes. In these cases, the rules that originated as common law evolve into statute law once they are codified by Parliament or a legislature.

Judges often use common law to interpret statutes. If a statute leaves a term — such as "weapon" — undefined or loosely defined, a judge can look through common law precedents to see whether other judges have defined the term. If they have, their definition may assist the judge in determining whether a broken beer bottle, for example, is a "weapon" in the circumstances of the case before him.

Statute Law

Statutes are written laws that are created by the federal Parliament or one of the provincial legislatures. They serve as codifications of various laws that govern particular areas of citizens' lives, such as rights and responsibilities within families. Statutes typically deal with subject matter that is reflected in their title — for example, the *Family Law Act*. Statutes are also known as "legislation," and municipal statutes are generally called "bylaws."

Canada is a federal country, which means that it is made up of a group of provincial governments existing within a larger national framework that is presided over by a federal government. The federal structure of Canada is described in the *Constitution Act, 1867*, a statute that was originally passed by the British Parliament. It established the terms for Canada's independence from Britain as well as Canada's federal structure.

The *Canadian Charter of Rights and Freedoms* now forms part of Canada's constitution. The Charter guarantees certain fundamental rights to Canadian residents. All laws and government actions must now conform to the requirements of the Charter. Any law or part of a law that violates the principles of the Charter can be declared unconstitutional, and thus rendered invalid, by a court.

Whether a statute is provincial or federal depends on its subject matter. Sections 91 and 92 of Canada's constitution create a framework that assigns certain subjects to either the federal or a provincial government.

For example, section 91(27) gives the federal government power to create criminal laws. The *Youth Criminal Justice Act* is an example of such a law.

Section 92(13) of the *Constitution Act, 1867* gives provincial governments the power to create laws that affect civil rights. The *Child and Family Services Act*, passed by Ontario, is an example of such an act.

jurisdictions areas over which the legal authority of a particular statute or court extends

Gradually, however, as the result of pressure from children's advocates — sometimes educators, clergy, or related organizations — the state began to set limits on the decision-making authority of parents.

In many **jurisdictions**, including Canada, the government's self-assigned authority over children's safety has steadily increased over the last several decades. Nowadays, if a child is at risk from parental harm, the decision to remove the child from the nuclear family is generally made not by extended family members or neighbours, but by government agencies. These agencies take responsibility for the care of children in need of protection.

The Role of Legislation

legislation law passed by a parliament and codified in writing

The government's modern child protection role is defined, in large part, by **legislation**. A wide range of statutes now include government-mandated parenting standards, and many statutes include penalties for failing to meet these standards. For example, section 3 of the Ontario *Immunization of School Pupils Act* requires that "[t]he parent of a pupil shall cause the pupil to complete the prescribed program of immunization in relation to each of the designated diseases," and section 4 of the Act imposes a fine on conviction for failure to comply.

PRESCRIPTIVE PARENTING STANDARDS

prescriptive standards standards that prescribe (require) specific action

Legislated parenting standards cover a wide range of topics. **Prescriptive standards** include those related to

- providing the necessities of life (*Criminal Code*, Ontario *Child and Family Services Act*);
- facilitating enrollment in public or approved private schools (Ontario *Education Act*);
- supervising young children (Ontario *Provincial Offences Act*, Ontario *Child and Family Services Act*);
- providing economic support from both parents, including the non-custodial parent, in the event of divorce or separation (Ontario *Family Law Act*);
- obtaining maternal medical care in childbirth (*Criminal Code*); and
- facilitating immunization and providing appropriate health care for sick and injured children (*Criminal Code*, Ontario *Immunization of School Pupils Act*).

However, governmental prescriptions for good parenting are not always free from controversy. Some parents object, for example, to compulsory school education, and must obtain special exemptions before homeschooling their children. Other parents support public schooling, but object to the compulsory immunization that is a condition of attendance.

It is useful to remember that the duties imposed on parents by governments reflect the subjective values of particular societies at particular times. In some countries, for example, legislation requires parents to support their children's participation in religious worship or practice. In Canada, a large proportion of citizens who happily accept public education would likely oppose prescribed religious observance.

As the government's child protection mandate has grown, opponents of particular laws have often sought to restrict state incursions into what was previously the decision-making territory of parents. In responding to this opposition, governments and courts have attempted to be mindful of the primary child-raising role of parents, and the enduring importance of the institution of the family. Courts have held that the state and its agents must reserve drastic measures (such as removal of children from the family home) for situations in which there is a clear need for protection. The judge in *Re Brown*, an Ontario County Court decision from the 1970s, offered the following comments:

> [T]he community ought not to interfere merely because our institutions may be able to offer a greater opportunity to the children to achieve their potential. Society's interference in the natural family is only justified when the level of care of the children falls below that which no child in this country should be subjected to.

PROSCRIPTIVE LIMITS AND PROHIBITIONS

Besides prescriptive standards, various statutes impose **proscriptive standards** that limit the authority of parents. Proscriptive legislation often applies not only to parents, but also to other adults that a child may encounter. For example:

proscriptive standards
standards that prohibit particular actions

- adults are prohibited from engaging in sexual activity with children (*Criminal Code*);

- adults are prohibited from facilitating or encouraging children to have sex with other adults, and from exploiting children through pornography (*Criminal Code*);

- adults are prohibited, in certain contexts, from exposing children to corrupting influences, such as sex, gambling, and violence (*Criminal Code*, Ontario *Theatres Act* (for movie ratings));

- adults are prohibited from selling or granting children access to dangerous goods, such as alcohol, tobacco, controlled substances, and weapons (*Criminal Code*, Canada *Controlled Drugs and Substances Act*, Canada *Firearms Act*, Ontario *Liquor Licence Act*);

- adults (and corporations) are prohibited from employing children of mandatory school attendance age during school hours, and underage children can be employed outside school hours only in limited contexts (*Canada Labour Code*, Ontario *Employment Standards Act*); and

- parents and other adults are prohibited from using corporal punishment as a means of disciplining children except in strictly limited circumstances (*Criminal Code*, Ontario *Child and Family Services Act*).

Again, proscriptive child protection rules can be controversial. For example, some groups in society support corporal punishment to a degree that is not permitted by existing law. Cultural and religious values also colour proscriptive rules. For example, male infant circumcision is currently legal in Canada and widely practised for both religious and secular reasons; however, female genital mutilation — a traditional practice in some cultures that is sometimes described as "female circumcision" — is illegal here.

Finally, many statutes that do not have a specific child protection purpose create special rules for children. These statutes recognize and incorporate either the concept of children's lack of legal capacity or the concept of children's vulnerability and need of protection. An example of a statute that recognizes age-based limits on legal capacity is the Ontario *Insurance Act*, which provides that a person 16 years or older is capable of making an insurance contract (the more commonly recognized age at which an adolescent can make a valid contract is 18). An example of a statute that recognizes the vulnerability of children is the Ontario *Highway Traffic Act*, which prohibits the issuance of drivers' licences to people under the age of 16.

Important examples of child protection legislation, such as the *Criminal Code*, the Ontario *Child and Family Services Act*, and the Ontario *Family Law Act* are discussed in detail in chapters 7, 8, and 4, respectively.

Child Protection in the Common Law

common law a legal rule or a body of legal principles, established through judicial decisions, that deal with a particular legal issue or subject area

Statutes are not the only source of legal rules for the protection of children. Another important source is the common law. The **common law** is a body of legal rules developed by many judges in deciding many cases over many years. Unlike a statute, the common law is not set out in a single code. Rather, it is found in the written decisions of many judges, which are published for public distribution.

Common law rules often predate the rules contained in statutes. If there is no statute to guide a judge, he must settle the legal problem before him on the basis of reason and his knowledge of the earlier decisions of other judges that make up the common law. His own resolution of the legal problem before him also becomes part of the common law.

Sometimes, but not always, the common law provides the basis of future statutory rules. For example, legal decisions in Ontario that interpreted the meaning of "spouse" to include same-sex spouses formed the basis for statutory recognition of the family law rights of same-sex spouses under the Ontario *Family Law Act*.

Common law rules can also exist in conjunction with statutory rules, providing guidelines and limits for their interpretation. For example, there is a statutory rule in section 88 of the *Criminal Code* that prohibits the possession of a weapon for a dangerous purpose. But what is a weapon? A loaded gun certainly qualifies, but what about a broken beer bottle? In deciding the matter, a judge examines common law rules related to the scope of the term "weapon" and then determines that, in appropriate factual circumstances, a "weapon" under section 88 of the *Criminal Code* can include a broken beer bottle. The judge's ultimate decision as to whether the person before him has been in possession of a weapon for a dangerous purpose is therefore informed both by statute and by the common law.

DUTY OF CARE

duty of care in negligence law, an obligation on the part of one person to take into account the effect of his or her actions on another person. The duty usually arises based on a recognized relationship

negligence the failure of a person to respect or carry out a duty of care owed to another

There are many common law rules that relate to children. One common law concept with special importance in the context of child protection is the duty of care.

The **duty of care** applies in many different areas of the law, but especially in the law of **negligence**. Negligence law assigns legal responsibility and liability to people who cause harm to others or who allow harm to come to others, whether or not they mean to do so. Legal responsibility for the safety of others increases when the person who causes or allows the harm owes a duty of care to the person harmed. If, for example, a daycare worker leaves a child unattended beside a wading pool, the worker is negligent if the child drowns, because he has breached his duty of care to the child. By contrast, if a passerby fails to notice that a child is unsupervised beside a pool and the child drowns, he is arguably not negligent since he owes no duty of care to the child.

Because we consider children to be vulnerable members of society, the law recognizes well-defined duties of care toward children. For example, adults have historically been held responsible for protecting children in situations where they might not necessarily be expected to protect other adults. Many of these situations are now governed by statute. For example, under the *Child and Family Services Act*, teachers are required to report signs of child abuse to the authorities, but they have no duty to report, for example, suspicious injuries suffered by a child's mother that they observed at pickup time.

FIDUCIARY DUTY

A related concept is that of **fiduciary duty**. Some relationships — including that of parent and child — involve an element of special trust and dependency. The trust is created because one person depends on the other for protection or guidance. As a result of the relationship, the dependent person may be particularly susceptible to any wrongdoing or negligence on the part of the other person. The other person, who is known as a fiduciary, is therefore charged with a fiduciary duty of care toward the dependent person. Fiduciary duty is discussed in detail in chapter 2.

The concepts of duty of care and fiduciary duty underpin all facets of child protection law. They are the basis of many statutory rules, and they guide the interpretation and application of statute law. Finally, when a novel legal issue appears — when there is no statutory answer to a particular question — the principles of duty of care and fiduciary duty serve as enduring touchstones for the courts.

fiduciary duty an enhanced duty of care that arises in a fiduciary relationship

KEY TERMS

age of majority	jurisdictions
common law	legal capacity
criminal law	legislation
criminal responsibility	negligence
Criminal Code	prescriptive standards
duty of care	proscriptive standards
fiduciary duty	statute

REFERENCES

Brown, Re. (1975), 21 RFL 315; 9 OR (2d) 185 (Ont. Co. Ct.).

Criminal Code. RSC 1985, c. C-46, as amended.

Immunization of School Pupils Act. RSO 1990, c. I.1.

REVIEW QUESTIONS

1. Which social and economic forces played a role in the segregation of children and adults that marked the 19th century?

2. Did the recognition of childhood and adolescence as distinct developmental stages diminish the legal rights of children? If so, how? In what ways did it enhance children's rights?

3. Describe three different kinds of statutes that treat children differently from adults.

4. List three prescriptive child protection rules. List three proscriptive child protection rules.

5. Who, apart from parents, protected children before the government became involved?

6. How does the common law affect statute law?

7. What is a duty of care? What is a fiduciary duty?

DISCUSSION QUESTIONS

1. Did you realize, before reading this chapter, how recently governments became involved in child protection? Do you think that protecting children, sometimes from the actions of their parents, is an appropriate role for government? Why or why not?

2. Many child protection issues that were originally the subject of common law rules have been incorporated into statutes. Why do you think this has happened?

3. Legal action is a common reaction to child abuse or neglect. Is law the best tool for preventing or redressing harm to children? What are its drawbacks? What non-legal strategies are available to society?

2 Adults With Special Child Protection Responsibility

CHILD WELFARE AND PROTECTION: WHOSE BUSINESS IS IT?

Parents

As natural and original caregivers, parents have almost always been seen as having primary responsibility for the welfare and protection of their children. Canadian law recognizes the unique status of parents in this regard. Many laws made for the benefit of children (for example, the *Immunization of School Pupils Act*) require *parental* compliance, emphasizing the principle of parental responsibility; and there are many legal offences directed at parental dereliction of duty.

Other Adults

Parents, however, are not the only adults in society who care for children. School-age children spend nearly half their waking hours in the education system, where they are under the care of teachers, principals, bus drivers, school counsellors, and other education professionals. Younger children may spend time in daycare or nursery school.

Other adults who have more occasional care of children provide services that imply a measure of protection and guidance. Most children are, at least occasionally, in the care of doctors and/ or therapists; others receive guidance and teaching from religious practitioners; and yet others have contact with public authorities, such as police.

Because of the inherent vulnerability of children, society considers it important that the non-parental adults in a child's life be held to a higher-than-usual interpersonal standard of care. This special standard helps parents entrust their children into the care of these other adults, and protects children from the people

CHAPTER OBJECTIVES

After reading this chapter,
you should be able to:

- Explain the concept of fiduciary duty.

- Describe the legal responsibilities owed by parents to their minor children.

- Explain how the common law gives certain non-parent adults special responsibility for the welfare of children.

- List at least three statutes that impose responsibility on adults for the protection of children.

- Describe at least three classes of professionals who have a special responsibility toward children in their care.

- Describe the consequences, under common law and statute, for failing to live up to a special responsibility to protect a child.

closest to them. This protection is important, because child welfare research has consistently shown that children are at greatest risk of harm not from strangers, but from familiar adults on whom they depend. And from a more positive perspective, adults who are closest to children are best placed to protect them; so it makes sense to make these adults accountable as protectors.

Fiduciary Duty Revisited

As noted in chapter 1, the common law ascribes an enhanced duty of care, called a fiduciary duty, to adults with whom children share a relationship of trust and dependence. The theory behind this duty suggests that trust and dependence increase the vulnerability of the dependent child, thereby exposing him to a risk of unusually serious harm if the trust is betrayed.

fiduciary somebody who is entrusted with the care of another person based on a relationship of service and/or dependence

standard of care the standard by which discharge of a duty of care is measured, which depends on the relationship between the parties and the circumstances under which the duty arises

guardian a person who, though not the parent of a child, has assumed or is charged with responsibility for his or her care

question of fact something that can only be determined by the court after an examination of the specific circumstances of the case

The adult's special status as a **fiduciary** means that he or she owes an unusually high **standard of care** to the child. A fiduciary must be especially careful to avoid harming a child, and may be held legally responsible for lapses in care that would not ordinarily attract legal liability.

Every parent who is also a legal **guardian** of a child under the age of majority owes a fiduciary duty to that child. Certain other non-parental adults may owe a fiduciary duty to children with whom they are in contact when a relationship of special trust and/or dependence exists. For example, the live-in boyfriend of a single mother who becomes emotionally close to her children and shares in their care will typically be found to owe a fiduciary duty to those children.

Some statutes impose specific fiduciary duties on particular adults. For example, the *Day Nurseries Act*, which governs most daycare centres and day camps, imposes such duties on workers. However, not all fiduciary relationships are created by statute. Whether or not an adult is in a fiduciary relationship with a child can be a **question of fact** that is determined by a court on the basis of the circumstances of the relationship. For example, to return to the example of the live-in boyfriend, if the boyfriend does shiftwork and is asleep when the children are home such that he has little or no responsibility for their care and no relationship with them, a court may not find that he has a fiduciary relationship with them.

Legislated Duties

Both the courts and society have consistently viewed certain kinds of adult–child relationships as leading to special protection responsibilities. These relationships include teacher–student, physician–patient, and religious leader–child. In many cases, the responsibilities created by these relationships have been codified and clarified by statute.

An adult who fails to discharge the child protection responsibilities that a statute has imposed must often face legal consequences. These consequences can include being charged with an offence, having a licence (such as a daycare operator's licence) suspended, or being prohibited from future contact with the affected child and/or other children. The specifics of these statutory duties and the consequences of non-compliance with them are discussed in future chapters.

■CLASSES OF INDIVIDUALS WITH SPECIAL RESPONSIBILITIES

Parents and Other Private Guardians

PARENTS

Biological and adoptive parents are the adults with primary responsibility for child welfare and protection in our society.

The law assumes that children are dependent on adults for at least some of the necessities of life until they reach the age of majority. In Canada, children cannot legally withdraw from the care of their parents until they reach the age of 16. A parent who refuses to shelter or care for a child under 16 may be found guilty of child neglect under the *Child and Family Services Act*. If the child is under 10 years of age, the parent may be found guilty of child abandonment under section 218 of the *Criminal Code*.

Section 215 of the *Criminal Code* requires parents of children under the age of 16 to provide them with the **necessaries of life**. Courts have decided that necessaries include food, acceptable shelter, and necessary medical treatment.

Statutes other than the criminal law add other responsibilities to this list. For example, as mentioned above, the *Child and Family Services Act* requires that parents provide appropriate care, supervision, and protection for children under the age of 16. The *Education Act* requires that parents enroll their children in school and ensure their attendance. The *Family Law Act* requires that both parents contribute to the economic support of their children.

necessaries of life
under the criminal law, a fairly narrowly defined list including food, shelter, clothing, and necessary medical treatment

---

ASIDE

CANADIAN FAMILIES: A NUCLEAR VIEW

In Canada, the legal responsibility for providing basic care and protection is ascribed to parents, and not to a child's extended family or community. This legal principle reflects the parenting practices of the majority of, but not all, Canadians. Most Canadian children now live with and are raised by their nuclear families: one or two parents and siblings, if any. However, in earlier times (and in current times in some cultures), an extended family household was more common. In an extended family, a child may have not only his parents but also his grandparents and/or aunts and uncles or other relatives living with him, all under the same roof. Some extended one-household families believe that all resident adults share primary responsibility for the basic care of all the resident children.

Some cultures even ascribe responsibility for children to an entire closely knit community. Better known examples of this form of child raising include some traditional First Nations cultures and Jewish kibbutz communities. For true extended families and for groups that practise communal parenting, the notion of limiting legal child protection responsibility to parents may seem somewhat foreign. It does, however, reflect the family experience of the majority of Canadian children.

PRIVATE GUARDIANS

private guardian
an individual who has
assumed responsibility for
a child (as distinguished
from an agent of the
province)

In some cases, a child may not live with her parents, but rather with a **private guardian** — that is, a person who is not part of the child protection system. The guardianship relationship may be either formal (court-ordered) or informal. For example, a formally appointed legal guardian may be a person to whom a court has granted custody of a child after the death of her parents, while an informal guardian may be a person, a grandparent or aunt, perhaps, whom the parents have simply asked to care for the child while they are away — for example, out of the country or in an inpatient treatment facility.

In undertaking guardianship of a child that is not his own, a guardian usually assumes the legal responsibilities of a parent. (A legal guardian often also requires rights in addition to responsibilities — for example, access to health information, or the right to make decisions about the child's education.)

in loco parentis Latin for
"in place of a parent"

A court may find that a particular adult has parental/guardian responsibilities for a child even if that adult has not consciously assumed guardianship. If an adult treats a child in the way that a parent normally does, and if the child responds to and depends on the adult in a manner usually reserved for parents, a court may find that the adult is *in loco parentis*. This means that the adult stands in the place of a parent with respect to that child. Where there is an *in loco parentis* relationship, the adult may be legally obliged to meet the standard of care usually reserved for a parent. *In loco parentis* relationships commonly arise when a new partner moves in with a child's single parent and participates in the child's care and upbringing.

in need of protection
in the context of child
protection, a court's
finding that action must be
taken to protect a child

The failure of a parent, guardian, or person who stands *in loco parentis* to carry out his responsibilities toward a child can result in a criminal charge. More commonly, however, it can lead to child protection proceedings under the *Child and Family Services Act.* These proceedings are based on evidence that the neglected or abused child is **in need of protection**. If such a finding is made, the child may be removed from the care of the parent, guardian, or person *in loco parentis*.

Guardians in the Child Protection System

A child who lives with neither a parent nor a private guardian is almost always in the care of the public child protection system. Following child protection proceedings, if a court decides that a child should be removed from her parents' care, she may be made a ward either of a child protection agency (children's aid society) or of the Crown (the government). The responsibilities associated with wardship are extensively covered by statutes and regulations, most importantly the *Child and Family Services Act.* Wardship is discussed in greater detail in chapters 8 and 9.

Education System Personnel

Because children spend many of their waking hours in school, school personnel have many special responsibilities for child safety under the Ontario *Education Act* (and other statutes, such as the Ontario *Building Code*). Schools are responsible for the safety of children on their premises during the school day. This responsibility requires measures such as maintaining school buildings and property in safe condition, monitoring systems such as water quality and ventilation, providing safe transportation to and from school, and planning for emergencies, such as fires and bomb threats.

School personnel are also responsible for protecting children against interpersonal threats. For example, school boards must carefully screen teachers, counsellors, and other individuals who will have contact with children to guard against the risk of violence or other abuse. Schools must also monitor and control situations such as bullying and fighting to prevent the risk of children harming each other. The Ontario Ministry of Health, under the *Health Protection and Promotion Act*, requires that schools take measures to contain outbreaks of disease by requiring proof of immunization, reporting outbreaks, and taking steps to prevent the transmission of communicable diseases within the school population.

In addition to their responsibilities with respect to in-school safety, educators have an additional child protection role in the form of a duty to report child abuse or neglect. Under the *Child and Family Services Act*, teachers, principals, counsellors, and school nurses are required to report signs of child abuse and/or neglect to a children's aid society. While this duty extends to all members of the public, the reporting duties of school personnel are backed up by penalties under the *Child and Family Services Act* for failure to report.

The child protection role of educators is covered in greater detail in chapter 5.

Daycare and Recreational Program Workers

Other adults charged with the regular care of children include daycare workers and recreation program personnel. These individuals and the organizations that employ them are subject to regulation under legislation such as the Ontario *Day Nurseries Act* and under operating licences that set standards for their work. Failure on the part of employees and organizations to meet these standards can lead to the suspension of an organization's licence. Harm to children that results from a serious dereliction of duty can form the basis of lawsuits brought by parents and guardians against employees and organizations.

Daycare and recreation workers are under an **enhanced duty to report** child abuse or neglect. This means that failure to report can, for these individuals, lead to their being charged under the *Child and Family Services Act.*

enhanced duty to report
a duty to report that, if ignored, can lead to the laying of charges

Health Care Personnel

Most children have at least periodic contact with doctors, nurses, dentists, and other members of the health care system, and members of this system often treat children who have suffered abuse-related injuries. The relationship between health professionals and their patients has long been recognized as a special one — a fiduciary one — that gives rise to particular duties.

Because treating children provides an opportunity to observe signs of abuse and neglect, health care personnel are required, under the *Child and Family Services Act*, to report suspicious findings to a children's aid society. Failure to report is an offence under the Act, and law enforcement personnel have proven their willingness to lay charges against offending health care workers.

Social Workers

The duties of workers who care for children who are under the formal protection of the state are well defined. Well-defined duties of care also extend to children who are not yet, and may never be, under this formal protection.

Section 72(1) of the *Child and Family Services Act* presents a detailed definition of the circumstances that create a duty to report child abuse or neglect. Many of the circumstances described in this section prompt investigation and intervention by social workers. Social workers may also come into contact with children indirectly — for example, in the course of working with another member of a child's family.

Regardless of the circumstances that bring a child to the attention of a social worker, the social worker has a duty to report any observation that suggests that the child has been subjected to, or is at risk of being subjected to, abuse or neglect. A social worker's failure to report suspicious observations can constitute an offence under section 72(5) of the *Child and Family Services Act*. In addition, if a child is harmed as a result of a dereliction of duty, the state may lay a criminal charge, or an injured party may institute a lawsuit, against the offending social worker.

CASE IN POINT

SOCIAL WORKER CHARGED WITH CRIMINAL NEGLIGENCE

In 1997, Angie Martin, a social worker with the Catholic Children's Aid Society of Toronto, was charged with criminal negligence causing death, in contravention of section 220 of the *Criminal Code*. A person found guilty of this offence can be sentenced to a maximum penalty of imprisonment for life.

Ms. Martin was assigned to monitor the case of Jordan Heikamp, an infant born on May 18, 1997 to a 19-year-old homeless woman. Jordan was released from hospital into his mother's care on May 29. By June 23, he was dead. An autopsy showed that he had died of starvation while living with his mother at a shelter for abused women.

preliminary inquiry
a judicial hearing where the prosecution must prove that it has enough evidence to prove, if uncontested and accepted by the trier of fact, that the accused is guilty of the charges against him or her; also called a charge screening device

coroner's inquest a court-like hearing, conducted by the coroner's office, designed to investigate a suspicious death and, often, to provide recommendations for avoiding similar incidents in the future

During the **preliminary inquiry** into the charges against Ms. Martin, evidence was presented about mistakes made by the social worker in monitoring the case. The evidence showed that the baby's mother had lied to the social worker about taking the baby to the doctor, and about the baby's weight gain. It also showed that Ms. Martin had relied on this misinformation in assuming that Jordan was receiving appropriate care. Nevertheless, the court found that this and other mistakes on the social worker's part were insufficient to support the charge under section 220 of the *Criminal Code*. The presiding judge found that Ms. Martin's work fell within the accepted standard of care for children's aid workers. Ms. Martin had not shown a wanton disregard for Jordan's life, and she had not directly contributed to his starvation. The state dropped the charge against the social worker.

A subsequent **coroner's inquest** into the case was very critical of the Catholic Children's Aid Society and Ms. Martin. The social worker endured substantial adverse publicity in the wake of the baby's death. While she escaped a penalty under the criminal law, Ms. Martin did not escape the impact of the baby's death, both from a personal and from a career perspective.

Child welfare experts suggest that social workers who perform their duties in good faith and to the best of their abilities within the standards of their profession can generally expect to be free from legal liability (Kanani et al., 2002, pp. 1029–43). However, the prosecution of Ms. Martin under the criminal law proves that law enforcement personnel will respond to the human cost of mistakes, and to the public outrage that follows the death of a child under agency supervision.

Counsellors, Religious Leaders, Lawyers, and Police

Other individuals who may have a special duty of care toward children include counsellors, religious professionals, lawyers, peace officers, and coroners. These professionals are named in section 72(5) of the *Child and Family Services Act* as being accountable, and subject to fines, for failing to report observations that are suggestive of child abuse and neglect.

From a broader perspective, however, all adults — and especially all service professionals — who develop a relationship with a child that places them in a position to observe signs of abuse or neglect should be mindful of the need to report suspicious observations to a children's aid society. Adults who interact with children on a regular basis should be alert at least to the more common signs of abuse, which can include physical injuries, changes in behaviour, and unusual conduct.

KEY TERMS

coroner's inquest

enhanced duty to report

fiduciary

guardian

in loco parentis

in need of protection

necessaries of life

preliminary inquiry

private guardian

question of fact

standard of care

REFERENCES

Child and Family Services Act. RSO 1990, c. C.11.

Criminal Code. RSC 1985, c. C-46, as amended.

Heikamp and Martin, R v. (December 3, 1999). Judgment at preliminary inquiry in the Ontario Court of Justice.

Kanani, Karima, Cheryl Regehr, and Marvin M. Bernstein. (2002). Liability considerations in child welfare: Lessons from Canada. *Child Abuse & Neglect, 26,* 1029–43.

REVIEW QUESTIONS

1. Why are parents primarily responsible for the welfare and protection of their children?

2. What does the criminal law require parents to provide for their children?

3. What is a fiduciary duty? Who decides who has a fiduciary relationship with a child?

4. List four statutes that impose child welfare or protection duties on non-parents.

5. List five classes of professionals who are subject to an enhanced duty to report child abuse or neglect.

6. Describe three different kinds of legal penalties that a person may suffer for failing to report observations that suggest child abuse or neglect.

DISCUSSION QUESTIONS

1. A professional who owes an enhanced duty to report child abuse or neglect may also have responsibilities to an abusive or neglectful parent. Consider, for example, a person who is offering counselling to an entire family, or a family's priest, rabbi, or imam. What problems does this present for the professional, and how might the professional overcome these problems?

2. In many common circumstances, our law requires an adult to participate in protecting a particular child whether or not the adult has expressed an intention or a desire to be responsible for that child.

   a. Name two circumstances in which an adult may have a fiduciary duty toward a child without knowing it.

   b. Explain why the law does not require that an adult express an intention to be responsible for a child in order to be charged with the child's protection.

   c. Defend or challenge this aspect of the law, and prepare arguments in support of your position.

3. While a child's adult relatives are arguably in an ideal position to observe and report child abuse or neglect, they are not listed in section 72(5) of the *Child and Family Services Act* as being under an enhanced duty to report their observations. Why? Do you think they should be listed?

PART II

Protecting Children's Rights

3 Children and the Civil Courts

■ INTRODUCTION: COURTS AND TRIBUNALS

The civil (non-criminal) court system provides a forum in which a person who has suffered an injury or a loss at the hands of another can seek legal redress. A civil **lawsuit** is essentially a request, made to a court (judge), for a court-ordered remedy that can be enforced against whoever caused the injury or loss. The most common remedy is **damages**, a monetary sum that is intended to represent the economic value of the loss or injury suffered.

There are remedies other than damages available through the civil courts. One of these is **restitution**, in which a court orders someone who has taken something away from a plaintiff to give it back to her. For example, if a guardian wrongly sells real estate instead of holding it in trust for a child until she reaches the age of majority, a court may cancel the sale and order that the property be given back to the child in restitution.

Besides deciding lawsuits, civil courts can also enforce statutes and legal documents, as well as hear appeals from the decisions of other courts or tribunals. As examples, consider the following:

- *Statutes.* Family courts, which are branches of the civil court system, can enforce statutes. They apply the provisions of the *Family Law Act*, which governs matters such as custody and child support, to specific family situations.

- *Legal documents.* Probate courts, which are also part of the civil court system, interpret and enforce the provisions of wills.

- Decisions of courts or tribunals. Some civil courts hear appeals from decisions of other civil courts that are lower than they are in the legal hierarchy. For example, decisions of the Ontario Superior Court of Justice can be appealed to the Ontario Court of Appeal. Others review

CHAPTER OBJECTIVES

After reading this chapter, you should be able to:

- Understand the concepts of legal capacity and standing.

- Describe the role of a litigation guardian.

- List three kinds of lawsuits that children may bring.

- Describe the role of the Children's Lawyer.

lawsuit a formal request, by one party, for the court's assistance in obtaining, through its processes, compensation or relief as against another party

damages monetary compensation for a legal wrong

restitution the act of putting someone back into the (usually economic) position that he or she enjoyed before a culpable event intervened

administrative tribunal
a decision maker or panel of decision makers who decide contentious issues that arise within a particular administrative framework—for example, the Ontario Labour Relations Board

the decisions of administrative tribunals. An **administrative tribunal** is a panel of decision makers who make decisions about disputes that are with a particular administrative system — for example, the Ontario Labour Relations Board. For example, section 202 of the *Child and Family Services Act* provides that a facility that has been denied a licence to operate a children's residence can appeal a decision of the Licence Appeal Tribunal to the Ontario Divisional Court.

AN EXAMPLE

DAMAGES IN A CIVIL LAWSUIT

Before being hit by Sylvie's car, 12-year-old Sanjit was a promising dancer who attended Canada's National Ballet School. Sanjit's accident resulted in injuries that caused him four months of pain and suffering. The injuries led to medical costs that were not covered by public health insurance. This forced Sanjit's parents to pay for a private tutor while he was in hospital. Although Sanjit will walk again, irreversible damage to his knee means that he will be unable to pursue a career as a professional ballet dancer.

In bringing a lawsuit against Sylvie, Sanjit might sue for the following damages:

- $14,000 for medical expenses, physiotherapy, and psychological counselling;

- $5,000 for the tutor;

- $40,000 for pain and suffering; and

- $225,000 for loss of future income, based on the following calculation: the $25,000 yearly difference between a professional ballet dancer's salary and a ballet teacher's salary for 18 years (a typical career length for a ballet dancer) multiplied by 50 percent (a number reflecting the probability, as predicted by expert witnesses, that Sanjit would have become a professional ballet dancer).

Sanjit's damages therefore total $284,000. (This amount is provided for illustration purposes only and does not take into account the need to express future losses in future dollars, and to make provision for inflation and salary growth.)

■CHILD PLAINTIFFS AND APPLICANTS: CAPACITY AND STANDING

plaintiff a person who commences a lawsuit

applicant a person who files an application for legal relief with a court or an administrative tribunal

standing the status of being recognized by a court as a legitimate party to a legal proceeding

A **plaintiff** is a person who brings a lawsuit. An adult plaintiff who has suffered a loss or an injury can bring a lawsuit on his own behalf. An **applicant** is a person who applies for an order, either of a court or of an administrative tribunal. If a plaintiff or applicant is a child, however, there are complications that relate to issues of standing and legal capacity.

Standing is a concept that describes a person's right to appear before a court or tribunal. Rules governing procedure in the civil courts dictate who can (and who cannot) bring a lawsuit. In Canada, children under the age of majority do not have standing before most courts and tribunals. While children *do* have legal rights, these rights must be enforced by adults. A child who wants to take legal action but who lacks standing must be represented either by a litigation guardian or by the Children's Lawyer. Both of these options are discussed below.

Legal capacity, which was touched on in chapter 1, is a concept that describes the ability of children to act in ways that are legally enforceable. For example, in most cases, young children lack the legal capacity to enter into contracts, sign leases, get married, or own property in their own names. The age of legal capacity varies in accordance with the legal activity that the child wishes to perform. Legal capacity is an issue separate from standing. For example, a 16-year-old may be legally capable of signing a valid lease, but may not have standing to enforce her rights as an applicant before the administrative tribunal that settles disputes between landlords and tenants.

In general, children who want to enter into legal transactions but who lack the legal capacity to do so must act through adults. For example, a child who inherits real estate usually must have the property held for him by an adult in trust until he comes of age.

CHILD DEFENDANTS

A child is sometimes required to participate in a civil case as a **defendant** — the person who is being sued. Children are less likely to find themselves in the role of defendant than plaintiff because of two important practical limits on lawsuits against children. First, children rarely have enough money of their own to pay the damages claimed by plaintiffs. Second, the law presumes that young children lack the intention to cause harm, an element that is essential to many lawsuits that arise as a result of injuries sustained by people or property.

There is a legal presumption that **children of tender years** — usually those under the age of 6 or 7 — and children with delays in mental development cannot intend to cause harm. The presumption is almost absolute and is rarely challenged. The presumptions that children between the ages of 7 and 12 cannot tell right from wrong, foresee harm, or intend harm are, however, open to challenge by a plaintiff with sufficient evidence. For example, a 10-year-old child who brags about his plan to burn down a neighbour's garage, or who carefully conceals the fact that he set an accidental fire might be ordered to pay damages to the plaintiff neighbour. However, a child of the same age who runs tearfully from a blazing garage into the neighbour's arms would be difficult to sue.

Child defendants, like child plaintiffs, must be represented before the court by litigation guardians or the Children's Lawyer.

LITIGATION GUARDIANS

Litigation is a general term that describes proceedings in courts. A **litigation guardian** is an adult who agrees to pursue or defend a lawsuit on behalf of a child. In many cases, that person is the child's parent. However, another adult can act as the child's litigation guardian if the parent is unavailable or unwilling to do so, or if the parent is herself the defendant.

defendant the accused in a criminal case; or, in a civil case, the person against whom a lawsuit is filed

children of tender years children whose limited development makes them incapable of intending harm in the legal sense, or who require a particular level of, often maternal, care

litigation legal action, usually with a court component—for example, a lawsuit

litigation guardian a person with legal capacity who pursues legal relief on behalf of a person who lacks legal capacity

affidavit a witness's written and sworn account of his or her own evidence. Sworn means the witness has promised, before a person who has taken the account, that the contents are true

The conditions governing the appointment of litigation guardians are found in rule 7.03 of the Ontario *Rules of Civil Procedure.* A person who wishes to act as a litigation guardian must prepare an **affidavit** (a sworn legal statement) that reveals information about himself and the child, including information about whether he stands to gain or lose as a result of the lawsuit. A person with a personal stake in the outcome of a lawsuit cannot act as a litigation guardian.

Once a lawsuit is under way, the person who wants to be a litigation guardian must apply to the court to appoint him to that role. In a case in which the defendant is a child, the plaintiff may need to apply to the court to appoint a litigation guardian if no one voluntarily comes forward on behalf of the child. In these cases, the court decides who is to be the litigation guardian. It often appoints the Children's Lawyer to perform this role.

costs the granting by a court, as a form of legal relief, of a sum, payable by one litigant (usually the unsuccessful one) to the other, to pay for (some) of the costs of the litigation

A litigation guardian must personally pay whatever costs a court awards against a child if the child cannot afford to pay these costs herself. **Costs** are not damages; rather, they are an amount formally determined by the court that is intended to cover part of the expense of bringing or defending the lawsuit.

THE CHILDREN'S LAWYER

The notion of having a court- or government-provided lawyer for children in Ontario dates back to 1826, when the government appointed a private lawyer to serve as guardian *ad litem* (for the lawsuit) for children who needed legal representation. This role is now filled by the **Children's Lawyer**, an office within the Ontario Ministry of the Attorney General. While an individual lawyer holds this titled position, she (currently Clare E. Burns) is supported by a staff that includes other lawyers who appear in court on behalf of the office's child clients.

Children's Lawyer a government office, headed by an individual lawyer, which provides legal assistance to unrepresented child litigants in certain kinds of cases or by order of a court

The Children's Lawyer represents children in a range of matters:

- property rights cases, such as disputes involving wills, trusts, and real estate;

- civil lawsuits, typically involving personal injuries;

- family law cases, such as custody and access disputes where the court thinks it is necessary for the child to have a lawyer (usually only the parents have lawyers); and

- child protection cases in which the court decides that it is necessary for the child to have a lawyer who is independent of those who represent the child's parents and/or a child protection agency.

CHILDREN'S LITIGATION

The following sections explore the most common types of litigation initiated by children. Litigation may also be initiated by others but involve children as defendants or other parties.

YOU DECIDE!

THE CHILDREN'S LAWYER

Ben, an 11-year-old, became a ward of a children's aid society and was placed in foster care when he was 8. At that time, his parents were still married, but his father was in prison, and his mother had been hospitalized for the third time for overdosing on pain medication. Because Ben's mother refused to enter a drug treatment program after being released from hospital, Ben, who had a history of being left alone in the family home, was kept in foster care.

About six months ago, Ben's father Chris, now out of prison and reportedly reformed, began writing letters to Ben in which he asked Ben to agree to see him. Chris began an application for access to Ben under section 58 of the *Child and Family Services Act*. The children's aid society decided, early in the proceedings, to oppose Chris's request for access to Ben.

When Chris began the application process, Ben told the society that he did not want visits from his father. However, recently he has changed his mind after corresponding with Chris for some time. In an interview with the judge, Ben expressed his desire that the access application succeed.

Questions

1. Should the court order that the Children's Lawyer represent Ben? Why or why not?

2. Given Ben's current views, what position is the Children's Lawyer likely to take on the application?

3. If Chris wants access and the society does not want him to have it, the court will hear arguments on both sides of the issue. Why would the court need or want a third point of view?

4. Would your answers to the above questions change if Ben were 6 years old instead of 11?

Personal Injury Cases

In personal injury litigation, a person brings a lawsuit against another for damages relating to intentional harm or negligence. (The example above about Sanjit, the ballet dancer, involves personal injury litigation.) In many cases, a lawsuit is the only means by which an injured child can obtain compensation for personal injuries that may have a lasting impact on her life. In cases of debilitating injury, failure to obtain compensation may mean that the disabled child will be unable to support herself (and pay for her own care) in the future. Because the law requires that personal injury litigation be brought in a timely manner, injured children must sue those who have harmed them as soon as possible, usually through litigation guardians.

A subclass of personal injury litigation involves lawsuits by children against people who have physically or sexually abused them. Because of the often secretive nature of these injuries, and the reluctance of children to report them, special rules apply with respect to the timing of litigation. These rules allow adults, in some cases, to sue their abusers for compensation in relation to abuse perpetrated upon them during childhood.

Property and Estate Cases

trustee a person who holds property in trust for another

Property-based litigation by children is less common than personal injury litigation, because children's property is typically managed by adult trustees. A **trustee** is a person who holds (owns) and administers property for another person under the terms of a trust, which is a legal arrangement. However, circumstances sometimes force children to become involved in property-based litigation. If, for example, a child believes that the trustee of his property has made a bad or negligent decision or has taken an action with regard to the property that is harmful to his interests, the child may need to bring his case before the courts.

Children also may be required to participate in estate or will litigation where there is a dispute over the inheritance of particular assets or property such as land or houses. Cases of this nature that affect the interests of children are generally handled by the Children's Lawyer.

Contract Cases

Children do not normally have the legal capacity to enter into contracts, so it is unusual for children to bring contract-based litigation. However, there is an exception to the legal capacity rules that allows children to enter into valid contracts for the necessities of life. This exception has led to some limited contract litigation by children, generally through a litigation guardian.

Children Suing Their Parents

A difficult subclass of children's litigation involves cases in which a child decides to sue one or both of his own parents. Often these cases involve personal injury to the child for which the parent was at fault (at least according to the child or his lawyer). Lawsuits by children against their parents are permitted under section 65 of the Ontario *Family Law Act*.

On occasion, children have sued their parents for physical or sexual abuse. Some of their lawsuits have been successful, even when they were brought many years after the abuse occurred. Children have also sued one parent for failing to protect them from abuse at the hands of the other parent. In the case of *J.(L.A.) v. J.(H.)*, a child sued her mother for failing to protect her from her father, and the court agreed that the mother had a duty to protect her daughter.

In rarer cases, children have sued parents for prenatal injuries, or even for failing to abort them after learning of birth defects. These cases are complicated and controversial. "Wrongful birth" is currently not recognized under Canadian law, but the courts have been somewhat more receptive to lawsuits involving a pregnant mother who has knowingly harmed a fetus in her womb. The Ontario *Family Law Act* states the following:

> No person is disentitled from recovering damages in respect of injuries for the reason only that the injuries were incurred before his or her birth.

AN EXAMPLE

LAWSUITS AGAINST PARENTS

Three-year-old Dagmar, who was riding in the front seat of a car with her mother, was seriously injured in a head-on collision after traffic lights at an intersection malfunctioned. The police charged the other driver with dangerous driving. They did not charge Dagmar's mother. However, the doctors treating Dagmar have advised her family that had she been riding in the back of the car in a toddler's car seat instead of in the front of the car with an adult's seat belt, Dagmar's injuries would have been much less serious. In fact, they might have been avoided altogether.

Dagmar's aunt acted as her litigation guardian. Dagmar sued both the other driver and her own mother for damages, including loss of future income and the cost of future care.

Understandably, lawsuits by children against their own parents can have a devastating effect on family relationships. Unless the suit is brought for the purpose of collecting insurance (as is the case in the Dagmar example above), it is unusual for a parent–child relationship to survive this type of litigation. Often children who sue their parents have already been formally determined to be in need of the state's protection.

KEY TERMS

administrative tribunal

affidavit

applicant

children of tender years

Children's Lawyer

costs

damages

defendant

lawsuit

litigation

litigation guardian

plaintiff

restitution

standing

trustee

REFERENCES

Child and Family Services Act. RSO 1990, c. C.11.

Family Law Act. RSO 1990, c. F.3.

J.(L.A.) v. J.(H.). (1993), 16 CCLT (2d) 254 (Ont. Div. Ct.).

Rules of Civil Procedure, RRO 1990, Reg. 194.

REVIEW QUESTIONS

1. What are damages? How do you think a court determines the economic value of the losses that a child suffers as a result of injury?

2. Why do you think children lack standing to initiate legal proceedings without the intervention of an adult?

3. Do you agree that children under the age of 7 cannot foresee or intend harm? Why or why not?

4. Why do you think a child cannot choose a litigation guardian who has a legal interest in the proceedings? What is a legal interest?

5. What difficulties might a child encounter in finding someone willing to act as his litigation guardian?

6. In the car seat example, why must Dagmar sue her mother? What would happen if Dagmar did not include her mother as a defendant?

DISCUSSION QUESTIONS

1. Lawyers are required to act according to their client's instructions, within the limits of the law and their own consciences. What special challenges might the Children's Lawyer face in having children as clients?

2. What factors might limit a child's ability to pursue a civil lawsuit? How are these issues addressed in our legal and/or child protection systems?

3. Is litigation an efficient method by which children can obtain compensation for losses and injuries? Why or why not? Can you suggest alternatives?

4 Children and the Family Law

■ INTRODUCTION: THE SCOPE OF FAMILY LAW

Divorce, family property, and child custody/access cases are among the most common types of litigation undertaken by Canadians. The Canadian divorce rate has hovered not far below the 50 percent mark for the last few decades, and most research suggests that common law partnerships break up at least as often as marriages.

Divorce and separation affect many families in the midst of their peak child-raising years. Family breakdown brings with it significant economic, logistic, and emotional challenges for all members of the family. Family law has evolved to address the wide range of needs of separating couples and their children:

- Divorce law defines whether and when the couple can consider their marriage ended, and themselves single again and free to remarry, if they wish.

- Family property law determines the appropriate division of assets and **real property** (land, real estate) brought into and accumulated during their union.

- Family support law ensures that economically dependent family members receive economic help from those who supported them during the union.

- Custody and access law seeks to ensure that the day-to-day care of children, and the children's ongoing relationships with parents, are arranged in a manner that reflects the children's best interests.

Because family law covers so many issues and takes into account unique circumstances of individual families, a comprehensive overview of family law is beyond the scope of this book. Instead, this chapter simply introduces those aspects of family law that affect the lives of children. It also describes situations in which family law and child protection law intersect.

real property land and/or buildings

CHAPTER OBJECTIVES

After reading this chapter, you should be able to:

- List the statutes that codify family law in Ontario.

- Understand the basics of child support, custody, and access.

- Understand the legal importance of the best interests of the child.

- Describe at least three situations in which child protection workers or agencies might become involved with family law.

■ FAMILY LAW STATUTES

Like most legislation, family law statutes evolved from the common law, and many of the directions they have taken over the years reflect significant court decisions that have preceded them. A few family law issues, notably **trust**-based claims to property, are still resolved under the common law.

Most modern family law, however, is statute-based. This means that statutes are created to provide a complete and exhaustive code for dealing with the issues that families face after the partners separate. Courts may be called upon to apply or interpret various aspects of family law statutes, but the statutes themselves represent the core of our family law.

trust a legal relationship under which one person (the trustee) holds and manages assets for the benefit of another person (the beneficiary), often until the beneficiary is able to manage the assets for himself or herself

The Divorce Act

Currently, the *Divorce Act*, a federal statute, applies to married heterosexual couples only. It does not apply to unmarried heterosexual couples or same-sex couples, whether married or not. There is currently a bill (Bill C-38) pending in the federal Parliament that would, if passed, extend the application of the *Divorce Act* to same-sex couples. The *Divorce Act* establishes marriage breakdown as the only ground for divorce. Marriage breakdown can be proven on the basis of

- one year's separation,

- adultery, or

- cruelty.

The great majority of Canadian divorces are based on one year's separation. The *Divorce Act* requires couples (at least in the absence of cruelty or abuse) to consider reconciliation. Failing reconciliation, it requires couples to come to an agreement about issues of support and custody through a mediated process.

The Family Law Act

FAMILY PROPERTY

The Ontario *Family Law Act* applies to both married couples and some common law couples, including same-sex married and common law couples. It establishes rules for the calculation and division of family property, so that the couple's property can be divided between them on separation. In general, partners who have lived together with some degree of permanence are entitled to an equal division of real property and other assets acquired during the course of their union. The *Family Law Act* creates special rules with respect to the **matrimonial home**.

matrimonial home defined under the *Family Law Act* as a property the value of which, due to its use as a primary residence during a marriage or common law union, must be divided equally between the divorcing spouses upon dissolution of the union

One of the reasons for dividing property equally regardless of who "owns" it or who paid for it during the course of a marriage (or common law union) is to attempt to balance the economic security of the ex-partners on separation. Marriage breakdown often has an especially negative economic impact on a parent who has opted to suspend or forgo a career while caring for children.

A partner who provides child care frees the other partner to engage in paid employment, and thereby provides the family unit with an economic benefit. Equal division of property on separation recognizes the contributions of both partners to the family. In addition, it provides a source of economic security to the more dependent partner (if there is one). Increased economic security for the dependent partner in turn can reduce the need for spousal and/or child support from the other partner.

The Divorce Act and the Family Law Act

SPOUSAL SUPPORT

If one partner was economically dependent on the other partner during the union, the dependent partner may be able to claim spousal support after the relationship breaks down. Married heterosexual partners can claim financial support from one another under the *Divorce Act* or the *Family Law Act*. Married same-sex partners can claim only under the *Family Law Act*. Common law partners, including same-sex partners, can claim only under the *Family Law Act*, and only if the common law relationship meets certain criteria. All people who have had a child with a person with whom they have cohabited are eligible to make a support claim if their relationship with that person involved some degree of permanence.

Eligibility to claim spousal support does not mean that a court will automatically grant support to an ex-partner. Courts grant support only if a dependent partner proves that she has a need for (and sometimes an expectation of) support from her ex-partner and that her need has arisen as a result of the union. Employed and readily employable ex-partners are less likely to be awarded support than ex-partners who are unemployed as a result of many years of marital dependency.

Other factors affecting spousal support awards include the ages of the partners, and the duration and nature of the union. If the partners are young, childless, and lived together for only a few years while each of them worked, it is unlikely that one partner will be awarded significant support from the other. On the breakdown of a long marriage or common law union, in which the partners assumed traditional breadwinner–homemaker roles, the likelihood of a significant support award is high.

When partners with young children separate during or just after a period in which they shared child care duties disproportionately, the caregiving parent may be entitled to support to assist him (or, more often, her) in returning to or entering the workplace.

CHILD SUPPORT

Both the *Divorce Act* and the *Family Law Act* provide for child support orders. An overview of child support is set out in the next section.

◼ CHILD SUPPORT

Under the Divorce Act

Under the *Divorce Act*, parents are required to contribute to the support of a **child of the marriage**. This term includes not only the biological children of the two partners, but also their adopted children, stepchildren to whom one of them has stood *in loco parentis*, and other non-biological children (once called "illegitimate children").

child of the marriage
any child conceived or adopted after a marriage and before a divorce

The *Divorce Act* requires parents to pay support until a child is 16 years old, or older if the child is incapable of supporting herself (for example, as a result of an intellectual deficit).

Under the Family Law Act

The *Family Law Act* requires parents to support children until they reach the age of 18, or after that age if they are enrolled in a full-time program of study. However, where a child is 16 years old or older and has withdrawn from parental control (something that must be proven through evidence), parents are no longer required to provide support.

Child Support Is an Independent Issue

Child support is paid by one parent to another, and is an issue separate from custody and access. Consider the following examples:

- *Child support as separate from custody.* Ethan divides his time equally between his two mothers' homes, but his higher-earning mother is still required to pay support for Ethan to his lower-earning mother.

- *Child support as separate from access.* Françoise's parents have separated, and she lives with her mother. The court has suspended her father's access because of threats that he will kidnap Françoise and take her to live with his parents in Haiti. However, Françoise's father is still required to continue paying child support for his daughter.

Child Support Is the Right of the Child

Child support payments are generally made by one parent to the other; however, family courts view child support as something that is owed by a parent to a child, and not by a parent to the other parent. The family court sees its role, in part, as the protector of the best interests of children of ended unions. The court does not look favourably on attempts by one parent to use the paying or withholding of child support as a means of influencing or punishing the other parent. The inclusion of support payments in the receiving parent's household income may appear to enrich that parent — for example, by allowing for the purchase of a more comfortable home. This enrichment is acceptable, however, since it provides an important support to the standard of living of the parents' children.

Because support is the right of the child, children are permitted to bring their parents to court to obtain it. While most children's family law rights are pursued on their behalf by a parent, section 33(2) of the *Family Law Act* allows a child to bring an application for support independently (through a litigation guardian).

An application for child support may also be brought by the Ministry of Children and Youth Services, or by any one of the following:

- a municipal corporation — for example, a subsidized housing corporation — including a metropolitan, district, or regional municipality, but not including an area municipality;

AN EXAMPLE

SUITS BY TEENS

Sixteen-year-old Gary's parents' breakup was acrimonious and sometimes violent. Before the separation, Gary himself had been having some serious conflicts with his father, and had run away twice, both times returning to the family home within the month. When his parents were separating, Gary could not tolerate being in the house with them, so he moved into the basement of his friend Hassan's family.

Now that his parents are officially apart, Gary has learned that his father has asked his mother to sign a "negotiated" separation agreement that contains a statement that his father is not obligated to support Gary because Gary has withdrawn from parental control.

While Hassan's mother has said Gary can stay until the end of the school year or until things settle down, Gary never meant to leave for good and eventually wants to move back in with his mother and finish school. He decides to ask Hassan's mother whether she will help him bring an application for child support.

- a district social services administration board under the *District Social Services Administration Boards Act*;

- a First Nations band approved under section 15 of the *Indian Welfare Assistance Act*; or

- a delivery agent under the *Ontario Works Act, 1997*.

All of these agencies provide services, such as housing, to individuals in need, and may apply for support to recover some of their costs. The Ministry of Children and Youth Services may pursue support to recover some of the living expenses of children in its care.

Amount of Support

Formerly, courts calculated the amount of support a child was entitled to on a case-by-case basis, factoring in such issues as the child's need and the supporting parents' ability to pay. In recent years, however, Ontario has moved to a system of guidelines that set out what is essentially a mathematical formula that produces a support payment based on the parents' income. The guidelines were designed to bring a measure of objectivity to the question of child support, and to assist parents who choose to negotiate outside court. The guidelines now assist parents in determining how much support a court would likely award in the event of litigation.

■ CUSTODY AND ACCESS

Custody is a legal arrangement governing the care (and usually the residency) of a child. Having custody of a child implies being charged with both the day-to-day physical care of the child, and the making of decisions with respect to matters

custody legal arrangement governing the care of a child; in the child protection context, being kept in a place of safety under the care of a children's aid society

access in the family law
context, a child and her
non-custodial parent's
opportunity to visit with
each other, and the right to
this opportunity

such as education, medical treatment, and religious observance. **Access** describes a formal arrangement that allows a non-custodial parent and child to spend time together.

Both custody and access are governed by legislation: the federal *Divorce Act*, and the Ontario *Children's Law Reform Act*.

Who Can Apply?

Under the *Divorce Act*, previously married heterosexual parents can automatically apply for custody or access. Other individuals can apply if they have the permission of the court. Under the *Children's Law Reform Act*, parents, including common law parents, "or any other person" can apply.

In Canada, non-parents are very unlikely to get permanent custody of children where at least one parent is able and willing to have custody. Non-parents are also unlikely to be granted formal access rights where parents object.

How Is Custody Decided?

best interests of the child
a legal principle, embraced
by several statutes and
areas of the common law,
as a basis for decision-
making

The most important principle in custody decisions is the **best interests of the child**. If there is a dispute about custody, the court is required to decide the issue not on the basis of who is the more "deserving" parent, but rather on the basis of whose custody will best serve the interests of the child.

The interests to be taken into account are varied. The court often tries to fashion a custody arrangement that fosters some degree of stability in the children's lives. For example, where the mother has left the matrimonial home and has moved to another city, the court might award primary custody to the father because, in living with him, the children will be able to continue to attend the same school and have regular contact with nearby grandparents.

The court also gives some weight to historical caregiving patterns. For example, if children have been cared for by a full-time stay-at-home mother who intimately knows their needs, habits, schedules, and preferences, a court will likely award custody to the mother, even if the divorce means that both parents will need to work outside the home.

The court tends to avoid awarding custody in a way that will exacerbate emotional turmoil, favouring arrangements that preserve relationships. For example, even if a mother has been very involved in her children's care, if she shows signs of obstructing the children's access to their father, a court may award custody to the father so that the children's relationship with both parents is preserved.

Finally, in some situations, a court will consider emotional ties and the preferences of the children. While it is not law, there is a long-standing practice (sometimes called the "tender years doctrine") in Canadian family law of awarding custody of infants and very young children to their mother. This doctrine is based on the cultural belief that mothers and babies share a special relationship, and that mothers are especially well-equipped for nurturing younger children — for example, through breast-feeding and baby-wearing. Once children are at least school age, their choices about the parent with whom they would like to live often become important, if not determinative. In considering a child's wishes, a judge must often exercise great sensitivity in determining whether the child's preference is genuine, or the result of parental pressure.

YOU DECIDE!

CUSTODY DILEMMA

Ian and Jill are the divorcing parents of two sons: Kevin, aged 13, and Luke, aged 2. Each parent wants full custody of the children. Since Jill is moving to Alberta and Ian is remaining in Ontario, joint custody is not a realistic option.

Both Ian and Jill are caring parents who have been involved in their children's lives. While Ian has worked full-time since before Kevin was born, he has always been careful to limit his overtime and to spend as much of the weekend as possible with the children. Jill stayed home with Kevin until he started grade 1. By the time Luke was born, after many years of fertility problems, her career had blossomed; she stayed home with Luke for one year and has now gone back to work. Luke had some trouble settling into daycare but finally seems to have adjusted. Having his mother sleep in his bed at night helps calm his anxieties.

Ian and Jill's separation was precipitated by Ian's involvement in an extramarital affair, which is now over. The affair was very hurtful to Jill, and she continues to be overwhelmingly angry with Ian, which is one of the reasons she is leaving the province.

Thirteen-year-old Kevin has found his parents' fighting very distressing. While he loves his school and his marks seem not to have suffered, he has lost all interest in sports and extracurricular activities. He has developed an unusually close relationship with his two-year-old brother, often choosing to stay home with Luke instead of playing at friends' homes. The counsellor Kevin has been seeing suggests that Kevin's attachment to Luke is a coping mechanism. Feeling powerless to keep his parents together, he seems to be putting his energy into being a brother, a relationship he can control. Kevin is angry with both his parents and refuses to state a preference for living with either of them.

Questions

1. How would you award custody in this case?

2. What are your reasons?

3. What are the potential disadvantages of your decision?

Possible Custody Arrangements

Custody is not always an all-or-nothing arrangement. **Sole custody** is a term sometimes used to describe a situation in which one parent is charged with almost all child care and all decision making. However, joint custody arrangements, in which parents share custody, have been steadily increasing in popularity.

To understand joint custody, it is important to remember that custody has two components: physical care plus residency, and decision-making authority. True joint custody, which is commonly referred to as **shared custody**, generally means that a child's parents share both aspects of custody, though not necessarily equally. A constantly changing residence can be hard on children, and shared custody arrangements are often subject to change and fine-tuning.

sole custody
an arrangement under which one parent is charged with almost all child care responsibilities and in which the child resides full-time with that parent

shared custody
(usually used to describe physical custody) an arrangement under which a child resides for part of the time with each of two or more parents

joint legal custody
an arrangement under which both parents of a child have the legal right to make decisions with respect to his or her care, and in which the child lives with one parent most of the time

With **joint legal custody**, children live with one parent most of the time, but both parents share equally in decision-making authority. Many shared custody arrangements evolve into joint legal custody.

All types of joint custody require considerable contact between the separated parents. For joint custody to work properly, the parents must be able to negotiate contentious issues, and accommodate each other's schedules. Courts rarely award joint custody to parents who are incapable of calm and rational contact; however, as parents adjust to their separation over the years, courts can revisit the issue of custody and change the arrangement from full custody to joint custody at the parents' request.

Access

Access, like custody, must be determined in the context of the best interests of the child. In the great majority of cases, courts believe that a relationship with both parents is consistent with a child's best interests. Courts even go so far, in some cases, as to award access to a parent against a child's expressed wishes. This kind of decision is always controversial. It is generally made when a court feels that a child's current views about a parent may be coloured by negative feelings flowing out of the separation, or other temporary reasons. Research suggests that in the absence of contact, parent–child relationships disintegrate very quickly. If there is no issue of child abuse, courts are very supportive of access.

Supervised Access

supervised access
access that is subject to supervision, usually by a social worker, to ensure the safety of the child

If a court is concerned about a child's safety in the care of a parent, it can award **supervised access**. The supervision is often provided by a social welfare agency, and involves the presence of a social worker during the parent's visits with the child. Reasons for ordering supervised access can include the following:

- substantiated suspicions that a parent will abduct a child during access periods;

- believable allegations of prior child abuse — whether emotional, physical, or sexual — or evidence of such abuse;

- believable allegations or evidence of child neglect;

- a court's belief that a parent is not fully capable of caring for a child by reason, for example, of substance addiction or mental illness; or

- a child's expressed fears or reservations about access.

When supervised access goes well, the parent under supervision may eventually be successful in having the access order changed to allow unsupervised visits.

Custody/Access Needs Assessments

Under section 30 of the *Children's Law Reform Act*, a court can order an assessment by a professional (usually a social worker or counsellor) of the needs of a child, and the ability of each of the child's parents to fulfill those needs. The purpose of such an assessment is to assist the court in making decisions about custody or access. Sometimes a court makes an assessment order at the request of a parent, but a court can also order an assessment on its own initiative. Where possible, the court appoints a professional selected and agreed upon by the parents. The assessor's report is filed with the court, and the assessor can be called as a witness in the proceedings.

In preparing a needs assessment report, the assessor must strive to consider only the best interests of the child, and not the interests or desires of either of the parents. Needs assessments usually involve interviewing all the parties. They provide one of the means by which the wishes of the child are communicated to the court. Children may be more comfortable expressing their preferences to an assessor who is experienced in interviewing children than to a judge in chambers or a courtroom.

Children's Representation

In most custody and access cases, only the parents are represented. However, where the wishes of (especially an older) child are inconsistent with those expressed by the parents, or where the child's interests do not appear to be fully represented by either parent, the court may order that the child have independent representation, usually by the Children's Lawyer. In many cases, full representation is not necessary, and issues of concern can be addressed by the Children's Lawyer's preparation and filing with the court of a custody and access report. The Children's Lawyer may also be involved as a guardian of a child's property, where property is at issue in the proceedings.

Enforcing Custody and Access Arrangements

Where a custody or access arrangement is not working, the *Children's Law Reform Act* provides mechanisms for the enforcement of orders made by the court in relation to the parties.

In cases of conflict between the parents or among the parents and others — grandparents, for example — the court can make an order under section 35 to restrain one party from harassing another.

Sometimes, contrary to the terms of a custody or access order, one person withholds a child from another. In this case, section 36 of the *Children's Law Reform Act* empowers the court to make an order that allows the person from whom the child is being withheld or his representative to "locate and apprehend" the child.

A court can also make an order to locate and apprehend a child if the person who applies for the order describes reasonable and probable grounds for believing that another party is likely to remove the child from Ontario in violation of a separation agreement or court order. The court can issue an order to prevent the removal of a child from Ontario. Under section 37 of the *Children's Law Reform Act*, a court can enforce its order by requiring a person to place property in trust until the child is returned (at the end of an access visit), to post a bond, or to surrender the child's passport to the court for safekeeping.

If a person takes a child from her province of residence to another province in contravention of a separation agreement or court order, there are legal mechanisms through which the two provinces can negotiate the return of the child. If a person takes a child outside Canada, the *Convention on the Civil Aspects of International Child Abduction* applies, provided that the country to which the child is taken has signed the convention. The **convention** is designed to assist countries that have signed it in obtaining the return of abducted children. However, the process can be complicated and frustrating; it is much easier for parents to prevent the removal of their children in the first place.

Finally, the court has a broad power, under section 38 of the *Children's Law Reform Act*, to punish those who exhibit "wilful contempt of or resistance to its process or orders in respect of custody of or access to a child." Disregard for a court's orders can result in a fine of up to $5,000 and/or 90 days' imprisonment.

convention usually, a traditional rule of law or policy that has persuasive value and tends to be applied by formal decision makers

■ ALLEGATIONS OF CHILD ABUSE IN THE CONTEXT OF FAMILY BREAKDOWN

When a couple separates, usually at least one ex-partner is plunged into a state of extreme emotional distress and insecurity. Coping with separation is difficult for everyone, but dealing at the same time with one's children's distress is a significant complicating factor. Separation can trigger a wide range of "normal" reactions, including a deep sense of betrayal, tremendous anger, and an instinct to "protect" the children from the other parent.

Where child custody becomes a contentious issue between the parties, an exchange of criticism over each other's fitness to parent is almost par for the course. In more unusual cases, criticism escalates into allegations of child neglect, or physical, emotional, or sexual abuse.

Child abuse allegations made in the context of a separation create an enormous challenge for all parties involved. Even the subtlest of suggestions of abuse can influence a court in making an interim (temporary) custody order. An interim custody placement is significant because it is highly predictive of what will happen when final custody is awarded. Attempts to influence interim custody by falsely suggesting that the other parent might be abusive are unethical and irresponsible.

Explicit or forceful allegations of abuse automatically require the involvement of child protection agencies in what is no longer a routine separation. Dealing with abuse allegations at the same time as standard custody issues is a very complex task. The timing of these abuse allegations makes them difficult to investigate. On the one hand, the accusing parent may be inventing the allegations to win an advantage when it comes to custody. On the other hand, research into abuse suggests that the stresses associated with separation can in fact lead to child abuse even when it has never happened in the family before.

Being labelled an abuser can have devastating consequences for an accused parent, the worst of which may be limitation of access to the point where the parent–child relationship is irreparably eroded.

Unless he is fabricating the whole thing, the parent who makes the allegations is also in a difficult situation. Before making the allegations public, he must decide whether the child who complains of abuse is telling the truth, and whether the conduct complained of is serious enough to justify a course of action that may destroy the child's relationship with the other parent. Some damaging parent–child interactions (including all forms of sexual abuse) clearly require investigation and should prompt protective action. However, some behaviour that might be labelled emotional abuse (name calling, for example) or physical abuse (forcing a toddler into a car seat, for example) may be more ambiguous. All parents make mistakes, and the high stress of separation may lead to a temporarily reduced ability to parent. If parental lapses in judgment are rare and subsequently regretted by the "offending" parent, to describe the behaviour as abuse can inflict disproportionate damage on the parent–child relationship.

Procedure in the Case of Abuse Allegations

If one parent makes a serious allegation of abuse against the other parent, the lawyer to whom the allegation is made must contact a children's aid society. If no lawyer is involved, a mediator usually reports the allegation. The reporting responsibilities of lawyers and mediators are set out in section 72 of the *Child and Family Services Act* and fully explained in chapter 8.

The children's aid society then investigates the allegation, and the results of the investigation will influence the custody/access dispute. The investigation will most likely include psychological assessments of both the child and the parent under suspicion of abuse. Child abuse investigations, while always difficult, can be even more so in the context of separation. In addition to suffering abuse, the child will be experiencing emotional insecurity from the breakup, and will be influenced by the conflict between her parents. The child may be afraid of the consequences of saying anything at all; and in most abuse situations, there are few independent witnesses who are able to provide evidence.

If the investigation does uncover credible evidence of abuse, a children's aid society will take a position with respect to custody that is designed to protect the child, and will inform the court of its opinion. If, in the opinion of the children's aid society, neither parent is capable of protecting the child, a court may find that the child is in need of state protection, and may make the child a ward of the society.

▇ADOPTION

The adoption of children within Canada is regulated by provincial legislation. Ontario law relating to adoption is found in the *Child and Family Services Act*.

Who Can Make Adoption Placements?

Under the *Child and Family Services Act*, legal adoption placements can be made, with court approval, only by the following:

1. *Certain classes of family members.* For example, the parents of a pregnant teenager can apply to adopt the baby, or a person who becomes the partner of a parent may apply to adopt that parent's children.

2. *A children's aid society.*

3. *A statutory licensee.* This is a person licensed under part IX of the *Child and Family Services Act* to make adoption placements.

It is illegal for anyone else to place children for adoption in Ontario or to bring children into Ontario for the purpose of adoption. It is also illegal to charge a fee for making adoption placements other than the licensee fee set out in the regulations under the *Child and Family Services Act*.

All permanent adoption placements must be finalized by court order. A child may be placed for adoption for a trial period before a court issues a final adoption order.

Who Can Be Placed for Adoption?

Crown ward a child or young person who, having been taken into protective custody of a children's aid society, will not be returned to the care of his or her parents and may be made available for adoption

As a general rule, unless a child is a **Crown ward** (which means that the child has been permanently removed from the care of his parents), the child's parents must consent to the placement of the child for adoption. This is true even where the child is a ward of a children's aid society. A ward of a children's aid society is not the same as a Crown ward; this distinction is discussed in chapter 8 under the heading "Dispositions."

For the purpose of consent to adoption, the *Child and Family Services Act* provides a complex definition of "parent." It is broad enough to include not only biological mothers and fathers but also other individuals who have assumed a parenting role with respect to the child.

A parent cannot give consent to have a child placed for adoption before the child is seven days old. Even after giving consent, a parent can withdraw her consent (and have the child returned, if the child has been placed for adoption) within 21 days. In some cases, courts permit parents to withdraw consent after the 21 days have passed, as long as the child has not yet been placed in the custody of the adopting parents.

A children's aid society (or other licensee) must advise a parent who contemplates giving consent to adoption of her right to withdraw consent. The society must also give the parent the opportunity to obtain independent legal advice. A parent who is under the age of 18 cannot give consent unless the Children's Lawyer is satisfied that the parent is fully informed about the implications of doing so. A child who is being placed for adoption and who is seven years old or older must also give his consent to the adoption.

The need for consent can be waived by a court in limited situations such as the following:

- the parent is incapable — for example, because of developmental disability;

- the consent requirement would cause emotional harm; or

- the best interests of the child require that the child be placed for adoption (but the parents withhold consent).

What Criteria Govern Adoption Placements?

As in other family law situations, the principle that governs adoption decisions is the best interests of the child. Children's needs and interests are determined by the court, often with help from a children's aid society or independent assessors.

The ability of parents to meet the needs of a child are determined by way of an adoption homestudy. A homestudy is an investigation by someone professionally trained to determine whether a particular person or family would provide a suitable home for an adopted child. Homestudies are usually conducted by social workers who have been approved by a director appointed under the *Child and Family Services Act*. Homestudies involve consideration of the following criteria, which are set out in section 136(2) of the *Child and Family Services Act*:

1. The child's physical, mental and emotional needs, and the appropriate care or treatment to meet those needs.

2. The child's physical, mental and emotional level of development.

3. The child's cultural background.

4. The religious faith, if any, in which the child is being raised.

5. The importance for the child's development of a positive relationship with a parent and a secure place as a member of a family.

6. The child's relationships by blood or through an adoption order.

7. The importance of continuity in the child's care and the possible effect on the child of disruption of that continuity.

8. The child's views and wishes, if they can be reasonably ascertained.

9. The effects on the child of delay in the disposition of the case.

10. Any other relevant circumstance.

Children in Need of Protection

Adoption placements of children who have been in the care of children's aid societies, either as society wards or Crown wards, pose some unique difficulties. Children who have been removed from unsafe family situations are often well past infancy by the time an adoptive placement can be considered, and placing older children is always more difficult than placing babies. Children under a society's care are also more likely than other children to have health, behavioural, or developmental problems. Most of these children have been required to adjust and re-adjust to changes in foster care placements and caregivers, and they may be very cautious about bonding with an adoptive family.

Children who have been taken into custody by a society may also have continuing connections with their birthparent(s). The *Child and Family Services Act* does not allow for the placement for adoption of any child to whom a parent continues to have access. It also requires that parents consent to the adoptive placement of children who are wards of a society. However, since apprehension by a society is often involuntary, there is always the chance that a birthparent will seek reunion with a child, especially after successfully resolving the personal problems that may have led to the child's apprehension. Because these reunions are often not in the best interests of adopted children, the *Child and Family Services Act* imposes strict limitations on the release of adoption records.

Children who are wards of a society are more likely than other adoptive children to have siblings who are also in need of adoption. There is a very strong legal preference for keeping siblings together by placing them with a family that is willing to take them all. In relatively rare cases, however, a court will find that separation of siblings is not inconsistent with the children's best interests, and will place one child alone.

International Adoptions

Where a child is adopted into Ontario from another country, the Ontario *Intercountry Adoption Act* applies. This Act incorporates the terms of the *Convention on Protection of Children and Co-operation in Respect of Intercountry Adoption*, an international agreement created by a group of nations. Not all nations have signed this convention, and the list of countries from which a child can be adopted into Canada is fairly limited.

The convention was drafted to give legal expression and support to the following principles, which are quoted from the convention's opening words:

> Recognizing that the child, for the full and harmonious development of his or her personality, should grow up in a family environment, in an atmosphere of happiness, love and understanding,
>
> Recalling that each State should take, as a matter of priority, appropriate measures to enable the child to remain in the care of his or her family of origin,
>
> Recognizing that intercountry adoption may offer the advantage of a permanent family to a child for whom a suitable family cannot be found in his or her State of origin,
>
> Convinced of the necessity to take measures to ensure that intercountry adoptions are made in the best interests of the child and with respect for his or her fundamental rights, and to prevent the abduction [of], the sale of, or traffic in children … .

The *Intercountry Adoption Act* requires parents who want to adopt a child internationally and bring the child into Ontario to proceed through an adoption licensee and participate in a successful homestudy. The only allowable fees for international adoptions are those approved under the general regulation, O. reg. 200/99, certain other approved expenses, and legitimate legal fees.

KEY TERMS

access

best interests of the child

child of the marriage

convention

Crown ward

custody

joint legal custody

matrimonial home

real property

shared custody

sole custody

supervised access

trust

REFERENCES

Child and Family Services Act. RSO 1990, c. C.11.

Children's Law Reform Act. RSO 1990, c. C.12.

Divorce Act. RSC 1985, c. 3 (2d Supp.).

Family Law Act. RSO 1990, c. F.3.

Hague Convention on Protection of Children and Co-operation in Respect of Intercountry Adoption (1993). Ratified by Canada in December 1996.

Intercountry Adoption Act, 1998. SO 1998, c. 29.

REVIEW QUESTIONS

1. Name the statutes that govern Ontario residents with respect to the matters listed below. Specify whether each statute applies to married heterosexual/same-sex couples and/or common law heterosexual/same-sex couples.

   a. divorce

   b. family property

   c. spousal support

   d. child support

   e. custody and access

   f. adoption

2. What is the purpose of child support? What parent is entitled to receive child support payments?

3. How is a parent's child support obligation calculated?

4. Until what age is a child entitled to be supported economically by his parents? Are there exceptions? If so, name them.

5. What overriding legal principle governs decisions about child custody and access?

6. What is custody? What is shared custody? What is joint legal custody? What is access?

7. Is being up to date with support payments a prerequisite to having access to a child? Why or why not?

8. How do children's agencies play a role in custody/access cases? Which kinds of agencies may be asked to assist the court in deciding questions about custody/access? What form does the assistance usually take?

9. Why are child abuse allegations made in the context of parental separation more difficult to investigate than allegations made during more stable times? Why must a children's aid society become involved as soon as child abuse is alleged in a separation context?

10. Which agencies or individuals can place a child for adoption?

11. Who must consent before a nine-year-old child is placed for adoption?

DISCUSSION QUESTIONS

1. Custody and access decisions are required to be made in the best interests of children. In the context of family litigation, who identifies these interests? Are separating parents capable of distinguishing their own interests from those of their children? Are children's interests adequately represented in our legal system? Why or why not?

2. Should a parent whose child has been taken into protective care be required to pay child support to the child protection agency? Should parents be allowed access to their children after the children have become wards of children's aid societies?

3. Does a family breakdown create fertile territory for child abuse allegations? Why or why not? Do you think that a family breakdown makes it more difficult for parents to judge the truth of their children's abuse allegations? Is there any reason to give less weight to allegations of abuse that occur in the context of a separation than in any other context?

4. Should Canadians be allowed to adopt children from overseas while there are Canadian children in protective care who are waiting for adoptive placements?

5 Children and the State

■ INTRODUCTION: SOCIAL WELFARE — THREE STREAMS

As explained in chapter 1, the state has become increasingly involved in child protection in the last 200 years or so. This involvement has been part of a broader social welfare movement. Social welfare programs, as they relate to children, have developed in three discrete streams: education, health care, and poverty relief. These three areas continue to be important today. Other areas in which the government involves itself in children's lives include cultural programs, early childhood development initiatives, and subsidized daycare.

While the existence of social programs for children is a very good thing, these programs are effective only when many children have access to them. Children must generally gain access to social programs through their parents. Where there are parenting problems, language barriers, or other obstacles that interfere with access, children may slip through the holes in the social welfare safety net. These children need the assistance of child and youth workers, other children's advocates — and sometimes the law — to ensure that they are benefiting from life in a country with a highly developed social welfare system.

CHAPTER OBJECTIVES

After reading this chapter, you should be able to:

- Describe the basic structure of Canada's social welfare system for children.

- Explain what happens when parenting decisions and government prescriptions conflict.

- Describe obstacles that some children may face in obtaining government support.

- Explain how children's advocates can improve children's access to social programs.

■ PUBLIC EDUCATION

Like most developed countries, Canada funds a public education system for Canadian children. This system is supported in part by property taxes.

Each province administers its own educational system. Responsibility for many aspects of public education within provinces is further delegated to regional school boards. The Ontario *Education Act* and the regulations made under it set out the legal framework for the education of Ontario children. The Ontario school system

secular not religious in
nature

is divided into two streams: **secular** public schools and Catholic schools (run by
"separate" school boards). Public funding of Catholic schools is a historical practice
that is authorized under the Canadian constitution.

Religious Schools

The government's funding of Catholic schools, and not other religious schools, has
long been a controversial issue. If given a choice, many parents would prefer that
their children receive a government-paid education in a school of another religious
denomination, such as a Jewish or Muslim school. The unfairness of funding only
Catholic schools has attracted international attention. In 1996, the United Nations
Human Rights Committee ruled that Canada was in violation of the *International
Covenant on Civil and Political Rights* because of Ontario's practice of funding Roman
Catholic schools and not those of other faiths. In response to the committee's rul-
ing, the Ontario government partially complied with the international covenant
by creating a system of educational vouchers designed to pay some of the cost of
sending children to other religious schools.

Compulsory Attendance, Homeschooling, and Non-Attendance as a Warning Sign

COMPULSORY ATTENDANCE

Another controversial issue in education is compulsory school attendance. Under
the *Education Act*, parents are required to ensure that their children between the
ages of 6 and 16 attend public or private school. Failure to enroll a child in school
or to take reasonable steps to ensure his daily attendance is an offence punishable
by a fine under section 30 of the Act.

There are some exceptions to the compulsory attendance requirement. The
principal one, under section 21(2)(a), exempts a child who "is receiving satisfactory
instruction at home or elsewhere." This exception allows children to attend schools
outside the public system, or to be homeschooled by their parents. Homeschooling
must be adequate in the eyes of the **provincial school attendance counsellor**.

**provincial school
attendance counsellor**
an agent of the Ministry
of Education charged with
confirming compliance
with compulsory school
attendance legislation

A child of school age who is not being sent to school is sometimes brought to
the attention of a school board by a neighbour or other adult who knows the child.
School boards are authorized under section 27 of the *Education Act* to confirm
compulsory attendance by conducting a census to identify persons under the age
of 21 in their districts.

HOMESCHOOLING

Homeschooling has always been a controversial subject, probably because a parent's
decision to homeschool her children amounts to a rejection, or at least a strong
criticism, of the public school system. A parent who is critical of the public system
is unlikely to provide instruction that is consistent with that system's curriculum.
Homeschoolers tend to focus on educational values and priorities that differ from
those of public schools. However, the adequacy of the instruction provided by
parents is subject to review by the provincial school attendance counsellor. In order
to satisfy himself that a homeschooled child is eligible for exemption from school

attendance under section 21(2) of the *Education Act*, the counsellor can launch an inquiry into the homeschooling program under section 24 of the Act.

Guidance in evaluating homeschooling is available through the government's *Policy/Program Memorandum No. 131: Home Schooling*, which was issued in 2002.

NON-ATTENDANCE AS A WARNING SIGN

A child's failure to attend school can sometimes be a warning sign that something is not right at home. There are many examples of children receiving high-quality homeschooling instruction. However, without evidence of such instruction, it is usually in the best interests of a child for the school board or the provincial school attendance counsellor to investigate cases of chronic non-attendance. In some cases, children who are subject to serious neglect may not make it to school because nobody is taking charge of waking, dressing, and feeding the children and shepherding them onto the bus. In more serious cases, a child may be away from school because she has been abducted and her abductor is hiding her from the authorities. Alternatively, a child may be the victim of physical, sexual, or emotional abuse, and her abuser may fear that school personnel will detect the abuse.

ASIDE

NON-ATTENDANCE AT SCHOOL AS A RED FLAG: REAL CASES

Randal Dooley

Randal Dooley, aged seven, died on September 25, 1998 of head injuries suffered in the course of physical abuse, perpetrated over a period of time, by his stepmother and biological father. Randal's parents had not enrolled the boy for the 1998 school year because he had visible injuries from an August 30 whipping, and the parents feared that school personnel would inform a children's aid society. The previous spring, Randal's grade 1 teacher, Gloria Robson, had noticed welts on the child's arm and had called both the police and a children's aid society.

Gavin Hollett

Gavin Hollett was taken out of Ontario by his mother in December 1994 in contravention of a custody/access order. He was 4 years old at the time. Gavin's father spent the next eight years searching for Gavin with the aid of missing children's agencies. Gavin's mother moved her residence (and the boy) several times in the intervening eight years, using pseudonyms to disguise Gavin's identity. In the spring of 2003, she and Gavin, then 12 years old, were living on an herb farm in a women's commune on Vancouver Island. Gavin, then called Leaf, was not enrolled in school. Leaf's absence from school was one of the factors that led a missing children's agency to investigate his identity. His mother was charged with parental abduction.

Parent–School Conflict Over Policies

HEALTH CONCERNS

In some cases, children may be unable to attend school because of their parents' decision not to comply with a school or school board policy. For example, a child may be prohibited from attending school because of a health concern that the parents have not resolved to the school's satisfaction.

Under the *Immunization of School Pupils Act*, children are required to receive a prescribed series of immunizations before attending school. Parents who object to the requirement must file a statement of their objection on one of three grounds:

- *Medical exemption.* A child's physician may advise that it would be unsafe for a particular child — for example, a child with immune problems — to receive a particular immunization. The physician may also provide evidence that the child is already immune to the disease sought to be prevented. Both exemptions arise under section 1 of the Act.

- *Religious exemption.* A child's parent may state in writing that the child's religion prohibits the administration of the medication. This exemption arises under sections 1 and 3 of the Act.

- *Conscience exemption.* A child's parent may state in writing that immunization of the child conflicts with the parent's sincere conscientious beliefs. This exemption arises under sections 1 and 3 of the Act.

Failure to produce proof of immunization or to file a statement of medical, religious, or conscience exemption can lead to the suspension of a child's attendance at school by order of a medical officer of health under section 6 of the *Immunization of School Pupils Act*.

While medical and religious exemptions are relatively clear-cut, exemptions based on conscience are more controversial. Childhood immunizations do carry some health risks. Most physicians agree that the protective effects of these immunizations, both from an individual and a community perspective, outweigh the risks; however, some health care practitioners and parents believe that there are strong links between immunization and serious health consequences. One link that is repeatedly drawn is between immunizations and the onset of **autism**. Parents may have a specific reason, such as the avoidance of autism, for expressing a conscientious objection. They may have a more amorphous reason, such as "nobody catches those diseases anymore" or "I believe in the body's ability to defend itself against disease without medical intervention."

The scientific basis of some sincere parental objections to immunization may be quite shaky. Conflict between the parents' wishes and what the school believes is good for a child may lead to allegations on the part of school personnel that the child is being cared for incompetently. The same kind of conflict can arise when school staff notice that a child has a health problem that is not, in their view, being adequately treated. Observations like this can be enough to trigger a teacher's duty to report suspected abuse (or in this case, usually neglect) under the *Child and Family Services Act*. This duty is described in detail in chapter 8 under the heading "Duty To Report."

autism a condition in which the sufferer's reaction to stimuli is impaired, often causing learning or behavioural problems

YOU DECIDE!

LICE CONTROL: SHOULD "NATURAL" APPROACHES BE ACCOMMODATED?

Marigold's mother, Natalie, practises natural living. For example, she buys only organic foods and cooks macrobiotically, dresses her family only in natural unbleached cotton, and uses vinegar and baking soda for household cleaning instead of strong chemicals. When one of her children is sick, she relies on the child's natural immune response, supplemented in some cases by gentle herbal remedies, to cure the illness. Natalie does not allow her children to take antibiotics or to receive immunizations, and will not take a child to the doctor unless she believes that the child's life is at risk.

Marigold is in grade 1. During a routine head check, a parent volunteer noticed that Marigold had head lice. Marigold's teacher, Oliver, sent her home with a notice requesting that the lice be treated and that she be kept out of school until she was lice-free. When Marigold returned, Oliver noticed that there were still lice in her hair. A call home revealed that Natalie had not used an insecticidal shampoo on Marigold, as the school recommended, but had begun rinsing her daughter's hair with tea tree oil, which she claimed "should work in time." Marigold's mother was not unduly concerned about the possibility that tea tree oil might not immediately solve the lice problem "because lice are just a harmless nuisance, but pesticides are dangerous to Marigold's health."

Fearing the reaction of other parents whose children might contract lice from Marigold, Oliver spoke to the principal. The principal suspended Marigold from school for two days with another request that Natalie treat the lice. Natalie again advised the school that she refused to use insecticidal shampoo. Marigold still had head lice on her return to school.

Questions

1. What would you do if you were the principal?

2. Is Oliver's continued observation of lice in Marigold's hair sufficient evidence of child neglect to trigger a reporting duty under the *Child and Family Services Act*? Why or why not?

3. What are Marigold's rights to public education?

4. Where might Natalie turn for help in dealing with the school on this issue?

STANDARDIZED TESTING

Another source of conflict between Ontario parents and schools in recent years is the standardized testing of students. The Education Quality and Accountability Office (EQAO) was established by the Ontario government in 1996 to evaluate the quality and effectiveness of elementary and secondary education.

The EQAO tests students in grades 3, 6, 9, and 10 to assess levels of literacy and competence in mathematics. While recent governments have promoted the testing as a means of ensuring government "accountability" in public education, parent reaction to the testing has been mixed. Some parents believe that intensive testing is stressful for children and of limited value in identifying specific problems with the educational system. Others are critical of the cost of the testing in the context of cuts to education. They question the value of test scores in the absence of follow-up funding to remedy problems.

These and other concerns have led some parents to keep children at home on test days, either as a form of protest or to spare children the stress associated with testing. While the EQAO policy permits schools, in some cases, to test absent children on their return, cases of conscientious objection are usually resolved between the school and the parents on an individual basis. Despite the "compulsory" nature of the testing, absenteeism on test days is typically higher than on other school days. However, because EQAO testing occupies most of a school day, a child's access to education is not seriously affected by a parental decision to keep a child home.

Language Barriers and Learning Problems

For some children, other barriers to education include language issues and/or developmental, intellectual, learning, or behavioural difficulties.

LANGUAGE BARRIERS

Especially in urban centres, the Canadian student population reflects considerable diversity with respect to culture and language. Canada is a popular destination for immigrants from all over the world. For many such immigrants, access to quality public education is a high family priority. However, children who enter Canadian schools without being fluent in either English or French are at a significant disadvantage in the classroom.

In areas where the first language of many children is neither English nor French, remedial programs exist to ease the transition of both children and their parents into English or French education. Schools tend to do a good job of identifying children who need this assistance, because struggling students put an increased demand on the time of classroom teachers. Often, a school's efforts on behalf of a child end up assisting the child's entire family. In smaller centres, however, or in times of economic cuts to education, access to language programs is limited. Social workers and children's advocates may need to become more active on behalf of children facing language barriers to education, for example, by advising parents about which schools offer the fullest range of language support programs, or by recommending other community resources.

LEARNING PROBLEMS

Another barrier to education appears in the form of learning and/or behavioural problems. About 10 percent of Canadian school children struggle, at some point in their education, with some kind of learning problem. Learning and behavioural problems are discussed together here because they can be closely related and difficult to distinguish, especially in younger children. Accommodating learning problems often requires support beyond the capacity of classroom teachers, with respect to both time and expertise. This means that in order to guarantee access to education for children with learning problems, schools must devote additional staff, specialized equipment, and classroom space specifically to the needs of these children.

Pressure on public budgets often threatens allocation of resources to special needs children. Many Ontario educators believe that the system is in a state of economic crisis. With schools experiencing cuts to programs that were once taken for granted — for example, physical education, music, and library programs — special needs programs have been reduced to minimal levels. The result is that children who once would have been identified as being in need of special support are being left to fend for themselves in regular classrooms. This practice not only undermines these children's rights to quality education, but often affects the rights of other children as well, by putting unrealistic demands on classroom teachers.

In cases of serious lack of special needs support, families may seek legal redress. For example, a strike by the Canadian Union of Public Employees in the spring of 2001 led to a request, by Ontario school boards, that parents of students with disabilities keep their children at home during the strike because of personnel absences. A group of these parents later launched a lawsuit seeking compensation for their children's lost access to public education.

■ PUBLIC HEALTH CARE

Perhaps the highest profile aspect of Canada's social welfare program is our public health care system. Each Canadian province offers a public health insurance scheme that covers the cost of a wide range of health care services and treatments.

The Ontario Health Insurance Plan (OHIP) offers coverage to Ontario residents who are either citizens or status immigrants. A **status immigrant** is a person who has been granted refugee status under a refugee convention, or a non-refugee immigrant who has met Canada's entry criteria. There are no premiums payable, and coverage is not based on employment. There is a residency stipulation, which requires claimants to live in Ontario for at least 153 of the first 183 days after applying for coverage, and 153 days of each year thereafter.

status immigrant
an immigrant who has been granted rights attendant with citizenship — for example, the right to work

Most children born in Ontario are registered under the plan before they leave the hospital after birth. Homebirthed children and new residents must be registered by their parents at an OHIP office.

At the moment, Ontario does not restrict a family's choice of physician, though it does restrict its choice to a medical doctor (MD). Families who seek alternative health care — such as naturopathy and homeopathy — for their children generally have to pay for it themselves. However, the services of certain alternative health practitioners — such as Ontario midwives — are now covered under the scheme.

OHIP does not generally cover the cost of drugs, either those sold over the counter or those sold by prescription; nor does it cover the cost of other health supplies, such as diabetic testing equipment. Some Ontario children enjoy full or partial coverage for drugs through an insurance plan of a parent's employer. Sometimes the cost of a child's medications, nutritional supplements, or health care equipment exceeds a threshold, established under the *Income Tax Act*. In this case, a parent may be able to claim an income tax deduction to help defray the cost. There is also a patchwork of other assistance programs for which families in need may qualify. Some are public (for example, the Trillium Drug Program and the Assistive Devices Program) and some are private (for example, the Easter Seals Society's programs).

Access Issues

The usefulness of public health care depends on the public's access to it. Barriers for children can include the following:

- lack of immigration status;

- language or other barriers related to a child's or family's problems in understanding health advice or communicating health information;

- residence in an isolated area where health care service is poor;

- residence in a populated area where high demands are placed on health care services;

- parents who fail to consent or facilitate access to health care;

- poverty, which results in an inability to pay for health care needs that are not covered by OHIP; and

- homelessness.

Social workers, child advocates, and other practitioners can sometimes help in overcoming some of these barriers. A child's poor access to health care, although difficult to identify, is perhaps most commonly observed by school personnel. An astute teacher may, for example, observe a symptom, such as vision or hearing loss, that has developed so gradually as to have escaped parental notice. A teacher may also form an opinion that a child has a chronic health problem — for example, sores, rashes, diarrhea, or a persistent cough — that is not being addressed through medical care. In these situations, the usual course of action is for the teacher or principal to discuss the observations with a parent. In serious situations where the parent does not act on the school's observations, the failure to obtain health care for the child may constitute neglect, and trigger the reporting duties set out in section 72 of the *Child and Family Services Act*. (Reporting duties are discussed in chapter 8 under the heading "Duty To Report."

Children under school age can be at increased risk from health care barriers related to parenting. When a child is not attending school or daycare, her health problems may go unnoticed by anyone other than a parent. Consider, for example, the Randal Dooley case study discussed earlier in this chapter. Some serious health problems can be difficult to detect, even by social workers. In this regard, consider the Jordan Heikamp case (discussed in chapter 2), where baby Jordan's life-threatening dehydration and malnutrition were not recognized by the social worker charged with supervising his care by an essentially homeless parent.

Luckily, general measures undertaken to protect children — for example, parent education, new-immigrant support programs, and income support programs — often tend to improve access to health care by extension.

Finally, when a child is found to be in need of protection, it is important to address his or her health problems and health care access issues as part of providing that protection.

■ POVERTY RELIEF

Assessing the prevalence of child poverty in Canada is a complicated, statistics-driven exercise. In general, a family is identified as living in poverty if the family income falls

ASIDE

CAN PATIENT–PHYSICIAN LANGUAGE BARRIERS AFFECT HEALTH CARE?

One of the most striking indications of the possible health outcomes of language barriers was described in a study by LeSon & Gershwin (1996) of young adults, aged 20–34, with asthma. The purpose of this study (and a companion study focusing on pediatric patients) was to determine the risk factors for intubation (the doctor's decision to place a breathing tube in the patient's throat). Intubation was used as a marker predicting death, which means that cases in which the patient was intubated were more likely to end in deaths than cases in which there was no intubation. This was a retrospective cohort study of hospitalized young adults, including all asthmatics aged 20–34 admitted over a 10-year period to a university medical centre in California. Of the 550 admissions, 209 were black, 180 were white, 118 were Hispanic, 27 American Indian; and 16 were Asian. Of all the patients, 34 required intubation. Severity of asthma was estimated as severe, moderate, or mild according to National Heart, Lung and Blood Institute guidelines. A large number of potential risk factors were included, including socio-economic variables and a variety of factors related to psychosocial functioning. … Patients with language barriers (defined as an inability to speak English) were over 17 times more likely to be intubated than patients with the same characteristics who were fluent in English. … A similar study of pediatric patients also found that a language barrier was a significant predictor, but the odds ratio fell to 3.3 (in other words, those with a language barrier were only 3.3 times more likely to be intubated than other patients). The study did not attempt to explain the link between a language barrier and greater risk of intubation. However, management of this chronic disease requires significant patient education and compliance with medication. Research on differences in asthma management by ethnicity has also found differences in patient understanding of the disease and self-management. … There is strong evidence that patient education, and therefore successful disease management, is impaired by the presence of a language barrier.

Source: Adapted from Bowen (2001, section 6.4.3).

below a "low income cutoff" that is propounded or accepted by the research agency seeking to quantify poverty. Dispute often surrounds the validity of these cutoffs and the definition of "necessities of life" upon which they are usually based.

According to David P. Ross, focusing on the calculation of the exact number of children living below an objective poverty line can lead analysts to miss the point. Especially where children are concerned, poverty means much more than not having adequate food and/or shelter. Low family income has consequences that pervade all aspects of children's lives.

In response to critics who suggest that it is enough to simply offer our poorest citizens bare physical survival, let me remind them that Canada is not a Third World country. Ours is a socially complex, economically advanced, and democratic society. In order for people to succeed in this society, they must do far more than just physically survive. They need a huge number of skills, many of which are learned during childhood. ...

What, then, are the potential threats to our envied status? I suggest there are at least two major concerns: the growth of earnings inequality in Canada, and the current trend towards slashing vital public services such as health care, education, and social assistance.

For the first time in Canada, there is abundant and compelling statistical evidence that family income has a major effect on child well-being. The data show that as family incomes rise, children's chances of developing to their full potential increase steadily. There is no magic poverty line above which children are guaranteed to thrive, and below which they are sure to fail. ...

Data from the surveys indicate that rates of poor health, hyperactivity, and delayed vocabulary development are much higher among children in low-income families than among children in middle- and high-income families. A child's likelihood of participating in organized sports activities is dramatically lower if they live in poor and modest-income families; rates of positive social relations and activities increase with family income. More than 16 per cent of older teens in poor families are at loose ends — they do not attend school, nor do they have a job — compared to less than four per cent of teens in high-income families. ...

Successful adults grow from successful children, and healthy child development requires more than just basic food and shelter. It is dependent upon access to economic resources, and shelter, access to good health care (including pre- and post-natal care, and dental care), positive parenting and child-care experiences, access to good schooling, to recreational and cultural opportunities, an involvement in community life, and a physical environment that is safe from pollution and crime. (Ross, 1999)

Income Support and Other Poverty Relief Programs

Reducing child poverty is a recurrent political issue in Canada. Income supplementation is primarily the responsibility of provincial governments, and the structure and philosophy of income support programs vary with the politics of successive governments. In the late 1990s and the early years of the 21st century, Ontario's government has favoured a strong "work incentive" philosophy in its provision of income relief programs, the pillar of which is called Ontario Works. Under the Ontario Works program, adult and teenage recipients of income support who are able to work or to attend school are required to do so, or to prove their need for and attendance in retraining programs. Parents receiving income support are given priority in obtaining subsidized daycare. Previous income support models have placed less emphasis on working, and have been more supportive of at-home parenting of young children.

Research results with respect to benefits to children from at-home parenting versus daycare have been mixed. For example, the health benefits of extended breast-feeding (which is really possible only if the mother is at home) are incontrovertible. On the other hand, some research suggests that very high quality daycare can improve the social and cognitive development of underprivileged children in relation to that of their wealthier peers.

The most common way that our society addresses child poverty is by attempting to improve the standard of living of parents. Income support programs pay parents, and those who design them can only assume, or hope, that the benefits are spent in ways that improve the standard of living of the whole family. However, income support payments can be very modest indeed. It is unrealistic to assume that even the most efficient welfare parent can adequately address a child's needs for shelter and nutrition, let alone a child's less tangible needs, such as recreation and intellectual stimulation.

In recognition of these shortfalls, many programs have emerged to tackle child welfare issues. These programs emanate from organizations as diverse as highly structured charitable institutions and informal community-based networks. Some programs, such as Food for Learning, are delivered within the education system, which has proven to be one of the best venues for identifying and addressing students' needs. Other community programs target young or single mothers. Finally, parenting programs are designed to assist parents in making good decisions with respect to their children's care.

Youth workers and social workers can help alleviate child poverty by educating both parents and children about the programs that exist in a particular community, and by facilitating access to these programs — for example, by helping with applications. They can also act as advocates for the rights of children when political decisions are being made about the future of income support and other key government programs.

Independent Teenagers

While our law currently requires parents to provide financial support to teenagers until they reach the age of 18, a teen can legally withdraw from parental control at age 16. A teen who can demonstrate that he receives no economic support from his family can apply for public income support. Obtaining access to support can be relatively difficult for teens (it is easier for teenage parents). A teen on income support must attend school to continue to qualify. Various support agencies can help teenagers with the application process. An example of such an agency is Ontario's Justice for Children and Youth, which also provides assistance to teens who are in trouble with the law.

KEY TERMS

autism

provincial school attendance
   counsellor

secular

status immigrant

REFERENCES

Bowen, Sarah. (2001). *Language Barriers in Access to Health Care.* Retrieved May 8, 2005 from http://www.hc-sc.gc.ca/hppb/healthcare/pubs/barriers/.

Child and Family Services Act. RSO 1990, c. C.11.

Education Act. RSO 1990, c. E.2.

Immunization of School Pupils Act. RSO 1990, c. I.1.

Ontario Ministry of Education. (2002). *Policy/Program Memorandum No. 131: Home Schooling.* Retrieved February 15, 2005 from http://www.edu.gov. on.ca/extra/eng/ppm/131.html.

Ross, David P. (1999). Insight: Rethinking child poverty. *Perception Magazine*, 23, no. 1. Retrieved May 8, 2005 from http://www.ccsd.ca/perception/221/cp.htm.

REVIEW QUESTIONS

1. Which tier of government (federal, provincial, or municipal) is responsible for delivering social welfare services, including education?

2. What are the three main branches of Canada's social welfare system for children?

3. In Ontario, school attendance is compulsory. What are a parent's legally acceptable alternatives to sending a child to public school?

4. How can a child's failure to attend school signal abuse?

5. How can social workers and youth workers promote or improve access to health care for children and youth?

6. In what ways can language or culture be a barrier to obtaining health care services?

7. Beyond limiting a child's access to bare necessities such as food and shelter, how does poverty affect children?

8. Why is it important to promote the development of parenting skills in families on income support?

DISCUSSION QUESTIONS

1. Is it important for school personnel to be trained in how to recognize child abuse? Why or why not?

2. Some parents avoid traditional health care practitioners and treatments (for themselves and for their children) for reasons of conscience or religion. What might be the implications of this kind of parental philosophy for child protection professionals? How can child protection professionals prepare themselves to deal with potential conflicts over these issues?

3. It is commonly thought that children living in poverty are at greater risk of abuse and neglect than other children. Determine on the basis of Internet research whether this view is supported by convincing authority. What reasons are suggested for an increased rate of child abuse in poor families? What strategies can you propose for reducing these risk factors?

6 Children and Criminality

◾ INTRODUCTION AND HISTORY OF CHILD CRIMINALITY

Every once in a while, usually in response to the commission of a particularly offensive crime by a particularly young offender, media attention focuses on "the problem of youth crime." In many cases, youth crime is portrayed as an emergent issue — a "sign of the times," a product of modern societal pressures, evidence that today's youth are growing up too fast, or evidence that they are more dangerous than the youth of previous generations.

The truth is, however, that children and youth — like adults — have always participated in a certain amount of criminality. In fact, before the middle of the 18th century, the notion of youth criminality was unheard of as an issue separate from adult criminality, because the concept of adolescence itself was only beginning to emerge. Before children and youth were recognized as developmentally different from adults, their crimes were simply that — crimes; and the punishment for those crimes was the same as it was for the crimes of adults.

CHAPTER OBJECTIVES

After reading this chapter, you should be able to:

- Explain how Canadian society deals with the "criminal" behaviour of children who are under the age of criminal responsibility.

- Identify the age of criminal responsibility, and the ages to which the *Youth Criminal Justice Act* applies.

- Describe the structure and principles of the *Youth Criminal Justice Act*.

- Describe the structure of the youth custody system and the rights of young inmates.

Implications of a Separate Category for Youth Crime

The evolution in society's view of childhood over the 18th and 19th centuries had two significant implications with respect to criminality. First, people began to believe that persons below a certain age did not have criminal responsibility. Second, people began to recognize that punishments given to adults who were found guilty of committing crimes were inappropriate for children and youth.

AGE OF CRIMINAL RESPONSIBILITY

Legal theorists of the 19th century began to advance the view that some children are not intellectually capable of forming a true criminal intent. Under the common

actus reus Latin for "guilty act"; the objective element of an offence, which may be an act, an omission, or a state of being

mens rea Latin for "guilty mind"; the subjective element of an offence that describes the state of mind or required intention of the accused

law, a crime has two elements: a guilty act (the **actus reus**), and a guilty intention (the **mens rea**). The absence of either of these elements generally means that no crime has been committed. Legal theorists began to consider that some young children were unable to understand the relationship of cause to effect and the logical consequences of their actions. This meant that those children could not be credited with the guilty intention necessary to bring their guilty acts within the common law's definition of crime. For example, an adult who throws a rock from an overpass into the path of traffic, causing a fatal car accident, might be charged with criminal negligence, or even manslaughter, because the adult would be expected to foresee the dangerous consequences of her act. A young child, by contrast, who throws the rock, and who lacks judgment and foresight, would likely be found to lack an intention to cause harm (manslaughter) or recklessness with respect to the consequences of her act (criminal negligence).

The logical consequence of this view is that children who are found, at trial, to have lacked the necessary *mens rea* to commit a crime are not guilty, and are entitled to leave court and resume their lives free of interference from the criminal justice system for the time being. However, determining the *mens rea* in every case is impractical — to conduct an investigation of the mental state of each child who has committed a guilty act would place an enormous burden on the resources of the justice system. In response to this dilemma, the concept of age of criminal responsibility began to emerge. Children below a certain age were simply deemed to be not criminally responsible for their guilty acts. In Canada, the age of criminal responsibility — that is, the age at which a child can be prosecuted for a crime — is 12 years. (This does not mean that all children who have reached the age of 12 are deemed to have the necessary criminal intention to commit a crime. The prosecution must always establish that the person accused of committing a crime — whether she is an adult or a child — had the guilty intention necessary to bring her guilty act within the sphere of the criminal law.)

While the creation of a "not criminally responsible" category addressed the situation of young children, it did nothing to recognize the unique developmental status of teenagers. As the concept of adolescence began to emerge, experts suggested that while in many ways teens think and act like adults, their powers of reasoning and judgment are still developing; additionally, they lack the life experience that helps inform adult decision making. These differences mean that teens are more likely than adults to make inappropriate decisions, including those related to the commission of crimes. The notion that teen criminality was somewhat more excusable than the adult variety helped to create, in many countries, justice systems for teens that are distinct in some ways from those for adults. In Canada, teen criminality is managed under the *Youth Criminal Justice Act*, which applies to crimes committed by persons between the ages of 12 and 17.

ADULT PUNISHMENT AS INAPPROPRIATE FOR CHILDREN AND YOUTH

The second crime-related idea that grew out of the evolution of the concept of childhood was the inappropriateness of punishing guilty children in the same way as guilty adults. There was a general sense that guilty children were perhaps not quite as guilty as their adult counterparts. The creation of an age of criminal responsibility was supposed to address this issue, but there remained a lingering uneasiness about subjecting children to the harshest penalties under the law. This uneasiness matured into a view that children, who are still developing intellectually and emotionally, should be especially susceptible to reform efforts. In other words, they ought to be given the chance to learn from their mistakes and to avoid making further mistakes in the future.

The idea that society should put effort into the rehabilitation of "delinquent" children led to the creation of reform schools. More recently, children who commit criminal acts have sometimes been deemed to be in need of protection, and their needs have been addressed under the *Child and Family Services Act.*

When a youth is convicted of a crime, our justice system very carefully considers the appropriate penalties. **Custody**, the harshest criminal penalty, is imposed only on serious offenders, and only when all alternatives have been considered and rejected. In most cases, youth in custody are kept separate from adults, ideally in separate facilities. The federal *Youth Criminal Justice Act* establishes guidelines for imposing criminal penalties on youth, as well as mechanisms for sentencing, custody transfers, appeals, reintegration into the community, and other key issues.

custody (in sentencing context) in the criminal law context, residence in a corrections facility

Facts About Youth Crime

Analysis of youth crime reporting suggests that the media consistently exaggerate and sensationalize both the prevalence and the seriousness of youth crime as a subcategory of crime in general (Tanner, 1996, p. 6). This kind of reporting, in turn, influences the public's perception of youth crime. When asked about the subject, adults typically overestimate the amount of crime committed by youth. The average member of the public is often unaware that patterns of crime by youth differ considerably from adult patterns. For example,

- the types of crimes most commonly committed by youth differ from those most commonly committed by adults;

- youth commit fewer violent crimes than do adults;

- the motivations for youth crime often differ from the motivations for adult crime;

- crime reduction strategies — such as **deterrence** and custody — are less effective against youth crime than against adult crime; yet

- youth criminals have a lower rate of **recidivism** (the commission of further offences) than do adult criminals.

deterrence in the criminal context, the use of sanctions against convicted offenders to discourage similar offending by those who might contemplate it

recidivism the tendency to revert to criminality and commit further offences

PATTERN OF CRIMES COMMITTED BY YOUTH

Certain kinds of crime are overrepresented when youth criminal activity patterns are compared with adult patterns. Crimes characteristic of the youth pattern include vandalism, shoplifting, break and enter, motor vehicle theft, joyriding, and crimes related to substance abuse.

While minor assaults (often in the course of fighting) are common, serious violence by youth is a rare occurrence. Some statistics show a disturbing increase in violent criminality on the part of adolescent girls (Leschied et al., 2000). However, since girls commit only about a quarter of all youth crimes, these offences represent only a tiny proportion of the broader picture of violent crime.

MOTIVATIONS FOR CRIMINAL ACTIVITY AND THE IMPACT OF DETERRENCE

One of the most important factors that distinguishes youth crime from adult crime is that many youths cite motivations for criminal activity that differ significantly from those of their adult counterparts. Recklessness, inappropriate risk taking, experimentation, and rebelliousness have long been recognized as characteristics of adolescent behaviour. These characteristics lead, in some cases, to criminal activity, particularly with respect to vandalism, joyriding, substance abuse, and petty theft. In many cases, a youth's foray into criminal activity can be more readily character- ized as an isolated mistake than a first step in a criminal career. Recidivism is lower among youths than it is among adults. Research suggests that the lower recidivism rate is associated less with the "success" of criminal penalties than with simple maturation; in other words, young people are more likely to "grow out of" crime than to learn to avoid it because they are deterred by sentences. Because many young people commit crimes out of impulsiveness or recklessness, traditional crime-reduction strategies based on deterrence appear to be less effective for youth. This fact has been taken into consideration in the emphasis placed by the *Youth Criminal Justice Act* on avoiding sentences that are designed to punish offenders (such as custody) in favour of rehabilitative approaches.

▉ CHILDREN UNDER THE AGE OF CRIMINAL RESPONSIBILITY

The belief that children under the age of 12 are not capable of forming a criminal intention is reflected, in our society, by a social welfare rather than a criminal justice approach to criminality for children aged 11 or younger. Where an underage child is suspected of committing an act that would otherwise be a crime, a **peace officer** can apprehend (take into custody) the child without a warrant under section 42 of the *Child and Family Services Act*. Section 40(13) of the Act gives peace officers the powers of child protection workers for the purpose of child apprehension. Section 40(8) allows a child protection worker to call in a police officer to assist with an apprehension.

peace officer a term that is usually broader than "police officer," that can be assigned to an individual (usually a government employee), and that is the basis for that individual's authority to take law enforcement or victim protection action

Section 42(1) of the *Child and Family Services Act* provides as follows:

> A peace officer who believes on reasonable and probable grounds that a child actually or apparently under twelve years of age has committed an act in respect of which a person twelve years of age or older could be found guilty of an offence may apprehend the child without a warrant and on doing so,
>
>> (a) shall return the child to the child's parent or other person having charge of the child as soon as practicable; or
>> (b) where it is not possible to return the child to the parent or other person within a reasonable time, shall take the child to a place of safety to be detained there until the child can be returned to the parent or other person.

■ THE YOUTH CRIMINAL JUSTICE ACT: AN OVERVIEW

The *Youth Criminal Justice Act* incorporates four general principles. These principles, which are expressed in section 3(1), can be summarized as follows:

1. the protection of the public;

2. a system separate from the adult system, with a separate procedure and an emphasis on rehabilitation;

3. sentencing that is culturally sensitive and promotes respect and reparations to victims "within the limits of fair and proportionate accountability"; and

4. special protections, including enhanced civil rights and a role for parents.

The *Youth Criminal Justice Act* was introduced in a complex political climate characterized by the recognition that widespread incarceration has a fairly poor track record for reducing youth crime and a (largely unsupported) public perception that violent youth crime is on the rise. Both in its provisions and in the way these provisions are applied by judges, the Act therefore reflects a tension between competing values within the law enforcement system.

From a child protection perspective, the most important improvements made by the *Youth Criminal Justice Act* (over the *Young Offenders Act*, which preceded it) may be refinements to sentencing and to the rights of youth in custody. The *Youth Criminal Justice Act* provides explicit sentencing principles designed to emphasize rehabilitation, the promotion of responsibility on the part of youth, and the obligation on judges to select the least restrictive sentence capable of protecting the public. When a judge believes that incarceration is necessary for public protection, rules regarding custody, facility choices, and placement review support the goal of minimum restrictions on freedom.

Sections 35 and 29(1) of the Act are also worthy of particular note for child protection workers. These sections hint at the complicated interplay between the child protection system and the youth criminal justice system.

Section 35 provides that a **youth justice court** may, in addition to making any other order at any stage in the criminal proceedings, "refer the young person to a child welfare agency for assessment to determine whether the young person is in need of child welfare services." This section requires courts to treat the youth criminal justice system as separate from the child protection system. This separation forces judges to sentence young offenders purely for criminal law reasons, and not for their own protection.

In the past, judges have ordered incarceration for youth whose needs for protection were at least as great as their needs for correction. This was partly the result of the fact that our modern youth criminal justice system had its roots in the juvenile delinquency reform school system, and partly the result of practical considerations. A very large proportion of cases of serious youth criminality are complicated by unmet needs for care, guidance, and protection on the part of the young offender. It is easy for experienced youth court judges to identify factors such as inadequate parenting, guidance, education, or housing as major contributors to a young person's problems with the law. Where a young person is in a difficult life situation, judges have sometimes imposed incarceration in the hope that the

youth justice court
a special court created by the *Youth Criminal Justice Act* for handling criminal cases where the accused was between the ages of 12 and 17 at the time of the alleged offence

conditions of custody — economic stability and access to education, for example — will satisfy some of the unmet needs of the youth.

Though based on an impulse to help, this response has been condemned by policy makers who see the dangers of using the criminal custody system in this way. In a nutshell, these policy makers believe that it is inappropriate to confuse the purpose of the criminal justice system with social welfare objectives. A more appropriate response, obviously, would be to devote the resources of the criminal justice system to crime control and the resources of the social welfare system to social welfare purposes.

The *Youth Criminal Justice Act* explicitly refers to the inappropriateness of using the criminal justice system for social welfare purposes in section 29(1):

> A youth justice court judge … shall not detain a young person in custody prior to being sentenced as a substitute for appropriate child protection, mental health or other social measures.

Of course, whether sufficient "child protection, mental health or other social measures" will be in place to take up the slack depends on complicated issues of access, accountability, and funding. This is an issue that child protection workers must grapple with throughout their careers.

Structure

The *Youth Criminal Justice Act* is made up of nine parts. Six of these — involving extrajudicial measures, organization of the youth criminal justice system, judicial measures, sentencing, custody and supervision, and publication and records — are discussed below. The other three parts — which involve procedural, transitional, and enactment issues — are beyond the scope of this text.

EXTRAJUDICIAL MEASURES

Extrajudicial measures can be described as ways in which police are authorized to handle youth crime without resort to the formal court system. These measures include cautioning a suspect, referring him to a social welfare agency, and referring him to a mental health facility or practitioner. They also include **sanctions**, a type of informal, extrajudicial sentence — for example, community service.

sanctions punishments imposed as a consequence for breaking a law

ORGANIZATION OF THE YOUTH CRIMINAL JUSTICE SYSTEM

This part of the *Youth Criminal Justice Act* provides for special courts and judges (youth justice courts) with authority over young suspects. Youth charged with crimes committed while they were between the ages of 12 and 17 fall into this category.

JUDICIAL MEASURES

This large part of the Act sets out the nuts and bolts of youth justice court procedure. Where a procedural matter is not specifically described, regular criminal procedure — that is, the procedure described in Canada's *Criminal Code* — applies. Issues covered under the judicial measures part of the *Youth Criminal Justice Act* include the following:

1. *The right to counsel.* All youth are entitled to be represented by a lawyer in criminal proceedings. This right arises early, at the stage when police are considering taking extrajudicial measures instead of prosecuting a youth. In order to encourage a young person to hire a lawyer, a youth's right to counsel is mentioned in a notice given by the police to the youth's parents after the youth is arrested, or served with a charging document (a ticket). If a young suspect cannot afford to hire a lawyer, the police generally refer her to legal aid. In some cases, a youth justice court can order the attorney general to appoint a lawyer for a youth, or it can order that a youth and her parents be represented by different lawyers.

2. *Notice to parents.* The police are required to give notice of a charge (and notice of a youth's right to counsel) to a parent; if no parent is available, the police must give notice to an adult relative or guardian of the youth. The purpose of this provision is to inform a responsible adult of the situation facing the youth so that she may assist the youth in hiring a lawyer and may provide support during the legal proceedings. An exception to the notice requirement exists where a youth is 20 or older at the time of his first court appearance (having been charged while under 18).

3. *Detention before sentencing.* In some criminal cases, a suspect is detained in custody before he is found guilty of having committed an offence and sentenced to incarceration. The usual reason for detention of this nature is that the suspect is deemed to be dangerous to society, or likely to escape before he can be tried. The *Youth Criminal Justice Act* imposes strict limits on the situations in which a young person can be detained before sentencing. The Act incorporates the pre-trial detention rules of Canada's *Criminal Code*, which are also applicable to adults charged with criminal offences. In addition, it adds its own rules, which are applicable only to youth. Under section 515(10) of the *Criminal Code*, a youth can be detained only if one or more of the following conditions are met:

   a. the detention is necessary to ensure that the youth will appear at his trial;

   b. the detention is necessary for the protection of the public — that is, to prevent the youth from offending again; and

   c. the detention is necessary to maintain public confidence in "the administration of justice."

   Section 29(2) of the *Youth Criminal Justice Act* imposes further restrictions on pre-sentencing custody by saying that a youth cannot be detained before being sentenced unless, if convicted, he would be subject to incarceration even after considering the restrictions on custody imposed by section 39(1) of the Act. These restrictions forbid a sentence that involves custody unless:

   a. the young person has committed a violent offence;

   b. the young person has failed to comply with previous sentences that have not involved custody; or

    c. the young person has committed a serious offence (an offence that would attract a two-year or longer term of imprisonment if committed by an adult), and the young person has a criminal record.

The combination of these restrictions means, in essence, that a young person cannot be detained before sentencing in the absence of violence, breach of probation, or the combination of a serious offence and a criminal record.

   4. *Medical or psychological assessment.* Part 3 of the *Youth Criminal Justice Act* also authorizes a court to order that a young person undergo a medical or psychological assessment. The court can order an assessment for one of a number of purposes. These include determining the appropriateness of pre-trial release (bail); assessing whether a young person can be subject to an adult sentence; supporting an appropriate choice of youth sentence; or supporting a choice of appropriate probation conditions. In some rare cases, a court can order the detention of a young person for the purpose of obtaining a medical or psychological assessment.

SENTENCING

As noted elsewhere in this chapter, the *Youth Criminal Justice Act* reflects a strong bias against incarceration for young people. The part of the Act that addresses sentencing provides greater detail about this issue. General principles of sentencing to be applied under the Act are expressed in section 38(2), which requires judges to choose a sentence that

- is consistent with other youth sentences for the same offence;

- is "proportionate to the seriousness of the offence and the degree of responsibility of the young person for that offence";

- is the least restrictive sentence available that is capable of achieving the purposes of sentencing (see below);

- is most likely to promote successful rehabilitation and reintegration into the community; and

- promotes a sense of responsibility in the young person, and acknowledges the harm done to the community.

The purpose of sentencing, as expressed by section 38(1), "is to hold a young person accountable for an offence through the imposition of just sanctions that have meaningful consequences for the young person and that promote his or her rehabilitation and reintegration into society, thereby contributing to the long-term protection of the public."

CUSTODY AND SUPERVISION

Part 5 deals with custody (incarceration) and supervision (probation). Once a youth has been tried and sentenced, she is generally dealt with not by youth court judges, but by administrators within the youth custody system. Part 5 is very detailed and covers many issues that can arise while a youth is in custody. These include the following:

- the level of custody, which involves matters such as the type of facility and amount of security;

- reviews of, and changes to, the level of custody;

- separating young offenders from adults (separation is necessary in most, but not all, cases — for example, all offenders 20 and older at the time of sentencing are incarcerated with adults);

- appeals by youth from administrative decisions about custody — for example, the level of custody;

- "reintegration leave," either on compassionate grounds — for example, for medical treatment — or as preparation for discharge;

- sentence review (commonly known as parole);

- appropriate conditions for supervision (parole) orders; and

- consequences of breach of supervision (parole) conditions.

From a child protection perspective, it is important to note that part 5 also provides for the "designation" of a youth worker for every young person sentenced to custody. According to section 90, the role of the youth worker is to "work with the young person to plan for his or her reintegration into the community, including the preparation and implementation of a reintegration plan that sets out the most effective programs for the young person in order to maximize his or her chances for reintegration into the community."

Part 5 of the *Youth Criminal Justice Act* should be read in conjunction with the *Child and Family Services Act*, which guarantees rights to, and provides protection for, youth in custody. A discussion of this aspect of the *Child and Family Services Act* appears below under the heading "Youth in Custody and the Child and Family Services Act."

PUBLICATION AND RECORDS

The *Youth Criminal Justice Act* reflects the principle that protecting the identity of young offenders reduces the hazard of "labelling" these youth as criminals. The avoidance of labelling was introduced by the *Juvenile Delinquents Act* and carried on by the *Young Offenders Act*, both of which were predecessors to the *Youth Criminal Justice Act*. Most psychologists agree that avoiding labelling can reduce the likelihood that a youth will continue to live up to a past reputation as a criminal. By not publishing identifying information about young offenders, the justice system seeks to protect their reputation in the community, recognizing that the young make mistakes because of their immaturity. By protecting the privacy of young people, the courts seek to eliminate limits on their future opportunities.

The publication ban imposed by the *Youth Criminal Justice Act* is not absolute. Section 110 prohibits the publication of information "that would identify the young person as a young person dealt with under this Act." However, there are exceptions, including cases where

- the young person is subject to an adult sentence; or

- the young person has been designated as a violent offender under the Act.

■STATUTORY OVERLAP

This book deals with two statutes in considerable depth: the *Youth Criminal Justice Act* (YCJA), a federal statute, and the *Child and Family Services Act* (CFSA), a provincial statute.

No statute is created in a vacuum. The drafters of the *Youth Criminal Justice Act* were conscious of a certain degree of overlap between child criminality and child protection. The drafters of the *Child and Family Services Act* have created a presumption that children under 12 years of age who engage in criminal behaviour are children in need of protection. Figure 6.1 is designed to assist child protection workers in understanding which statute applies to the various circumstances in which their clients may find themselves.

FIGURE 6.1　WHICH STATUTE APPLIES?

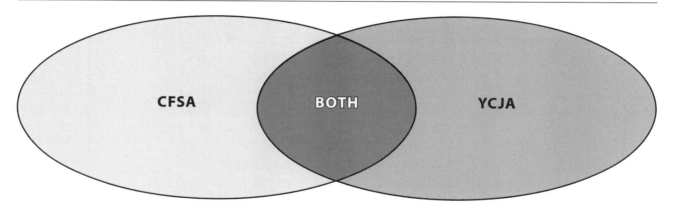

CFSA

- A child under 12 commits acts that would be crimes if she were older, especially if she is apprehended by police.

- A youth (12 or over) is convicted of crimes that require social services or protective care, but not criminal custody.

- A non-self-supporting youth (12 to 18) is released from criminal custody without a safe place to live.

- A youth (under 18) who is not being prosecuted for a crime is homeless and a nuisance.

YCJA

- A child (12 or over) is charged with a crime, but is not in need of protective care.

- a child (12 or over) is released from criminal custody into the care of parents or guardians, sometimes with probation terms.

BOTH

- A youth (12 to 17) who is being prosecuted for a crime has suffered or is at risk of suffering abuse or neglect.

- A youth (12 to 18) is sentenced to criminal custody in a provincial facility.

- A youth (12 to 18) is released from criminal custody into a residential facility for his protection, and is subject to sentencing conditions such as probation or supervision.

■ YOUTH IN CUSTODY AND THE CHILD AND FAMILY SERVICES ACT

Canada's *Constitution Act, 1867* gives the federal government power to legislate in relation to criminal law. Statutes such as the *Criminal Code* and the *Youth Criminal Justice Act* are laws passed in accordance with this power. The establishment and administration of custody facilities, however, is a responsibility that is shared between the federal and provincial governments. Section 91(28) of the *Constitution Act, 1867* gives the federal government the power to establish and maintain penitentiaries; section 92(6) gives the provincial governments power over "Public and Reformatory Prisons."

Under Canada's current custody system, whether a convict is sentenced to serve time in a federal penitentiary or a provincial reformatory depends on the length of the sentence; the length of the sentence depends on the seriousness of the offence, and whether or not the convicted person is deemed to be dangerous.

Because of the anti-custody emphasis of the *Youth Criminal Justice Act*, it is uncommon for a young offender to serve a sentence in a federal penitentiary. A judge would impose a penitentiary sentence under section 76 of the Act only if the young person were (1) sentenced as an adult as permitted under the *Youth Criminal Justice Act*, (2) 18 years of age or older at the time of sentencing, and (3) sentenced to imprisonment for a period of two years or more.

In the vast majority of cases, young convicts serve their sentences in provincial youth custody facilities.

Provincial Youth Custody Facilities Under the Child and Family Services Act

The establishment, designation, and administration of provincial youth custody facilities is governed, in Ontario, by many statutes, including the *Youth Criminal Justice Act* and the *Child and Family Services Act*. A detailed summary of Ontario's prison system is beyond the scope of this book. For our purposes, it is important to know that the *Youth Criminal Justice Act* requires the province to administer its prison system by establishing and maintaining at least two different levels of custody for youth, and by keeping youth separate from adults in most cases.

Part IV of the *Child and Family Services Act* authorizes the minister to establish and maintain custody programs for youth, including open, temporary, medium security, and maximum security programs. "Open" custody is distinguished from "secure" custody. Whether a facility or portion of a facility is designated as secure custody generally depends on the degree of restrictions on personal freedom for the offender. For example, an offender in open custody may have considerable freedom to move about the facility, and, to some extent, the community. A secure custody facility will usually have locked doors, guards, and other restraints. Medium- and maximum-security facilities are two forms of secure custody. Maximum-security facilities incorporate sophisticated restraint and monitoring features — for example, isolation cells, closed-circuit television (CCTV) surveillance, and high-security perimeter fencing.

Section 90 of the *Child and Family Services Act* provides for the designation of probation officers who can act both as youth workers under the *Youth Criminal*

Justice Act and as probation officers under the *Provincial Offences Act*. The duties of youth workers under the *Youth Criminal Justice Act* are set out above under the heading "Custody and Supervision."

If a judge orders the temporary detention of a young person, section 93(2) of the *Child and Family Services Act* calls for open detention of that person unless

- she has been charged with an offence for which an adult would be liable to serve five years' imprisonment or more *and* either the offence was a violent one, she has a history of failure to appear at trial, or she has a serious, recent criminal record (a record involving another offence for which an adult might serve five years' imprisonment that she has committed within the previous 12 months); or

- she has escaped or has tried to leave open detention without consent.

Section 94 of the *Child and Family Services Act* also expresses a presumption that young persons will be held in medium-security custody unless certain conditions are met to qualify them for maximum-security custody. These conditions, in a nutshell, turn on the violent nature of the offence and whether, if tried as an adult, the young person would have received a sentence of five years or more.

The Act also provides for the apprehension of young people who have escaped open detention. In addition, it grants powers of search and entry to police officers to assist in apprehending escapees.

The Rights of Youth in Custody

Part V of the *Child and Family Services Act* recognizes that young people serving custodial sentences have specified rights. These rights, which are listed below, are guaranteed by section 99 of the Act to any "child in care" — namely, any child

- who is in the care of a foster parent, or

- who is detained in a place of temporary detention or committed to secure or open custody under the *Youth Criminal Justice Act*.

The rights of children in care or custody are discussed in detail in chapter 9. For the purpose of this chapter, it is important to know that children in care are guaranteed a number of basic rights, which can be summarized as follows:

- the right to receive regular visits from family members (there is an exception for Crown wards, who must make a special application to receive these visits);

- the right to receive visits from a lawyer, an advocate, the Ombudsman, or a member of provincial or federal Parliament;

- the right to send and receive mail that is not opened or read by others (there is an exception that allows examination of mail, in the child's presence, for things such as weapons and drugs);

- the right to have reasonable privacy and to their own possessions;

- the right to receive religious instruction and participate in religious activities of their own choosing;

- the right to have a plan of care provided for them within 30 days of coming into care;

- the right to participate in the development of the plan of care;

- the right to eat appropriate food of good quality;

- the right to wear appropriate well-fitting clothing;

- the right to receive medical and dental care;

- the right to receive an education that meets their aptitudes and needs, preferably in a community setting — that is, outside the care facility, although usually youth in custody receive their schooling inside the custody facility;

- the right to participate in recreational and athletic activities;

- the right to express their views on any issue that affects them, to the extent that they are mature enough to do so; and

- the right to be informed of their rights and how they can be enforced, the rules of the care or custody facility, and their responsibilities while in care.

The *Child and Family Services Act* provides a complaints procedure under which children in care can seek to enforce rights that they feel are being denied. This procedure is discussed in detail in chapter 9.

Extraordinary Measures for Serious Mental Disorders

Part VI of the *Child and Family Services Act* deals with measures that may be taken, in extraordinary circumstances, to treat or manage the behaviour of children with serious mental disorders. Again, these measures are discussed more fully in chapter 9. For the purpose of this chapter, mental disorder is defined under section 112 of the Act as "a substantial disorder of emotional processes, thought or cognition which grossly impairs a person's capacity to make reasoned judgments."

Where a young person (who may also be a young offender) is suffering from a mental disorder, the administrators of a secure treatment program may be authorized to use certain measures to modify the young person's behaviour. These measures include locking up the young person, administering psychotropic drugs (drugs that affect mental/emotional function), and using mechanical restraints or other techniques that may be prescribed to control behaviour.

Because these treatments are physically intrusive and can have side effects, their use is very closely controlled. Part VI of the *Child and Family Services Act* establishes a procedure for deciding whether the use of a particular treatment is warranted. It also empowers a young person and his representative to challenge a decision to use a particular technique. These provisions are discussed in greater detail in chapter 9.

KEY TERMS

actus reus

custody (in sentencing context)

deterrence

mens rea

peace officer

recidivism

sanctions

youth justice court

REFERENCES

Child and Family Services Act. RSO 1990, c. C.11.

Constitution Act, 1867. 30 & 31 Vict., c. 3 (UK).

Leschied, Alan W. et al. (2000). *Female Adolescent Aggression: A Review of the Literature and the Correlates of Aggression.* Retrieved May 8, 2005 from Public Safety and Emergency Preparedness Canada website: http://www.sgc.gc.ca/publications/corrections/200004_Leschied_report_e.pdf.

Tanner, Julian. (1996). *Teenage Troubles: Youth and Deviance in Canada.* Toronto: Nelson.

Youth Criminal Justice Act. SC 2002, c. 1.

REVIEW QUESTIONS

1. Is youth crime an emergent issue? Why or why not?

2. List at least two ways in which our society treats the criminal behaviour of young people differently from the criminal behaviour of adults.

3. List at least three reasons why our society differentiates between the criminal behaviour of young people and the criminal behaviour of adults.

4. What happens when a child under the age of 12 commits an act that would be a crime if it were committed by an adult?

5. Why is deterrence a less important principle under the *Youth Criminal Justice Act* than under the criminal law generally?

6. Why does the provincial *Child and Family Services Act* deal with custody when criminal law is the responsibility of the federal government?

7. What is an extrajudicial measure under the *Youth Criminal Justice Act*? Why does the Act provide for extrajudicial measures?

8. Why are there restrictions on the publication of identifying information about a young person who is suspected of or convicted of committing an offence?

9. Why does the *Youth Criminal Justice Act* require that parents be given notice when a young person is charged with a crime? What happens if parents cannot be identified or will not get involved?

10. List five rights of a young person in custody.

DISCUSSION QUESTIONS

1. The *Youth Criminal Justice Act* strongly emphasizes rehabilitation in its sentencing principles. However, even people within the justice system often admit that the system does not provide an environment that is well suited to the task of rehabilitating young people with problems.

    a. Do the media affect the ability of law enforcement personnel to focus on rehabilitation when dealing with young offenders, especially violent ones? Why or why not?

    b. In what ways does the *Youth Criminal Justice Act* attempt to address the apparent conflict between its own principles and the realities of criminal justice and secure custody?

2. Under the *Youth Criminal Justice Act*, a judge can no longer sentence a young person to custody in an attempt to get him off the streets and to force the system to address his unmet needs. How, in the absence of a sentencing option, can the justice system bring a young person to the attention of the social welfare system? Skim the *Youth Criminal Justice Act* to identify at least two opportunities for referring a young offender to a social welfare service provider.

PART III

Protecting Children's Safety

7 Child Protection Under the Criminal Code

■ INTRODUCTION TO THE CRIMINAL CODE'S ENHANCED PROTECTION FOR CHILDREN

As discussed in previous chapters, Canada (along with most other countries) recognizes that children and young people have a special status in society. The physical vulnerability of children is obvious to everybody. Children cannot take care of many of their fundamental needs. Young children, especially, require help with very basic functions, such as eating, dressing, and bathing. Older children, who have the physical coordination to handle these tasks, still need help with other aspects of their lives. For example, a sick 10-year-old may not be able to judge whether he needs just rest and fluids, or whether he needs to see a doctor. He also needs his parents to arrange the visit to the doctor and to provide transportation. Finally, even young people who act like adults most of the time are still not completely capable of managing their own needs. As any parent who has packed a fiercely independent 18-year-old off to an out-of-town university knows from the regular "help me!" calls, adult-looking teenagers can have great difficulty coping with the vagaries of adult existence. Young people simply lack the judgment that comes with experience.

Our criminal law recognizes the fact that children are a dependent, and sometimes vulnerable, class of people. As vulnerable people, they are more easily victimized than their adult counterparts. The *Criminal Code* provides enhanced protection for children in an attempt to offset this vulnerability, and to inform would-be victimizers that Canada's criminal justice system has a low tolerance for those who take advantage of children.

Responsibility for the protection of children in Canada is assumed jointly by the provincial and federal governments. The introduction to a

CHAPTER OBJECTIVES

After reading this chapter, you should be able to:

- Explain why the *Criminal Code* extends enhanced protection to children.

- List at least five *Criminal Code* offences against children.

- Give an example of an offence that is rendered more serious if the victim is a minor.

- Give an example of an offence that is rendered more serious because the offender has a special responsibility toward the young victim.

- List at least three offences with which a child protection worker or a social welfare administrator could be charged in the course of her professional duties.

- Describe *Criminal Code* provisions designed to facilitate children's testifying in court.

- Explain the purpose and role of sex offender registries.

1999 federal Department of Justice consultation paper expresses this joint responsibility as follows:

> Developing and maintaining effective measures to protect children compre-
> hensively from serious injury and death at the hands of adults requires the
> best efforts of the provinces and territories and the Government of Canada
> working together. Providing services to children in need of protection is the
> responsibility of the provinces and territories; ensuring that appropriate of-
> fences and penalties are available is the responsibility of the Government of
> Canada. Through the *Criminal Code*, the Government of Canada provides
> strong support for provincial and territorial initiatives to protect children.

Child protection under the *Criminal Code* is expressed in a number of ways.
First, there are some actions that are offences only if they are perpetrated in relation
to children — for example, invitation to sexual touching (section 152) or luring
(section 172.1). Second, there are some actions that are always offences, but that are
more serious offences (often carrying harsher penalties) when they are perpetrated
in relation to children — for example, procuring (pimping) (section 212). Third,
there are some actions that are either criminal offences, or more serious criminal
offences, if the perpetrator violates a responsibility toward a young person — for
example, sexual exploitation (section 153).

This chapter provides a brief overview of *Criminal Code* offences in relation
to minors (typically, people under the age of 18). It also introduces offences that
can be charged against child protection professionals. It provides an overview of
Criminal Code provisions designed to make it easier for children to testify in court,
and finally it introduces the federal and provincial sex offender registries.

Criminal procedure is a fairly detailed and complicated area of the law, and a
thorough discussion of it is well beyond the scope of this book. For basic and general
information about Canadian criminal law and procedure, you may wish to consult
Foundations of Criminal and Civil Law in Canada (Hoag and Rock, forthcoming).

Offences Against Children

It is important to remember that the *Criminal Code*, in its entirety, applies to children as well as adults. As a result, almost any offence that has a victim can have a
child victim. In other words, an offence need not mention children specifically in
order to apply to an event that has involved an adult and a child.

General provisions with respect to violent offences — such as assault, sexual
assault, and murder — apply when these offences are committed against children.
A discussion of the full range of criminal offences is beyond the scope of this book;
however, some offences more commonly charged in cases of child abuse are worth
exploring here. The *Criminal Code* is divided into parts. For simplicity, this chapter
lists offences in the order in which they appear in the *Criminal Code*, and refers to
the parts of the Code in which they are contained.

PART VII: DISORDERLY HOUSES (PROSTITUTION), GAMING AND BETTING

Part VII of the *Criminal Code* deals with prostitution. Section 212, which covers
procuring (pimping), makes it illegal to procure, attempt to procure, or solicit a

person to have illicit sexual intercourse with another person. The section prohibits a wide range of behaviour that falls within the act of procuring — for example, bringing someone under false pretenses to a "common bawdy-house" for the purpose of recruiting that person as a prostitute, and living "on the avails of prostitution" (earning a living as a pimp).

While section 212(1) makes no reference to age, in practice the people most likely to be recruited as prostitutes are teenagers and very young adults of both sexes. Street youth are at particular risk of being the victims of procuring offences.

Non-aggravated procuring, under section 212(1) of the *Criminal Code* is an **indictable offence**. A person convicted of this offence could be imprisoned for a maximum of 10 years. The offence of aggravated procuring, under section 212(2), consists of living on the avails of prostitution of a person under the age of 18 years; a person convicted of this offence could be imprisoned for a maximum of 14 years. Furthermore, under section 212(2.1), a person who is convicted of aggravated procuring *must* be sentenced to at least 5 years' imprisonment if he uses violence or threats of violence in the course of committing the offence.

Related to procuring is prostitution (see section 213). Stopping a pedestrian or motorist, blocking traffic, or communicating with a person for the purpose of prostitution (often called "soliciting") is an offence for both the prostitute and the client — it can be charged against either or both parties. Communicating for the purpose of prostitution is a **summary conviction offence**.

indictable offence
a serious crime that is subject to stiff penalties and that is prosecuted using the more formal of two possible sets of criminal procedures

summary conviction offence a less serious crime than an indictable offence that carries a light penalty; the accused may be tried in Provincial Court without the benefit of a jury or a preliminary hearing

hybrid offence a crime that allows the prosecution to proceed by way of either summary conviction or indictment

ASIDE

SUMMARY CONVICTION, INDICTABLE, AND HYBRID OFFENCES

This chapter mentions three kinds of offences: summary conviction offences, indictable offences, and hybrid offences. In a nutshell, the difference involves the procedure that the Crown follows in prosecuting the person who is accused of committing the offence. The *Criminal Code* defines all offences as being either summary conviction, indictable, or hybrid.

Summary Conviction Offences

In general, summary conviction offences are less serious and carry lighter penalties than indictable offences. They are tried before a Provincial Court judge without a jury. There is no hearing preliminary to the trial itself.

Indictable Offences

Indictable offences are more serious than summary conviction offences. In Ontario, they are tried in one of three ways: before a Provincial Court judge, before a judge of the Ontario

Superior Court of Justice, or before a judge and jury of the Ontario Superior Court of Justice. The person accused of having committed a criminal offence is entitled to choose her mode of trial. In most cases, a hearing is held before trial (pre-trial hearing) to ensure that there is enough evidence to warrant a trial.

Hybrid Offences

If a person is charged with a **hybrid offence**, the Crown has the option of using either the summary conviction procedure or the indictable procedure in prosecuting the case. Where the Crown is anxious to secure a more significant penalty for the accused — for example, if a hybrid offence has been charged, but the Crown strongly suspects that the accused has committed other, more serious offences that cannot be proven — the Crown may opt for the more complicated, slower indictable procedure because on conviction a higher penalty is available.

PART VIII: OFFENCES AGAINST THE PERSON AND REPUTATION

Part VIII contains most of the violent offences created by the *Criminal Code* (other than those related to terrorism).

Criminal Negligence

Sections 215 through 221 deal with crimes based on harm caused through negligence (failing to perform a duty or performing it poorly). Sections 215 and 218 cover crimes against children, and therefore are discussed below under the heading "Neglect-Related Offences."

Criminal negligence is defined in section 219 of the *Criminal Code*. Under that section, a person is criminally negligent if, in doing something or in failing to perform a duty imposed by law, she "shows wanton or reckless disregard for the lives or safety of other persons." If a person's criminal negligence causes **bodily harm** to another person, the negligent person is guilty of committing an indictable offence, and she may be sentenced to a maximum 10-year jail term under section 221.

Criminal negligence causing death is also an indictable offence. If the negligence involves the use of firearms, a person convicted of the offence is subject to a minimum of four years' imprisonment and a maximum of life imprisonment. The actual length of a particular convict's sentence is determined by a court. If the negligence that causes a victim's death does not involve the use of a gun, a person convicted of criminal negligence causing death is subject to a maximum sentence of life imprisonment under section 221. There is no minimum sentence.

Criminal negligence is a very important offence with respect to the protection of children. Less serious cases of child neglect may be dealt with under section 215 of the Code (failure to provide necessaries). However, courts have not hesitated to charge parents under sections 219 to 221 where the circumstances warrant such a charge, typically where there has been a death or a serious injury.

Criminal negligence can also be charged against child protection and youth workers. Child protection and youth workers have a "duty imposed by law" to care for the children in their charge; failure to discharge this duty appropriately falls squarely within the definition of criminal negligence under section 219. The liability of child protection workers and youth workers to charges of criminal negligence is discussed below under the heading "Child Protection, Child Care, and Youth Workers."

Criminal negligence does not necessarily involve an intention to cause harm. A person can be charged with criminal negligence merely because he acts in a way that is indifferent to the consequences of his actions. For example, he leaves a sick baby unattended while he goes to a ballgame. This action is a marked departure from the standard of care that a reasonable person would exercise in the same situation. Any such action that results in harm or death almost always substantiates a criminal negligence charge. Actions that courts have found to be criminally negligent include the following:

- failing to obtain treatment for a sick baby or child;

- leaving a child unattended in a hot car with the windows up, so that the child succumbs to heatstroke;

- very reckless or dangerous driving resulting in harm to another; and

bodily harm usually, an injury to the body that has some degree of persistence — that is, it takes time to heal and limits activity

- a parent's leaving a child in the care of another parent whom she knows to be physically abusive.

Homicide

Sections 222 through 240 deal with causing death by means other than negligence. Terms used to describe causing death are: homicide (sections 222–228), murder (sections 229–231), and manslaughter (sections 232, 234, 239, and 240). Infanticide, a form of killing that is treated somewhat differently from other forms, is discussed later in this chapter.

The law of homicide, murder, and manslaughter is very complicated. The distinctions among these crimes involve a range of factors, particularly issues of intention. From the perspective of a child protection or youth worker, it is not necessary to understand the distinctions. It is the police, usually in close consultation with the Crown, who decide the nature of a charge to lay against anyone who is involved in the killing of another. For a child protection worker, it is important only to know that killing a child by a means other than criminal negligence is a serious indictable offence.

One point that does bear mention is the issue of baby shaking. Unfortunately, some parents or caregivers react to the stress of a baby's inconsolable crying by shaking the baby. While this act may seem only mildly harmful to the person doing it, shaking places stress on a baby's spinal cord and brain, and it can easily cause death or serious neurological injury. Shaking a baby is a violent act, and deaths that result from shaking are likely to culminate in the laying of a charge of manslaughter (or even murder), not criminal negligence, against the shaker.

Administering a Noxious Thing

Section 245 creates the offence of administering a noxious thing, such as poison. This section deals with intentional poisoning. This means that the person administering the noxious thing intends to cause harm, death, or at least discomfort to the victim. There have been occasional cases of adults administering drugs to children that could fall within the prohibited conduct outlined in this section. For example, a person who gives a child an inappropriate dose of a sedating medicine — such as Benadryl (an antihistamine) or Gravol (an anti-nauseant) — in order to control the child's behaviour could be charged under this section.

Similarly, a person who gives a child a drug or poison to intentionally produce symptoms could be charged. There is a rare psychological disorder called Munchausen syndrome by proxy. People who suffer from this syndrome feel compelled to attract attention to themselves or their children by causing the children to become (or appear) ill so that they need medical care. Munchausen's syndrome by proxy formed the basis of a charge in the case of *Children's Aid Society of Belleville (City), Hastings (County) and Trenton (City) v. L(S)*.

Criminal Harassment

Section 264 establishes the offence of criminal harassment. Where a person knowingly (or recklessly) harasses another person to the point that the harassed person has a reasonable fear for his own safety, the harasser can be charged with criminal harassment. Criminal harassment is a hybrid offence, which means that the Crown attorney can choose the method by which the case proceeds through the courts. A person found guilty of committing this offence could be sentenced to as much as 10 years' imprisonment. Criminal harassment can include unwanted communications (through phone calls or email, for example), watching a person's house or workplace, or threatening a person.

restraining order
a court order that imposes restrictions on the person to whom it applies — for example, restrictions on movement

Sometimes, as part of the sentencing process, a judge may impose a restraining order on a person found guilty of committing a criminal offence. A **restraining order** is a court order, with specific terms prohibiting certain actions — for example, coming within 20 metres of a particular house. If the conditions are broken, the person who is subject to the order can be charged with the offence of violating a court order. If a person who is subject to a restraining order commits the offence of criminal harassment in contravention of the restraining order, the contravention of the order becomes an aggravating factor in sentencing. This means that a judge may choose to impose a higher sentence than she would have imposed had the aggravating factor not been present. It may also mean that the Crown may choose to prosecute the case by way of indictment because this mode of procedure allows for higher penalties.

Section 264 of the *Criminal Code* is an important section for child protection and youth workers because it is often charged in cases of domestic abuse, especially where the parents have separated, and the parent without custody is harassing the parent with custody. Child protection workers should not ignore harassment that seems to target only the harasser's ex-partner (and not the children). Inevitably, the ex-partner's well-being influences the children, and observing the harassment is in itself harmful to the children.

Criminal harassment may also occur between young people. For example, one teenager may harass another in the wake of a failed dating relationship.

Assault

assault under the *Criminal Code*, any unwanted touching; under the common law, a threat of injury with no touching can be an assault

Sections 264.1 through 270.1 of the *Criminal Code* deal with assault. In simplest terms, an **assault** is any unwanted touching or credible threat of unwanted touching, even where no physical harm is caused.

Under the criminal law, an assault based on a threat must meet certain criteria of seriousness. According to section 264.1, the threat must be a threat of death or bodily harm (to anybody, not just the person being threatened), a threat of damage to property, or a threat of death or injury to a pet. Issuing a threat of death or bodily harm to a person is an indictable offence that carries a maximum penalty of five years' imprisonment; other kinds of threats carry a maximum two-year penalty if the Crown chooses to proceed by indictment.

Physical assaults are defined under section 265. The sections of the *Criminal Code* that follow section 265 define and create offences with respect to particular forms of assault. The following provides a summary:

- Section 266: simple assault.

- Section 267: assault with a weapon, and assault causing bodily harm.

- Section 268: aggravated assault, in which a suspect "wounds, maims, disfigures or endangers the life" of the victim. This section specifically includes female genital mutilation, an illegal practice in which a girl's or woman's clitoris is excised for religious or cultural purposes. Female genital mutilation is a procedure that causes extreme and permanent disfigurement, sexual dysfunction, and often lifelong pain for the girls and women subjected to it.

- Section 269: unlawfully causing bodily harm (the offence of unlawfully causing bodily harm) is similar to the offence of assault causing bodily harm, but is generally charged in cases that are somewhat less serious — for example, where the person causing the harm considers himself a "healer" and does harm while (illegally) practising "medicine."

- Section 269.1: torture (by officials).

- Sections 270 and 270.1: assaulting a peace officer, and disarming a peace officer.

Sexual abuse and other forms of physical abuse of a child constitute assault whether or not there is lasting physical injury. Unwanted touching, the essence of any physical assault, is touching to which the person being touched does not consent. **Consent**, in law, is a complicated issue, some aspects of which are addressed in section 265.

Failing to resist an assault does not amount to consent if the lack of resistance is motivated by certain causes, such as an assailant's threats or his position of authority in relation to the victim. Positions of authority in relation to a child victim include those of parent, guardian, or teacher. Therefore, for an unwanted touching to constitute assault against a child, the child need not express his lack of consent to the touching. At most, he must communicate that the touching is unwanted, and he can do this by any kind of negative reaction, such as squirming, crying, trying to evade the touching, or even frowning.

The one exception to the law of assault arises in the area of physical discipline. Some forms of physical discipline, such as spanking, are still permitted under our law. Section 43 of the *Criminal Code* states the following:

> Every schoolteacher, parent or person standing in the place of a parent is justified in using force by way of correction toward a pupil or child … who is under his care, if the force does not exceed what is reasonable under the circumstances.

Section 43 is very controversial, and has been recently challenged in the courts, where it was upheld. However, Canadian courts closely monitor cases involving spanking and other forms of physical discipline. Today, a parent, guardian, or teacher would be hard pressed to establish that spanking on a regular basis or spanking to the point of injury was reasonable under any circumstances.

Caring for a child involves a great deal of touching that may or may not be completely welcome by the child. Consider, for example, taking the hand of an eight-year-old boy to cross the street. The boy might find this kind of touching embarrassing, but a solicitous parent might very well be justified in feeling that the boy lacks the ability to safely cross the street alone. It is highly unlikely that a court would ever rule this kind of touching to be an assault.

However, imagine a situation in which a three-year-old girl refuses to get into her car seat for a trip to the doctor, and the parent uses so much force in putting

consent the informed, voluntary, and demonstrated approval by one party of the actions of another

YOU DECIDE!

IS CIRCUMCISION AN ASSAULT?

The circumcision of male infants and children is a surgical procedure in which the foreskin of the patient's penis is removed. The procedure is performed for a variety of reasons in our society: religion, aesthetics, and (in unusual cases) health. Many Canadian infants are circumcised shortly after birth, before being discharged from hospital. Until the mid-1980s, doctors performed the procedure routinely on most male babies. By 1997, medical evidence strongly suggested that, in the absence of health problems, circumcision did not afford substantial health benefits to patients; accordingly, all provincial health insurance schemes, except those of Manitoba and the Northwest Territories, had stopped funding routine circumcisions.

In the absence of a medical problem that establishes the need for circumcision, parents must now specifically request the procedure, and pay for it out of pocket. In families where circumcision is not motivated by religion, one of the most common reasons cited by parents for requesting the procedure is to have the baby boy "look like" other males in the family or in the community. This motivation may soon become less common: the rate of circumcision of male babies in Canada has decreased from about 60 percent in 1971 to about 15 percent in 2003.

Boys are typically circumcised in childhood, without consenting to the procedure and before they can fully understand its implications. Complications have been associated with the operation, ranging from excessive bleeding to permanent disfigurement and complete sexual dysfunction. A few deaths have been associated with the procedure. The failure to provide adequate pain relief to an infant during the procedure has drawn significant criticism from both inside and outside the medical community. There are medical studies suggesting that the experience of pain during circumcision can have a lifelong influence on the pain perceptions and reactions of an adult. Circumcision is also believed to reduce sexual sensitivity and pleasure for most men.

Some people believe that circumcision is an assault. Some men have sought compensation (usually in the civil, rather than the criminal, courts) for having been circumcised as babies. These lawsuits have not been widely successful, but they certainly supply food for thought.

Questions

1. Use the Internet to research the arguments currently being made for and against circumcision of healthy babies. In the absence of medical problems, do you think parents should be allowed to consent to the alteration of their children's bodies?

2. Elective circumcision (circumcision for non-health reasons) does not constitute an assault under the *Criminal Code*. What does this teach you about the role of culture, values, and other subjective factors in Canada's criminal law?

the child in the seat that it breaks her collarbone. This situation is much more ambiguous. The parent may be justified in requiring her daughter to ride in the car seat to comply with the law and for her own safety, and may feel that the visit to the doctor is essential for the child's health. The parent may feel that she had no choice in the situation. However, it is possible that a court would find that the parent's forceful and unwanted touching constituted an assault.

In interpreting touch between children and adults, child protection workers must draw on their judgment, as informed by experience. Accidents happen; however, abusers routinely characterize abuse as an unfortunate series of accidents. For this reason, it is important for child protection workers to be trained to understand the patterns, motivations, and symptoms of child abuse.

Sexual Assault

Sections 271 to 273.2 deal with sexual assault. It is important to note that the *Criminal Code* includes another set of provisions that deal specifically with sexual situations involving children. These provisions are found in sections 150 to 173 of the Code and are discussed below under the heading "Actions That Are Crimes Because They Involve Young People." This does not mean, however, that the offences in sections 271 to 273.2 cannot be charged when children are involved; they can. The police, possibly in conjunction with a Crown attorney, determine which charge is the most appropriate based on the circumstances of each case. The important thing for child protection workers to remember is that the criminal law that covers sexual situations is different — and much more restrictive — where one or more of the people involved in the situation is a child. This reflects society's ideas about consent to sexual activity, and the inappropriateness of certain sexual activities for young people.

Section 271 establishes the penalties for sexual assault, which is a hybrid offence. The maximum penalty, when prosecuted by way of indictment, is 10 years' imprisonment. (By way of comparison, the maximum penalty for incest, which is discussed later in this chapter, is 14 years' imprisonment, and the maximum penalty for sexual exploitation of a minor is 5 years' imprisonment.) Section 272 deals with sexual assaults that involve the use of a weapon, threats, and/or bodily harm. All of these factors render the offence more serious, and raise the maximum penalty to 14 years' imprisonment. Section 272 also makes it an offence to be a party to a sexual assault. A person may become a party to a sexual assault by, for example, finding a victim for a sexual offender, or being present at an assault and assisting the offender while failing to do anything to help the victim. In some cases, a parent who has never touched a child in a sexual way may be a party to the other parent's sexual assault by acquiescing in the assault and failing to protect the child.

Section 273 creates the offence of aggravated sexual assault, which means an assault in which the victim is wounded, maimed, disfigured, or has his life endangered. This offence carries a maximum sentence of life imprisonment. Where an offender uses a firearm in the course of committing the offence, there is a minimum sentence of four years' imprisonment.

Sections 273.1 and 273.2 are complicated sections intended to clarify the issue of consent; their content is beyond the scope of this chapter. Sections 274 through 277 deal with issues involving evidence and procedure. For example, section 276 limits the extent to which a victim's prior sexual history is relevant to a trial on a charge of sexual assault. These sections, while beyond the scope of this book, are sometimes important in cases involving teenage victims, including prostitutes.

Kidnapping and Hostage Taking

Section 279 covers kidnapping, and section 279.1 covers hostage taking. These sections apply to victims of any age. A person may be convicted of kidnapping regardless of whether she makes a ransom request, engages in violence, or injures her victim. Section 279(2) establishes the offence of forcible confinement, which is similar to the offence of kidnapping, though somewhat less serious. Section 280 and 281, which are discussed below under the heading "Abduction," deal with child abduction.

Actions That Are Crimes Because They Involve Young People

In recognition of the vulnerability of children, some offences under the *Criminal Code* require that one of the people involved in the offence (typically a victim or a witness) is below a specified age. That is to say, the identical activity would not be a crime if one of the people involved were not a minor. Who is a "child" or a "teenager" depends on which section of the *Criminal Code* is under consideration. There is no general definition of "child" (or minor, or teenager) that pertains to the Code as a whole. There is, however, a definition of "newly-born child" in section 2, which makes "a person under the age of one year" a newly born child throughout the entire Code.

Some sections of the Code provide their own definitions of "child." For example, section 172, which deals with "corrupting" children, defines a child as anyone under the age of 18. However, other sections dealing with sexual activity define a child as a person under the age of 14. Section 151, which deals with sexual interference with minors, is an example of such a section.

The different definitions of "child" reflect, to some degree, the piecemeal evolution of Canada's criminal law. For example, inciting bestiality (section 163) is an old offence that defines a child as someone below the traditional age of sexual consent, which is 14 years. However, section 172.1, a much newer provision that deals with "luring" a child (usually over the Internet) defines a child as a person under the age of 18. This discrepancy reflects changes in the way we have come to view child sexuality. In general, society has become increasingly concerned about the sexual exploitation of young people in the last half-century or so. This concern has led to an impulse to protect older teens from sexual exploitation by adults.

Many (but not all) experts now feel that it is unreasonable to assume that a 14-year-old is sufficiently mature to protect her own safety and other interests in sexual situations. When the Department of Justice conducted a consultation in 1999 about changes to the criminal law, the possibility of raising the age of sexual consent was discussed. Although the government did not raise the age of consent at that time, there has been a clear trend toward defining a child as a person under 18, not under 14, in new sexual offence provisions.

CHAPTER 7   Child Protection Under the Criminal Code

SEXUAL OFFENCES

Sections 150.1 through 172.1 deal primarily with sexual situations involving children. Section 150.1 establishes the general age at which young people are legally capable of consenting to sexual activity, which is 14 years. However, a court may still find that a child over the age of 14 is incapable of consenting to sexual acts, or that the child did not in fact consent in particular circumstances.

Section 150.1 contains certain exceptions for actions that would otherwise constitute sex crimes when these actions take place between children of similar ages, typically less than 2 to 3 years apart. For example, sexual acts between children aged 12 to 15 years are not criminal in the absence of factors such as violence, threats, or a relationship that involves authority and dependence. These provisions are intended to address the realities of teen sex.

Sexual Interference

Section 151 creates the offence of sexual interference:

> Every person who, for a sexual purpose, touches, directly or indirectly, with a part of the body or with an object, any part of the body of a person under the age of fourteen years is guilty of an indictable offence and liable to imprisonment for a term not exceeding ten years or is guilty of an offence punishable on summary conviction.

Sexual interference is a hybrid offence, which means that the Crown can choose to proceed by way of summary conviction or indictable procedure. The Crown's election will often depend on factors that may never form part of the evidence in the case. For example, a long history of unprovable sexual advances against the same child may prompt the Crown to proceed by way of indictment. The jury will never have the past conduct evidence, but the evidence will have influenced the case nonetheless.

Sexual Touching

Section 152 creates the offence of invitation to sexual touching:

> Every person who, for a sexual purpose, invites, counsels or incites a person under the age of fourteen years to touch, directly or indirectly, with a part of the body or with an object, the body of any person, including the body of the person who so invites, counsels or incites and the body of the person under the age of fourteen years, is guilty of an indictable offence and liable to imprisonment for a term not exceeding ten years or is guilty of an offence punishable on summary conviction.

Again, this is a hybrid offence, and is designed to cover sexual situations in which the child does the touching, under duress.

Sexual Exploitation

Section 153 creates the offence of sexual exploitation, an offence somewhat more detailed than those outlined in sections 151 and 152. In a nutshell, sexual exploitation means doing anything prohibited under sections 151 and 152 in relation to a child between the ages of 14 and 18 (as opposed to a child under 14); however, section 153 requires that the exploiter is "in a position of trust or authority towards a young person or is a person with whom the young person is in a relationship of dependency." Sexual exploitation is a hybrid offence with a maximum penalty of five years' imprisonment if the Crown proceeds by indictment. Categories of adults whom courts have found to fall into "a position of trust or authority towards a young person" include: teachers, coaches, physicians, therapists, psychologists, guardians, relatives, and child protection or youth workers.

Incest

Section 155 establishes the offence of incest, an offence that establishes no age limits. This means that the victim need not be a child. "Sexual intercourse" is the only sexual act that qualifies as incest under section 155.

Bestiality

Section 160(3) makes it a hybrid offence to commit bestiality (have sex with an animal) in the presence of a child under the age of 14.

Restrictive Orders Under Section 161

Section 161 allows courts to make special orders concerning people who have committed sexual offences relating to children. These orders typically restrict offenders, after release from custody, from going to places where children might be (such as schools, playgrounds, and recreational centres); from doing work that requires being with children; or from communicating with children over the Internet. Orders under section 161 may extend for a temporary period or for the lifetime of the offender.

Child Pornography

Sections 163.1 through 164.3 create a comprehensive regime for the control of child pornography. These detailed sections make it a crime not only to produce child pornography, but to sell, possess, or have access to it as well. For the purpose of these sections, a child is anyone under the age of 18 years.

Corrupting a Child

Section 172 makes it illegal to "corrupt" a child by engaging in certain activities in the child's home (such as adultery, sexual immorality, or habitual drunkenness) and thereby making the child's home unfit for the child to live in. Charges under section 172 are uncommon, but the section creates an indictable offence and carries a sentence of up to two years' imprisonment.

Luring a Child

Section 172.1 creates the relatively new offence of "luring" a child, by means of a computer system, for the purpose of doing something that would constitute an offence under one of the sexual offence sections. For the purpose of this provision, a child is someone who meets the definition of "child" under the relevant sexual offence section. For example, if a person is accused of luring a child for the purpose of sexual exploitation (as defined in section 153), the luring charge under section

172.1 applies to activities involving a child between the ages of 14 and 17 because these are the ages that meet the definition of child under section 153.

Indecent Exposure to a Child

Finally, section 173(2) makes it a crime to expose one's genitals in the presence of a child under the age of 14.

NEGLECT-RELATED OFFENCES

Abandonment or Exposure

Section 214 defines "abandon" or "expose" in the following manner:

> (a) a wilful omission to take charge of a child by a person who is under a legal duty to do so, and
>
> (b) dealing with a child in a manner that is likely to leave that child exposed to risk without protection.

These definitions relate primarily to section 218, which makes it an offence to abandon or expose a child under 10 years of age in circumstances where the child's life is at risk or the child's health is at risk of permanent injury.

The offence requires that the person who abandons or exposes the child intends to do so. Section 218 does not apply, for example, if a child wanders away from her house in the middle of the night.

A person's intention to abandon or expose a child in dangerous circumstances and his act of leaving the child in these circumstances are all that the Crown need prove in order to convict the person under section 218. It is irrelevant whether or not the child is rescued before her life or health is actually threatened, and it does not matter whether the child manages, by luck, to escape harm. This section is also applicable in cases where a child is abandoned in relatively safe environs, from a physical standpoint, but where there is a risk that the child will be abducted.

Failing To Provide Necessaries

Section 215 is of particular concern for child protection workers. It creates a duty on the part of a "parent, foster parent, guardian or head of a family" to "provide necessaries" for a child under the age of 16 years. Failing to provide necessaries (for a period of at least one month) that results in the child's being "in destitute circumstances" or that results in the endangerment of the child's life or health is a hybrid offence. It carries a maximum penalty of two years' imprisonment. Courts have taken a relatively narrow view of what constitutes necessaries; in general, they include the basics of food, shelter, clothing, supervision, and medical care.

Child protection workers are commonly required to determine whether or not a child is in need of protection. The kinds of neglect that can establish a need for protection under the *Child and Family Services Act* are considerably broader than those that can establish the failure to provide necessaries under the *Criminal Code*. However, it is important to distinguish between the purpose of these two statutes. The description of a child's needs under the *Child and Family Services Act* is designed to support the provision of social services to a child, whereas an analysis of neglect based on section 215 of the *Criminal Code* is intended to form the basis of a criminal charge against neglectful parents or guardians. Parents and guardians are not charged under the criminal law in most circumstances where a child is offered services under the *Child and Family Services Act*. Neglect in the context of the *Child and Family Services Act* is reviewed in chapter 8 under the heading "When Is the Duty Triggered?"

Infanticide

Section 223 of the *Criminal Code* states that "a child becomes a human being ... when it has completely proceeded, in a living state, from the body of its mother" regardless of whether the following events have occurred:

(a) it has breathed;

(b) it has an independent circulation; or

(c) the navel string is severed.

This definition is provided to support section 223(2), which provides that killing a child is homicide. Therefore, the relevant sections of the Code involving homicide (sections 222–228), murder (sections 229–231), and manslaughter (sections 232, 234, 239, and 240) apply. These provisions are discussed briefly above under the heading "Homicide."

Infanticide, described in section 233 of the Code, is a form of killing that is treated somewhat differently from any other form. Infanticide can be committed only by the mother of the victim and only under these particular circumstances:

> when by a wilful act or omission she causes the death of her newly-born child, if at the time of the act or omission she is not fully recovered from the effects of giving birth to the child and by reason thereof or of the effect of lactation consequent on the birth of the child her mind is then disturbed.

FYI

INFANTICIDE: A COMMON PHENOMENON

"It is estimated that infanticide has been responsible for the death of more children than any other single cause with the possible exception of bubonic plague." (Solomon, 1980)

Infanticide by a mother has been recognized as a unique situation for centuries. The effect of section 233 is to attribute a lower level of intention to mothers who kill their infants than to others who commit various forms of homicide, and, as a result, a lower penalty. Infanticide is an indictable offence that carries a maximum sentence of five years' imprisonment. In modern terms, infanticide is typically charged when a killing is proven to have been motivated by postpartum psychosis (an extreme form of postpartum depression) or severe postpartum depression.

Neglect in Childbirth and Related Offences

An offence related to infanticide is neglect in childbirth under section 242 of the *Criminal Code*. A mother who is about to give birth and who fails to obtain medical assistance can be charged under section 242 if the baby dies or is permanently injured. This indictable offence carries a maximum sentence of five years' imprisonment. The intention required by section 242 is quite specific: the mother must neglect to seek assistance "with the intent that the child shall not live" or with the intent to conceal the birth. Section 243 makes it an indictable offence to conceal the body of a child with the intent to conceal its birth. A person other than the mother can also be charged under section 243.

A person other than the mother who kills a baby during its birth can be charged under section 238, unless the actions that led to the baby's death were done in a sincere belief that they would save the baby's or the mother's life.

ABDUCTION

Section 273.3 makes it a hybrid offence with a maximum sentence of 5 years' imprisonment to "do anything for the purpose of removing a child from Canada" in order to perform an action that would be a crime in Canada under specified sections of the *Criminal Code*, typically those that involve sexual offences.

Section 280 makes it an indictable offence with a maximum sentence of 5 years' imprisonment to take a person who is under the age of 16, against his will, out of the care and control of his parent or guardian.

Section 281 makes it a crime to take a child under the age of 14 from the care and control of her parent or guardian (regardless of the child's wishes), or to harbour a child who has been abducted in this manner. This is an indictable offence with a maximum penalty of 10 years' imprisonment.

Section 282 deals with the hybrid offence of child abduction by a parent in contravention of a custody order. Section 283 covers child abduction by a person whose intention is to deprive another person of a child lawfully in the other person's care (in the absence of a custody order). This is a hybrid offence with a maximum indictable penalty of 10 years' imprisonment.

Section 285 creates an exemption from criminal responsibility for child abduction for a person who abducts a child on the basis of a reasonable belief that it is necessary to do so in order to protect the child from harm. For a person to escape criminal responsibility under section 285, a court must be satisfied, based on the facts, that the threat of harm was real and imminent, and that the abduction was necessary to avoid it.

Offences Made More Serious Because They Involve Children

Some offences are rendered more serious — which means that they carry a higher penalty — when the victim of the offence is under a specified age.

As mentioned above, procuring (pimping) under section 212 is more serious when the victim is a young person. Aggravated procuring — living on the avails of prostitution of a person under the age of 18 — carries a maximum 14-year sentence. Using violence or threats of violence to do so carries a *minimum* sentence of five years' imprisonment under section 212(2.1).

In preference to creating a "tiered" offence, in which penalties differ according to the age of the victim, the *Criminal Code* sometimes creates a separate offence for situations involving children. Consider, for example, the difference between kidnapping (under section 279) and child abduction (under sections 280–283). Kidnapping is discussed above under the heading "Kidnapping and Hostage Taking," and child abduction is discussed above under the heading "Abduction."

Child Protection, Child Care, and Youth Workers

Child protection workers and youth workers are by no means immune from charges under the criminal law. As noted in chapter 2, a children's aid society worker was charged with criminal negligence causing death under section 220 of the *Criminal Code* as a result of the death of baby Jordan Heikamp in 1997.

Although the charge in the Heikamp case was eventually dropped, it serves to demonstrate the vulnerability of well-meaning social workers who fail to meet the appropriate standard of care in dealings with young people under their supervision.

A child protection or youth worker who is less than well-meaning, and who exploits his position for the purpose of victimizing children, could very easily be charged under one or more of the sexual offence sections of the *Criminal Code*. Sadly, there are numerous historical examples, in Canada, of offences committed against children while they are in the care of supposedly charitable agencies. For this reason, children's aid societies, government ministries, schools, religious organizations, recreation facilities, and other employers who hire people to work with children typically conduct extensive background and criminal checks on all of their volunteers, employees, and potential employees in an attempt to identify potential offenders. Pedophiles (adults who crave sexual contact with children) and other criminals often actively seek employment in child care settings in order to gain access to children.

A child care worker who has no criminal motivations can still get into legal trouble by doing her job negligently. As discussed above, a number of *Criminal Code* sections — for example, failure to provide necessaries (section 215), and criminal harassment (sections 219–221) impose penalties for harming children through negligence. Finally, it is possible for a child protection worker who fails to properly supervise a child under her care to be charged with abandonment and/or exposure under section 218.

The best way for child protection and youth workers to avoid criminal charges is to be competent, responsible, and compassionate. Competence means having sufficient training to do the job required, being willing to ask for help when help is needed, being observant, being honest in reporting one's observations; and taking care always to act in the interests of the client being served — the child. Even when the child's interests conflict with other interests — for example, one's own employment interests, the interests of a parent, or the interests of an employer — it is the interests of the child that must remain paramount.

A practical difficulty facing many child protection and youth workers is overwork. A caseload that is too heavy can make it difficult for even the most well-intentioned worker to do his job competently.

◼ CHILDREN'S EVIDENCE

In recognition of the vulnerable status of children, the *Criminal Code* contains special provisions that are designed to promote the successful prosecution of people who victimize children. For example, section 477.1 of the Code facilitates the prosecution of sexual offences against children by allowing a Canadian court to hear cases that involve offences that occurred outside Canada, provided that the person accused of committing an offence is a Canadian citizen or resident.

Other provisions are intended to make it easier for children to give evidence. Some examples of these are as follows:

- Section 486(1.1) allows a court to exclude the public from a courtroom in some cases when a person under 18 is giving evidence.

- Section 486(1.2) permits a child under 14 to have a support person present while she gives evidence.

- Section 486(2.1) allows a person under 18 to give evidence outside the courtroom or behind a screen where these accommodations would assist him in making full and candid disclosure.

- Section 486(2.3) prevents a person accused of committing an offence from herself cross-examining a witness under the age of 18 in most cases. The accused person's lawyer may, however, cross-examine the witness on the accused person's behalf.

It may be appropriate for a child protection or youth worker who has cared for a child and gained his trust to act as a support person in court under section 486(1.2). However, this is usually impossible in cases where the child protection or youth worker is also a witness in the proceedings.

■ SEX OFFENDER REGISTRIES

Pedophiles share certain characteristics when they commit offences against children. The rate of recidivism is very high among these offenders. Perhaps because sex offences against children are driven by the offender's sex drive (and not by the more cerebral factors that motivate, say, economic crime), deterrent strategies are often ineffective in preventing repeat offences. Some pedophiles commit dozens of offences over the course of their criminal careers.

sex offender registry
a government database in which indentifying information about people who have committed sexual offences in the past is collected

Sex offences against children are often accompanied by additional violence. In some cases, the offender seeks and is stimulated by violence; in others, harming or murdering the child seems, to the offender, to be the only way of avoiding detection and prosecution. Where a child is murdered by a sex offender, the killing typically follows swiftly after the abduction. According to the Ontario **sex offender registry**:

Data indicates that a rapid response during an investigation of a child abduction for a sexual purpose is critical. Of those victims who were murdered:

- 44% were dead within one hour after the abduction;

- 74% within three hours; and

- 91% within 24 hours.

The unique nature of sex crimes has led to the development of sex offender registries. In Ontario, a statute known as Christopher's Law paved the way for the creation of a searchable registry containing information about sex offenders.

> ### FYI
>
> ### CHRISTOPHER'S LAW
> The Christopher of Christopher's Law was 11-year-old Christopher Stephenson, a child who was brutally murdered by a pedophile who was on federal statutory release (parole). A 1993 inquest following Christopher's death produced recommendations that formed the foundation of Ontario's registry.

The Ontario sex offender registry began functioning in April 2001. Registration with the database is mandatory for residents of Ontario who have been convicted of a "criteria sex offence" (as defined by statute) in Canada and

- were serving a sentence on the day Christopher's Law was proclaimed;

- were convicted of a sex offence on or after the statute came into force;

- have been found not criminally responsible for a sex offence by reason of a mental disorder on or after the statute came into force; or

- are young persons convicted of a criteria sex offence and serving an adult sentence.

The Ontario registry records a wide range of information including name, date of birth, current address (with an update obligation), and current photograph. According to Bernie Cowan, manager of the registry, other useful information can be added to a person's file. For example, details about distinctive strategies and methods used in committing previous crimes can be included, as can expressions and mannerisms characteristic of the offender. For example, if an offender has an unusual nickname that he uses when addressing children, this information is searchable. Information about an offender's idiosyncrasies can be highly useful to law enforcement personnel. For example, if a child disappears in the company of a man who has been overheard calling him "my fine young fellow," database information about a known pedophile who uses this phrase when approaching victims could lead to the speedy apprehension of an offender. However, the database is merely an investigative tool, and law enforcement personnel must take great care that they are apprehending the correct suspect. The Ontario registry incorporates several useful functions, including geographic information systems (GIS) mapping, to locate offenders. It is not available to the public, but can be used by law enforcement personnel for general investigative purposes when a child goes missing.

More recently, the federal government established a registry of its own. The legislation establishing the national sex offender registry came into force on December 15, 2004. The national registry is administered by the Royal Canadian Mounted Police. Like the Ontario registry, the national registry makes registration mandatory for individuals who meet specified criteria.

Bernie Cowan of the Ontario registry confirms that the national registry will not replace the Ontario registry; rather, both registries will exist in parallel. Perhaps the most important difference between the two registries is that the national registry can be accessed only when investigators have reasonable and probable grounds to believe that a crime will be committed. Unlike the Ontario registry, it cannot be used for general investigative purposes. Also, the information collected by the national registry is more limited than that collected by the Ontario registry and currently lacks some of the search functions available at the provincial level.

■ THE ROLE OF THE CHILD PROTECTION OR YOUTH WORKER

This chapter has provided considerable detail with respect to the criminal law. The reason for this is that while child protection workers have a limited role in enforcing the law, they must be familiar with the kinds of actions that constitute crimes against children. It is important, however, that child protection workers not lose sight of their primary responsibility, which is the best interests of children. This responsibility is very different from that of the police, who are responsible not only for protecting victims, but also for apprehending offenders.

It is comforting to know that those who victimize children are punished by the criminal law. However, from a child protection perspective, the much more relevant issue is the immediate safety of children. As a child protection worker, it is your job to keep this priority at the forefront of your mind in everything that you do. In some ways, whether or not the state characterizes an action as criminal or non-criminal is not especially relevant to the issue of child welfare. Also, it is important to know that a view of child welfare that takes only the criminal law into account is narrow. In fact, it is usually much narrower than the definition of risk to a child under provincial child protection legislation, which is discussed in chapter 8.

In the context of the criminal law, a child protection worker's role is primarily a reporting role. When something happens that renders a child in need of protection, a chain of events is triggered under provincial legislation. As part of that chain of events, it is often important for a child protection worker to make a report to police, who then launch a criminal investigation.

In making a report to police, a child protection worker should usually make the report personally, though it is a good idea for the worker to advise her supervisor of her intention to do so. It is generally not necessary, and not a good idea, for the worker to warn the person suspected of committing a crime of her intention to report his behaviour to the police. However, it is usually appropriate to ask a suspect to stop engaging in harmful behaviour.

Reporting a crime to the police does not, in itself, discharge a child protection worker's duty under provincial legislation. Once the police report is made, a child protection worker must take additional steps, under provincial legislation, to secure the child's safety. These steps occur irrespective of and parallel to any investigation by the police. *For this reason, where the commission of a crime is suspected, a child protection worker should report relevant information both to the police and to a child protection agency.*

In the course of their investigation, police may question a child protection worker about a crime or may request that he appear in court as a witness. A child protection worker's responsibility to the justice system is separate from his responsibility to the child. As far as possible, the child protection worker should attempt to comply with police requests while keeping his responsibility to the child as his chief priority. In some cases, involvement as a criminal witness may limit the child protection worker's ability to work with the child. In these cases, it is appropriate to ask the police whether the evidence they seek can be collected in a way that minimizes disruption of the worker–child relationship.

KEY TERMS

assault

bodily harm

consent

hybrid offence

indictable offence

restraining order

sex offender registry

summary conviction offence

REFERENCES

Canada Department of Justice. (1999). *Child Victims and the Criminal Justice System: A Consultation Paper.* Retrieved February 25, 2005 from http://canada.justice.gc.ca/en/cons/child/toc.html.

Children's Aid Society of Belleville (City), Hastings (County) and Trenton (City) v. L (S). (December 13, 1999). Ontario Court of Justice. Doc. Belleville 258/99.

Criminal Code. RSC 1985, c. C-46, as amended.

Ontario Ministry of Community Safety and Correctional Services. (2004). *Ontario Sex Offender Registry.* Retrieved February 25, 2005 from http://www.mpss.jus.gov.on.ca/english/police_serv/sor/sor.html.

Hoag, Valerie, and Nora Rock. (forthcoming). *Foundations of Criminal and Civil Law in Canada,* 2nd edition. Toronto: Emond Montgomery.

Solomon, T. (1980). History and demography of child abuse. In J.V. Cook and R.T. Bowles (Eds.), *Child Abuse: Commission and Omission.* Toronto: Butterworths.

REVIEW QUESTIONS

1. Why does the *Criminal Code* provide greater protection for children and young people than it does for adults by, for example, making certain actions criminal only when at least one participant is a child?

2. Explain how the responsibility for protecting children is shared by the federal and provincial governments. Which aspects of that responsibility fall within each sphere?

3. What is the difference between the offence of procuring under section 212, and the offence described in section 213 of the Code (soliciting prostitution)?

4. Why do you think the offence of failure to provide necessaries under section 215 carries a lighter penalty than the offence of criminal negligence under section 219 of the Code?

5. Why does the offence of "luring" apply to victims under the age of 18 when the general age of consent to sexual activity is 14?

6. Is it necessary for a parent to be charged with a criminal offence in order for a child to be found to be in need of protection under the *Child and Family Services Act*? Why or why not? Provide an example to justify your answer.

7. List three offences that might be charged against child protection workers.

DISCUSSION QUESTIONS

1. There is some overlap among the sexual offence provisions of the *Criminal Code*. Identify some factors and motivations that might affect whether someone is charged with one offence rather than another. For example, why might someone be charged with sexual assault (under section 271) instead of sexual exploitation (under section 153)? Assume that the facts of the case could support either charge.

2. Why might it be inappropriate for a child protection worker to collaborate closely with a criminal prosecution when a child in the worker's charge was the victim of the crime?

3. Why do you think the creators of the national sex offender registry chose to make access to a registrant's information accessible only when investigators have reasonable and probable grounds to suspect that an offence is going to occur? Make reference in your answer to the Ontario registry, which permits access to the database for general investigative purposes.

8 The Child and Family Services Act

INTRODUCTION TO THE OBJECTIVES OF THE CHILD AND FAMILY SERVICES ACT

The *Child and Family Services Act* was introduced in chapter 2 and has already been mentioned many times in this book. Chapters 8 and 9 provide a detailed overview of the Act and of the non-criminal child protection system in Ontario. Chapter 8 focuses on child protection that does not involve residential placement and on the steps that lead to the placement of a child in care. Chapter 9 focuses on children and youth in residential care.

The object of the *Child and Family Services Act* is expressed in section 1:

> The paramount purpose of this Act is to promote the best interests, protection and well being of children.

The requirement that the Act be applied according to the best interests of the child is not unique. The high value placed on the best interests of children is a theme that runs through Ontario family law in general and the Ontario *Family Law Act* in particular. Understanding the concept of a child's best interests is critical for child protection workers. When working with parents, and members of the child protection system, the education system, and the justice system, child protection workers will come into contact with a large number of well-meaning adults. Many of these people hold strong opinions with respect to the treatment of children and young people. In some cases, these opinions may be in conflict. It is easy for child protection workers to be influenced by strong opinions, and just as easy to feel torn between conflicting points of view. However, it is essential that child protection workers, regardless of their sympathy for the positions taken by adults, never lose sight of their duty to act in the best interests of their clients:

CHAPTER OBJECTIVES

After reading this chapter, you should be able to:

- Explain the objectives and describe the structure of the *Child and Family Services Act*.

- Explain the role of children's aid societies in administering the *Child and Family Services Act*.

- List at least 10 factors that trigger a duty to report under the Act, and explain the consequences for a child protection worker who fails to report.

- Explain the basic steps in investigating a report of abuse or neglect, and describe factors that support the need for taking a child into care.

- Explain how the justice system determines whether a child is in need of protection, and the various consequences of such a determination.

- Describe the rights of parents and children during an investigation or intervention under the *Child and Family Services Act*.

children. Deciding on the course of action that best supports these interests is not always easy, but many decisions become clearer when the decision maker focuses on who her client is, and views all situations from the vantage point of her client's best interests.

Besides its paramount purpose of promoting the best interests, protection, and well-being of children, the *Child and Family Services Act* has secondary purposes, which are set out in section 1(2). The Act sets out the secondary purposes, which are to be achieved only as long as they are consistent with the paramount purpose, in the following way:

1. To recognize that while parents may need help in caring for their children, that help should give support to the autonomy and integrity of the family unit and, wherever possible, be provided on the basis of mutual consent.

YOU DECIDE!

WHO IS MY CLIENT?

You are a child protection worker. Your newest client is Paulette, a 15-year-old who was referred to you by a centre for pregnant teenagers. Paulette, who is now seven months' pregnant, concealed her pregnancy for six months. When Paulette began to show, her mother, Réjeanne, told Paulette that she would help care for and provide for the baby, but only if Paulette agreed to stop seeing or communicating with her boyfriend, Seth. Paulette refused. Mother and daughter have had many arguments over the issue. When Paulette was referred to you, she was living in a shelter for street youth, after being told to leave Seth's home by his parents.

After interviewing Paulette, you decide that she is quite unprepared for independent living. She has problems making decisions and taking initiative. Despite being in her seventh month of pregnancy, she has seen a doctor only twice: once for a pregnancy test at four months, and once with her mother immediately after Réjeanne discovered the pregnancy. When you ask Paulette what kinds of preparations she has made for motherhood, she seems completely at a loss. The only thing that she has a definite opinion about is that she does not want to live with her mother any longer.

Two days after you interview Paulette, you get a call from Réjeanne, who got your name from the teenage mothers' centre. Réjeanne is worried about both Paulette and the baby. She tells you she is prepared to help her daughter care for the baby, if only she will move back home. Your impression is that Réjeanne, though disapproving of her daughter's relationship and pregnancy, is a sensible, sincere, and concerned mother. Réjeanne pleads with you to encourage Paulette to move home.

Questions

1. Paulette is clearly your client. Is Paulette's unborn baby also your client? Why or why not?

2. Do you believe that Paulette's best interests would be served by living with her mother? If so, what should you do? If not, what living arrangement is in Paulette's best interests?

3. What are the dangers in advocating to Paulette the course of action suggested by her mother?

4. Is your concern for the unborn baby an appropriate motivator for your actions on Paulette's behalf? Why or why not?

5. What are your obligations with respect to the baby?

6. How might any actions you take to protect the baby put you in a conflict of interest with Paulette?

2. To recognize that the least disruptive course of action that is available and is appropriate in a particular case to help a child should be considered.

3. To recognize that children's services should be provided in a manner that,
   i. respects children's needs for continuity of care and for stable family relationships, and
   ii. takes into account physical and mental developmental differences among children.

4. To recognize that, wherever possible, services to children and their families should be provided in a manner that respects cultural, religious and regional differences.

5. To recognize that Indian and native people should be entitled to provide, wherever possible, their own child and family services, and that all services to Indian and native children and families should be provided in a manner that recognizes their culture, heritage and traditions and the concept of the extended family.

As you can see, the secondary purposes of the *Child and Family Services Act* reflect a strong bias in favour of deference to and preservation of the family unit. Assisting children within the context of family relationships is a theme that is reflected in many parts of the Act. The sections that most obviously reflect this theme

ASIDE

DEFERENCE TO THE FAMILY: A LEGAL TRADITION

The *Child and Family Services Act* clearly states that primary responsibility for child protection lies not with the state, but with parents. Most Canadians believe that most children are best served when they are allowed to remain in their family homes, even when these homes are not perfect.

The notion that children belong at home is frequently espoused by children themselves, even in cases of serious abuse. For example, after Randal Dooley died as a result of abuse by his father and stepmother, his brother Teego Dooley expressed a desire to remain in the custody of his father. (The court ordered that Teego Dooley be returned to his family in Jamaica; his father is currently serving a prison sentence.)

The *Child and Family Services Act* reflects the belief that the state should intervene in the affairs of a family against the will of the parents only in very serious cases. This belief, which continues to guide child protection law today, was expressed in the following way in *Re Brown*, a 1975 court decision:

> [T]he community ought not to interfere merely because our institutions may be able to offer a greater opportunity to the children to achieve their potential. Society's interference in the natural family is only justified when the level of care of the children falls below that which no child in this country should be subjected to.

provide for services to be provided to children with the consent of their parents, and sometimes with the participation of their parents or other family members.

Secondary purpose number 2 makes it clear that, when a child requires assistance, those providing the assistance are bound to choose the course of action that is the "least disruptive." Disruptive here usually means disruptive to the child's existing environment, including his family unit, community and educational setting, and housing situation. Secondary purpose number 1 mentions services that are provided to children with the consent of their parents; these services are typically less disruptive than non-consensual interventions by child protection workers, including the apprehensions of children.

Recent interest in "differential response," a system for distinguishing between serious cases (requiring apprehension) and less serious cases (addressed while the child remains at home), is in line with these purposes. For more on differential response, see chapter 10 under the heading "Working With Parents and Others."

The secondary purposes of the Act also recognize the important role of culture, religion, heritage, tradition, regional differences, and community values. As much as possible, a child's ties to these aspects of life should be preserved even when the child is in need of assistance or protection. For example, a child in care should be given a chance to attend services at a place of worship for her own faith. Children's aid societies often attempt to place children with foster families who share their culture.

Secondary purpose number 5 provides that native children should receive, where possible, services from organizations managed by First Nations bands that are operated with respect for their heritage and traditions. Services run by native adults for native children are available in many parts of the province, and especially on First Nations reserves. Over the past two or three decades, control over the administration of government social services funding to First Nations communities has been placed largely (though not completely) in the hands of these communities.

■ OVERVIEW OF THE CHILD AND FAMILY SERVICES ACT

Duties of Service Providers

Immediately following the purposes section of the *Child and Family Services Act*, and preceding the main body of the statute, is section 2(2), entitled "Duties of Service Providers." This section appears early in the statute because its drafters wanted the importance of the section to be understood. Section 2(2) has two requirements:

1. that service providers ensure that children and their parents "have an opportunity where appropriate to be heard and represented when decisions affecting their interests are made and to be heard when they have concerns about the services they are receiving"; and

2. that decisions affecting the rights of children and their parents be made "according to clear, consistent criteria and are subject to procedural safeguards."

procedural fairness
fairness that flows from the observance of procedures designed to promote the protection of individual rights

Section 2(2) is designed to ensure **procedural fairness** in the application of the statute. In a nutshell, this means that built-in procedures must allow for the disclosure to children and parents of information that affects their interests; these procedures must also provide children and parents with the opportunity to challenge decisions that affect their interests. Many sections of the *Child and Family Services Act* are designed to ensure procedural fairness. For example, any section that requires that notice of a decision or an action be given to a parent or child creates procedural fairness by facilitating disclosure to and challenge by people affected by the decision or action.

Definitions

Section 3 of the *Child and Family Services Act* provides definitions of many important terms. Some of these terms are discussed later in this chapter in their relevant contexts. For now, it is worth noting that defined terms include the following:

- child (person under the age of 18);
- parent (see section 3(2));
- child development service;
- child treatment service;
- child welfare service;
- community support service;
- residential service;
- young offender's service;
- developmental disability;
- foster care;
- Indian, native person, and native community;
- program supervisor;
- society (children's aid society); and
- service provider.

Parts I to XII: The Body of the Child and Family Services Act

Following its introductory provisions, the *Child and Family Services Act* contains 12 parts. The listing below explains, in very general terms, the contents of each part.

PART I: FLEXIBLE SERVICES

Part I of the Act covers a number of administrative issues with respect to the creation of programs and services, the designation of facilities and programs as agencies, the designation of agencies as children's aid societies, and the appointment and powers of society directors and program supervisors. It provides for remedies — typically the suspension of services — if an agency fails to meet the prescribed standards.

PART II: VOLUNTARY ACCESS TO SERVICES

Part II provides additional definitions: advisory committee (residential placement advisory committee), institution, record, and special need. It also covers consent to services, with respect to residential and non-residential services, and with respect to children aged 16 to 17 and under 16. It allows a child who is 12 or older to consent to counselling without the need for parental consent. It provides for voluntary temporary care agreements between parents and guardians on the one hand and children's aid societies on the other; it also prescribes terms to be included in those agreements in section 29(8). In addition, part II covers the making of voluntary special needs agreements, which are governed by terms similar to those that govern the making of voluntary temporary care agreements.

This part also creates a detailed procedure for the review of residential placements, including voluntary placements, in sections 34 through 36.

PART III: CHILD PROTECTION

Part III of the Act begins with its own definitions section. Section 37(2) contains the extremely important definition of a "child in need of protection." If a court finds that a child is in need of protection, important consequences flow from the legislation. The most significant consequence, in many cases, is the placement of a child in care, irrespective of whether his parents or guardians consent to the placement. The definition of a child in need of protection is provided below under the heading "Child Protection Proceedings."

Part III contains many other provisions that are of key importance to child protection workers, including those relating to:

- legal representation for children;

- parties to child protection proceedings;

- notice of child protection proceedings;

- commencement of child protection proceedings (including court orders);

- apprehension of children (including apprehension of children already in care, search and entry rules, and cooperation between child protection workers and law enforcement personnel);

- rules and procedures for child protection hearings;

- rules and procedures for the assessment of children's needs;

- wardship (including society wardship, Crown wardship, and placement decisions);

- status reviews and appeals of wardships;

- records and access to records;

- child abuse register; and

- offences related to non-compliance with part III.

Finally, part III also contains section 72, which makes all people responsible for reporting their suspicions of child abuse and neglect. This duty is enhanced for child protection workers and certain other people. The enhanced reporting duty was touched on in chapter 2. It is covered in detail below under the heading "Duty To Report."

PART IV: YOUNG OFFENDERS

Part IV of the Act deals with young offenders: children between the ages of 12 and 17 who have been convicted of a criminal offence. This part was covered extensively in chapter 6.

PART V: RIGHTS OF CHILDREN

This part of the *Child and Family Services Act* is designed to protect the rights of children in residential placements and in criminal custody. The rights of children in criminal custody were introduced in chapter 6 under the heading "Rights of Youth in Custody." The rights of children in all types of care are covered further in chapter 9 under the heading "Rights of Youth in Residential Care."

PART VI: EXTRAORDINARY MEASURES

Part VI of the Act deals with the use of extraordinary measures in the care of certain children. These may include measures necessary for the control of children (for example, locking them up) or for the treatment of their behavioural problems and mental illnesses. The provisions of this part were introduced in chapter 6. They are covered further in chapter 9 under the heading "Extraordinary Measures." Here the focus is on the role of the child protection worker in the administration of extraordinary measures.

PART VII: ADOPTION

Part VII of the Act deals with adoption. Children who are Crown wards are typically available for adoption. The legal framework relating to adoption is to some degree beyond the scope of this book, but is touched on in chapter 5.

PART VIII: CONFIDENTIALITY AND ACCESS TO RECORDS

The protection of a child's privacy is a high priority within the child protection and youth criminal justice systems. Part VIII of the Act provides detailed rules with respect to records. The role of child protection workers in handling confidential records is introduced in chapter 9.

PART IX: LICENSING

Part IX of the Act provides for the licensing of facilities that provide residential care. This subject is covered in chapter 9 under the heading "Licensing of Residential Facilities."

PART X: FIRST NATIONS CHILD AND FAMILY SERVICES

First Nations communities are encouraged to administer their own social services, including the provision of services to children. Part X of the Act covers such issues as agreements between the government and band councils that provide child protection services. Considerations that are of particular concern when providing services to native children are discussed in chapter 10 under the heading "Race, Ethnicity, Religion, and Culture."

PART XI: REGULATIONS

Part XI provides for the creation of regulations to assist the administration of the *Child and Family Services Act*. A **regulation** is a legal instrument designed to provide guidance with respect to administrative aspects of a statute.

regulation a legal instrument that is subservient to a statute and created to provide guidance for the administration of the statute

PART XII: REVIEW

Part XII provides for the periodic review of the *Child and Family Services Act* by the minister of community and social services.

■SOCIETIES, AGENCIES, AND LICENSING

The *Child and Family Services Act* falls under the responsibility of the Ministry of Community and Social Services. However, the Act is administered in large part by children's aid societies.

Agencies that are approved under section 8 of the *Child and Family Services Act* act as service providers under section 7. The minister of community and social services may provide services directly or by purchase, and may use public money to fund service providers. In many cases, the minister makes agreements with municipalities for the shared provision of child protection programs and services. In approving an agency as a service provider under the *Child and Family Services Act*, the minister is authorized under section 10 of the Act to impose terms and conditions on the agency. Once approved, an agency must prepare and file a copy of its bylaws with the minister. A **bylaw** is a rule or policy of an organization that is often the subject of voting by the organization's board of directors. The content of the bylaws and the terms and conditions that the minister may impose are to some extent governed by regulations made under the Act.

bylaw a rule, policy, law, or regulation, chosen by the organization's members, that governs the operations of a private organization

Section 9 of the Act requires the minister to approve any buildings in which services are provided. Section 11 of the Act empowers the minister to fund advisory groups that support the provision of services.

Agencies that have been approved under the Act can be further designated as children's aid societies. In Ontario, there are over 50 agencies designated as children's aid societies under the *Child and Family Services Act*. This designation is subject to its own set of terms and conditions. A society's designation can be restricted with respect to geographical area or mandate (functions and objectives). The functions of a children's aid society are described in section 15(3) as follows:

> (a) investigate allegations or evidence that children who are under the age of sixteen years or are in the society's care or under its supervision may be in need of protection;
>
> (b) protect, where necessary, children who are under the age of sixteen years or are in the society's care or under its supervision;
>
> (c) provide guidance, counselling and other services to families for protecting children or for the prevention of circumstances requiring the protection of children;
>
> (d) provide care for children assigned or committed to its care under this Act;
>
> (e) supervise children assigned to its supervision under this Act;

(f) place children for adoption under Part VII; and

(g) perform any other duties given to it by this or any other Act.

The mandate of an agency (including a society) may be set out in the regulations under the Act or in the terms and conditions of its designation, or in both sources. If an agency is not carrying out its mandate in compliance with the standards imposed on it, the minister can take actions to enforce these standards. In an effort to enforce standards, the minister can exercise a number of powers provided by the Act. She can order an agency to stop doing something that is causing or threatening harm to a person's health, safety, or welfare under section 23. She can, under section 22, revoke a designation altogether or take over the operations of the agency.

The licensing of residential facilities is governed by part IX of the *Child and Family Services Act*. It is discussed in chapter 9 under the heading "Licensing of Residential Facilities."

The Ontario Association of Children's Aid Societies (OACAS) is an organization devoted to the needs of its children's aid society members. Nearly all Ontario societies are members of OACAS (a list of Ontario societies and a description of each society's geographical area of operation are available at the association's website). The OACAS provides various services, both to its society members and to children at large, through its advocacy of child welfare issues.

Among the services offered by the OACAS to its members are the following:

- accreditation,

- consultation services,

- French language services support,

- information and database services,

- the Ontario child protection training program,

- training and support for foster parents, and

- the youth in care network support program.

The OACAS praises Ontario's organization of child protection services delivery for the following reasons:

> We are in a unique position in Canada because child welfare services in Ontario are based in the community and governed by voluntary boards of directors. State-run child welfare delivery systems cannot advocate for best practices and other critical issues because the political and service arms are one and the same. Children's aid societies in Ontario are non-profit transfer payment agencies that have a unique capacity to advocate for children and families, community services and best practices in service delivery. (OACAS, 2004)

Each society has its own mission and vision of the way in which child protection services can most effectively be delivered. For information on individual societies, the Internet is a good place to start. Many societies have websites accessible via links from the OACAS website.

■DUTY TO REPORT

The *Child and Family Services Act* does not refer to the duty to report child abuse and/or neglect until section 72. However, this duty provides a good place to begin a discussion of the child protection system. In most cases, the making of a report about a child is the source from which all further actions and consequences flow under the Act. This is not only true of non-consensual actions, such as the apprehension of a child. It is also true of actions to which parents voluntarily consent. All societies encourage parents who are struggling with parenting problems to get in touch with a society for support.

A parent's report about a child, or a report made by a concerned person outside the family, can result in the parent's voluntary acceptance of assistance by a society. In practice, this kind of self-reporting is fairly rare, because many parents worry that disclosing the fact that they are having problems with their children might lead to unwanted consequences, such as the apprehension of a child. However, in many communities there are programs in place (that have some connection to a society) to encourage parents to seek help on their own. These programs are discussed further under the heading "Services to Which Parents or Guardians Consent," below.

When Is the Duty Triggered?

As mentioned in chapter 2, section 72 of the *Child and Family Services Act* makes it mandatory for *all* people to report a belief that a child — any child — has suffered or is at risk of suffering from abuse or neglect. Read section 72(1) carefully in its entirety:

> Despite the provisions of any other Act, if a person, including a person who performs professional or official duties with respect to children, has reasonable grounds to suspect one of the following, the person shall forthwith report the suspicion and the information on which it is based to a society:
>
> 1. The child has suffered physical harm, inflicted by the person having charge of the child or caused by or resulting from that person's,
>   i. failure to adequately care for, provide for, supervise or protect the child, or
>   ii. pattern of neglect in caring for, providing for, supervising or protecting the child.
>
> 2. There is a risk that the child is likely to suffer physical harm inflicted by the person having charge of the child or caused by or resulting from that person's,
>   i. failure to adequately care for, provide for, supervise or protect the child, or
>   ii. pattern of neglect in caring for, providing for, supervising or protecting the child.
>
> 3. The child has been sexually molested or sexually exploited, by the person having charge of the child or by another person where the person having charge of the child knows or should know of the possibility of sexual molestation or sexual exploitation and fails to protect the child.

4. There is a risk that the child is likely to be sexually molested or sexually exploited as described in paragraph 3.

5. The child requires medical treatment to cure, prevent or alleviate physical harm or suffering and the child's parent or the person having charge of the child does not provide, or refuses or is unavailable or unable to consent to, the treatment.

6. The child has suffered emotional harm, demonstrated by serious,
   i. anxiety,
   ii. depression,
   iii. withdrawal,
   iv. self-destructive or aggressive behaviour, or
   v. delayed development,

   and there are reasonable grounds to believe that the emotional harm suffered by the child results from the actions, failure to act or pattern of neglect on the part of the child's parent or the person having charge of the child.

7. The child has suffered emotional harm of the kind described in subparagraph i, ii, iii, iv or v of paragraph 6 and the child's parent or the person having charge of the child does not provide, or refuses or is unavailable or unable to consent to, services or treatment to remedy or alleviate the harm.

8. There is a risk that the child is likely to suffer emotional harm of the kind described in subparagraph i, ii, iii, iv or v of paragraph 6 resulting from the actions, failure to act or pattern of neglect on the part of the child's parent or the person having charge of the child.

9. There is a risk that the child is likely to suffer emotional harm of the kind described in subparagraph i, ii, iii, iv or v of paragraph 6 and that the child's parent or the person having charge of the child does not provide, or refuses or is unavailable or unable to consent to, services or treatment to prevent the harm.

10. The child suffers from a mental, emotional or developmental condition that, if not remedied, could seriously impair the child's development and the child's parent or the person having charge of the child does not provide, or refuses or is unavailable or unable to consent to, treatment to remedy or alleviate the condition.

11. The child has been abandoned, the child's parent has died or is unavailable to exercise his or her custodial rights over the child and has not made adequate provision for the child's care and custody, or the child is in a residential placement and the parent refuses or is unable or unwilling to resume the child's care and custody.

12. The child is less than 12 years old and has killed or seriously injured another person or caused serious damage to another person's property, services or treatment are necessary to prevent a recurrence and the child's parent or the person having charge of the child does not provide, or refuses or is unavailable or unable to consent to, those services or treatment.

13. The child is less than 12 years old and has on more than one occasion injured another person or caused loss or damage to another person's property, with

the encouragement of the person having charge of the child or because of that person's failure or inability to supervise the child adequately.

In summary, everyone has a duty to report *a suspicion based on reasonable grounds* that a child has suffered or is at risk of suffering:

1. physical harm through

    a. abuse, or

    b. neglect;

2. sexual molestation or exploitation, either

    a. directly, or

    b. by not being protected;

3. a deprivation of necessary medical treatment;

4. emotional harm through

    a. abuse, or

    b. neglect;

5. a deprivation of treatment for emotional or developmental problems, whatever the cause of the problems;

6. abandonment;

7. a deprivation of services or treatment designed to prevent the child (under 12) who has killed or seriously injured someone from doing so again; and

8. a risk of doing serious harm to a person or property as a result of encouragement by another person, or through insufficient supervision, if the child is under 12.

The duty to report arises as soon as the person making the relevant observations has reasonable grounds to suspect that harm has occurred, is occurring, or is threatened. There is no requirement that the person be certain of the harm. For example, a gym teacher who observes bruises on a child's body that are not consistent with normal play — for example, bruises on the back, neck, or upper arm — almost certainly has reasonable grounds to make a report. In some cases, a gym teacher who observes symptoms such as these has a duty to make a report despite hearing an account from the child that points to an innocent explanation for the bruises.

Section 72 is purposely broad and general. It is designed to include a very broad range of situations that may be abusive or neglectful. The reason for the breadth of section 72 is that adults may have difficulty interpreting the true scope and nature of harm being suffered by a child. In many cases, abusers go to considerable lengths to conceal their actions, and victims may further conceal the problem. By providing a very general duty to report, the statute aims to catch as many cases of serious harm as possible.

The breadth of the Act may result in reports being made in situations where a child is not in fact subject to, or threatened with, abuse or neglect. Society employees are trained to assess reports and to conduct investigations to determine whether child protection actions are warranted. A broad duty to report ensures that the task of weighing the evidence in a particular situation lies not with the person making the report, but with the (expert) agency receiving it. As explained above, the *Child and Family Services Act* expresses the paramount purpose of providing protection that is in the best interests of a child, and secondary purposes that reflect a preference to maintain families intact. Any assessment made by a society of a report received about a child should be conducted with these purposes in mind.

YOU DECIDE!

DO YOU HAVE A DUTY TO REPORT?

After considering the following facts, decide whether they create a duty to report. In each instance, also consider whether your observations relate to abuse, the threat of abuse, neglect, or the threat of neglect.

1. You are an administrator in the office of a large high school. Terry, a 10th grade student, has been sent to the office, along with two of his friends, for discipline in connection with a prank played on the basketball coach (the students filled his shoes and desk drawer with shaving cream). You advise Terry that entering the coach's office without permission and making a mess constituted bad judgment. Since this is Terry's second offence of this nature, you also tell him that he will be suspended for two days and his parents will be informed of the suspension. Terry looks panic-stricken and begs you to reconsider, saying, "My dad is gonna kill me."

2. You are the lunchroom supervisor at an elementary school. For the third time this week, Vezna, a second-grader, has not brought her lunch. She tells you that her mom forgot to make it. You encourage other students to share their lunches with her. You have noticed that Vezna often looks unkempt. She dresses inappropriately for the weather, her hair is often hopelessly tangled, and she smells bad. This freezing January day, Vezna is wearing a pair of cropped pants in a thin summery fabric and sandals with socks. You ask Vezna whether her mother helped her pick out these clothes, and

Vezna tells you that her mother is "never awake in the mornings before school, but I'm old enough to choose my own clothes."

3. You are the superintendent of a small apartment building. While carrying out your nightly rounds, you discover Uma, a 12-year-old girl whom you recognize as being the daughter of a third-floor tenant, asleep in a sleeping bag underneath a flight of stairs. Uma and her father share a bachelor apartment. You wake Uma and ask what she is doing there. Very embarrassed, she tells you that her father "brought home a date and locked me out. I'm fine, I'm warm. I'd rather be out here than in there with them anyway."

4. You are a passenger on a city bus. You take the same bus every morning. Most mornings, a woman gets on with a boy who looks to be about three years old and a newborn. The boy is fairly well behaved on the bus, but the mother, it seems to you, responds extremely harshly to any transgression on his part. Within the space of about two blocks, she has yelled at the boy three times for kicking the seat in front of him. The fourth time he kicks the seat, she grabs his foot and shoves it violently downwards. The force of her action causes his body to lurch forward, and he bumps his head hard against the handrail on the seat in front. He begins to cry, and his mother immediately apologizes and rubs his forehead. However, within 10 minutes, she yells at him again, this time for humming.

How To Make a Report

Once a person has reasonable grounds to suspect that anything listed in section 72 is happening to a child, the duty to report arises. The specifics of this duty, as expressed by the *Child and Family Services Act*, can be paraphrased as follows:

- Make the report "forthwith" — that is, immediately or as soon as is practically possible.

- Report "the suspicion and the information upon which it is based."

- Give the report to a children's aid society (reports to police are discussed below).

- Make the report personally (the person whose duty to report is triggered must be the person who makes the report, according to section 72(3)).

- Be aware of the ongoing duty to report (if a person who has already made a report has new observations, even about the same child, he must make a new report, according to section 72(2)).

While the Act requires that people make reports promptly, the timing of the report is to some degree influenced by the perceived seriousness of the harm observed, or the presence of an ongoing threat. For example, if you observe an adult in the process of beating a child, it is usually appropriate to call the police immediately, and to call a society next. Where the circumstances are more ambiguous (as in the example about Vezna at lunch), it is sometimes acceptable to wait and see whether you have observed an isolated incident or a pattern of inadequate parenting (all parents have the occasional bad morning). However, it is never appropriate to ignore signs of abuse or neglect in the hope that they will be resolved on their own, or reported by someone else.

When making a report by telephone, be prepared before dialing with notes about your observations and suspicions. Society employees will often ask questions designed to elicit the kind of information that is most useful to them. In making a report, it is important to be calm, impartial, and open, and to refrain from using the reporting process as a personal attack on the suspected abuser. Personnel receiving reports, despite their efforts to remain impartial, may have difficulty in avoiding being influenced by your tone. If your report sounds malicious or exaggerated, the credibility of your information is tainted. No matter what your feelings about the abuse or neglect you have witnessed, a calm, impartial, factual report is the most likely one to be helpful to the child.

Even though many people may not be specifically aware of their duty to make a report under the *Child and Family Services Act*, they are aware of the existence and purpose of children's aid societies. The telephone numbers of these societies are readily accessible. If someone makes her initial report to the police, a police officer should advise her of her duty to make a report to a society and if possible, provide her with a telephone number. *Calling the police is not enough to satisfy the duty to report abuse or neglect under the Child and Family Services Act.* In some situations, it is appropriate to call both the police and a society about the same incident.

If you are an employee of a society and you witness events that trigger your duty to make a report about a client or a ward, you have a duty to report your observations to the director of the society (in cases of abuse of a child in care) under section 72.1. Alternatively, and provided that it is within the scope of your work, you can take appropriate protective actions with respect to the information.

The requirement under section 72(3) that reports be made directly means that you cannot delegate your reporting duty to someone else, even your supervisor. You must make the call yourself.

In many cases, it will be appropriate to advise another person of your suspicions, and in some cases, to consider that person's advice with respect to reporting.

SAMPLE DIRECT REPORTING POLICY

Jessie's Centre for Teenagers is an independent organization (not connected with a society) that provides various services to pregnant teenagers and their children. Children visit Jessie's drop-in centre with their parents, and Jessie's volunteers are sometimes in a position to observe reportable child abuse or neglect. Jessie's has developed a policy for making reports under the *Child and Family Services Act*. The following is an excerpt from that policy:

Volunteer/Student Reporting Procedure

Where a volunteer or a student witnesses or suspects that a child is in need of protection, they are expected to follow the procedure outlined below:

1. Speak to the staff involved in the program area before making the report.

2. Where possible make the report to a child protection worker in the presence of Jessie's staff or program manager during program time.

3. The normal consultation process is strongly encouraged prior to making the report. This consultation will be done with Jessie's staff. [The consultation process, described in another part of the guidelines, requires staff and/or volunteers to discuss their concerns about a child's care in a friendly and supportive manner with the child's parent.]

4. A follow-up letter outlining the nature of the report and follow-up agreement with child welfare should be done by the staff person involved within 24 hours of the report.

5. Direct service staff/program manager will be present to provide additional confidential information as required, as well as to write the follow-up letter to child welfare.

6. Students/volunteers should expect to be supported through the process by direct service staff.

The person having the most direct information bears the responsibility of making the report to the children's aid society using the supportive procedure outlined above.

Where delay could place the child at risk, the volunteer/student suspecting abuse or neglect should make the report immediately, and then inform the direct service staff for appropriate follow-up (Jessie's Centre for Teenagers, n.d., p. 7).

However, the duty to report is always yours personally, and if you fail to make a report in circumstances where you should have done so, you may be charged with an offence.

While the duty to report applies to everybody, certain people have an enhanced duty to report in the sense that failing to do so may result in the person's being charged with an offence. Section 72(4) of the *Child and Family Services Act* states that if a person

- falls within a stipulated list of types of persons,

- obtains information triggering a duty to report in the course of his professional duties, and

- does not make a report,

that person can be charged with an offence that can attract a fine of up to $1,000.

It is important to remember, however, that a $1,000 fine is not the worst possible consequence of failing to report information about child abuse. As explained in chapter 7, there are several offences under the criminal law that can be charged against child protection workers who are negligent in carrying out their duties. Failure to satisfy a duty to report would be important evidence in a criminal proceeding. Another legal consequence of failing to satisfy a reporting duty could include a lawsuit brought against a child protection worker in the civil (non-criminal) courts. Lawsuits designed to obtain monetary compensation for harm suffered by children are discussed in chapter 3.

The professionals who may be subject to being charged with an offence under section 72(4) are listed in section 72(5):

Subsection (4) applies to every person who performs professional or official duties with respect to children including,

(a) a health care professional, including a physician, nurse, dentist, pharmacist and psychologist;

(b) a teacher, school principal, social worker, family counsellor, priest, rabbi, member of the clergy, operator or employee of a day nursery and [a non-volunteer] youth and recreation worker;

(c) a peace officer and a coroner;

(d) a solicitor; and

(e) a service provider and an employee of a service provider.

■INVESTIGATING A REPORT

Initial Steps

When a society receives a report under section 72, the society is obliged to investigate to determine whether a child is in need of protection, and how the child might be protected. The first step is usually a thorough interview by a society employee of the person who made the report.

In some cases, an investigation proceeds from this point on a consensual basis: the parents give permission for the society to interview and/or more formally assess the child, and the person who is suspected of abuse or neglect consents to being interviewed as well. The results of a consensual investigation could satisfy the society that the child is not, in fact, in need of protection. In this case, no further action is taken, though a schedule of follow-up visits or reporting may be proposed.

In other cases, a problem may be uncovered, and the people involved may agree that the society or another suitable agency will provide necessary services. Services provided on a consensual basis can be either residential (the child goes to live somewhere else temporarily) or non-residential. Consensual services are discussed below under the heading "Services to Which Parents or Guardians Consent."

In other cases, the investigation will not be consensual. The parents may not consent to the child's being interviewed, and the suspected abuser (parent or otherwise) may not consent to being interviewed either.

Where the situation does not appear to present an immediate danger, a caseworker may attempt to gather information from other sources — for example, by speaking to a child's teachers, neighbours, or other people who know the child. These inquiries may be made in an attempt to determine whether a child is in need of protection and should be apprehended by the society for her own protection.

A society that suspects that a child may be in need of protection usually refers the case to a review team under section 73 of the Act. If the child's parents consent, the review team can then assess the child without apprehending her. However, if a society cannot adequately review a child's case because her parents will not consent to an assessment, the society may need to take the child into custody.

If a society has a sufficient suspicion of abuse or neglect to begin the apprehension process, it can elect — instead of actually apprehending the child — to have a homemaker remain with the child in her home. This option is described under section 78 of the Act. A homemaker cannot live with the child for more than 30 days; at the end of that time, if the parent is not able to care for the child, a society usually apprehends the child. Reliance on a homemaker is not appropriate in situations where a child is suffering abuse. Homemakers tend to be used in circumstances in which, for some extraordinary reason, a good parent is temporarily unable to care for a child and there are no relatives available to help out — for example, a parent suddenly falls ill, is detained out of the country, or is detained in criminal custody pending a bail hearing.

Apprehension of a Child

The **apprehension** of a child who is suspected to be in need of protection is governed by part III of the *Child and Family Services Act*. Part III opens with a definition of "child in need of protection," which is reproduced below under the heading "Child Protection Proceedings." For the purposes of part III, a child is a person aged 16 or under. Whether or not a child is in need of protection is a decision made by a court after a hearing.

apprehension in the child protection context, the taking into protective custody of a child

Section 38 provides that a child may be represented by a lawyer from the beginning of the child protection process. In practical terms, this generally means from the point at which a conflict of interest between children and parents develops. A conflict of interest usually arises when it becomes clear that apprehension may be necessary. It is not necessary for a child to wait until court proceedings are commenced in order to obtain a lawyer. A child's options with respect to legal representation are discussed further under the heading "Child Protection Proceedings," below.

justice of the peace
an officer of the court
who makes administrative
decisions — for example,
issuing warrants

warrant a document
(or occasionally, oral
statement) providing court
authorization for certain
described action (such
as the apprehension of a
child)

Where a society — or, in practice, an employee of a society — has *reasonable and probable grounds* to believe that a child is in need of protection, the society can apply to a justice of the peace for a warrant to apprehend a child under section 40(2). A **justice of the peace** is an officer of the court who makes decisions with respect to various issues, notably the issuance of search warrants. A **warrant** is an authorization to do something (search a location, apprehend a person, etc.) with the court's blessing. A justice of the peace will issue the warrant if

1. he is satisfied that the reasonable and probable grounds, as described, do exist on the part of the society; and

2. "a less restrictive course of action is not available or will not protect the child adequately."

In order to prove that a less restrictive course is not available, a child protection worker must generally provide evidence. Common examples of evidence that is relevant in this regard include failed attempts to obtain information that is sufficient to assess the child's case; or lack of parental response to suggestions or warnings given by a society about the child's treatment or care.

The *Child and Family Services Act* contains the following requirements for apprehending a child:

- A warrant to apprehend a child need not specify the child's name or location (section 40(5)).

- A child protection worker may enter any location specified in the warrant, by force if necessary, to look for and apprehend the child (section 40(6)).

- A child protection worker may apprehend a child *without a warrant* where reasonable and probable grounds exist to believe that the child is in need of protection, and where "there would be a substantial risk to the child's health or safety during the time necessary to apply for a warrant (section 40(7)).

- A child protection worker can call for the assistance of a peace officer in apprehending a child, and the officer has the powers of a child protection worker when acting in this capacity (sections 40(8) and 40(13)).

- A child protection worker who apprehends a child with or without a warrant can order a medical examination of the child without the parent's consent (section 40(9)).

- Where no "less restrictive alternative" exists, a child can be placed in "open temporary detention" as defined under the federal *Youth Criminal Justice Act*.

- A child protection worker or peace officer is protected from legal action relating to actions taken in the process of apprehending a child where the child protection worker or peace officer acts in good faith in carrying out the apprehension (section 40(14)).

Section 41 of the Act provides a similar scheme for the apprehension of a child who has already been placed in the care of a society, when that child has left or has been removed from care without authorization.

Section 42 of the *Child and Family Services Act* provides for the apprehension of a child under the age of 12 who has committed an act which, if the child were 12 or older, could form the basis for a criminal charge. As explained in chapter 6, the *Youth Criminal Justice Act* applies to youth aged 12 and older. Children under the age of 12 are considered to be incapable of forming a criminal intention, and therefore incapable of committing crimes. However, the fact that a child performs criminal-type actions can constitute evidence that the child is in need of protection (see sections 37(2)(j), 37(2)(k), 72(1)12, and 72(1)13 of the *Child and Family Services Act*). When a child is apprehended under section 42, the peace officer who apprehends the child must give notice to the child's parent(s), and deliver the child into the parent(s)'s care as soon as possible. Where it is not possible to turn the child over to his parents within 12 hours, the child must be dealt with under section 46, which requires a hearing concerning what is to be done with him.

Finally, section 43 deals with the apprehension of runaways — that is, children under the age of 16 who have "withdrawn from the care and control" of parents, guardians, or agencies approved under the *Child and Family Services Act*. Where a child under 16 runs away, and a parent, guardian, or society believes that the child's health or safety may be at risk if the child is not apprehended, a justice of the peace can issue a warrant to apprehend the child. The warrant will either order that the child be returned to the parent, guardian, or society, or that the child be brought to a place of safety to await a child protection hearing.

YOU DECIDE!

MOTHER IS "VERY STRICT"

Xavier's teacher, Zara, has noticed that 10-year-old Xavier seems to be losing hair around his temples. The skin in the area is raw and red. After much questioning by Zara, Xavier admits, through tears, that his hair loss is the result of "stress." It appears that Xavier has been pulling out his own hair in an effort to calm his fear of his "very strict" mother. Zara called Xavier's mother to talk about this problem, but Xavier's mother was completely unwilling to discuss the issue.

After the phone call, Xavier stopped coming to school. Zara became concerned and reported her concerns to the children's aid society. Two months later, Xavier had not yet returned to school, and Zara made a follow-up call to the society. She learned from a society employee that the society decided not to commence child protection proceedings after speaking with Xavier's mother. Zara feels quite strongly that Xavier may be suffering or be at risk of suffering serious emotional abuse, and that action is needed to protect him, even if this means apprehension by the society.

Questions

1. After reading sections 40 to 44 of the *Child and Family Services Act*, decide what Zara should do.

2. In what section of the Act did you find your solution?

place of safety under the *Child and Family Services Act*, a hospital, foster home, or other residential facility or place designated as a place of safety under section 17

Once a child is apprehended, he is taken to a **place of safety**, which is defined under the *Child and Family Services Act* as a hospital, foster home, or other residential facility or place designated as a place of safety under section 17 (often a group home established for the temporary care of children awaiting child protection proceedings).

Where a child has been apprehended, there are three options, one of which must be chosen by the child protection agency that has taken charge of the child no later than five days after the apprehension. Section 46(1) provides that a child must be

- returned to his parent(s) or guardian,
- brought before the court for a child protection hearing, or
- made the subject of a temporary care agreement.

These options are discussed below.

The decision to apprehend a child can be a very difficult one to make, especially if scant information is available about the child's situation. Where parents, other adults, and even the child herself are not cooperating with a child protection worker's attempts to investigate a report, it is easy to draw the inference that someone is hiding something, and that the child is at significant risk. However, the upheaval and turmoil that a child may suffer in being removed from her home should never be underestimated. In some cases, parents may resist cooperating with a society purely out of fear or misunderstanding of the society's motives. Wherever possible, workers should try to gather comprehensive information about the child's situation before making a decision to apprehend the child, unless there are clear indications that the child is at risk of suffering serious harm. When those indications are present, child protection workers should feel comfortable in moving quickly to remove a child from a dangerous situation. It is always possible to return the child to the home if suspicions prove to be unwarranted; it is not so easy to undo abuse or neglect that occurs as a result of inaction.

Sometimes a society refers a child's case to a review team before an apprehension. It always does so after an apprehension. Section 73 provides that a review team must consist of

(a) persons who are professionally qualified to perform medical, psychological, developmental, educational or social assessments; and

(b) at least one legally qualified medical practitioner.

The review team assesses all information available about the child's case so that it can make recommendations about how the child can best be protected.

■ SERVICES TO WHICH PARENTS OR GUARDIANS CONSENT

Agencies within communities can provide services to which parents or guardians consent without the need for a court's finding that a child is in need of protection. The availability of community child care services are consistent with the secondary purposes of the *Child and Family Services Act*, which are set out above under the heading "Introduction to the Objectives of the Child and Family Services Act."

The nature of available services will vary from community to community. While children's aid societies may provide some services, different kinds of agencies may provide other services. Services can include parenting classes, drop-in centres where staff supervise children so that parents can run errands (these centres often also provide parent education programs), and programs designed to address particular situations, such as parenting children with developmental problems, disabilities, or behavioural problems. Many communities offer parent relief programs. In these programs, parents experiencing burn-out — or who need free time to travel for job interviews, etc. — can temporarily turn the care of their children over to volunteers or staff who supervise the children overnight in either the parent's home or in their own home. These arrangements typically last only a few nights.

The *Child and Family Services Act* offers residential placements on a voluntary, or consensual, basis. These placements are generally reserved for children whose problems are relatively serious or will take considerable time to resolve, such as a parent's serious drug addiction and need for rehabilitation. A child may be placed in care on the parent's initiative, or (perhaps more commonly) after apprehension. Placement in care is an alternative to child protection proceedings that preserves the participation of parents.

Voluntary residential placements are governed by sections 29 to 36 of the *Child and Family Services Act*. Section 29 provides for the making of a written **temporary care agreement**, which is essentially a contract between a child's parent or guardian and a children's aid society. Where a child is between the ages of 12 and 15 (or 12 and 17, if the child has special needs), the child is also involved in the contract.

Temporary care agreements are made for specific time periods, but can be extended (or shortened) where appropriate. Section 29(8) provides that a temporary care agreement must contain the following:

1. A statement by all the parties to the agreement that the child's care and custody are transferred to the society.

2. A statement by all the parties to the agreement that the child's placement is voluntary.

3. A statement, by [the parent or guardian], that he or she is temporarily unable to care for the child adequately and has discussed with the society alternatives to residential placement of the child.

4. An undertaking by [the parent or guardian] to maintain contact with the child and be involved in the child's care.

GETTING PRACTICAL

WHAT'S AVAILABLE IN YOUR COMMUNITY?

Using the telephone directory, the Blue Book, the Internet, and any other resources you find helpful, research the voluntary services provided by, or recommended by, children's aid societies in your community. Choose one facility to visit or one care provider to interview. Visit the facility or interview the provider to learn about the program. The following questions might provide you with a starting point:

- How do children find your program?

- Is your program run by a children's aid society, associated with a society, or recommended by a society?

- Is the program staffed by volunteers or employees?

- What training and credentials do the staff have?

- What types of problems does your program address?

- What types of problems are beyond your program's mandate?

- Does your program have a policy for identifying participants in need of protection? If so, what is it?

Give a presentation to your class about the program or facility.

---

temporary care agreement under the *Child and Family Services Act*, a voluntary agreement between a society and a child's parent(s) or guardian that provides for residential care of the child on a temporary basis

5. If it is not possible for [the parent or guardian] to maintain contact with the child and be involved in the child's care, the person's designation of another named person who is willing to do so.

6. The name of the individual who is the primary contact between the society and [parent or guardian].

7. Such other provisions as are prescribed [by the regulations].

As you can see, temporary care agreements are made with the expectation that the child and her parent or guardian will maintain contact during the course of the agreement, and that the parent or guardian will remain "involved in the child's care." This level of involvement distinguishes the temporary care arrangement from society wardship, which is discussed below under the heading "Society Wardship." Children who are society wards are allowed contact with parents or guardians in most cases, but there is no statutory provision for direct parental involvement in the child's care. How exactly a parent or guardian will participate in a child's care during a voluntary placement will vary from society to society. It will also depend on the reasons for the child's placement in care, and factors concerning the child's parent or guardian, such as whether the placement was required because of health or other problems on the part of the parent that might prevent significant involvement in the child's care. In almost all cases, societies will, at least, provide opportunities for parents or guardians and children to visit each other.

Section 30 provides for temporary placements of children with special needs. These needs may arise from a disability, developmental delay, emotional problem, or serious behavioural problem. Temporary placements are often made where no parenting problem exists, but where the child is not thriving at home because his parent or guardian cannot address the child's needs. Children aged 16 and 17 can be placed in these programs (regular temporary care placements end at age 16).

In some cases, a parent or guardian is still not able to care for a child after a voluntary placement ends. In these circumstances, section 33(5) of the *Child and Family Services Act* gives the minister the following three choices:

1. to return the child to the parent or guardian who made the care agreement;

2. to place the child in the care of a person who has obtained a custody order since the making of the agreement (even if this person was not the adult who entered into the agreement); or

3. to bring child protection proceedings with a view to making the child a society or Crown ward if the minister (via the society) believes that the child is in need of protection.

■ CHILD PROTECTION PROCEEDINGS

A children's aid society can commence child protection proceedings at any time. In general, however, these proceedings are begun at the time the society decides to apprehend a child.

From the point of view of a society, the purpose of a child protection hearing is to obtain a legal determination that a child is in need of protection. No services to which a child's parent or guardian fails to consent can be delivered to the child until a court finds that the child is in need of protection.

The finding that a child is in need of protection is made on the basis of evidence presented to a court. This evidence must establish that it is more likely than not that the child either has suffered abuse or neglect or is at risk of suffering abuse or neglect, and requires protection to be safe from future abuse or neglect.

Section 37(2) provides the definition of child in need of protection. You will find that it covers much of the territory covered in section 72, which sets out the duty to report. This makes good sense, of course, because the intent of section 72 is to impose a duty on people to report information that suggests that a child is in need of protection. Section 37(2) provides that a child is in need of protection in the following circumstances:

> (a) the child has suffered physical harm, inflicted by the person having charge of the child or caused by or resulting from that person's,
>
> > (i) failure to adequately care for, provide for, supervise or protect the child, or
> >
> > (ii) pattern of neglect in caring for, providing for, supervising or protecting the child;
>
> (b) there is a risk that the child is likely to suffer physical harm inflicted by the person having charge of the child or caused by or resulting from that person's,
>
> > (i) failure to adequately care for, provide for, supervise or protect the child, or
> >
> > (ii) pattern of neglect in caring for, providing for, supervising or protecting the child;
>
> (c) the child has been sexually molested or sexually exploited, by the person having charge of the child or by another person where the person having charge of the child knows or should know of the possibility of sexual molestation or sexual exploitation and fails to protect the child;
>
> (d) there is a risk that the child is likely to be sexually molested or sexually exploited as described in clause (c);
>
> (e) the child requires medical treatment to cure, prevent or alleviate physical harm or suffering and the child's parent or the person having charge of the child does not provide, or refuses or is unavailable or unable to consent to, the treatment;
>
> (f) the child has suffered emotional harm, demonstrated by serious,
>
> > (i) anxiety,
> >
> > (ii) depression,
> >
> > (iii) withdrawal,
> >
> > (iv) self-destructive or aggressive behaviour, or
> >
> > (v) delayed development,
>
> and there are reasonable grounds to believe that the emotional harm suffered by the child results from the actions, failure to act or pattern of neglect on the part of the child's parent or the person having charge of the child;
>
> (f.1) the child has suffered emotional harm of the kind described in subclause (f) (i), (ii), (iii), (iv) or (v) and the child's parent or the person having

charge of the child does not provide, or refuses or is unavailable or unable to consent to, services or treatment to remedy or alleviate the harm;

(g) there is a risk that the child is likely to suffer emotional harm of the kind described in subclause (f) (i), (ii), (iii), (iv) or (v) resulting from the actions, failure to act or pattern of neglect on the part of the child's parent or the person having charge of the child;

(g.1) there is a risk that the child is likely to suffer emotional harm of the kind described in subclause (f) (i), (ii), (iii), (iv) or (v) and that the child's parent or the person having charge of the child does not provide, or refuses or is unavailable or unable to consent to, services or treatment to prevent the harm;

(h) the child suffers from a mental, emotional or developmental condition that, if not remedied, could seriously impair the child's development and the child's parent or the person having charge of the child does not provide, or refuses or is unavailable or unable to consent to, treatment to remedy or alleviate the condition;

(i) the child has been abandoned, the child's parent has died or is unavailable to exercise his or her custodial rights over the child and has not made adequate provision for the child's care and custody, or the child is in a residential placement and the parent refuses or is unable or unwilling to resume the child's care and custody;

(j) the child is less than twelve years old and has killed or seriously injured another person or caused serious damage to another person's property, services or treatment are necessary to prevent a recurrence and the child's parent or the person having charge of the child does not provide, or refuses or is unavailable or unable to consent to, those services or treatment;

(k) the child is less than twelve years old and has on more than one occasion injured another person or caused loss or damage to another person's property, with the encouragement of the person having charge of the child or because of that person's failure or inability to supervise the child adequately; or

(l) the child's parent is unable to care for the child and the child is brought before the court with the parent's consent and, where the child is twelve years of age or older, with the child's consent, to be dealt with under this Part.

A court determines whether or not a particular child falls within this definition on the basis of many forms of evidence. The main form is testimony — verbal questioning of individuals by lawyers acting for each of the parties in the case. A **party** is a person or organization with an interest in (and who will be affected by) the litigation. The parties in a child protection hearing are listed in section 39 of the *Child and Family Services Act* as follows:

party an individual or corporation with an interest in — who will be affected by — legal proceedings

- the applicant (whoever requested the hearing; this is usually a children's aid society, but can be someone else);

- the society;

- the child's parent; and

- "where the child is an Indian or a native person, a representative chosen by the child's band or native community."

A director of a children's aid society can request to be added to the proceedings as a party.

Any person who has cared for a child (in the sense of living with the child and being his sole caregiver), including a foster parent, can participate in the hearing. Although such a person does not have the status of a party in the proceedings, she has many of the same privileges. These privileges include the right to have notice of decisions and the progress of proceedings, to be represented by a lawyer, and to state her case to the court.

A child aged 12 or over who is the subject of the hearing is generally entitled to attend the proceedings, though not as a party. Children are not entitled to attend if the court thinks that the child's presence will cause the child emotional harm. A child under the age of 12 is generally not entitled to attend the hearing unless the court decides otherwise. A court would make such a decision on the basis that the child is capable of understanding the hearing and would not suffer emotional harm as a result of being present.

Section 38 of the *Child and Family Services Act* allows a child to have a lawyer at any time in the course of child protection efforts. However, it is not mandatory that a child have a lawyer. Most children do not have the funds necessary to hire a lawyer independently. In certain cases, a court will decide that it is desirable for a child to have legal representation, and will make an order that the child is to be represented by the Children's Lawyer, a public official. A court usually makes such an order if it thinks that a child's interests, as expressed by the child, are not identical to the society's view of the child's interests. This kind of situation might arise if an older child was expressing a very strong desire to remain in the care of an abusive parent.

Witnesses who are likely to give evidence in a child protection hearing include the following: people who have observed the circumstances that provoked the making of a report about the child, experts (such as doctors and therapists) who have assessed the child, investigators who have uncovered evidence about the treatment of the child, people who have evidence tending to support the contention that abuse or neglect did *not* occur, and any other person who has information that is useful to the court. Section 49 of the *Child and Family Services Act* gives the court itself the power to require any witness to appear to give testimony at a child protection hearing.

Child protection workers are often called as witnesses in child protection cases. In most circumstances, giving evidence is a fairly simple matter. It involves telling the truth in response to questions asked, without exaggerating or concealing anything, and without making inappropriate or biased judgments about people or facts. In the occasional case, however, the child protection worker may find himself at odds with the position taken by the children's aid society for which he works. For example, a child protection worker may believe, on the basis of the interactions that he has observed, that a child has not been abused, though the society may believe, on the basis of the history of the people involved, that the child has been abused. This is a difficult situation, because it means that the child protection worker is at odds with his own employer.

PREPARING TO GIVE EVIDENCE IN COURT

Child protection workers are frequently asked to appear in court to give evidence at child protection hearings and criminal trials. Giving verbal evidence is nerve-wracking for anybody. Some degree of anxiety is to be anticipated, but good preparation can assist a witness in being more comfortable on the witness stand.

Before court, the following steps may be useful:

- Review any notes you have made about the case, the child's file, and any other documents that may be useful in refreshing your memory of the events.

- Bring your notes to court.

- Confirm the time and exact location of the hearing the night before. Be sure you know how to find the courtroom.

- Speak to a supervisor who has attended this kind of hearing before. What was the experience like? What kinds of questions were asked? Is there anything you should know to help you give your evidence most effectively?

- Speak to the lawyer representing the party who has called you as a witness. Ask her any questions that you have about the process or your role in it. Inquire about the types of questions you may be asked.

- Try to predict the questions that you may be asked in court, and think about how you will answer them in advance. What will your side ask? What will the other side ask?

- Dress professionally.

- Arrive on time.

While giving evidence, consider the following tips:

- Ask the judge's permission if you would like to consult the notes that you have brought with you.

- Speak clearly and slowly.

- Keep all of your answers brief. If a lawyer wants more information, he will ask you a follow-up question. Do not elaborate your answers unless you are prompted to do so by a lawyer or the judge.

- Tell the truth. Do not exaggerate or speculate.

- If you do not know the answer to a question, say so. Do not guess.

- If you make a mistake, say so, and correct it if possible.

- Keep your personal views of the other parties, especially the suspected abuser, to yourself. Objectivity makes your evidence more credible; bias makes it less so. Credible evidence is the most helpful thing you can offer your child client.

- Stay calm, and try to avoid reacting emotionally to upsetting questions.

- Remember that you have a duty at all times to tell the truth and to act in the best interests of the child as far as is consistent with telling the truth.

- Understand the difference between the child's interests, your own interests, and the interests of your employer.

The answer as to how to handle this kind of situation, though not easy, is clear: the child protection worker has a duty, as a representative of a children's aid society, to act in the best interests of the child. If the best interests of the child, as understood by the worker, require that the worker give evidence that is not helpful to the society's case, the child protection worker must give his evidence in any event.

Another challenge can arise where a child protection worker's own interests are in conflict with the interests of her client, the child. Consider, for example, a case in which a worker made a mistake by failing to follow through on a report of abuse, and this resulted in the child's being subjected to further abuse because the child was not apprehended soon enough. Testifying about her involvement in this situation might cost the worker her job or, worse, attract a lawsuit or criminal prosecution. Again, however, the child protection worker is required to act in the best interests of the child, even if it means telling an uncomfortable truth.

Child protection hearings are usually held in private. They are an exception to the general rule that court proceedings are open to the public. Society keeps child protection hearings private to protect children from suffering emotional harm. However, a court has the power to order that the public be admitted in appropriate cases, and has a certain amount of control over the admission and exclusion of the media. It is never permissible to identify the child, or to publish any information that would identify him. The court can also make an order prohibiting the publication of information that would identify an adult who is charged with an offence under the *Child and Family Services Act*.

DISPOSITIONS

Plans and Assessments

The purpose of a child protection hearing, as mentioned above, is to determine whether a child is in need of protection, and to provide for the child's care. In some cases, a court will make a care order under section 56 of the *Child and Family Services Act*, which is based on a plan of care that has been prepared by a society.

A **plan of care** prepared by a society must include the following:

> (a) a description of the services to be provided to remedy the condition or situation on the basis of which the child was found to be in need of protection;

> (b) a statement of the criteria by which the society will determine when its wardship or supervision is no longer required;

> (c) an estimate of the time required to achieve the purpose of the society's intervention;

> (d) where the society proposes to remove or has removed the child from a person's care,
>
> > (i) an explanation of why the child cannot be adequately protected while in the person's care, and a description of any past efforts to do so, and
> >
> > (ii) a statement of what efforts, if any, are planned to maintain the child's contact with the person; and

> (e) where the society proposes to remove or has removed the child from a person's care permanently, a description of the arrangements made or being made for the child's long-term stable placement.

plan of care a personalized statement of a child's needs and the strategies that will be undertaken to meet those needs that is generally prepared by a child protection agency and approved by a court

Child protection workers employed by societies may be involved in the preparation of plans of care, and may be required to testify in court about the plans.

A court may order its own assessment to determine a child's needs under section 54 of the Act if it feels that an assessment is necessary for a just determination of the case. A child can be assessed by one or more of a variety of specialists, such as doctors, psychologists, and behavioural therapists. A completed assessment becomes evidence in the case.

In making an order, a court need not endorse or follow a plan of care exactly as it was prepared. However, a plan of care often provides a judge with a very useful starting point when making an order concerning a child. As noted above, a child protection order must be made in the best interests of the child. Section 37(3) sets out the following factors that a judge must consider in determining the best interests of a child:

1. The child's physical, mental and emotional needs, and the appropriate care or treatment to meet those needs.

2. The child's physical, mental and emotional level of development.

3. The child's cultural background.

4. The religious faith, if any, in which the child is being raised.

5. The importance for the child's development of a positive relationship with a parent and a secure place as a member of a family.

6. The child's relationships by blood or through an adoption order.

7. The importance of continuity in the child's care and the possible effect on the child of disruption of that continuity.

8. The merits of a plan for the child's care proposed by a society, including a proposal that the child be placed for adoption or adopted, compared with the merits of the child remaining with or returning to a parent.

9. The child's views and wishes, if they can be reasonably ascertained.

10. The effects on the child of delay in the disposition of the case.

11. The risk that the child may suffer harm through being removed from, kept away from, returned to or allowed to remain in the care of a parent.

12. The degree of risk, if any, that justified the finding that the child is in need of protection.

13. Any other relevant circumstance.

Although a court must consider a child's ethnic and cultural background in all cases, it has a special responsibility to do so with respect to First Nations children. Under section 37(4) of the *Child and Family Services Act*, any person who makes an order with respect to a child in need of protection must "take into consideration the importance, in recognition of the uniqueness of Indian and native culture, heritage and traditions, of preserving the child's cultural identity."

Care Orders

If a child has been brought before the court with the participation of her parent(s), or with her own consent (in the case of children aged 12 and over), the court can make a **consent order**. This is an order that has received the consent of the parent(s) and/or the child, and has been created with their input.

If the court does not make a consent order, section 57 provides the court with three choices of orders that it can make on behalf of a child. The court may make a supervision order, an order of society wardship, or an order of Crown wardship.

SUPERVISION ORDERS

If the court makes a **supervision order**, the child is permitted to remain in the care of his parent(s) or guardian. The society provides supervision for a period of at least 3 and at most 12 months, providing guidance to the parent or guardian and making sure that the child is safe and well cared for.

ORDER OF SOCIETY WARDSHIP

If the court feels that a child cannot be adequately protected in her own home, but that it is appropriate for the child to continue to have contact with her parent(s), the court usually makes an order of **society wardship**. This kind of order is made only if non-residential services cannot adequately protect the child. It results in the child's placement in residential custody for a maximum of 12 months. Society wardship can, in some cases, be extended by court order.

As an alternative to society wardship, a court should consider the placement of a child in the care of a relative, friend, neighbour, or, in the case of First Nations children, a member of the child's band. Courts make these orders in appropriate cases with the consent of the person who will be taking charge of the child.

Children who are wards of a society have the right to visit their parents. The parents (and sometimes others, such as grandparents or guardians) have the right to apply under section 58 of the Act for access orders that permit them to visit the child. A court will make an access order only if it is in the best interests of the child.

A variation on a society wardship order is a "consecutive order." This is an order of society wardship followed by supervision in the care of a parent or guardian.

If a court makes a child the ward of a society but later determines that it would be inappropriate to return the child to the care of her parent or guardian, the court can make an order of Crown wardship in respect of the child.

ORDER OF CROWN WARDSHIP

If a court determines that a child's parents are unlikely ever to be able to care for the child adequately — for example, in cases of serious child abuse — the court can make an order of Crown wardship. Orders for Crown wardship are not made for specific periods of time. When a child becomes a ward of the Crown, the child is not expected ever to be returned to the care of his parents or guardian. A child who has been made a Crown ward may ultimately be made available for adoption. In general, courts do not make access orders for Crown wards. Parents and others are not permitted to visit Crown wards, unless a court determines that contact with

consent order in the context of child protection services, an agreement arrived at voluntarily by two parties that is given legal status as an order by the court

supervision order an order by the court that provides that certain activities (for example, a child's residence in the family home after a period of society care) will be monitored by a third party (usually a government employee)

society wardship term that describes the status of a child in care who is considered to be under the temporary care of a society and who will eventually be returned to his or her parent(s)

the person who desires access would be beneficial to the child (which is rarely the case) and that the contact would not jeopardize the child's chances of being placed in a stable home.

Supervision, society wardship, and (in more restricted cases) Crown wardship can be reviewed, usually after at least six months from the time that the order is made, under section 64. Reviews are generally conducted for the purpose of changing an order. For example, a children's aid society might apply for a review after it takes a child who was under supervision into care or if it feels that a society ward should be made a Crown ward. Parents are also entitled to request a review in most cases (but never after a child has been adopted; and only with permission of the court in the case of Crown wards). All placement orders end on the day the child turns 18.

Restraining Orders

Instead of, or in addition to, making a supervision, society wardship, or Crown wardship order, a court can make an order under section 80 of the *Child and Family Services Act*. A section 80 order is a restraining orders. It does not provide for the care of the child; rather, it protects the child from another person by restricting that person's access to the child.

Restraining orders can provide an appropriate solution in cases in which the child has been abused by a person other than the custodial parent — for example, a member of the extended family, a family friend, or a neighbour. In some cases, a restraining order may be effective against a parent who does not have custody of a child.

Restraining orders last for specific periods of time that are imposed by the judge who makes them. They can last for a maximum initial period of six months, but they can be renewed by the court if the person who initially sought the order applies for its renewal.

KEY TERMS

apprehension	procedural fairness
bylaw	regulation
consent order	society wardship
justice of the peace	supervision order
party	temporary care agreement
place of safety	warrant
plan of care	

REFERENCES

Brown, Re. (1975), 21 RFL 315; 9 OR (2d) 185 (Ont. Co. Ct.).

Child and Family Services Act. RSO 1990, c. C.11.

Jessie's Centre for Teenagers. (n.d.). Jessie's Volunteer Child Abuse and Neglect Reporting Policies and Procedures. Unpublished.

Ontario Association of Children's Aid Societies. *About Us.* Retrieved March 1, 2005 from http://www.oacas.org/aboutoacas/index.htm.

Ontario Association of Children's Aid Societies. *List of CASs in Ontario.* Retrieved March 1, 2005 from http://www.oacas.org/resources/members.htm.

REVIEW QUESTIONS

1. What is the primary purpose of the *Child and Family Services Act*?

2. To which section of the Act do judges look for guidance in determining the best interests of a child in need of protection? Paraphrase the relevant considerations that are listed in this section.

3. Other than a child protection worker, who has a duty to report a reasonable belief that a child is subject to or threatened with abuse or neglect? Which section of the *Child and Family Services Act* establishes the duty to report?

4. Can the duty to report be delegated to another person — for example, one's supervisor?

5. Must a society obtain a warrant before apprehending a child who may be in need of protection?

6. When seeking a warrant to apprehend a child, what kinds of information will a society employee need to provide to a justice of the peace? What kind of information is not essential?

7. List an alternative to apprehension for a child who is found to be temporarily without adult supervision overnight because of a family emergency.

8. Who decides that a child is in need of protection? Which section of the *Child and Family Services Act* defines "child in need of protection"?

9. Why might a child protection worker be called as a witness in a child protection hearing?

10. Why is a voluntary residential placement preferable to society wardship in most cases? Is a child protection hearing required before a society can make a voluntary residential placement?

11. What is the purpose of a plan of care? Who prepares a plan of care? What is the role of the plan in a child protection hearing?

12. What orders can a court make after finding that a child is in need of protection? Describe the differences between these orders.

13. In a child abuse case, does the holding of a child protection hearing mean that there will be no criminal trial? Does the judge in a child protection hearing have the power to sentence an abuser, or recover monetary compensation for abuse on a child's behalf?

14. What is procedural fairness? Skim the *Child and Family Services Act* to find three examples of provisions that are designed to promote procedural fairness.

15. When might a court that finds a child to be in need of protection make a restraining order instead of a residential placement order?

DISCUSSION QUESTIONS

1. In serious cases of child abuse, there can be a child protection hearing, a criminal trial, and a civil lawsuit for compensation. Imagine a case in which a parent has subjected a child to physical abuse that has caused permanent disabling injuries. All three types of proceedings are being contemplated on behalf of this child. Answer the following questions:

    a. What is the purpose of the child protection hearing? What kind of order or remedy will be sought in this hearing? Who typically initiates these proceedings?

    b. What is the purpose of the criminal trial? What kind of order or remedy will be sought in this hearing? Who typically initiates these proceedings?

    c. What is the purpose of the civil lawsuit? What kind of order or remedy will be sought in this hearing? Who typically initiates these proceedings?

2. Review the primary and secondary purposes of the *Child and Family Services Act*. How do these purposes affect the mandate of a children's aid society? Does the society have a duty to consider the interests of the parents, or is this solely the responsibility of the court? Discuss the issues raised by your answer.

3. As a child protection worker, what challenges do you expect to encounter in your attempts to act in the best interests of children?

9 Children in Residential Care

■ INTRODUCTION: WHAT IS CARE OR CUSTODY?

As you have already learned in the earlier chapters of this book, there are three ways in which a child can find herself removed from the care of her family and taken into the physical care or custody of an agency of the state.

1. The child may be sentenced to criminal custody after a court finds her guilty of having committed a crime.

2. The child may be placed in the residential care of a children's aid society with the consent of her parent. In some cases, the child may herself consent to her own residential placement.

3. The child may be placed in the residential care of a children's aid society, without her parent's consent (and either with or without her own consent), after a court finds her to be in need of protection.

But what exactly is care or custody? Where does a child in care live? A child's residential placement depends on why the child is in care or custody, how long she is in care or custody, and the nature of the resources and facilities available in her community.

CHAPTER OBJECTIVES

After reading this chapter, you should be able to:

- Describe the types of facilities that house children in care.

- Describe the licensing regime for residential care facilities.

- Explain the role of foster families.

- List at least six rights of children in residential care.

- Discuss the issues of abuse and neglect of children in residential care.

- Explore the limited use of extraordinary measures permitted for behaviour control and mental health treatment.

- Explain what happens to children when they leave the care of a children's aid society.

Criminal Custody

Criminal custodial facilities differ from other residential facilities for several reasons. Criminal facilities usually require security, such as locked doors or gates. As an additional security measure, these facilities often isolate residents from each other for part of the day in individual rooms or cells. These measures are designed not only to prevent inmates from escaping, but also to protect guards and staff from inmates, and to protect inmates from each other.

Unlike other residential care facilities, criminal facilities do not focus on creating a family-like atmosphere. While schooling is provided (sometimes within the facility, sometimes at community schools) and certain ties to the outside community are sometimes fostered, criminal custody is not like home. The law prescribes a strong focus on rehabilitation and preparation of young offenders for reintegration into society; however, prison sentences are meant to include an aspect of deterrence. In other words, life in prison is not supposed to be much fun. The daily routine is governed by strict rules, including penalties for non-compliance. If an inmate is not willing to obey the rules in return for the relative freedom that minimum-security custody offers, she faces the threat of transfer to a higher-security institution.

Young people (aged 12 and up) who are sentenced to criminal custody are almost always placed in provincial facilities. (Occasionally, an older youth who has committed a serious crime and/or is a repeat offender may be sentenced as an adult to serve a term in federal prison.) As explained in chapter 6, the judicial system strongly prefers to separate young offenders from adult criminals, either in separate facilities or in youth-only areas of mixed facilities. After leaving a prison, young people may spend time in a smaller group residence (often called a "halfway house") in preparation for independent living.

Hospitals and Mental Health Facilities

Children and youth with serious mental health problems may spend part of their custodial time in a hospital or mental health clinic. Patients in these facilities may or may not have histories of criminal activity. In general, all mental health patients are subjected to some level of security, and increased security is provided for those who have committed violent crimes or are at risk of committing suicide.

In some cases, a judge may send a young person who is convicted of a crime to a mental health facility, rather than a prison. In this case, the facility generally retains control of the young convict until he is well enough to resume a normal life and interact appropriately with others. If there is still time remaining on the convict's criminal sentence after he has recovered his mental health, the authorities may transfer him to prison. If there is no time remaining, he may be transferred to a small group residence, or released into his own or his parents' care. In some cases, a mentally ill criminal will actually spend longer in mental health care than he would have spent in prison.

Group Residences

The child protection system prefers to provide children in care with placements that closely mimic family life. This means that, where possible, children in care are placed with foster families (discussed below under the heading "Foster Care"). However, these placements are not always available.

Where it is impractical or inappropriate to place a child with a foster family, a society may place the child in a group residence. These residences range in size from house-sized facilities to large, multi-unit buildings designed to house many children.

In some cases, children stay at a group residence while a children's aid society makes foster care arrangements for them. Children may also stay in group residences if a society anticipates that the children will be in care for a very short time.

Children with significant disabilities or special needs are sometimes cared for in a group residence. Group residences are often appropriate for children who need around-the-clock supportive care — for example, children with no mobility who wake regularly during the night. These residences can prove beneficial when a single foster family cannot meet a child's significant needs for care, or when they offer therapies and services that are particularly useful for individual children. Group residences often allow the disabled children to heal, learn, or otherwise flourish more readily than they could at home, where therapies, technologies, and services are not available. Some of these facilities specialize in providing care to children with specific kinds of problems, such as serious brain injuries or autism.

Another reason why a child may be placed in group residential care is that foster care has been tried, but the child has not coped well, often as a result of serious behavioural or mental health problems — for example, fetal alcohol syndrome, substance addiction, serious attention deficit disorder, or autism. A group residence with strict rules, constant supervision, and some security may provide the only option for a child who just cannot seem to thrive in foster care, or who poses a risk to the foster family or the community.

ASIDE

FETAL ALCOHOL SYNDROME

Fetal alcohol syndrome (FAS) is a condition that can cause a child to experience significant problems in coping with life and behaving appropriately with others. A milder version of the syndrome is called fetal alcohol effects (FAE). FAS describes a multitude of physical and behavioural characteristics that are observed in some children who were exposed to alcohol in the womb. Medicine does not yet understand how alcohol causes FAS, or why some children of mothers who drank alcohol during their pregnancies contract FAS and others do not. The simple volume of alcohol consumed over the course of a pregnancy does not seem to be the deciding factor; a pregnant woman's binge drinking, or drinking at critical periods of fetal development, may be the cause.

Children with FAS or FAE can have physical deformities that include low birth weight, small size, bone deformities, organ deformities, skin webbing between fingers and toes or at the corner of the eyes, and mouth and ear deformities. Some children can show the classical FAS facial deformities but exhibit no behavioural problems. Others have a completely normal appearance but have serious neurological or behavioural problems. Neurological, learning, and behavioural problems can include cognitive deficits, learning disabilities, irritability, hyperactivity, inappropriate risk taking, poor impulse control, social problems, and poor physical coordination.

FAS is incurable, though affected children can improve their capacity for learning and social functioning with proper support. Adults with FAS can experience difficulty holding a job, memory problems, difficulty in managing money, troubled interpersonal relationships, and poor judgment generally.

Finally, while children's aid societies are strongly biased in favour of foster care for young children, this bias does not always extend to teenagers. Teens may struggle to adapt to foster care and may prefer (and cope better in) group care, particularly if they are old enough to be preparing themselves for independent living.

Foster Care

foster family a family authorized by a children's aid society to provide residential care for children in need of protective services

Where possible, children's aid societies place a child in need of protection in the care of a **foster family** in her own community. The *Child and Family Services Act* expresses a preference that children grow up in a family environment. A family setting is less intimidating than other placement options for most children. A family lifestyle encourages children to interact both with the adults and with any other children in the home, and it provides for the individualized attention that helps children feel secure. Foster families include foster children in their usual activities, such as chores, recreational events, sports, trips to the grocery store and the library. These activities are familiar to children and encourage them to interact with members of the community.

Children's aid societies carefully screen and train foster parents. While "perfect parenting" is not required, foster parents must be caring, patient, and able to handle the unique needs of children who have been removed from abusive or neglectful situations. Children's aid societies pay foster parents for the services they provide and usually give them emotional support. Foster parents may choose to be members of a foster parenting association, such as the Foster Parents Society of Ontario, where they can share experiences and work together to find solutions for common child care issues.

Where possible, children's aid societies attempt to place children with foster families that are compatible with their culture, ethnicity, and religion. Children therefore have continuing opportunities to retain familiar cultural practices, celebrate their religions, and maintain their ties to ethnic communities. The *Child and Family Services Act* requires that, where possible, aboriginal children be fostered in aboriginal families.

Foster placements can range in duration from a few days to many years. A "permanent" placement lasts until a child reaches the age of 18, or earlier if the child chooses to move out on her own after her 16th birthday. Permanent foster placements are not adoptions, although it is possible for foster parents to adopt foster children. Rather, they are placements in circumstances where it is not expected that a child will ever be able to return to her original home, where adoption is unlikely, and where the child and foster family are interested in remaining together until the child is self-supporting.

Rights of Children in Residential Care

The rights of children in care were introduced in chapter 6, under the heading "The Rights of Youth in Custody." Although these rights were described in the context of criminal custody, they bear repeating since they also apply to children in protective care:

■ the right to receive regular visits from family members (there is an exemption for Crown wards, who may make a special application to receive these visits);

- the right to receive visits from a lawyer, an advocate, the Ombudsman, or a member of provincial or federal Parliament;

- the right to send and receive mail that is not opened or read by others (there is an exception that allows examination of mail, in the child's presence, for things such as weapons and drugs);

- the right to have reasonable privacy and his own possessions;

- the right to receive religious instruction and participate in religious activities of his own choosing;

- the right to have a plan of care provided for him within 30 days of coming into care;

- the right to participate in the development of the plan of care;

- the right to eat appropriate food of good quality;

- the right to wear appropriate, well-fitting clothing;

- the right to receive medical and dental care;

- the right to receive an education that meets his aptitudes and needs, preferably in a community setting — that is, outside the care facility;

- the right to participate in recreational and athletic activities;

- the right to express his views on any issue that affects him, to the extent that he is mature enough to do so; and

- the right to be informed of his rights and how they can be enforced, the rules of the care or custody facility, and his responsibilities while in care.

A child's religious, educational, and health care rights are subject to her parents' rights to guide her in these areas and to consent to her activities (see section 106 of the *Child and Family Services Act*). Parental rights are not absolute; they are typically limited by the age of the child. In the case of Crown wards, they are suspended altogether.

The *Child and Family Services Act* provides a complaints procedure (see section 109) under which children in care may attempt to enforce any right that they feel is being denied them. When a child lodges a complaint, a facility is required to conduct a review. If the child is not satisfied with the results of the review, she can apply to the minister of children and youth services to appoint a person who is not an employee of the facility to conduct a further review. This external reviewer must make a report to the minister within 30 days, and the minister must make a decision and communicate it to both the child and the facility administration.

Section 102 of the *Child and Family Services Act* establishes the Office of Child and Family Service Advocacy, which assists children in care and their families in obtaining legal and advocacy support.

◼ LICENSING OF RESIDENTIAL FACILITIES

As noted in chapter 8, the minister of children and youth services has the power to create or designate facilities as agencies, children's aid societies, and residential facilities for the purpose of carrying out the mandate of the *Child and Family Services Act*. Part IX of the Act deals with the licensing of residential facilities.

Section 192 defines a "children's residence" to mean the following:

> (a) a parent model residence where five or more children not of common parentage, or
>
> (b) a staff model residence where three or more children not of common parentage,

live and receive residential care, and includes a foster home or other home or institution that is supervised or operated by a society.

Section 192 goes on to exclude certain other places from the definition of children's residence. Not governed by part IX are private hospitals, day nurseries (daycare facilities), recreational camps, public and private schools, hostels, hospitals, and group homes that receive financial assistance from the minister of correctional services.

A **parent-model residence** is defined as "a building, group of buildings or part of a building where not more than two adult persons live and provide care for children on a continuous basis." A **staff-model residence** is defined as "a building, group of buildings or part of a building where adult persons are employed to provide care for children on the basis of scheduled periods of duty."

All children's residences must be licensed under the Act, and nobody can place a child for adoption without having a children's residence licence. All placements of children in children's residences have to be made in accordance with the Act. This means that nobody can place a child in a children's residence without a (voluntary) temporary care agreement, or a child protection order.

Only individuals and non-profit agencies can be granted children's residence licences.

Section 194 authorizes a "program supervisor" to enter a children's residence at any time to ensure that the conditions of licensing are being met — that is, that the residence is being run in accordance with the terms of its licence and the regulations made under the *Child and Family Services Act.* The program supervisor is entitled to inspect the premises as well as its books and records.

Under section 195 a director can refuse to issue a licence where, in the director's opinion, the licence seeker is not competent to run the residence appropriately or has a history that suggests an inability to run a residence appropriately, or where the residence is not being run according to the regulations. The director can refuse to renew or can revoke a licence for various reasons, including the following:

- there has been a contravention of the *Child and Family Services Act* or the regulations;

- the premises fail to comply with the regulations;

- "the activity for which the licence is required is carried on in a manner that is prejudicial to the children's health, safety or welfare"; or

- the licence holder or its employees have made misrepresentations in the application or in their reports under the terms of the licence.

Part IX sets out a procedure by which revocations and non-renewals can be made provisionally (until problems are remedied), suspended, or appealed. It also provides for the extension of licences in some cases.

---

parent-model residence
a children's residence that is structured like a family home, with one or two adult caregivers and a small number of children

staff-model residence
a children's residence in which care is provided by staff to a number of children not related to the staff or to each other

The status of a residence may be uncertain if, for example, the director has refused to renew the licence, and the licence holder is appealing the director's refusal; in these cases, section 204 of the Act authorizes the minister to seek a court order that allows the minister to "occupy" the residence and run it on an interim basis while the matter is resolved. In this way, disruption to the children is kept to a minimum in situations where it appears possible that the licence will be reinstated or renewed.

If a licence is finally revoked, section 203(2) requires the minister to find other suitable placements for the children living in the residence as soon as is practicable. In finding placements, the minister must consider the children's best interests.

■ STANDARDS FOR RESIDENTIAL CARE FACILITIES

Standards for the operation of children's residences are set out in several sources. In understanding the standards that apply to a particular children's residence, child protection workers will need to take into account:

- the specific terms of the licence issued to the residence;

- any internal policies developed by the residence for its own management (sometimes the content of these are dictated by regulations);

- and the regulations made under the *Child and Family Services Act*.

This part of the chapter discusses the standards imposed by the general regulation made under the *Child and Family Services Act*.

General Standards

The general regulation authorized under the *Child and Family Services Act* deals with many aspects of licensing and facility standards. Some of these requirements are listed below.

RESIDENTIAL BUILDING LAWS

Under section 64 of the general regulation, a children's residence must comply with all relevant laws and regulations dealing with residential buildings in the area — for example, the building code, the fire code, and local board of health regulations.

NUMBER OF RESIDENTS

Under section 66 of the general regulation, a children's residence must comply with any conditions made by the director with respect to the maximum number of children who can live there.

ASIDE

NETWORKING FOR YOUTH IN CARE

Residential care may be necessary in the best interests of a young person; however, living away from family in a foster home or children's residence can be isolating and can pose major challenges for older children and teens. The Ontario Association of Children's Aid Societies (OACAS) has established a program called "Youth in Care Connections." There is also a National Youth in Care Network.

Youth in Care Connections, established in 1992, is administered by a youth liaison worker with the OACAS. The program offers peer mentoring. It also puts young people in touch with each other so that they can identify issues of mutual concern and work to resolve these issues, sometimes by communicating them to advocates. Youth in Care Connections publishes a newsletter called *NOTICE* (*Needs of Teens in Care Everywhere*).

Under section 104 of the general regulation, a children's residence must comply with the regulations with respect to minimum numbers of staff. The staff-to-child ratio in a staff-model residence is a minimum of one staff member for every eight children averaged over a 24-hour period. A maximum of eight children are allowed to live in a parent-model residence.

POLICIES

Section 73 of the general regulation requires a children's residence to have in place, and available for consultation by staff, an up-to-date set of policies that state:

(a) the purpose of the residence;

(b) the program provided in the residence;

(c) procedures relating to the admission and discharge of residents;

(d) the planning, monitoring and evaluation of care provided to residents;

(e) procedures for the maintenance of case records;

(f) methods of maintaining discipline;

(g) the health program provided for residents;

(h) the methods of maintaining security of the residence;

(i) the methods for involving a resident's parent with the program of the residence;

(j) the administrative structure of the residence;

(k) staff and supervisory practices to be followed by staff persons in the residence;

(l) the conduct and discipline of persons employed in the residence;

(m) procedures to be followed in emergencies;

(n) the financial administration of the residence;

(o) the methods employed to encourage residents to participate in community activities;

(p) articles prohibited by the licensee for the purposes of [inspecting mail under section 103(3) of the *Child and Family Services Act*];

(q) procedures governing the expression of concerns or complaints by residents; and

(r) procedures governing punishment and isolation methods that may be used in the residence.

REGISTER

Section 100 of the general regulation requires a children's residence to maintain a register of its residents.

CASE RECORDS

Section 99(1) of the general regulation obliges a children's residence to maintain a written case record for every resident child. The residence must retain this record for 20 years after the final entry is made. The record must include the following:

(a) the resident's full name, sex and birth date;

(b) the name, address and telephone number of the resident's parents or the society or other person placing the resident;

(c) any personal, family and social history and assessment that has been prepared by the [licence holder] or provided to the [licence holder];

(d) the reason for admission of the resident;

(e) reports of all medical examinations and treatment given to the resident upon admission and while in the residence;

(f) where obtainable, any legal document that is concerned with the resident's admission to and stay in the residence including any consent to admission, treatment and release of information;

(g) a copy of the agreement for service with respect to the resident including any revisions to the agreement and particulars of any reviews of the agreement;

(h) school records and reports concerning the resident, where applicable;

(i) the plan of care developed for the resident and particulars of any review of the plan of care or of the resident's status;

(j) reports of any serious occurrence involving the resident;

(k) where applicable, documentation of the circumstances of transfer or discharge of the resident, the name, address and relationship of the person to whom the resident is transferred or discharged and the summary report [provided to the residence to which the resident is transferred or to the person or agency to whom the resident is discharged];

(l) where [a particularly serious incident referred to in section 102(1) of the general regulation occurs], the time of the occurrence, the name of the person reporting it and the person to whom the report was made; and

(m) such other information or documents with respect to the resident in addition to those referred to in clauses (a) to (l) as are considered appropriate by the [licence holder].

DAILY LOG

Section 74 of the general regulation requires a children's residence to keep a daily log of incidents that "may affect the health, safety or well being" of a staff person or resident.

FINANCIAL INFORMATION AND INSURANCE

Under sections 77 to 79 of the general regulation, a children's residence must prepare a budget and proper financial statements. It must also obtain an insurance policy.

SERVICE AGREEMENTS

Section 81 of the general regulation requires that a children's residence create a written agreement for the provision of service to each child in care. This agreement must contain such things as the terms of the care placement, financial arrangements for the child, and statements with respect to who must consent to medical treatment. These agreements are negotiated in consultation with everyone affected by them. They are to be signed by the following parties:

    (a) the [licence holder];

    (b) the parent of the child or the society or other person placing the child;

    (c) a children's aid society in whose care the child is where the child is in care … ;

    (d) the child, where the child is sixteen years of age or over;

    (e) the child's nearest relative, where the child is unable to sign and there is no parent; and

    (f) where the agreement concerns a child who is a party to a temporary care agreement, the child.

FOOD AND CLOTHING

Sections 88 and 89 of the general regulation require a children's residence to provide nutritious food and clothing suitable to the weather and the child's size respectively.

EDUCATION

A children's residence must provide its residents with a suitable education, generally in the community at large.

HEALTH CARE

Section 91(1)(c) of the general regulation requires a children's residence to provide "at least an annual assessment of the health, vision, dental and hearing condition of the residents," as well as health education and access to medical care.

The residence must also provide prescription medicines where required, and maintain accurate records for their administration. Under section 92 of the general regulation, "a record is kept of all medication given to each resident, including the type of medication, the period for which it is prescribed, when each dose is to be given and is given and by whom each dose is given." Children aged 16 and older should be provided, where appropriate, with a lockable storage locker for possessions, including medicine, and should be allowed to self-administer medication if they are sufficiently responsible to do so.

Finally, a children's residence must maintain a first aid kit, and isolate children who have communicable diseases, as appropriate in accordance with its obligations under sections 93 and 94 of the general regulation.

MAIL

A children's residence must allow its residents free and private access to their mail; section 98 of the general regulation obliges it to provide reasons in the case record if staff members open mail or remove objects from mail.

Plans of Care

An important requirement imposed on operators of children's residences is the need to prepare a plan of care. A draft or provisional plan of care is typically prepared before a court makes a child protection order. In any event, a plan of care must be finalized within 30 days of a child's placement in a residential facility. A plan is prepared in consultation with the people who will be affected by it, including the child's parent(s), a society, and the child herself. Under section 86 of the general regulation, a plan of care must include the following:

(a) a description of the resident's needs that is developed with reference to the findings of current or previous assessments of the resident;

(b) a statement of goals to be achieved for the resident while the resident is in the residence;

(c) a statement of the means to be used to achieve the goals referred to in clause (b);

(d) a statement of the educational program that is developed for the resident in consultation with the school boards in the area in which the residence is located;

(e) where applicable, a statement of the ways in which a parent of the resident will be involved in the plan of care including arrangements for contact between the resident and a parent of the resident and the resident's family;

(f) particulars of any specialized service to be provided directly or arranged for by the [licence holder];

(g) particulars of the dates for review of the plan of care;

(h) a list of revisions, if any, to the plan of care; and

(i) a statement of the anticipated plan for discharge of the resident.

Plans of care can be revised from time to time as a child progresses, or develops new care needs. A schedule of regular reviews must be part of the plan of care. In the first six months, the licensee must review the care of a child every 30 days, giving the child the opportunity to comment. After six months, general reviews of a child's care should occur at least every six months.

The plan of care and documentation relating to reviews form part of a resident's case record.

Discipline

Another closely regulated issue is the administration of discipline and punishment, and the use of isolation. Children's residences must have policies about discipline, and these policies must be communicated to, understood by, and consistently applied by all staff of the children's residence. Section 95 of the general regulation requires the following:

- Discipline policies must be in writing.

- Discipline policies must be communicated to staff as soon as they are formulated, and reviewed at least annually.

- Staff must be informed of the types of behaviour that warrant the administration of discipline or punishment.
- Only staff trained in discipline policies are allowed to discipline children.
- Interventions involving discipline or punishment must be recorded in the resident's case record and reported to the licence holder.

Section 96 of the general regulation prohibits harsh or degrading punishments, or punishments that involve depriving a child of his basic needs, such as shelter, clothing, food, or bedding.

Serious Occurrences

Section 102 of the general regulation addresses serious occurrences, which include situations in which a child

- dies,
- suffers serious injury,
- suffers any injury at the hands of a staff member or licence holder,
- suffers abuse or mistreatment,
- is physically restrained by a staff member or licence holder, or
- makes a complaint or is the object of a complaint that the licensee deems to be of a serious nature.

Serious occurrences also include

- a fire or "other disaster" at the residence, or
- any other occurrence that the licence holder thinks is serious.

These occurrences must be recorded in the child's case record; they must also be reported to the child's parent(s), to the person who placed the child (usually a child protection worker) if possible, to a children's aid society, and to a director.

A licence holder also has reporting obligations, including the obligation to make a report to local police, if a resident is absent without permission for 24 hours, or for less time if the licence holder considers the situation to be serious.

Accommodation Standards

Section 106 of the general regulation sets out standards for accommodation as follows:

1. No room without a window is used as a bedroom.

2. No basement area or room is used for sleeping accommodation unless such use is approved by a Director.

3. Each bedroom has a minimum area of five square metres of floor space for each resident over the age of eighteen months and under the age of sixteen years.

4. Each bedroom has a minimum of seven square metres of floor space for each resident sixteen years of age or over.

5. A residence that accommodates residents under the age of eighteen months has a minimum area of 3.25 square metres of floor space for each resident and at least 7.5 square metres of floor space in every bedroom where residents under the age of eighteen months are accommodated.

6. Each resident is provided with his or her own bed and clean mattress suitable for the resident's age and size, together with bedding that is appropriate according to the weather and climate.

7. No resident over six years of age shares a bedroom with another resident of the opposite sex unless the sharing is approved by a Director.

8. The residence has a minimum of one wash basin with hot and cold water and one flush toilet for every five residents or fewer and one bath or shower with hot and cold water for every eight residents or fewer and, where there is more than one toilet in any one room, each toilet has a separate compartment.

9. The water temperature in a washroom or bathroom in a residence does not exceed 49 degrees Celsius.

10. The residence has an outdoor play space that is equivalent in area to at least nine square metres for each resident based on the maximum number of children permitted in the licence except where an alternative arrangement is approved by the Director.

11. The outdoor play space is maintained in a safe and sanitary condition.

12. The temperature of the residence is maintained at not less than 17 degrees Celsius.

Section 107 of the general regulation prescribes safety standards for medicine cabinets, "fuel-fired appliances" (such as furnaces, barbecues, and gas dryers), and chimneys. Sections 108 and 109 prescribe fire safety standards, practices, and procedures. Section 108 prohibits the storage of firearms and unnecessary hazardous substances or materials in a children's residence.

Physical Restraint

Sections 109.1 through 109.3 of the general regulation set out a scheme for the use of physical restraint that is so complex and detailed that all employees are required to receive extensive training in the subject before using physical restraint of any kind.

In very brief summary, physical restraint is considered to be inherently dangerous to the safety of children. It is an intrusion on their rights to bodily integrity and personal freedom. As such, it is not to be used unless specific conditions demand it.

Physical restraint can be used only

- to prevent a resident from injuring herself or others,

- to prevent a young offender from escaping from a residence, or

- to prevent a young offender from causing significant property damage.

Even if one of the above conditions exists, physical restraint may not be used unless

- there is a "clear and imminent risk" that the injury, escape, or damage will otherwise occur, or

- there is no less intrusive means that would be effective in preventing the anticipated harm.

Requisite staff training is specified in section 109.3 of the general regulation. Staff can use only the restraint holds in which they have been trained, and they must choose the technique that involves the least amount of force that will be effective in the circumstances. While physically restraining a resident, they must monitor the resident's condition continuously.

The facility must have a written physical restraint policy, and staff must comply with it. The use of physical restraint must be documented in the resident's file, and those involved in a restraint incident (including the resident) must be debriefed afterwards in accordance with section 109.2 of the general regulation.

YOU DECIDE!

WHAT WOULD YOU DO?

Review the following observations of life in a children's residence or foster home, and explain how you would respond in each situation.

1. You are a foster parent with two children of your own (boys aged 4 and 8) and two foster children (girls aged 3 and 12). Your house has three bedrooms: one is your own; one is shared by the boys; and one is shared by the girls. The older girl, Meiying, complains that 3-year-old Starr is constantly going through her things, talking when she is trying to read, and otherwise bothering her. Meiying is becoming increasingly vocal about her concerns, and you need a solution. There is a room available in the basement, but when the children's aid society inspected the house, you told them that the girls would be sharing an upstairs room.

2. You are a staff person in a staff-model children's residence. Sixteen-year-old Keith is a diabetic resident who needs to take insulin daily by injection. On three occasions in the past month, Keith has left an injection needle on his nightstand or on the bathroom counter, instead of placing it in the safety container that the residence has provided. You are worried that another child will get hold of one of Keith's needles and injure himself.

3. You work in a parent-model children's residence. Jem, a 6-year-old boy living in the residence has frequent nightmares. Three mornings in a row, you have found him asleep in bed with Ziporah, the 11-year-old girl in the room next door. Ziporah does not mind; she has a close relationship with Jem and clearly takes pleasure in "mothering" him when he needs comfort at night.

4. You work in a staff-model children's residence. The residence has an outdoor play yard with a climber. On two separate occasions, two different children have fallen from the climber where the ladder meets the upper level, and you suspect a design defect. The children love the climber, and the residence does not have the funds to replace it.

Foster Care Standards

The standards under the general regulation to Ontario's *Child and Family Services Act* for foster care placements are somewhat less formal than those for children's residences. Before placing a child in foster care, the licensee must conduct a preliminary assessment under section 111(1)(a) to determine

(i) the immediate needs of the child,

(ii) where it can be ascertained, whether the child is likely to be returned to his or her home,

(iii) available identifying information concerning the child,

(iv) the child's legal status, and

(v) any other information that is, in the opinion of the [licence holder], relevant to the immediate care of the child.

This preliminary assessment is followed by a more thorough assessment that must be conducted within 21 days after a child is placed in care. The formal assessment then forms the basis of a foster care plan, which is developed in consultation with the child's foster parents.

Section 111(5) of the general regulation requires that children with special needs that arise from physical, developmental, learning, emotional, or behavioural problems must be fully assessed so that their needs are understood and an appropriate plan of special care is developed for them.

The child protection case worker assigned to the child must review foster care plans every three months, or whenever there is a change in care. A change in care occurs, for example, when another child is placed in the same home where a child is currently receiving foster care.

Section 112 requires a licence holder to assess and approve a foster family before making a foster care placement. Licence holders that place children in foster care must develop appropriate screening and placement procedures for foster families. These procedures should include the development of objectives for foster families, annual review of foster families, and a system for supervising foster care.

In general, no more than four foster children can be placed in one foster home, and no more than two of these children can be under the age of two years.

Section 118 of the general regulation sets out screening procedures that should be performed before a licence holder approves a foster home. For example, the licence holder or someone designated by the licence holder must interview every adult in a foster home and inspect the premises. The accommodation standards for foster homes, which are set out in section 119 of the general regulation, are somewhat more relaxed than those for children's residences:

1. No room without a window is used as a bedroom.

2. No bedroom is in a building detached from the foster home, an unfinished attic or unfinished basement or a stairway hall.

3. Each foster child has a bed and clean mattress suitable for the age of the foster child together with bedding that is appropriate according to the weather and climate.

4. No foster child shares a bed or sleeping room with an adult couple or adult of the opposite sex. [There are exceptions for infants and sick children.]

5. No foster child over six years of age shares a bedroom with another child of the opposite sex.

Foster families sign foster care service agreements that constitute their contract with the licence holder. Some of the terms of these agreements are described in section 120 of the general regulation. The licence holder assigns each foster family a staff person who provides supervision and liaison with the licence holder. The staff person also arranges any services that are provided for under the foster care service agreement, such as arrangements for relief care.

■ EXTRAORDINARY MEASURES

extraordinary measures under the *Child and Family Services Act*, severe measures used to control the symptoms or behaviour of a child with mental health or behavioural problems — for example, the use of physical restraints or the administration of psychotropic drugs

Part V of the *Child and Family Services Act* prohibits the locking-up of children except as permitted under part VI of the *Child and Family Services Act* and part IV the *Youth Criminal Justice Act*. It also prohibits the use of corporal punishment. Practices and treatments that are physically intrusive or that impose strict limits on personal freedom are characterized as **extraordinary measures**. The use of such measures is governed by part VI of the *Child and Family Services Act* and sections 42 to 49 of the general regulation.

Section 112 of the *Child and Family Services Act* defines "intrusive procedures" as follows:

(a) a mechanical means of controlling behaviour,

(b) an aversive stimulation technique, or

(c) any other procedure that is prescribed as an intrusive procedure ...

Secure Treatment Programs

Secure treatment programs are programs approved by the minister of children and youth services in which children with severe mental disorders are housed and treated in secure facilities. Facilities that offer secure treatment differ from regular residential care facilities because they constantly restrict the liberty of residents in locked premises.

A child can be placed in a secure treatment program in two situations:

1. after a court makes an order in the course of a hearing under section 117 of the *Child and Family Services Act*, or

2. on an emergency basis under section 124 of the Act.

Where the situation is not an emergency, a person in charge of a child with a severe mental disorder may apply to have the child committed to a secure treatment facility. Section 114(1) of the Act allows a child aged 16 or older to consent to her own commitment, and also allows a physician to commit a child aged 16 or over.

Commitment hearings must be held within 10 days of the application. The hearing is held in private. Children, who are usually entitled to be present, are required to have legal representation (by court order, if necessary).

A court can order an assessment of the child to assist it in making its decision about committing the child to a secure treatment program. If necessary, the court can make a temporary commitment order before the hearing is completed. Child protection workers may be called to give oral testimony at a commitment hearing.

Section 117 of the Act requires that a child be committed into a secure treatment program if the following circumstances exist:

- The child has a mental disorder.

- The child has caused or attempted to cause serious bodily harm to himself or another person in the 45 days preceding the hearing, the imposition of a criminal sentence, or the child's admission into a psychiatric facility.

- The child has seriously threatened someone (other than in an incident referred to above) or made a death threat within the past year.

- The secure treatment program would be effective in protecting the child or others.

- Treatment appropriate to the child's condition is offered in the secure treatment facility.

- There is no less restrictive method of providing the child with the treatment necessary for his condition.

A court can commit a child for up to 180 days. After 60 days, there is an automatic review. During the review, a parent can request an additional period of commitment, or the child can be made a Crown ward and the Crown can request the extension. The maximum time that a child can be committed is 180 days.

As part of the commitment order, the court must include a statement about plans for the child's care after release. For example, the statement should clarify whether the child is to be returned to her parent, placed in society care, or returned to criminal custody.

Where a person in charge of the child believes that the child needs secure treatment on an emergency basis, the administrator of the secure treatment facility can admit the child. Persons in charge of children under 16 can include a parent, guardian, child protection worker, or a children's aid society. Persons in charge of children 16 and older can include the child, a parent, a society, or a physician.

In emergencies, the criteria for admission to a secure treatment facility are similar to those that are applied in a commitment hearing. The consent of the minister of children and youth services consent is required before a child under the age of 12 can be admitted. When a child is admitted on an emergency basis, any interested party can bring an application for the child's release, and the application must be heard within five days. Interested parties include the child, who must receive notice of his rights to apply for release, and who is entitled to representation by the Children's Lawyer. If the court finds that the criteria for admission were not met, it orders the release of the child.

Secure Isolation

Secure isolation differs from secure treatment because it is a very temporary cooldown measure, typically used in a crisis, to protect a child (or protect others from a child) who is living in a children's residence. Section 44 of the general regulation made under the *Child and Family Services Act* prescribes rules for the use of secure isolation. A facility that would like to use a secure isolation room must have the room and its policies for the room's use approved by a director under section 48 of the general regulation.

Secure isolation rooms cannot be used as bedrooms, must have an unbreakable window and sufficient light for continuous monitoring of the child through the window, and cannot contain objects that the child could use to injure herself.

Section 45 of the general regulation requires that secure isolation must be carried out in accordance with a written policy and must be reviewed with all staff members who are involved in strict isolation at least annually. Children in secure isolation must be continuously observed. Where a child is placed in secure isolation for longer than an hour, the supervising staff person must review the need for secure isolation at least every 30 minutes.

Section 127(3) of the *Child and Family Services Act* imposes guidelines for the use of secure isolation. It allows for the placement of a child in a secure isolation room in the following circumstances:

> (a) in the service provider's opinion,
>
> (i) the child's conduct indicates that the child is likely, in the immediate future, to cause serious property damage or to cause another person serious bodily harm, and
>
> (ii) no less restrictive method of restraining the child is practicable; and
>
> (b) where the child is less than twelve years of age, a Director gives permission for the child to be placed in a secure isolation room because of exceptional circumstances.

Section 46 of the general regulation requires the documentation of all uses of secure isolation in the child's case record.

Psychotropic Drugs

The use of psychotropic drugs is considered to be an extraordinary measure under the *Child and Family Services Act*. The general regulation provides a schedule that lists drugs that are deemed to be psychotropic. This schedule includes anti-psychotic drugs, anti-depressant drugs, sedative and hypnotic drugs, anti-anxiety drugs, anti-hyperkinetic drugs, and the anti-bipolar drug Lithium Carbonate.

Residential facilities are prohibited from giving psychotropic drugs to a child in care without his consent if the child is 16 or older. Before administering psychotropic drugs to a child under 16, a facility must obtain the consent of the child's parent(s) or a society, according to section 132 of the Act. Where a child under 16 is to be given a drug, her views and preferences must be taken into account.

A consent to the administration of a psychotropic drug must be in writing. It must also provide information about the nature of the drug, its purpose, its possible side effects, the dosage ranges, the frequency of its administration, and the length of time that the drug needs to be taken.

Other Intrusive Procedures

Certain portions of the *Child and Family Services Act* have been passed by Ontario's legislature but not proclaimed into law, which means they do not yet have legal force. Some of these sections deal with the emergency administration of psychotropic drugs and "other intrusive procedures." These procedures are not defined in the unproclaimed sections. However, section 133, which is currently in force, allows a facility to create a team to review recommendations (usually from a family physician or psychiatrist) for the use of electroconvulsive (shock) therapy and sterilization that is not required to cure a medical condition.

At the moment, because the sections are not yet proclaimed, the use of these as-yet undefined intrusive procedures is not a part of the child protection scheme.

■ DUTIES OF A CHILD PROTECTION WORKER

As you can see from the material in this chapter, the care standards for children's residences and other care and custody facilities are enormously detailed. Society expects that children in care will live in healthy and comfortable conditions, and fully exercise their human rights and personal freedoms, except in very narrow circumstances.

The *Child and Family Services Act* and its regulations are designed to leave no room for the mistreatment of children. Children in care have typically come from difficult living circumstances and are physically and emotionally vulnerable. The quality of the treatment that they receive in care may make the difference between their healthy or unhealthy emotional development for life.

Child protection workers can improve the lives of children in care by knowing the living standards that apply to them, and by actively working to enforce these standards. The following list of recommendations may serve as a summary of actions that child protection workers can take to promote the health of their young clients.

Physical Environment

- Report any damage to the facility or its furnishings.

- Report uncomfortable conditions — for example, leaks, inappropriate room temperatures, fumes, or mould.

- Report any hazards or dangers that you observe — for example chemicals stored in unlocked cabinets, fire hazards, or missing handrails.

- Report complaints from children about matters such as room sharing, crowding, or invasion of privacy.

Physical Integrity

- Never touch a child in any way without his consent.

- Do not use restraint holds unless the conditions for their use have been met, and you have been trained in using a particular hold.

- Report all fighting, threats, teasing, and bullying to a supervisor to protect children from harm by other children.

- Respect the right of children to keep their possessions secure.

- Respect children's right to personal freedom. Do not violate anti-lock-up provisions, and do not isolate or contain children without having appropriate grounds for doing so.

Emotional Integrity and Human Rights

- Respect children's right to know their rights. Ensure that they receive the required notice of all decisions made about their care, and do not restrict access to advisers, such as parents or lawyers.

- Respect children's right to privacy. This includes both physical privacy and the right to have private conversations.

- Respect the right of children who are not Crown wards to have contact with their families, including visits and correspondence.

Record Keeping

Keep immediate, complete, and accurate medical records and records of all note-worthy events, including the following:

- the use of restraints, secure isolation, and other correction methods;

- violent incidents;

- accidents;

- complaints by and about children;

- the administration of medicines, including the dose, timing, amount, and any side effects observed; and

- legal hearings, including reviews, and all outcomes and decisions affecting a child's care.

Reporting Mistakes

If you make a mistake in carrying out your duties, it is important to report it immediately to a supervisor, assist in documenting the error, and apologize to the child involved. Attempting to cover up an accident or an error in judgment is a second, more serious, error that could result in legal or employment consequences to you.

■ NEGLECT OR ABUSE OF CHILDREN IN CARE

Unfortunately, placing a child in the care of a children's aid society does not guarantee that the child will be safe from abuse or neglect. The quality of the care that a child receives depends to a very great extent on the people who are directly in charge of the child.

As you have almost certainly learned from news reports, children suffer accidents, mistreatment, and abuse in some residential care settings. Some prominent examples include the mistreatment of First Nations children in residential schools run by the Canadian government; sexual abuse of children in Catholic residences and orphanages in Canada and the United States; and a sexual abuse scandal at Upper Canada College, one of Toronto's elite private schools.

In some ways, the nature of residential care can itself place children at risk of victimization. Children who are placed in care are generally especially vulnerable, because they are working to recover from the abuse or neglect they have suffered at home. They may not yet have an understanding of how to build healthy relationships with adults. Residential care puts children in ongoing close contact with each other and non-family adults, creating opportunities for both beneficial and harmful interactions. For example, children in care may not be able to discern which kinds of physical contact between adults and children are inappropriate, and may therefore be vulnerable to abuse.

Adults who have a tendency to victimize children — either by abusing them sexually or by exerting inappropriate control over them — may seek employment that puts them in the company of children. Careful screening by child protection employers should be designed to identify and exclude these individuals, but screening practices are not foolproof.

Finally, child abuse and neglect thrives best in an organizational climate of intimacy, secrecy, and collusion. In a recent child abuse case — *John Doe v. Bennett* — the Supreme Court of Canada held a bishop, an archbishop, and an Episcopal corporation directly liable for a priest's sexual abuse of 36 children. The bishop and archbishop were held responsible for the priest's abuse because they knew or ought to have known that the priest was assaulting children, but they chose to allow the matter to remain secret instead of taking effective action to prevent harm. Facilities governed by unwritten rules that require those who observe signs of abuse to "look the other way," "give the benefit of the doubt," or "deal with the matter internally" encourage the unfettered abuse of vulnerable children. Foster families that are governed by cultures of secrecy are equally prone to be breeding grounds for the abuse of adult power.

As a child protection worker, you have a duty to challenge an organizational culture that allows troubling interactions between adults and children to go unchecked. Your duty to report child abuse and neglect does not end at the door of a children's aid society. Your exposure to fines under the *Child and Family Services Act*, for failure to exercise that duty, does not end there either, because the Act's duty to report, under section 72, is an ongoing one. Criminal and civil liability for child abuse and neglect extends beyond the person directly responsible for the abuse. Employees of residential care facilities who assist or fail to prevent or terminate child mistreatment can be held liable too, as can the organization as a whole.

Children must be protected not only from abuse by adults, but also from mistreatment by other children within a facility. For example, children in care must be protected from bullying at the hands of other children. A serious incident of mistreatment can lead to both a criminal charge and a civil lawsuit brought on behalf of the mistreated child.

Caring for children, especially troubled children who have been removed from their homes, is a challenging career that will involve daily crises and frustrations. Occasional feelings of anger and resentment toward children are to be expected. Learning how to manage those feelings constructively, without suffering overwhelming personal stress or abusing your power over the children in your charge, is a significant employment challenge. Supporting your fellow employees as they deal with the same issues is important too, but you must never confuse being supportive with covering a co-worker's back. The *Child and Family Services Act* demands that every decision you make and every action you are part of be informed by the paramount principle of the best interests of the child. If you remember this, any mistake you inadvertently make will at least be an honest one.

KEY TERMS

extraordinary measures

foster family

parent-model residence

staff-model residence

REFERENCES

Child and Family Services Act. RSO 1990, c. C.11.

General regulation (made under the *Child and Family Services Act*). RRO 1990, reg. 77/02, amended to O. reg. 77/02.

John Doe v. Bennett. [2004] 1 SCR 436.

REVIEW QUESTIONS

1. List three ways in which criminal custody differs from residential care. List three similarities between criminal custody and residential care.

2. List three types of facilities in which children may live that are *not* covered by the residential facility provisions of the *Child and Family Services Act* and its regulations.

3. Why does the child protection system express a preference for family-model care and foster care for children?

4. List three kinds of laws that apply to a children's residence (other than the *Child and Family Services Act*).

5. List everyone who must be involved in the development of a plan of care for a society ward who is placed in a children's residence. List everyone involved when the child is a Crown ward.

6. If a child is unhappy with the details of her care placement, what can she do about it?

7. Can a parent of a society ward challenge the terms of the child's placement? Why or why not?

8. If an agency were searching for a suitable facility in which to establish a children's residence, where would management look for information about standards governing washrooms and bedrooms?

9. What conditions must exist before a child can be committed to secure treatment under a court order?

10. List three conditions that must be met for the use of secure isolation.

11. What consequences might befall the management of a children's residence that routinely uses illegal physical restraint on its residents? List at least three consequences.

DISCUSSION QUESTIONS

1. Identify five goals that should form part of a child's plan of care.

2. Devise 10 work practices or ideas that might improve the quality of care that children receive in a children's residence or foster home. (Examples might include instituting a meal-planning process that allows children to have input into menu choices, or raising funds to allow staff to attend a workshop in recreation planning.)

3. How can the staff in a children's residence create an atmosphere that minimizes the risk that children will suffer abuse or neglect in the facility?

10 Special Issues

▪ INTRODUCTION: LEGAL DUTIES, PRACTICAL CHALLENGES, AND CONTEMPORARY ISSUES

Choosing a career in child protection is a brave step. Few other jobs demand such a high level of personal and professional responsibility on the part of practitioners.

Perhaps one feature that helps to ease the burden of child protection work is the fact that the philosophy of the profession is so clear: for child protection employees, the central guiding principle is the best interests of the child. Workday decisions made in a sincere attempt to pursue the best interests of children are automatically protected, at least to a certain degree, from criticism by employers, clients, and the public at large.

Unfortunately, the challenges of child protection can make it difficult, in some cases, to identify the best interests of children, or to choose from among alternative courses of action. It is difficult for a child protection worker not to be influenced by interests other than those of the child — for example, the interests of parents and employers, or even the worker's own self-interest.

There are also practical obstacles in child protection work. As a largely state-funded function, child protection is limited by government budgets. This translates into personnel limitations, space limitations, and limitations in the range of programs available to meet the needs of children. Making the most of limited resources requires careful compromise and good judgment, even under significant job stress.

While errors made in the course of sincere efforts can usually be corrected and forgiven, errors made out of incompetence, negligence, or wilful blindness can attract serious legal consequences not only for a child protection worker personally, but also for the worker's employer.

CHAPTER OBJECTIVES

After reading this chapter, you should be able to:

- Understand the legal duties of a child protection worker.

- Understand the potential legal consequences, both for workers and employers, of failing to discharge their legal duties.

- Describe some of the practical challenges facing child protection workers.

- Discuss contemporary issues in child protection, such as the use of community resources, advocacy on behalf of children, and sensitivity to cultural diversity.

▧ IMPORTANT ISSUES FACING CHILDREN TODAY

The study of child protection in the London and Middlesex region, referred to in the previous section, linked the increase in the number of children in care to several factors. These include "child maltreatment, woman abuse, poverty, maternal depression, parenting capacity, and intergenerational CAS involvement."

This is only a shortlist. There are many other issues encountered by child protection workers, and the issues often vary from place to place. For example, child protection workers invited to comment on the London and Middlesex region study expressed surprise that the study did not place more emphasis on the impact of immigration, and the challenges that face new Canadians.

A key problem for those working in child protection is ensuring that children's issues receive sufficient advocacy. Because children are young and are not an organized group, they lack their own political voice. Other groups, such as commercial associations or teachers' unions, may more readily clamour for the attention of politicians. Providing a voice for children requires initiative on the part of adults who have a chance to observe children, listen to their concerns, and understand their needs. Children's aid societies, and all of their employees, have an important responsibility to be advocates for children, as well as service providers. The best way to change a system is from within. As a child protection worker, you are uniquely placed to understand the needs of the community you serve, and to communicate its problems and ideas to those who are in a position to address them.

Poverty

According to the London and Middlesex region study, the number of children admitted to society care who were living in poverty in 2001 was almost twice as great as the number admitted to care in 1995.

The rate of child poverty is consistently higher than the poverty rate for the general population. This means that simply being a child puts a person at a higher risk of having unmet needs. Poverty within a family places significant stress on all family members, and is associated with mental health problems, illness, learning problems, and parenting problems.

Programs that alleviate child poverty support child protection initiatives by relieving the strain on families. Subsidies that assist families in obtaining good-quality daycare help parents earn a living, and can help bring a measure of stability and predictability to the often chaotic lives of poor children.

Poverty is usually related to problems with housing. A 2000 Ontario study identified housing problems as a factor in 20 percent of child protection placements. For example, the fact that a child's mother is homeless is a very important factor in determinations of whether the child is in need of protection. Apprehension of the newborn children of mothers who live on the streets is a regular occurrence.

Even where a child's basic needs are met, the growing gap between the standard of living of the rich and the poor can create difficulties. Children who do not have the same access as their peers to items such as personal computers, cellular phones, and video games often suffer stigmatization.

Understanding the impact of poverty on family dynamics and individual development is an important part of child protection work. Child protection workers should consider themselves political advocates for initiatives designed to remedy child poverty. Helping a child may require child protection workers to assist the child's parents in gaining access to the income support programs that are available in their community, helping to arrange for relief care so that the parents can search for work, or assisting with applications for subsidized daycare. In addition, child protection workers can inform parents of community resources such as subsidized recreational programs, toy lending libraries, and clothing exchanges. In order to succeed in this aspect of their work, child protection workers must maintain a comprehensive and up-to-date knowledge of the resources and services available in their client's community.

Race, Ethnicity, Religion, and Culture

A child's race, ethnicity, religion, and culture are important aspects of her identity. The *Child and Family Services Act* emphasizes the importance of maintaining a child's connections with her ethnic or cultural community. Section 1(2), for example, expresses this goal in delineating some of the purposes of the Act:

4. To recognize that, wherever possible, services to children and their families should be provided in a manner that respects cultural, religious and regional differences.

5. To recognize that Indian and native people should be entitled to provide, wherever possible, their own child and family services, and that all services to Indian and native children and families should be provided in a manner that recognizes their culture, heritage and traditions and the concept of the extended family.

Section 34(10)(f) of the *Child and Family Services Act* requires a committee that is assessing whether a child who "is an Indian or native person" has a special need to "consider the importance, in recognition of the uniqueness of Indian and native culture, heritage and traditions, of preserving the child's cultural identity."

Under section 37(3), a court that is determining the best interests of a child must consider the following:

3. The child's cultural background.

4. The religious faith, if any, in which the child is being raised.

In addition, section 37(4) states:

Where a person is directed in this Part to make an order or determination in the best interests of a child and the child is an Indian or native person, the person shall take into consideration the importance, in recognition of the uniqueness of Indian and native culture, heritage and traditions, of preserving the child's cultural identity.

Section 61(2) of the Act requires that a residential placement chosen for a child be one that,

(b) where possible, respects the religious faith, if any, in which the child is being raised;

(c) where possible, respects the child's linguistic and cultural heritage;

(d) where the child is an Indian or a native person, is with a member of the child's extended family, a member of the child's band or native community or another Indian or native family, if possible.

Where the suitability of an adoption placement is being considered for a child, section 136(2) requires that the best interests of the child be considered. In analyzing the best interests of the child, the person seeking to place the child for adoption should consider, if he deems it relevant:

3. The child's cultural background.

4. The religious faith, if any, in which the child is being raised.

In addition, section 136(3) states the following:

Where a person is directed in this Part to make an order or determination in the best interests of a child and the child is an Indian or native person, the person shall take into consideration the importance, in recognition of the uniqueness of Indian and native culture, heritage and traditions, of preserving the child's cultural identity.

The general regulation made under the *Child and Family Services Act*, which was extensively discussed in chapter 9, establishes guidelines and rules for the management of a children's residence. One of the requirements for residential care facilities is the promotion of a child's connections with his ethnic, religious, and cultural community.

Respecting a child's heritage can involve taking a number of practical steps, among which are the following:

- Where a child's religion or culture incorporates food rules, the foster family or residence staff must respect these rules by providing well-balanced and nutritious meals that do not violate any of the child's religious or cultural laws.

- Where a child celebrates particular cultural or religious holidays, care providers should take steps to help the child to observe these holidays, ideally among other members of her community. For example, they should escort a child to a place of worship on religious holidays. On holidays that are generally celebrated in non-religious ways, care providers might encourage the child to participate in festivals, parades, or other social events at a cultural community centre.

- Children in care are entitled to wear clothing appropriate to their cultural traditions and religious beliefs. Care providers should allow them to wear hairstyles and makeup that reflect their cultural traditions.

- Care providers should ensure that children in care have access to ceremonial, religious, and other articles appropriate to their culture, such as religious books, candles, or shrines.

- Where possible, care providers should offer children in care the opportunity to attend schools, clubs, and recreational programs appropriate to their culture or religion.

- Care providers should encourage children in care to maintain or develop ties with religious and cultural mentors, and with peers who share their culture, religion, or ethnicity. Religious and cultural ties can be strengthened if care providers allow children to attend recreational and social events within their culture and at places of religious worship. Care providers should give children ample opportunity to visit friends and relatives who share their background.

FIRST NATIONS

As some of the above excerpts from the *Child and Family Services Act* suggest, the statute treats aboriginal children as a special group. Part X of the Act creates a framework for the provision of child protection services by First Nations communities. The minister of community and social services contracts with these communities in the same way as he contracts with other agencies, in non-native communities, that seek status as designated agencies or societies.

First Nations child protection organizations have the option of providing customary care for the children in their communities. **Customary care** is defined as "the care and supervision of an Indian or native child by a person who is not the child's parent, according to the custom of the child's band or native community."

Customary care reflects a traditional First Nations view that child raising is the responsibility of the child's community, and not only of the child's parents. In a native community that has been granted the power to provide customary care by the minister, a child who is in need of protection may be cared for by individuals such as band elders in a living situation unlike that of a traditional (non-native) foster home. For example, the child may live in various different homes, depending on who is available to care for him directly at a particular time. Where a customary care agreement is in place, the minister can grant a subsidy to the care provider to help support the child.

Finally, section 213 of the Act requires that a society that is involved in protecting and placing First Nations children consult regularly with the native band to which the children belong about issues that include the following:

> (a) the apprehension of children and the placement of children in residential care;

> (b) the placement of homemakers and the provision of other family support services;

> (c) the preparation of plans for the care of children;

> (d) status reviews under Part III (Child Protection);

> (e) temporary care and special needs agreements under Part II (Voluntary Access to Services);

> (f) adoption placements;

> (g) the establishment of emergency houses; and

> (h) any other matter that is prescribed.

customary care in the context of the *Child and Family Services Act,* "the care and supervision of an Indian or native child by a person who is not the child's parent, according to the custom of the child's band or native community"

PHYSICAL CORRECTION

Child protection workers should be alert to the fact that different cultures have different views about how children should be raised. For example, some cultures routinely permit physical correction, such as caning, which is considered a violent offence in Canada.

Cases of physical abuse in families where caning or beating is considered culturally acceptable must be handled with sensitivity by child protection workers. In some cases, the parents who use these methods may do so in an effort to conform with the traditional child-raising values of their culture, and may be motivated by the desire to help their children learn appropriate behaviour. Children who receive these beatings may not view them as cruel in the same way that children of non-beating cultures do. Nevertheless, while section 43 of the *Criminal Code* allows "reasonable" physical correction by a parent, violent or regular beatings that result in injury are unlikely to be tolerated under Canada's criminal law. It is the responsibility of child protection workers to inform the parents, in such cases, of the unacceptable nature of their actions, and to warn that continued use of violent physical correction will result in the institution of child protection proceedings.

FEMALE GENITAL MUTILATION

Another cultural problem that a child protection worker may encounter is the mutilation of the genitals of female children. Female genital mutilation is practised in certain countries to reinforce patriarchal values and to subjugate women and girls. The mutilation is extremely painful, leaves permanent damage, and usually impairs sexual expressiveness for life. Female genital mutilation is illegal in Canada under section 268 of the *Criminal Code*. Any child protection worker who encounters a case in which such a mutilation took place on Canadian soil should do what is necessary to ensure that the matter is prosecuted under the criminal law. This includes reporting the observations to the police. However, such a report must be handled with sensitivity to the victim; if possible, the victim should be given the opportunity to make the report herself, perhaps with the child protection worker's support.

Immigrant female children who have suffered genital mutilation in their home countries before coming to Canada may exhibit physical and psychological effects. They may experience chronic pain, fear doctors, and they may avoid public nudity or medical examinations, as well as necessary health treatments. Child protection workers should be alert to these signs in immigrant children and, where appropriate, arrange for counselling to support their recovery.

■ LEGAL DUTIES REVISITED

This book has provided an overview of the legal framework that protects children in Canada. For the most part, the focus has been on children, and the laws that society has devised to protect them and remedy any harm that they have suffered. This book has also touched on the laws that apply to those who administer child protection law. This section of the book provides a summary of the legal duties of child protection workers and agencies.

Like all members of society, child protection workers are subject to all of the statutes and common law in force in the place where they live and work. However, by virtue of undertaking to work with children, some people — including child protection workers — may be subject to a higher standard of care than other people. They may also find themselves in a position where their mistakes are more likely to affect the safety and security of children.

Duty To Report

The duty to report child abuse and neglect, as expressed in section 72 of the *Child and Family Services Act*, is shared by all adults. However, for certain individuals, including child protection workers, specific legal sanctions can flow from the failure to properly discharge this duty.

The duty to report is an ongoing obligation. This means that until abuse or neglect or the threat of it stops, a person who observes its signs has a continuing obligation to do something about it. The duty to report is discussed in chapter 8 under the heading "Duty To Report."

Duty To Take Protective Action

Once a children's aid society receives a report concerning the abuse or neglect of a child, it has a duty to act. Failure to provide protection for a child who is identified as being at risk is in itself a neglectful act. The *Child and Family Services Act* provides various mechanisms by which a children's aid society can be required to reconsider decisions it has made about a child. For example, where a person who has made a report to a society is unsatisfied with the action that the society has taken, the report maker or another interested party can apply to a court; the court can then order that the child be brought before it so that the matter can be reviewed. This protective mechanism is set out in section 40(4) of the Act.

An agency that fails to provide protection and service to a child as required by the Act can lose its designation as a child protection agency or its licence to run a children's residence.

ASIDE

SUING A CHILD WELFARE DEPARTMENT

Two interesting lawsuits have been filed in Alberta recently. Both claim damages against the provincial Department of Child Welfare for administrative decisions made in the 1970s and 1980s.

In one case, *Mr. K v. E.K.*, the plaintiff, who is now a young man, is suing the Department of Child Welfare for allegedly failing to take adequate measures to protect him from abuse at the hands of his mother (another defendant in the lawsuit). A number of complaints were made to the department on Mr. K's behalf when he was a child.

In another case, a sexual assault victim is suing her young assailant (a criminal trial has already been held; the assailant was convicted). The plaintiff has named the Department of Child Welfare as an additional defendant in the lawsuit. Her claim against the department stems from her allegation that it failed to protect her rapist from abuse as a child, and thus it contributed to an upbringing that made him likely to use violence against her.

Both cases are still pending as this book goes to press.

There is also the potential that a civil lawsuit can arise from the failure of a worker or agency to protect a child. Section 81 of the Act permits the Children's Lawyer to bring a civil lawsuit for damages on behalf of a child against the child's abuser. The relevant definition of abuse in this context is set out in section 79 of the Act. It includes the failure "to care and provide for or supervise and protect the child adequately" in circumstances that

(i) permit the child to suffer abuse, or

(ii) permit the child to suffer from a mental, emotional or developmental condition that, if not remedied, could seriously impair the child's development.

A civil lawsuit can be brought under this section against an individual child protection worker, or against a children's aid society or other child protection agency or residence. The negligence or misconduct of a single worker has the potential to lead to liability for that worker's employer, and this liability could result in the closure of the employer's facility, to the detriment of the children that are its clients. Civil lawsuits are discussed in chapter 3.

Neglect Under the Criminal Law

Failing to address, with an appropriate service response, child abuse or neglect can attract both criminal and civil sanctions that go beyond those set out in the *Child and Family Services Act*. As noted in chapter 7, section 218 of the *Criminal Code* makes it an offence to abandon or expose a child to harm where his life or health is put permanently at risk. The definition of "abandon or expose" extends the scope of liability beyond the child's parents. Under section 214, abandonment or exposure means

(a) a wilful omission to take charge of a child by a person who is under a legal duty to do so, and

(b) dealing with a child in a manner that is likely to leave that child exposed to risk without protection.

Section 215 of the *Criminal Code* is also directly applicable to child protection workers, in that it imposes "a duty to provide necessaries" for a child on a "parent, foster parent, guardian or head of a family." The duty to provide necessaries is discussed in chapter 7.

Section 220 of the Code creates the offence of criminal negligence. This was the offence charged against the child protection worker assigned to the case of baby Jordan Heikamp; the baby died in his mother's care in 1997 despite the involvement of a children's aid society. Criminal negligence is discussed in chapter 7.

■ PRACTICAL CHALLENGES

Besides having to work within a complicated legal framework, child protection workers are also faced regularly with the practical challenges posed by interpersonal relationships and budgetary constraints. Some of these challenges are explored below.

Working With Parents and Others

The *Child and Family Services Act* gives preference to service initiatives that allow parents to have a role in their children's lives. Families are very important to children. Research proves that children develop best within a family setting, even where parenting is less than ideal. Child protection workers commonly encounter cases in which children who have suffered parental abuse or neglect express a strong preference, nonetheless, to maintain close ties with their parents.

SUPPORTING FAMILIES

In your work, you will encounter many family situations that give you cause for concern. As a trained child protection worker, you will probably have an unusually good grasp of the kind of care and living environment that is ideal for children. Your vision of an ideal situation may sharply contrast with the kinds of parenting you observe. However, it is important to remember that parenting skills are acquired through a learning process, and that some people master these skills better and more quickly than others do. You will need to learn to cooperate effectively and respectfully with parents who fall short of your expectations, because to do so is to support the best interests of the children who love these parents.

Effective cooperation with struggling parents is best accomplished when you learn to view the system as primarily supportive of families, and not in conflict with them. Many children in care return to their families eventually. Building supportive relationships with the parents you encounter in the course of your work ensures the best possible chances of an improved future for your child clients.

DIFFERENTIAL RESPONSE

An increase in caseloads, combined with the recognition that children benefit when it is possible for them to safely remain with their families, has resulted in a recent interest in **differential response**. Differential response is like triage. Serious cases, such as serious physical abuse or any incident of sexual abuse, result in apprehension of the child or removal of the offender. Less serious cases, such as neglect, are handled in a less extreme and disruptive manner. Children may stay in their own homes while child services works with the family to improve parenting skills. The goal is to strengthen the family rather than break it up. Access to other resources, such as housing assistance, may also promote stability and lessen stress levels in the home.

differential response
a system for distinguishing between serious cases and less serious cases

Differential response has been embraced in Alberta and in several American jurisdictions. It is being explored as an alternative in Ontario as well. The Alberta model emphasizes community-based partnerships and utilizes the support of extended family members, such as grandparents, godparents, and aunts and uncles, where appropriate. Community partners include government services, municipalities, non-profit organizations, businesses, schools, and religious-based institutions.

Significant training is required for differential response to work effectively. Workers require the knowledge and skills to accurately evaluate the seriousness of each case, and to determine which level of response best serves the needs of the child. Where a community and home-based intervention plan is implemented, workers will face the challenge of working collaboratively with parents and families.

WHO IS YOUR CLIENT?

While building cooperative relationsips with parents is important, you must not let these relationships cloud the issue of who your client is. In some cases, a parent may be a highly sympathetic character with her own understandable problems. For example, your client may be a very difficult child and the child's behaviour problems, not the parenting, may seem to be at the root of the family's troubles. In the case of the children of teen parents, your client's parent may be a child in need of protection herself. Finally, your client may be a child who is in the child protection system against his own wishes — as a result, for example, of being under 12 and in conflict with the law — and he may resist help at every turn.

In each of these situations, you will find that your loyalties are tested. Allowing your actions and decisions to be influenced by the interests of people who are not your client can put you in an awkward position. It is important, at all times, to be clear in your own mind about whom you are supposed to be serving. Where necessary, you will also need to remind others that while you are willing to take their views into account, you are bound by law to act in the best interests of the child. In some cases, the nature of those interests will have been determined by a court; in other cases, they may be expressed in a plan of care on file for a child. However, particularly at the earlier stages of an investigation, you yourself will be required to identify them as best you can on the basis of the information at your disposal.

Working Within a Budget

A very important issue facing child protection workers throughout most of Canada is the apparent lack of sufficient resources, in the system, to address the needs of all children requiring protection and other services.

Between 1995 and 2001, the number of children in society care in the London and Middlesex region of Ontario increased by 70 percent, and the growth has shown no sign of slowing. This alarming statistic prompted the United Way to commission a study by experts from the University of Western Ontario. The study, which was released in October 2003, focused on possible causes for the massive increase. It has been described as the most comprehensive study of its type in Canada.

While the study "found no evidence that the CAS is not fully meeting its mandate to protect vulnerable children," child protection workers identified 14 different barriers to the adequate protection of children in the community. Lack of funding was identified as a key aspect of many of these barriers.

Concerns about the funding of child welfare initiatives persist despite recent attempts to improve funding. As a result of inquests and investigations into a number of deaths of children in society care in the 1990s, Ontario created a child mortality task force. In response to the findings of this task force and to the recommendations of a child welfare reform agenda in 1998, the province put in place a new funding formula for child welfare. The new formula incorporated an increase in government funding to $870 million in 2002 (from $542 million in 1998).

Regardless of the precise level of funding, all child protection agencies must work within a specified budget, and with a set complement of staff. Increases in investigative and service caseloads force staff to prioritize the delivery of services to individual clients.

Making decisions about priorities while striving to maintain a focus on the best interests of children creates significant job stress for child protection workers. Some child protection agencies offer mentoring and counselling programs to help employees deal with these sources of stress.

Working With Other Resources in the Community

Another way child protection workers can cope with the limitations on services available directly from children's aid societies is by learning as much as possible about other services and resources available in the community. By making appropriate referrals, a child protection worker can use these programs and resources to help address the needs of clients and their families who do not require the full protective services of a society.

Each community has a different spectrum of family services at its disposal. Most larger communities publish information about community services in a guide that is often referred to as a "Blue Book." Similar index-style guides are available on the Internet. Knowing which services are available in your community and how to access them is a key job responsibility for all child protection workers.

KEY TERMS

customary care
differential response

REFERENCES

Blais, Tony. (2004, July 24.) Victim suing for sex attack. *Edmonton Sun.*

Child and Family Services Act. RSO 1990, c. C.11.

Cohen-Schlanger, M., A. Fitzpatrick, J.D. Hulchanski, and D. Raphael. (1995). Housing as a Factor in Admission of Children to Temporary Care. *Child Welfare, 74*(3): 547–62.

Leschied, A.W., D. Chiodo, P.C. Whitehead, and D. Hurley. (2003). *Protecting Children Is Everybody's Business.* Retrieved May 8, 2005 from University of Western Ontario website: http://www.edu.uwo.ca/CAS/.

Mr. K v. E.K. 2004 ABQB 159.

Ontario Association of Children's Aid Societies. (July 1997). Final Report of the Child Mortality Task Force. *Journal,* 1–47 (Special Edition).

REVIEW QUESTIONS

1. Which interests, other than the best interests of your child clients, can threaten to influence your work decisions? Why?

2. How does inadequate housing influence the number of child protection cases? Is a child protection response an appropriate solution to affordable housing shortages? Why or why not?

3. Child protection workers have a duty to promote a child's connections with his ethnic, religious, and cultural community. How can a worker learn about a child's culture and ethnicity?

4. What is customary care?

5. What does the *Child and Family Services Act* mean when it characterizes the duty to report child abuse and neglect as an "ongoing" duty?

6. List at least two potential consequences for a child protection agency that could flow from its failure to protect a child client.

7. List three potential consequences for a child protection worker who physically abuses a child in her care.

8. If a child is a society ward, why is it essential that child protection workers cooperate effectively with the child's parents in making decisions about the child's care?

DISCUSSION QUESTIONS

1. Define "advocacy." Then, using the Internet and other resources, research advocacy groups, associations, or organizations in your community. Identify at least three different ways in which you can support advocacy efforts on behalf of children.

2. As a class, create a list of examples of how family poverty can adversely affect the lives of children. Choose three items from your list, and brainstorm ways in which child protection workers can address these problems.

3. Imagine that you are the supervisor of a residential care facility that provides relief care — that is, temporary care for children during times when their parents cannot cope, need a break, or require hospitalization, for example. You have noticed that recent conflicts between parents, children, and staff have caused significant stress for certain members of staff, particularly those new to the job. What steps can you take to create a working environment that supports your staff and resolves the outstanding stress-related issues? List at least three initiatives.

Appendixes

A Selected Statutes and Regulations Affecting Children and Their Rights

FEDERAL STATUTES

Children's Special Allowances Act, SC 1992, c. 48

Criminal Code, RSC 1985, c. C-46, as amended

Divorce Act, RSC 1985, c. 3 (2d Supp.)

Family Orders and Agreements Enforcement Assistance Act, RSC 1985, c. 4 (2d Supp.)

Garnishment, Attachment and Pension Diversion Act, RSC 1985, c. G-2

Sex Offender Information Registration Act, SC 2004, c. 10
[not yet in force at the time of publication of this book]

ONTARIO STATUTES

Child and Family Services Act, RSO 1990, c. C.11 (see the full text in appendix B)

- General (including standards for children's residences), RRO 1990, reg. 70

- Register (child abuse register), RRO 1990, reg. 71

- Procedures, Practices and Standards of Service for Child Protection Cases (fast track information system), O. reg. 206/00

Children's Law Reform Act, RSO 1990, c. C.12

Christopher's Law (Sex Offender Registry) Act, 2000, SO 2000, c. 1

Developmental Services Act, RSO 1990, c. D.11

Day Nurseries Act, RSO 1990, c. D.2

Domestic Violence Protection Act, 2000, SO 2000, c. 33
[not yet in force at the time of publication of this book]

Education Act, RSO 1990, c. E.2

Education Quality and Accountability Office Act, SO 1996, c. 11

Family Law Act, RSO 1990, c. F.3

Family Benefits Act, RSO 1990, c. F.2

Family Responsibility and Support Arrears Enforcement Act, 1996, SO 1996, c. 31

Immunization of School Pupils Act, RSO 1990, c. I.1

Intercountry Adoption Act, 1998, SO 1998, c. 29

Interjurisdictional Support Orders Act, 2002, SO 2002, c.13

Parental Responsibility Act, 2000, SO 2000, c. 4

Reciprocal Enforcement of Support Orders Act, RSO 1990, c. R.7

Rescuing Children from Sexual Exploitation Act, 2002, SO 2002, c. 5
     [not yet in force at the time of publication of this book]

B Child and Family Services Act

RSO 1990, c. C.11

CONTENTS

Paramount purpose and other purposes

Paramount purpose
1. (1) The paramount purpose of this Act is to promote the best interests, protection and well being of children.

Other purposes
(2) The additional purposes of this Act, so long as they are consistent with the best interests, protection and well being of children, are:
  1. To recognize that while parents may need help in caring for their children, that help should give support to the autonomy and integrity of the family unit and, wherever possible, be provided on the basis of mutual consent.
  2. To recognize that the least disruptive course of action that is available and is appropriate in a particular case to help a child should be considered.
  3. To recognize that children's services should be provided in a manner that,
       i.   respects children's needs for continuity of care and for stable family relationships, and
       ii. takes into account physical and mental developmental differences among children.
  4. To recognize that, wherever possible, services to children and their families should be provided in a manner that respects cultural, religious and regional differences.
  5. To recognize that Indian and native people should be entitled to provide, wherever possible, their own child and family services, and that all services to Indian and native children and families should

be provided in a manner that recognizes their culture, heritage and traditions and the concept of the extended family.

Note: Despite the proclamation of the Statutes of Ontario, 1999, chapter 2, section 1, section 1 of this Act, as it read before March 31, 2000, continues to apply with respect to any proceeding under Part III, including a status review proceeding, that was commenced before March 31, 2000. See: 1999, c. 2, ss. 37 (5), 38.

Duties of service providers

French language services
2. (1) Service providers shall, where appropriate, make services to children and their families available in the French language.

Duties of service providers
(2) Service providers shall ensure,

(a) that children and their parents have an opportunity where appropriate to be heard and represented when decisions affecting their interests are made and to be heard when they have concerns about the services they are receiving; and

(b) that decisions affecting the interests and rights of children and their parents are made according to clear, consistent criteria and are subject to procedural safeguards.

Interpretation

Definitions
3. (1) In this Act,

"agency" means a corporation;

"approved agency" means an agency that is approved under subsection 8 (1) of Part I (Flexible Services);

"approved service" means a service provided,

(a) under subsection 7 (1) of Part I or with the support of a grant or contribution made under subsection 7 (2) of that Part,

(b) by an approved agency, or

(c) under the authority of a licence;

"band" has the same meaning as in the *Indian Act* (Canada);

"Board" means the Child and Family Services Review Board continued under Part IX (Licensing);

"child" means a person under the age of eighteen years;

"child development service" means a service for a child with a developmental disability or physical disability, for the family of a child with a developmental disability or physical disability, or for the child and the family;

"child treatment service" means a service for a child with a mental or psychiatric disorder, for the family of a child with a mental or psychiatric disorder, or for the child and the family;

"child welfare service" means,

(a) a residential or non-residential service, including a prevention service,

(b) a service provided under Part III (Child Protection),

(c) a service provided under Part VII (Adoption), or

(d) individual or family counselling;

"community support service" means a support service or prevention service provided in the community for children and their families;

"court" means the Ontario Court of Justice or the Family Court of the Superior Court of Justice;

"developmental disability" means a condition of mental impairment present or occurring in a person's formative years that is associated with limitations in adaptive behaviour;

"Director" means a Director appointed under subsection 5 (1) of Part I (Flexible Services);

"foster care" means the provision of residential care to a child, by and in the home of a person who,

(a) receives compensation for caring for the child, except under the *Ontario Works Act, 1997*, the *Ontario Disability Support Program Act, 1997* or the *Family Benefits Act*, and

Note: On a day to be named by proclamation of the Lieutenant Governor, clause (a) is repealed by the Statutes of Ontario, 1999, chapter 2, subsection 2 (3) and the following substituted:

(a) receives compensation for caring for the child, except under the *Ontario Works Act, 1997* or the *Ontario Disability Support Program Act, 1997*, and

See: 1999, c. 2, ss. 2 (3), 38.

(b) is not the child's parent or a person with whom the child has been placed for adoption under Part VII,

and "foster home" and "foster parent" have corresponding meanings;

"Indian" has the same meaning as in the *Indian Act* (Canada);

"licence" means a licence issued under Part IX (Licensing), and "licensed" and "licensee" have corresponding meanings;

"local director" means a local director appointed under section 16 of Part I (Flexible Services);

"Minister" means the Minister of Community and Social Services;

"municipality" does not include a lower-tier municipality that is situated within a regional municipality;

"native community" means a community designated by the Minister under section 209 of Part X (Indian and Native Child and Family Services);

"native person" means a person who is a member of a native community but is not a member of a band, and "native child" has a corresponding meaning;

"order" includes a refusal to make an order;

"prescribed" means prescribed by the regulations;

"program supervisor" means a program supervisor appointed under subsection 5 (2) of Part I (Flexible Services);

"regulations" means the regulations made under this Act;

"residential service" means boarding, lodging and associated supervisory, sheltered or group care provided for a child away from the home of the child's parent, and "residential care" and "residential placement" have corresponding meanings;

"service" means,

    (a) a child development service,

    (b) a child treatment service,

    (c) a child welfare service,

    (d) a community support service, or

    (e) a young offenders service;

"service provider" means,

    (a) the Minister,

    (b) an approved agency,

    (c) a society,

    (d) a licensee, or

    (e) a person who provides an approved service or provides a service purchased by the Minister or an approved agency,

but does not include a foster parent;

"society" means an approved agency designated as a children's aid society under subsection 15 (2) of Part I (Flexible Services);

"Tribunal" means the Licence Appeal Tribunal;

"young offenders service" means a service provided under Part IV (Young Offenders) or under a program established under that Part.

Idem: "parent"

(2) In this Act, a reference to a child's parent shall be deemed to be a reference to,

    (a) both parents, where both have custody of the child;

    (b) one parent, where that parent has lawful custody of the child or the other parent is unavailable or unable to act as the context requires; or

    (c) another individual, where that individual has lawful custody of the child,

except where this Act provides otherwise.

Consents and Participation in Agreements

Consents and agreements

4. (1) In this section,

"capacity" means the capacity to understand and appreciate the nature of a consent or agreement and the consequences of giving, withholding or revoking the consent or making, not making or terminating the agreement;

"nearest relative", when used in reference to a person who is less than 16 years old, means the person with lawful custody of him or her, and when used in reference to a person who is 16 years old or more, means the person who would be authorized to give or refuse consent to a treatment on his or her behalf under the *Health Care Consent Act, 1996* if he or she were incapable with respect to the treatment under that Act.

Elements of valid consent or agreement, etc.

(2) A person's consent or revocation of a consent or participation in or termination of an agreement under this Act is valid if, at the time the consent is given or revoked or the agreement is made or terminated, the person,

    (a) has capacity;

    (b) is reasonably informed as to the nature and consequences of the consent or agreement, and of alternatives to it;

    (c) gives or revokes the consent or executes the agreement or notice of termination voluntarily, without coercion or undue influence; and

    (d) has had a reasonable opportunity to obtain independent advice.

Where person lacks capacity

(3) A person's nearest relative may give or revoke a consent or participate in or terminate an agreement on the person's behalf if it has been determined on the basis of an assessment, not more than one year before the nearest relative acts on the person's behalf, that the person does not have capacity.

Exception

(4) Subsection (3) does not apply to a consent under section 137 (consents to adoption) of Part VII (Adoption) or to a parent's consent referred to in clause 37 (2) (l) (child in need of protection) of Part III (Child Protection).

Consent, etc., of minor

(5) A person's consent or revocation of a consent or participation in or termination of an agreement under this

Act is not invalid by reason only that the person is less than eighteen years old.

PART I
FLEXIBLE SERVICES

Directors and Program Supervisors

Directors and program supervisors

Appointment of Director

5. (1) The Minister may appoint any person as a Director to perform any or all of the duties and functions and exercise any or all of the powers of a Director under this Act and the regulations.

Appointment of program supervisor

(2) The Minister may appoint any person as a program supervisor to perform any or all of the duties and functions and exercise any or all of the powers of a program supervisor under this Act and the regulations.

Limitations, etc., on appointments

(3) The Minister may set out in an appointment made under this section any conditions or limitations to which it is subject.

Remuneration and expenses

(4) The remuneration and expenses of a person appointed under this section who is not a public servant under the *Public Service Act* shall be fixed by the Minister and shall be paid out of legislative appropriations.

Reports and information

(5) A service provider shall,

    (a) make the prescribed reports and furnish the prescribed information to the Minister, in the prescribed form and at the prescribed intervals; and

    (b) make a report to the Minister whenever the Minister requests it, in the form and containing the information specified by the Minister.

Powers of program supervisor

6. (1) For the purpose of ensuring compliance with this Act and the regulations a program supervisor may, at all reasonable times, upon producing proper identification, enter premises where an approved service is provided, inspect the facilities, the service provided, the books of account and the records relating to the service, and make copies of those books and records or remove them from the premises to copy them as may be reasonably required.

Offence

(2) No person shall hinder, obstruct or attempt to hinder or obstruct a program supervisor in the performance of the program supervisor's duties or knowingly give false information about an approved service to a program supervisor.

Idem

(3) No service provider or person in charge of premises where an approved service is provided shall refuse to give a program supervisor access to the books and records referred to in subsection (1) or refuse to give a program supervisor information about the approved service that the program supervisor reasonably requires.

Regulations re exercise of power of entry

(4) A program supervisor shall exercise the power of entry set out in subsection (1) in accordance with the regulations.

Approvals and Funding

Provision of services directly or by purchase

7. (1) The Minister may,

    (a) provide services and establish, operate and maintain facilities for the provision of services; and

    (b) make agreements with persons, municipalities and agencies for the provision of services,

and may make payments for those services and facilities out of legislative appropriations.

Grants and contributions for services, consultation, etc.

(2) The Minister may make grants and contributions, out of legislative appropriations, to any person, organization or municipality for consultation, research and evaluation with respect to services and for the provision of services.

Approval of agencies

8. (1) Where the Minister is satisfied that an agency is, with financial assistance under this Part and the regulations, financially capable of establishing, maintaining and operating a service and that its affairs are carried on under competent management in good faith, the Minister may approve the agency to provide that service.

Funding for establishment of services

(2) Where the Minister intends to approve an agency to provide a service under subsection (1), the Minister may enter into an agreement with the agency for the establishment of the service.

Financial assistance, etc.

(3) Where the Minister approves an agency to provide a service under subsection (1), the Minister may give the agency financial and other assistance, in accordance with the regulations.

Effective date

(4) The Minister's approval under subsection (1) shall be deemed to have retroactive effect if the Minister so specifies.

Approval of premises for provision of services

9. (1) Where the Minister is satisfied that premises are suitable for providing a service, the Minister may approve all or any part of the premises for the provision of the service by an approved agency and may give the agency financial and other assistance in accordance with the regulations, for the maintenance and operation of the premises and the provision of the service.

Approval may relate to all or part of building, etc.
(2) The Minister's approval under subsection (1) may specify a building, a group of buildings, part of a building or a location in a building as the approved premises.

Effective date
(3) The Minister's approval of premises under subsection (1) shall be deemed to have retroactive effect if the Minister so specifies, but it shall not be deemed to take effect on a day before the Minister's approval of the agency concerned becomes effective under section 8.

Terms and conditions and services to adults

Terms and conditions
10. (1) The Minister may impose terms and conditions on an approval given under subsection 8 (1) or 9 (1) and, upon reasonable written notice to the approved agency, may vary, remove or amend the terms and conditions or impose new terms and conditions.

Duty of Director
(2) A Director shall review any objections from an approved agency which has received notice under subsection (1).

Transfer of assets
(3) An approved agency shall not transfer or assign any of its assets acquired with financial assistance from the Province of Ontario, except in accordance with the regulations.

Services to persons over eighteen
(4) The Minister may,
   (a) provide services under clause 7 (1) (a);
   (b) make agreements for the provision of services under clause 7 (1) (b);
   (c) make grants and contributions for the provision of services under subsection 7 (2);
   (d) approve agencies for the provision of services under subsection 8 (1);
   (e) approve premises for the provision of services under subsection 9 (1),
to persons who are not children, and to their families, as if those persons were children.

Co-ordinating or advisory groups

11. The Minister may make agreements with persons, organizations or municipalities for the establishment, support and operation of co-ordinating or advisory groups or committees, may make payments for the purpose out of legislative appropriations and may give other assistance for the purpose.

Security for payment of funds

12. The Minister may, as a condition of making a payment under this Part or the regulations, require the recipient of the funds to secure them by way of mortgage, lien, registration of agreement or in such other manner as the Minister determines.

Approved agency

13. (1) An approved agency shall file a certified copy of its by-laws and of any amendment to them with the Minister forthwith after they are made.

Idem
(2) The by-laws of an approved agency shall contain the prescribed provisions.

Band or native community representatives
(3) An approved agency that provides services to Indian or native children and families shall have the prescribed number of band or native community representatives on its board of directors, appointed in the prescribed manner and for the prescribed terms.

Employee may not sit on board
(4) An employee of an approved agency shall not be a member of the agency's board of directors.

Placements must comply with Act and regulations

14. No approved agency shall place a child in a residential placement except in accordance with this Act and the regulations.

Children's Aid Societies

Children's Aid Society

15. (1) In this section,

"prescribed" means prescribed in a regulation made by the Minister under subsection 214 (4) of Part XI (Regulations).

Designation of children's aid society
(2) The Minister may designate an approved agency as a children's aid society for a specified territorial jurisdiction and for any or all of the functions set out in subsection (3), may impose terms and conditions on a designation and may vary, remove or amend the terms and conditions or impose new terms and conditions at any time, and may at any time amend a designation to provide that the society is no longer designated for a particular function set out in subsection (3) or to alter the society's territorial jurisdiction.

Functions of society
(3) The functions of a children's aid society are to,
   (a) investigate allegations or evidence that children who are under the age of sixteen years or are in the society's care or under its supervision may be in need of protection;

(b) protect, where necessary, children who are under the age of sixteen years or are in the society's care or under its supervision;

(c) provide guidance, counselling and other services to families for protecting children or for the prevention of circumstances requiring the protection of children;

(d) provide care for children assigned or committed to its care under this Act;

(e) supervise children assigned to its supervision under this Act;

(f) place children for adoption under Part VII; and

(g) perform any other duties given to it by this or any other Act.

Prescribed standards, etc.
(4) A society shall,

(a) provide the prescribed standard of services in its performance of its functions; and

(b) follow the prescribed procedures and practices.

(5) REPEALED.

Protection from personal liability
(6) No action shall be instituted against an officer or employee of a society for an act done in good faith in the execution or intended execution of the person's duty or for an alleged neglect or default in the execution in good faith of the person's duty.

Appointment of local director

16. Every society shall appoint a local director with the prescribed qualifications, powers and duties.

Duties of Director with respect to societies

17. (1) A Director,

(a) shall advise and supervise societies;

(b) shall inspect or direct and supervise the inspection of the operation and records of societies;

(c) shall exercise the powers and duties of a society in any area in which no society is functioning;

(d) shall inspect or direct and supervise the inspection of places in which children in the care of societies are placed; and

(e) shall ensure that societies provide the standard of services and follow the procedures and practices required by subsection 15 (4).

Director may designate places of safety
(2) A Director may designate a place as a place of safety, and may designate a class of places as places of safety, for the purposes of Part III (Child Protection).

18. REPEALED.

Financial provisions

19. (1) REPEALED.

Payments by Minister
(2) The Minister shall pay to every society out of legislative appropriations an amount determined in accordance with the regulations.

(3) REPEALED.

How society's estimates determined
(4) A society's estimated expenditures shall be determined and shall be approved by the Minister in accordance with the regulations.

(5) REPEALED.

Manner of payment
(6) An amount payable to a society under subsection (2), including advances on expenditures before they are incurred, shall be paid at the times and in the manner determined by the Minister.

Local board

20. (1) REPEALED.

Society deemed to be a local board
(2) A society shall be deemed to be a local board of each municipality in which it has jurisdiction for the purposes of the *Ontario Municipal Employees Retirement System Act* and the *Municipal Conflict of Interest Act*.

Directives to societies

20.1 A Director may issue directives to one or more societies, including directives respecting their provision of services under this Act.

Agreements with other Governments

Minister may make agreements with other governments

21. The Minister may, with the approval of the Lieutenant Governor in Council, make agreements on behalf of the Government of Ontario with the Crown in right of Canada and with the Crown in right of any other province of Canada respecting services under this Act or the care or protection of children.

Revocation and Take-Over Powers

Powers of Minister

22. (1) Where the Minister believes on reasonable grounds that,

(a) an approved agency is not providing services in accordance with this Act or the regulations or in accordance with any term or condition imposed on the approval under subsection 8 (1) or 9 (1) or, in the case of a society, on the designation under subsection 15 (2);

(b) a director, officer or employee of an approved agency has contravened or knowingly permitted any person under his or her control and direction to contravene any provision of this Act or the regulations or any term or condition imposed on the approval under subsection 8 (1) or 9 (1) or, in the case of a society, on the designation under subsection 15 (2);

(c) approval of the agency under subsection 8 (1) or of the premises under subsection 9 (1) would be refused if it were being applied for in the first instance; or

(d) in the case of a society, the society,

(i) is not able to or fails to perform any or all of its functions under section 15,

(ii) fails to perform any or all of its functions in any part of its territorial jurisdiction, or

(iii) fails to follow a directive issued under section 20.1,

the Minister may,

(e) revoke or suspend the approval; or

(f) in the case of a society,

(i) revoke or suspend the designation under subsection 15 (2),

(ii) remove any or all of the members of the board of directors and appoint others in their place, or

(iii) operate and manage the society in the place of the board of directors.

Notice of proposal

(2) Where the Minister proposes to act under clause (1) (e) or (f), the Minister shall serve notice of the proposal and written reasons for it on the approved agency, unless the agency has requested that the Minister so act or has consented to the Minister's proposal.

Request for hearing

(3) A notice under subsection (2) shall inform the agency that it is entitled to a hearing under this section if the agency mails or delivers to the Minister, within sixty days after the notice under subsection (2) is served, a written request for a hearing.

Where agency does not request hearing

(4) Where the agency does not require a hearing under subsection (3), the Minister may carry out the proposal stated in the Minister's notice under subsection (2) without a hearing.

Hearing

(5) Where the agency requires a hearing under subsection (3),

(a) if the Minister proposes to act under clause (1) (e) only, the Minister; and

(b) in all other cases, the Lieutenant Governor in Council,

shall appoint one or more persons not employed by the Ministry to hear the matter and recommend whether the Minister should carry out the proposal.

Procedure

(6) Sections 17, 18, 19 and 20 of the *Statutory Powers Procedure Act* do not apply to a hearing under this section.

Report to Minister

(7) The person or persons appointed under subsection (5) shall hold a hearing and make a report to the Minister setting out,

(a) recommendations as to the carrying out of the proposal; and

(b) the findings of fact, any information or knowledge used in making the recommendations and any conclusions of law arrived at that are relevant to the recommendations,

and shall provide a copy of the report to the agency.

Minister's decision

(8) After considering a report made under this section, the Minister may carry out the proposal and shall give notice of the Minister's decision to the agency with reasons.

Provisional suspension

(9) Despite subsection (2), the Minister, by notice to the agency and without a hearing, may provisionally exercise any of the powers set out in clauses (1) (e) and (f) where it is necessary to do so, in the Minister's opinion, to avert an immediate threat to the public interest or to a person's health, safety or welfare and the Minister so states in the notice, with reasons, and thereafter the Minister shall cause a hearing to be held and subsections (3) to (8) apply with necessary modifications.

Minister's order to cease activity

23. (1) Where the Minister is of the opinion, upon reasonable grounds, that an activity carried on, or the manner of carrying on an activity, in the course of the provision of an approved service is causing or is likely to cause harm to a person's health, safety or welfare, the Minister may by order require the service provider to suspend or cease the activity and may take such other action as the Minister deems to be in the best interests of the persons receiving the approved service.

Notice of proposal

(2) Where the Minister proposes to make an order requiring the suspension or cessation of an activity under subsection (1), the Minister shall serve notice of the proposal and written reasons for it on the service provider, and subsections 22 (3) to (8), except clause (5) (b), apply with necessary modifications.

Where order may be made immediately

(3) Despite subsection (2), the Minister, by notice to the service provider and without a hearing, may require that the service provider immediately suspend or cease the activity where the continuation of the activity is, in the Minister's opinion, an immediate threat to the public interest or to a person's health, safety or welfare and the

Minister so states in the notice, with reasons, and thereafter the Minister shall cause a hearing to be held and subsections 22 (3) to (8), except clause (5) (b), apply with necessary modifications.

Minister has powers of board

24. (1) Where the Minister operates and manages a society under subclause 22 (1) (f) (iii), the Minister has all the powers of its board of directors.

Idem

(2) Without restricting the generality of subsection (1), where the Minister operates and manages a society under subclause 22 (1) (f) (iii), the Minister may,

- (a) carry on the society's business;
- (b) enter into contracts on the society's behalf;
- (c) arrange for bank accounts to be opened in the society's name, and authorize persons to sign cheques and other documents on the society's behalf;
- (d) appoint or dismiss employees of the society; and
- (e) make by-laws.

Occupation and operation of premises

(3) Without restricting the generality of subsection (1), where the Minister operates and manages a society under subclause 22 (1) (f) (iii), the Minister may,

- (a) despite sections 25 and 41 of the *Expropriations Act*, immediately occupy and operate, or arrange for the occupation and operation by a person or organization designated by the Minister, of any premises occupied or used by the society for the provision of approved services; or
- (b) apply without notice to the Superior Court of Justice for an order directing the sheriff to assist the Minister as may be necessary in occupying the premises.

Maximum period

(4) The Minister shall not occupy and operate premises under subsection (3) for a period exceeding one year without the society's consent, but the Lieutenant Governor in Council may extend the period from time to time.

Offences

Offence

25. A person who knowingly,

- (a) fails to furnish a report required by the Minister under subsection 5 (5);
- (b) contravenes subsection 6 (2) or (3) (obstructing program supervisor, etc.); or
- (c) furnishes false information in an application under this Part or in a report or return required under this Part or the regulations,

and a director, officer or employee of a corporation who authorizes, permits or concurs in such a contravention or furnishing by the corporation, is guilty of an offence and is liable upon conviction to a fine of not more than $2,000.

PART II
VOLUNTARY ACCESS TO SERVICES

Definitions

26. In this Part,

"advisory committee" means a Residential Placement Advisory Committee established under subsection 34 (2);

"institution" means,

- (a) a children's residence, other than a maternity home, operated by the Minister or under the authority of a licence issued under Part IX (Licensing) with the capacity of providing residential services to ten or more children at a time, or
- (b) premises designated by a Director under subsection 34 (5);

"record", when used in reference to a person, has the same meaning as in Part VIII (Confidentiality of and Access to Records);

"special need" means a need that is related to or caused by a developmental disability or a behavioural, emotional, physical, mental or other disability.

Consents

Consent to service

Consent to service: person over sixteen

27. (1) A service provider may provide a service to a person who is sixteen years of age or older only with the person's consent, except where the court orders under this Act that the service be provided to the person.

Consent to residential service: child under sixteen

(2) A service provider may provide a residential service to a child who is less than sixteen years of age only with the consent of the child's parent or, where the child is in a society's lawful custody, the society's consent, except where this Act provides otherwise.

Exception

(3) Subsections (1) and (2) do not apply where a service is provided to a child under Part IV (Young Offenders).

Discharge from residential placement

(4) A child who is placed in a residential placement with the consent referred to in subsection (2) may only be discharged from the placement,

- (a) with the consent that would be required for a new residential placement; or
- (b) where the placement is made under the authority of an agreement made under subsection 29 (1) (temporary care agreements) or subsection 30 (1) or (2) (special needs agreements), in accordance with section 33 (termination by notice).

Transfer to another placement

(5) A child who is placed in a residential placement with the consent referred to in subsection (2) shall not be transferred from one placement to another unless the consent that would be required for a new residential placement is given.

Child's wishes

(6) Before a child is placed in or discharged from a residential placement or transferred from one residential placement to another with the consent referred to in subsection (2), the service provider shall take the child's wishes into account, if they can be reasonably ascertained.

Counselling service: child twelve or older

28. A service provider may provide a counselling service to a child who is twelve years of age or older with the child's consent, and no other person's consent is required, but if the child is less than sixteen years of age the service provider shall discuss with the child at the earliest appropriate opportunity the desirability of involving the child's parent.

Temporary Care Agreements

Temporary care agreement

29. (1) A person who is temporarily unable to care adequately for a child in his or her custody, and the society having jurisdiction where the person resides, may make a written agreement for the society's care and custody of the child.

Child's age

(2) No temporary care agreement shall be made in respect of a child,

(a) who is sixteen years of age or older; or

(b) who is twelve years of age or older, unless the child is a party to the agreement.

Exception: developmental disability

(3) Clause (2) (b) does not apply where it has been determined on the basis of an assessment, not more than one year before the agreement is made, that the child does not have capacity to participate in the agreement because of a developmental disability.

Duty of society

(4) A society shall not make a temporary care agreement unless the society,

(a) has determined that an appropriate residential placement that is likely to benefit the child is available; and

(b) is satisfied that no less disruptive course of action, such as care in the child's own home, is appropriate for the child in the circumstances.

Term of agreement limited

(5) No temporary care agreement shall be made for a term exceeding six months, but the parties to a temporary care

agreement may, with a Director's written approval, agree to extend it for a further period or periods if the total term of the agreement, as extended, does not exceed an aggregate of twelve months.

Time limit

(6) No temporary care agreement shall be made or extended so as to result in a child being in a society's care and custody, for a period exceeding,

(a) 12 months, if the child is less than 6 years of age on the day the agreement is entered into or extended; or

(b) 24 months, if the child is 6 years of age or older on the day the agreement is entered into or extended.

> **Note: For the purposes of subsection (6), as re-enacted by the Statutes of Ontario, 1999, chapter 2, subsection 8 (2), no period that a child was in a society's care and custody before March 31, 2000 shall be counted. See: 1999, c. 2, s. 37 (1).**

> **Note: Despite the proclamation of the Statutes of Ontario, 1999, chapter 2, subsection 8 (2), subsection (6) of this section, as it read before March 31, 2000, shall continue to apply with respect to a child who is in the care and custody of a society on March 31, 2000 so long as that child continues to be in the care and custody of a society. See: 1999, c. 2, ss. 37 (2), 38.**

Same

(6.1) In calculating the period referred to in subsection (6), time during which a child has been in a society's care and custody,

(a) as a society ward under paragraph 2 of subsection 57 (1);

(b) under a temporary care agreement under subsection 29 (1); or

(c) under a temporary order made under clause 51 (2) (d),

shall be counted.

Previous periods to be counted

(6.2) The period referred to in subsection (6) shall include any previous periods that the child was in a society's care and custody as described in subsection (6.1) other than periods that precede a continuous period of five or more years that the child was not in a society's care and custody.

> **Note: For the purposes of subsections (6.1) and (6.2), as enacted by the Statutes of Ontario, 1999, chapter 2, subsection 8 (2), no period that a child was in a society's care and custody before March 31, 2000 shall be counted. See: 1999, c. 2, s. 37 (1).**

*Authority to consent to medical
treatment may be transferred*
(7) A temporary care agreement may provide that the society is entitled to consent to medical treatment for the child where a parent's consent would otherwise be required.

Contents of temporary care agreement
(8) A temporary care agreement shall include:

1. A statement by all the parties to the agreement that the child's care and custody are transferred to the society.

2. A statement by all the parties to the agreement that the child's placement is voluntary.

3. A statement, by the person referred to in subsection (1), that he or she is temporarily unable to care for the child adequately and has discussed with the society alternatives to residential placement of the child.

4. An undertaking by the person referred to in subsection (1) to maintain contact with the child and be involved in the child's care.

5. If it is not possible for the person referred to in subsection (1) to maintain contact with the child and be involved in the child's care, the person's designation of another named person who is willing to do so.

6. The name of the individual who is the primary contact between the society and the person referred to in subsection (1).

7. Such other provisions as are prescribed.

Designation by advisory committee
(9) Where the person referred to in subsection (1) does not give an undertaking under paragraph 4 or designate another person under paragraph 5 of subsection (8), an advisory committee that has jurisdiction may, in consultation with the society, name a suitable person who is willing to maintain contact with the child and be involved in the child's care.

Variation of agreement
(10) The parties to a temporary care agreement may vary the agreement from time to time in a manner that is consistent with this Part and the regulations made under it.

Special Needs Agreements

Special needs agreements

Special needs agreement with society
30. (1) A person who is unable to provide the services required by a child in his or her custody because the child has a special need, and a society having jurisdiction where the person resides, may with a Director's written approval make a written agreement for,
  (a) the society's provision of services to meet the child's special need; and

  (b) the society's supervision or care and custody of the child.

Special needs agreement with Minister
(2) A person who is unable to provide the services required by a child in his or her custody because the child has a special need, and the Minister, may make a written agreement for,
  (a) the Minister's provision of services to meet the child's special need; and
  (b) the Minister's supervision or care and custody of the child.

Term to be specified
(3) A special needs agreement shall only be made for a specific period, but may be extended, with a Director's written approval in the case of an agreement with a society, for a further period or periods.

s. 29 (7-10) apply

(4) Where a special needs agreement provides for a child's residential placement, subsections 29 (7), (8), (9) and (10) (authority to consent to medical treatment, contents of agreement, variation) apply with necessary modifications, and subsection 29 (4) (duty of society) applies to the society or the Minister, as the case may be, with necessary modifications.

Sixteen and seventeen year olds

Society agreements with sixteen and seventeen year olds
31. (1) A child who is sixteen years of age or older and is not in the care of his or her parent and has a special need, and the society having jurisdiction where the child resides, may with a Director's written approval make a written agreement for the society's provision of services to meet the child's special need.

Idem: special needs agreement with Minister
(2) A child who is sixteen years of age or older and is not in the care of his or her parent and has a special need, and the Minister, may make a written agreement for the Minister's provision of services to meet the person's special need.

Contents of agreements
(3) An agreement made under subsection (1) or (2) shall contain the prescribed provisions.

s. 29 (10) applies

(4) Subsection 29 (10) (variation) applies to an agreement made under subsection (1) or (2).

Expiry and Termination of Agreements

Agreement expires at eighteen

32. No agreement made under section 29, 30 or 31 shall continue beyond the eighteenth birthday of the person who is its subject.

Notice of termination of agreement

33. (1) A party to an agreement made under section 29, 30 or 31 may terminate the agreement at any time by giving every other party written notice that the party wishes to terminate the agreement.

When notice takes effect

(2) Where notice is given under subsection (1), the agreement terminates on the expiry of five days, or such longer period not exceeding twenty-one days as the agreement specifies, after the day on which every other party has actually received the notice.

Return of child, etc., by society

(3) Where notice of a wish to terminate an agreement for care and custody made under subsection 29 (1) or 30 (1) is given by or to a society under subsection (1), the society shall as soon as possible, and in any event before the agreement terminates under subsection (2),

    (a) cause the child to be returned to the person who made the agreement, or to a person who has obtained an order for the child's custody since the agreement was made; or

    (b) where the society is of the opinion that the child would be in need of protection within the meaning of subsection 37 (2) of Part III (Child Protection) if returned to the person referred to in clause (a), bring the child before the court under that Part to determine whether the child would be in need of protection in that case, and thereafter Part III applies to the child, with necessary modifications.

Idem: Minister

(4) Where notice of a wish to terminate an agreement for care and custody made under subsection 30 (2) is given by or to the Minister under subsection (1), subsection (3) applies to the Minister, with necessary modifications.

Idem: expiry of agreement

(5) Where a temporary care agreement expires or is about to expire under subsection 29 (6), and where a temporary care agreement or a special needs agreement that provides for care and custody expires or is about to expire according to its own terms and is not extended, the society or the Minister, as the case may be, shall before the agreement expires or as soon as practicable thereafter, but in any event within twenty-one days after the agreement expires,

    (a) cause the child to be returned to the person who made the agreement, or to a person who has obtained an order for the child's custody since the agreement was made; or

    (b) where the society or the Minister, as the case may be, is of the opinion that the child would be in need of protection within the meaning of subsection 37 (2) of Part III (Child Protection) if returned to the person referred to in clause (a), bring the child before the court under that Part to determine whether the child would be in need of protection

in that case, and thereafter Part III applies to the child, with necessary modifications.

Review by Residential Placement Advisory Committee

Residential placement review

34. (1) In this section,

"residential placement" does not include,

    (a) a placement made under the *Young Offenders Act* (Canada) or under Part IV (Young Offenders),

    (b) commitment to a secure treatment program under Part VI (Extraordinary Measures), or

    (c) a placement with a person who is neither a service provider nor a foster parent.

Residential placement advisory committees

(2) The Minister may establish residential placement advisory committees each consisting of,

    (a) persons engaged in providing services;

    (b) other persons who have demonstrated an informed concern for the welfare of children;

    (c) one representative of the Ministry; and

    (d) if the Minister wishes, another person or persons, including a representative of a band or native community, whom the Minister considers appropriate,

and shall specify the territorial jurisdiction of each advisory committee.

Payments, etc., to members

(3) The Minister may pay allowances and reasonable travelling expenses to any or all of the members of an advisory committee, and may authorize an advisory committee to hire support staff.

Duties of committee

(4) An advisory committee has a duty to advise, inform and assist parents, children and service providers with respect to the availability and appropriateness of residential services and alternatives to residential services, to conduct reviews under this section, and to name persons for the purpose of subsection 29 (9) (contact with child under temporary care agreement), and has such further duties as are prescribed.

Designation by Director

(5) A Director may designate a building, group of buildings or part of a building in which residential services can be provided to ten or more children at a time as an institution for the purposes of this section.

Mandatory review by committee

(6) An advisory committee shall review,

    (a) every residential placement in an institution of a child who resides within the advisory committee's jurisdiction, if the placement is intended to last or actually lasts ninety days or more,

(i) as soon as possible, but in any event within forty-five days of the day on which the child is placed in the institution,

(ii) unless the placement is reviewed under sub-clause (i), within twelve months of the establishment of the committee or within such longer period as the Minister allows, and

(iii) while the placement continues, at least once during each nine month period succeeding the review under subclause (i) or (ii);

(b) every residential placement of a child twelve years of age or older who objects to the placement and resides within the advisory committee's jurisdiction,

(i) within the week immediately following the day that is fourteen days after the child is placed, and

(ii) while the placement continues, at least once during each nine month period succeeding the review under subclause (i); and

(c) an existing or proposed residential placement of a child that the Minister refers to the advisory committee, within thirty days of the referral.

Discretionary review

(7) An advisory committee may at any time review or re-review, on a person's request or on its own initiative, an existing or proposed residential placement of a child who resides within the advisory committee's jurisdiction.

Review to be informal, etc.

(8) An advisory committee shall conduct a review under this section in an informal manner, in the absence of the public, and in the course of the review may,

(a) interview the child, members of the child's family and any representatives of the child and family;

(b) interview persons engaged in providing services and other persons who may have an interest in the matter or may have information that would assist the advisory committee;

(c) examine documents and reports that are presented to the committee; and

(d) examine records of the child and of members of the child's family, as defined in Part VIII (Confidentiality of and Access to Records), that are disclosed to the committee in accordance with that Part.

Service providers to assist advisory committee

(9) At an advisory committee's request, a service provider shall assist and co-operate with the advisory committee in its conduct of a review.

What committee shall consider

(10) In conducting a review, an advisory committee shall,

(a) determine whether the child has a special need;

(b) consider what programs are available for the child in the residential placement or proposed residen-

tial placement, and whether a program available to the child is likely to benefit the child;

(c) consider whether the residential placement or proposed residential placement is appropriate for the child in the circumstances;

(d) if it considers that a less restrictive alternative to the placement would be more appropriate for the child in the circumstances, specify that alternative;

(e) consider the importance of continuity in the child's care and the possible effect on the child of disruption of that continuity; and

(f) where the child is an Indian or native person, consider the importance, in recognition of the uniqueness of Indian and native culture, heritage and traditions, of preserving the child's cultural identity.

Recommendations

35. (1) An advisory committee that conducts a review shall advise,

(a) the service provider;

(b) any representative of the child;

(c) the child's parent or, where the child is in a society's lawful custody, the society;

(d) the child, where it is reasonable to expect him or her to understand; and

(e) where the child is an Indian or native person, a representative chosen by the child's band or native community,

of its recommendations as soon as the review has been completed, and shall advise the child of his or her rights under section 36 if the child is twelve years of age or older.

Report of review to Minister

(2) An advisory committee that conducts a review shall, within thirty days of completing the review, make a report of its findings and recommendations to the Minister.

Recommendation for less restrictive service

(3) Where an advisory committee considers that the provision of a less restrictive service to a child would be more appropriate for the child than the residential placement, the advisory committee shall recommend in its report under subsection (2) that the less restrictive service be provided to the child.

Additional reports at Minister's request

(4) An advisory committee shall make a report of its activities to the Minister whenever the Minister requests it, in addition to making the reports required by subsection (2).

Review by Child and Family Services Review Board

36. (1) A child who is twelve years of age or older and is in a residential placement to which he or she objects may, if the placement has been reviewed by an advisory committee under section 34 and,

(a) the child is dissatisfied with the advisory committee's recommendation; or

(b) the advisory committee's recommendation is not followed,

apply to the Board for a determination of where he or she should remain or be placed.

Duty of Board

(2) The Board shall conduct a review with respect to an application made under subsection (1) and may do so by holding a hearing.

Idem

(3) The Board shall advise the child whether it intends to hold a hearing or not within ten days of receiving the child's application.

Parties

(4) The parties to a hearing under this section are,

(a) the child;

(b) the child's parent or, where the child is in a society's lawful custody, the society;

(c) where the child is an Indian or native person, a representative chosen by the child's band or native community; and

(d) any other persons that the Board specifies.

Time for determination

(5) The Board shall complete its review and make a determination within thirty days of receiving a child's application, unless,

(a) the Board holds a hearing with respect to the application; and

(b) the parties consent to a longer period for the Board's determination.

Board's recommendation

(6) After conducting a review under subsection (2), the Board may,

(a) order that the child be transferred to another residential placement, if the Board is satisfied that the other residential placement is available;

(b) order that the child be discharged from the residential placement; or

(c) confirm the existing placement.

PART III
CHILD PROTECTION

Interpretation

37. (1) In this Part,

"child" does not include a child as defined in subsection 3 (1) who is actually or apparently sixteen years of age or older, unless the child is the subject of an order under this Part;

"child protection worker" means a Director, a local director or a person authorized by a Director or local director for the purposes of section 40 (commencing child protection proceedings);

"extended family", when used in reference to a child, means the persons to whom the child is related by blood, marriage or adoption;

"parent", when used in reference to a child, means each of,

(a) the child's mother,

(b) an individual described in one of paragraphs 1 to 6 of subsection 8 (1) of the *Children's Law Reform Act*, unless it is proved on a balance of probabilities that he is not the child's natural father,

(c) the individual having lawful custody of the child,

(d) an individual who, during the twelve months before intervention under this Part, has demonstrated a settled intention to treat the child as a child of his or her family, or has acknowledged parentage of the child and provided for the child's support,

(e) an individual who, under a written agreement or a court order, is required to provide for the child, has custody of the child or has a right of access to the child, and

(f) an individual who has acknowledged parentage of the child in writing under section 12 of the *Children's Law Reform Act*,

but does not include a foster parent;

"place of safety" means a foster home, a hospital, and a place or one of a class of places designated as such by a Director under subsection 17 (2) of Part I (Flexible Services), but does not include,

(a) a place of secure custody as defined in Part IV (Young Offenders), or

(b) a place of secure temporary detention as defined in Part IV.

Child in need of protection

(2) A child is in need of protection where,

(a) the child has suffered physical harm, inflicted by the person having charge of the child or caused by or resulting from that person's,

(i) failure to adequately care for, provide for, supervise or protect the child, or

(ii) pattern of neglect in caring for, providing for, supervising or protecting the child;

(b) there is a risk that the child is likely to suffer physical harm inflicted by the person having charge of the child or caused by or resulting from that person's,

(i) failure to adequately care for, provide for, supervise or protect the child, or

(ii) pattern of neglect in caring for, providing for, supervising or protecting the child;

(c) the child has been sexually molested or sexually exploited, by the person having charge of the child or by another person where the person having charge of the child knows or should know of the possibility of sexual molestation or sexual exploitation and fails to protect the child;

(d) there is a risk that the child is likely to be sexually molested or sexually exploited as described in clause (c);

(e) the child requires medical treatment to cure, prevent or alleviate physical harm or suffering and the child's parent or the person having charge of the child does not provide, or refuses or is unavailable or unable to consent to, the treatment;

(f) the child has suffered emotional harm, demonstrated by serious,
   (i) anxiety,
   (ii) depression,
   (iii) withdrawal,
   (iv) self-destructive or aggressive behaviour, or
   (v) delayed development,
and there are reasonable grounds to believe that the emotional harm suffered by the child results from the actions, failure to act or pattern of neglect on the part of the child's parent or the person having charge of the child;

(f.1) the child has suffered emotional harm of the kind described in subclause (f) (i), (ii), (iii), (iv) or (v) and the child's parent or the person having charge of the child does not provide, or refuses or is unavailable or unable to consent to, services or treatment to remedy or alleviate the harm;

(g) there is a risk that the child is likely to suffer emotional harm of the kind described in subclause (f) (i), (ii), (iii), (iv) or (v) resulting from the actions, failure to act or pattern of neglect on the part of the child's parent or the person having charge of the child;

(g.1) there is a risk that the child is likely to suffer emotional harm of the kind described in subclause (f) (i), (ii), (iii), (iv) or (v) and that the child's parent or the person having charge of the child does not provide, or refuses or is unavailable or unable to consent to, services or treatment to prevent the harm;

(h) the child suffers from a mental, emotional or developmental condition that, if not remedied, could seriously impair the child's development and the child's parent or the person having charge of the child does not provide, or refuses or is unavailable or unable to consent to, treatment to remedy or alleviate the condition;

(i) the child has been abandoned, the child's parent has died or is unavailable to exercise his or her custodial rights over the child and has not made adequate provision for the child's care and custody, or the child is in a residential placement and the parent refuses or is unable or unwilling to resume the child's care and custody;

(j) the child is less than twelve years old and has killed or seriously injured another person or caused serious damage to another person's property, services or treatment are necessary to prevent a recurrence and the child's parent or the person having charge of the child does not provide, or refuses or is unavailable or unable to consent to, those services or treatment;

(k) the child is less than twelve years old and has on more than one occasion injured another person or caused loss or damage to another person's property, with the encouragement of the person having charge of the child or because of that person's failure or inability to supervise the child adequately; or

(l) the child's parent is unable to care for the child and the child is brought before the court with the parent's consent and, where the child is twelve years of age or older, with the child's consent, to be dealt with under this Part.

Best interests of child

(3) Where a person is directed in this Part to make an order or determination in the best interests of a child, the person shall take into consideration those of the following circumstances of the case that he or she considers relevant:

1. The child's physical, mental and emotional needs, and the appropriate care or treatment to meet those needs.

2. The child's physical, mental and emotional level of development.

3. The child's cultural background.

4. The religious faith, if any, in which the child is being raised.

5. The importance for the child's development of a positive relationship with a parent and a secure place as a member of a family.

6. The child's relationships by blood or through an adoption order.

7. The importance of continuity in the child's care and the possible effect on the child of disruption of that continuity.

8. The merits of a plan for the child's care proposed by a society, including a proposal that the child be placed for adoption or adopted, compared with the merits of the child remaining with or returning to a parent.

9. The child's views and wishes, if they can be reasonably ascertained.

10. The effects on the child of delay in the disposition of the case.

11. The risk that the child may suffer harm through being removed from, kept away from, returned to or allowed to remain in the care of a parent.

12. The degree of risk, if any, that justified the finding that the child is in need of protection.

13. Any other relevant circumstance.

Where child an Indian or native person

(4) Where a person is directed in this Part to make an order or determination in the best interests of a child and the child is an Indian or native person, the person shall take into consideration the importance, in recognition of the uniqueness of Indian and native culture, heritage and traditions, of preserving the child's cultural identity.

Note: Despite the proclamation of the Statutes of Ontario, 1999, chapter 2, section 9, section 37 of this Act, as it read before March 31, 2000, continues to apply with respect to any proceeding under Part III, including a status review proceeding, that was commenced before March 31, 2000. See: 1999, c. 2, ss. 37 (5), 38.

Legal Representation

Legal representation of child

38. (1) A child may have legal representation at any stage in a proceeding under this Part.

Court to consider issue

(2) Where a child does not have legal representation in a proceeding under this Part, the court,

    (a) shall, as soon as practicable after the commencement of the proceeding; and

    (b) may, at any later stage in the proceeding,

determine whether legal representation is desirable to protect the child's interests.

Direction for legal representation

(3) Where the court determines that legal representation is desirable to protect a child's interests, the court shall direct that legal representation be provided for the child.

Criteria

(4) Where,

    (a) the court is of the opinion that there is a difference of views between the child and a parent or a society, and the society proposes that the child be removed from a person's care or be made a society or Crown ward under paragraph 2 or 3 of subsection 57 (1);

    (b) the child is in the society's care and,

        (i) no parent appears before the court, or

        (ii) it is alleged that the child is in need of protection within the meaning of clause 37 (2) (a), (c), (f), (f.1) or (h); or

    (c) the child is not permitted to be present at the hearing,

legal representation shall be deemed to be desirable to protect the child's interests, unless the court is satisfied, taking into account the child's views and wishes if they can be reasonably ascertained, that the child's interests are otherwise adequately protected.

Where parent a minor

(5) Where a child's parent is less than eighteen years of age, the Children's Lawyer shall represent the parent in a proceeding under this Part unless the court orders otherwise.

Note: Despite the proclamation of the Statutes of Ontario, 1999, chapter 2, section 10, section 38 of this Act, as it read before March 31, 2000, continues to apply with respect to any proceeding under Part III, including a status review proceeding, that was commenced before March 31, 2000. See: 1999, c. 2, ss. 37 (5), 38.

Parties and Notice

Parties

39. (1) The following are parties to a proceeding under this Part:

    1. The applicant.

    2. The society having jurisdiction in the matter.

    3. The child's parent.

    4. Where the child is an Indian or a native person, a representative chosen by the child's band or native community.

Director to be added

(2) At any stage in a proceeding under this Part, the court shall add a Director as a party on his or her motion.

Right to participate

(3) Any person, including a foster parent, who has cared for the child continuously during the six months immediately before the hearing,

    (a) is entitled to the same notice of the proceeding as a party;

    (b) may be present at the hearing;

    (c) may be represented by a solicitor; and

    (d) may make submissions to the court,

but shall take no further part in the hearing without leave of the court.

Child twelve or older

(4) A child twelve years of age or more who is the subject of a proceeding under this Part is entitled to receive notice of the proceeding and to be present at the hearing, unless the court is satisfied that being present at the hearing would cause the child emotional harm and orders that the child not receive notice of the proceeding and not be permitted to be present at the hearing.

Child under twelve

(5) A child less than twelve years of age who is the subject of a proceeding under this Part is not entitled to receive

notice of the proceeding or to be present at the hearing unless the court is satisfied that the child,

(a) is capable of understanding the hearing; and

(b) will not suffer emotional harm by being present at the hearing,

and orders that the child receive notice of the proceeding and be permitted to be present at the hearing.

Child's participation

(6) A child who is the applicant under subsection 64 (4) (status review), receives notice of a proceeding under this Part or has legal representation in a proceeding is entitled to participate in the proceeding and to appeal under section 69 as if he or she were a party.

Dispensing with notice

(7) Where the court is satisfied that the time required for notice to a person might endanger the child's health or safety, the court may dispense with notice to that person.

Commencing Child Protection Proceedings

Warrants, orders, apprehension, etc.

Application

40. (1) A society may apply to the court to determine whether a child is in need of protection.

Warrant to apprehend child

(2) A justice of the peace may issue a warrant authorizing a child protection worker to bring a child to a place of safety if the justice of the peace is satisfied on the basis of a child protection worker's sworn information that there are reasonable and probable grounds to believe that,

(a) the child is in need of protection; and

(b) a less restrictive course of action is not available or will not protect the child adequately.

Idem

(3) A justice of the peace shall not refuse to issue a warrant under subsection (2) by reason only that the child protection worker may bring the child to a place of safety under subsection (7).

Order to produce or apprehend child

(4) Where the court is satisfied, on a person's application upon notice to a society, that there are reasonable and probable grounds to believe that,

(a) a child is in need of protection, the matter has been reported to the society, the society has not made an application under subsection (1), and no child protection worker has sought a warrant under subsection (2) or apprehended the child under subsection (7); and

(b) the child cannot be protected adequately otherwise than by being brought before the court,

the court may order,

(c) that the person having charge of the child produce him or her before the court at the time and place

named in the order for a hearing under subsection 47 (1) to determine whether he or she is in need of protection; or

(d) where the court is satisfied that an order under clause (c) would not protect the child adequately, that a child protection worker employed by the society bring the child to a place of safety.

Child's name, location not required

(5) It is not necessary, in an application under subsection (1), a warrant under subsection (2) or an order made under subsection (4), to describe the child by name or to specify the premises where the child is located.

Authority to enter, etc.

(6) A child protection worker authorized to bring a child to a place of safety by a warrant issued under subsection (2) or an order made under clause (4) (d) may at any time enter any premises specified in the warrant or order, by force if necessary, and may search for and remove the child.

Apprehension without warrant

(7) A child protection worker who believes on reasonable and probable grounds that,

(a) a child is in need of protection; and

(b) there would be a substantial risk to the child's health or safety during the time necessary to bring the matter on for a hearing under subsection 47 (1) or obtain a warrant under subsection (2),

may without a warrant bring the child to a place of safety.

Police assistance

(8) A child protection worker acting under this section may call for the assistance of a peace officer.

Consent to examine child

(9) A child protection worker acting under subsection (7) or under a warrant issued under subsection (2) or an order made under clause (4) (d) may authorize the child's medical examination where a parent's consent would otherwise be required.

Place of open temporary detention

(10) Where a child protection worker who brings a child to a place of safety under this section believes on reasonable and probable grounds that no less restrictive course of action is feasible, the child may be detained in a place of safety that is a place of open temporary detention as defined in Part IV (Young Offenders).

Right of entry, etc.

(11) A child protection worker who believes on reasonable and probable grounds that a child referred to in subsection (7) is on any premises may without a warrant enter the premises, by force, if necessary, and search for and remove the child.

Regulations re power of entry
(12) A child protection worker authorized to enter premises under subsection (6) or (11) shall exercise the power of entry in accordance with the regulations.

Peace officer has powers of child protection worker
(13) Subsections (2), (6), (7), (10), (11) and (12) apply to a peace officer as if the peace officer were a child protection worker.

Protection from personal liability
(14) No action shall be instituted against a peace officer or child protection worker for any act done in good faith in the execution or intended execution of that person's duty under this section or for an alleged neglect or default in the execution in good faith of that duty.

Special Cases of Apprehension of Children

Apprehension of children in care

Warrant to apprehend child in care
41. (1) A justice of the peace may issue a warrant authorizing a peace officer or child protection worker to bring a child to a place of safety if the justice of the peace is satisfied on the basis of a peace officer's or child protection worker's sworn information that,
   (a) the child is actually or apparently under the age of sixteen years and has left or been removed from a society's lawful care and custody without its consent; and
   (b) there are reasonable and probable grounds to believe that there is no course of action available other than bringing the child to a place of safety that would adequately protect the child.

Idem
(2) A justice of the peace shall not refuse to issue a warrant to a person under subsection (1) by reason only that the person may bring the child to a place of safety under subsection (4).

No need to specify premises
(3) It is not necessary in a warrant under subsection (1) to specify the premises where the child is located.

Apprehension of child in care without warrant
(4) A peace officer or child protection worker who believes on reasonable and probable grounds that,
   (a) a child is actually or apparently under the age of sixteen years and has left or been removed from a society's lawful care and custody without its consent; and
   (b) there would be a substantial risk to the child's health or safety during the time necessary to obtain a warrant under subsection (1),
may without a warrant bring the child to a place of safety.

Apprehension of child absent from place of open temporary detention
(5) Where a child is detained under this Part in a place of safety that has been designated as a place of open temporary detention as defined in Part IV (Young Offenders) and leaves the place without the consent of,
   (a) the society having care, custody and control of the child; or
   (b) the person in charge of the place of safety,
a peace officer, the person in charge of the place of safety or that person's delegate may apprehend the child without a warrant.

Idem
(6) A person who apprehends a child under subsection (5) shall,
   (a) take the child to a place of safety to be detained until the child can be returned to the place of safety the child left; or
   (b) return the child or arrange for the child to be returned to the place of safety the child left.

Apprehension of child under twelve

42. (1) A peace officer who believes on reasonable and probable grounds that a child actually or apparently under twelve years of age has committed an act in respect of which a person twelve years of age or older could be found guilty of an offence may apprehend the child without a warrant and on doing so,
   (a) shall return the child to the child's parent or other person having charge of the child as soon as practicable; or
   (b) where it is not possible to return the child to the parent or other person within a reasonable time, shall take the child to a place of safety to be detained there until the child can be returned to the parent or other person.

Notice to parent, etc.
(2) The person in charge of a place of safety in which a child is detained under subsection (1) shall make reasonable efforts to notify the child's parent or other person having charge of the child of the child's detention so that the child may be returned to the parent or other person.

Where child not returned to parent, etc., within twelve hours
(3) Where a child detained in a place of safety under subsection (1) cannot be returned to the child's parent or other person having charge of the child within twelve hours of being taken to the place of safety, the child shall be dealt with as if the child had been taken to a place of safety under subsection 40 (7) and not apprehended under subsection (1).

Runaways

43. (1) In this section,

"parent" includes,

    (a)   an approved agency that has custody of the child,

    (b)   a person who has care and control of the child.

Warrant to apprehend runaway child

(2)   A justice of the peace may issue a warrant authorizing a peace officer or child protection worker to apprehend a child if the justice of the peace is satisfied on the basis of the sworn information of a parent of the child that,

    (a)   the child is under the age of sixteen years;

    (b)   the child has withdrawn from the parent's care and control without the parent's consent; and

    (c)   the parent believes on reasonable and probable grounds that the child's health or safety may be at risk if the child is not apprehended.

Idem

(3)   A person who apprehends a child under subsection (2) shall return the child to the child's parent as soon as practicable and where it is not possible to return the child to the parent within a reasonable time, take the child to a place of safety.

Notice to parent, etc.

(4)   The person in charge of a place of safety to which a child is taken under subsection (3) shall make reasonable efforts to notify the child's parent that the child is in the place of safety so that the child may be returned to the parent.

Where child not returned to parent within twelve hours

(5)   Where a child taken to a place of safety under subsection (3) cannot be returned to the child's parent within twelve hours of being taken to the place of safety, the child shall be dealt with as if the child had been taken to a place of safety under subsection 40 (2) and not apprehended under subsection (2).

Where custody enforcement proceedings more appropriate

(6)   A justice of the peace shall not issue a warrant under subsection (2) where a child has withdrawn from the care and control of one parent with the consent of another parent under circumstances where a proceeding under section 36 of the Children's Law Reform Act would be more appropriate.

No need to specify premises

(7)   It is not necessary in a warrant under subsection (2) to specify the premises where the child is located.

Child protection proceedings

(8)   Where a peace officer or child protection worker believes on reasonable and probable grounds that a child apprehended under this section is in need of protection and there may be a substantial risk to the health or safety of the child if the child were returned to the parent,

    (a)   the peace officer or child protection worker may take the child to a place of safety under subsection 40 (7); or

    (b)   where the child has been taken to a place of safety under subsection (5), the child shall be dealt with as if the child had been taken there under subsection 40 (7).

Power of Entry and Other Provisions for Special Cases of Apprehension

Authority to enter, etc.

44. (1)   A person authorized to bring a child to a place of safety by a warrant issued under subsection 41 (1) or 43 (2) may at any time enter any premises specified in the warrant, by force, if necessary, and may search for and remove the child.

Right of entry, etc.

(2)   A person authorized under subsection 41 (4) or (5) or 42 (1) who believes on reasonable and probable grounds that a child referred to in the relevant subsection is on any premises may without a warrant enter the premises, by force, if necessary, and search for and remove the child.

Regulations re power of entry

(3)   A person authorized to enter premises under this section shall exercise the power of entry in accordance with the regulations.

Police assistance

(4)   A child protection worker acting under section 41 or 43 may call for the assistance of a peace officer.

Consent to examine child

(5)   A child protection worker who deals with a child under subsection 42 (3) or 43 (5) as if the child had been taken to a place of safety may authorize the child's medical examination where a parent's consent would otherwise be required.

Place of open temporary detention

(6)   Where a person who brings a child to a place of safety under section 41 or 42 believes on reasonable and probable grounds that no less restrictive course of action is feasible, the child may be detained in a place of safety that is a place of open temporary detention as defined in Part IV (Young Offenders).

Protection from personal liability

(7)   No action shall be instituted against a peace officer or child protection worker for any act done in good faith in the execution or intended execution of that person's duty under this section or section 41, 42 or 43 or for an alleged neglect or default in the execution in good faith of that duty.

Hearings and Orders

Rules re hearings

45. (1) In this section,

"media" means the press, radio and television media.

Application
(2) This section applies to hearings held under this Part, except hearings under section 76 (child abuse register).

> **Note: On a day to be named by proclamation of the Lieutenant Governor, subsection (2) is repealed by the Statutes of Ontario, 1999, chapter 2, section 11 and the following substituted:**

Application
(2) This section applies to hearings held under this Part.

> **See: 1999, c. 2, ss. 11, 38.**

Hearings separate from criminal proceedings
(3) A hearing shall be held separately from hearings in criminal proceedings.

Hearings private unless court orders otherwise
(4) A hearing shall be held in the absence of the public, subject to subsection (5), unless the court, after considering,

   (a) the wishes and interests of the parties; and

   (b) whether the presence of the public would cause emotional harm to a child who is a witness at or a participant in the hearing or is the subject of the proceeding,

orders that the hearing be held in public.

Media representatives
(5) Media representatives chosen in accordance with subsection (6) may be present at a hearing that is held in the absence of the public, unless the court makes an order excluding them under subsection (7).

Idem
(6) The media representatives who may be present at a hearing that is held in the absence of the public shall be chosen as follows:

   1. The media representatives in attendance shall choose not more than two persons from among themselves.

   2. Where the media representatives in attendance are unable to agree on a choice of persons, the court may choose not more than two media representatives who may be present at the hearing.

   3. The court may permit additional media representatives to be present at the hearing.

Order excluding media representatives or prohibiting publication
(7) The court may make an order,

   (a) excluding a particular media representative from all or part of a hearing;

   (b) excluding all media representatives from all or a part of a hearing; or

   (c) prohibiting the publication of a report of the hearing or a specified part of the hearing,

where the court is of the opinion that the presence of the media representative or representatives or the publication of the report, as the case may be, would cause emotional harm to a child who is a witness at or a participant in the hearing or is the subject of the proceeding.

Prohibition: identifying child
(8) No person shall publish or make public information that has the effect of identifying a child who is a witness at or a participant in a hearing or the subject of a proceeding, or the child's parent or foster parent or a member of the child's family.

Idem: order re adult
(9) The court may make an order prohibiting the publication of information that has the effect of identifying a person charged with an offence under this Part.

Transcript
(10) No person except a party or a party's solicitor shall be given a copy of a transcript of the hearing, unless the court orders otherwise.

Time of detention limited

46. (1) As soon as practicable, but in any event within five days after a child is brought to a place of safety under section 40 or subsection 79 (6) or a homemaker remains or is placed on premises under subsection 78 (2),

   (a) the matter shall be brought before a court for a hearing under subsection 47 (1) (child protection hearing);

   (b) the child shall be returned to the person who last had charge of the child or, where there is an order for the child's custody that is enforceable in Ontario, to the person entitled to custody under the order; or

   (c) a temporary care agreement shall be made under subsection 29 (1) of Part II (Voluntary Access to Services).

Idem: place of open temporary detention
(2) Within twenty-four hours after a child is brought to a place of safety that is a place of open temporary detention, or as soon thereafter as is practicable, the matter shall be brought before a court for a hearing and the court shall,

   (a) where it is satisfied that no less restrictive course of action is feasible, order that the child remain in the place of open temporary detention for a period or periods not exceeding an aggregate of thirty days and then be returned to the care and custody of the society;

   (b) order that the child be discharged from the place of open temporary detention and returned to the care and custody of the society; or

(c) make an order under subsection 51 (2) (temporary care and custody).

Child protection hearing

47. (1) Where an application is made under subsection 40 (1) or a matter is brought before the court to determine whether the child is in need of protection, the court shall hold a hearing to determine the issue and make an order under section 57.

Child's name, age, etc.

(2) As soon as practicable, and in any event before determining whether a child is in need of protection, the court shall determine,

   (a) the child's name and age;
   (b) the religious faith, if any, in which the child is being raised;
   (c) whether the child is an Indian or a native person and, if so, the child's band or native community; and
   (d) where the child was brought to a place of safety before the hearing, the location of the place from which the child was removed.

Where sixteenth birthday intervenes

(3) Despite anything else in this Part, where the child was under the age of sixteen years when the proceeding was commenced or when the child was apprehended, the court may hear and determine the matter and make an order under this Part as if the child were still under the age of sixteen years.

Territorial jurisdiction

48. (1) In this section,

"territorial jurisdiction" means a society's territorial jurisdiction under subsection 15 (2).

Place of hearing

(2) A hearing under this Part with respect to a child shall be held in the territorial jurisdiction in which the child ordinarily resides, except that,

   (a) where the child is brought to a place of safety before the hearing, the hearing shall be held in the territorial jurisdiction in which the place from which the child was removed is located;
   (b) where the child is in a society's care under an order for society or Crown wardship under section 57, the hearing shall be held in the society's territorial jurisdiction; and
   (c) where the child is the subject of an order for society supervision under section 57, the hearing may be held in the society's territorial jurisdiction or in the territorial jurisdiction in which the parent or other person with whom the child is placed resides.

Transfer of proceeding

(3) Where the court is satisfied at any stage of a proceeding under this Part that there is a preponderance of convenience in favour of conducting it in another territorial jurisdiction, the court may order that the proceeding be transferred to that other territorial jurisdiction and be continued as if it had been commenced there.

Orders affecting society

(4) The court shall not make an order placing a child in the care or under the supervision of a society unless the place where the court sits is within the society's territorial jurisdiction.

Power of court

49. The court may, on its own initiative, summon a person to attend before it, testify and produce any document or thing, and may enforce obedience to the summons as if it had been made in a proceeding under the *Family Law Act*.

Evidence

Past conduct toward children

50. (1) Despite anything in the *Evidence Act*, in any proceeding under this Part,

   (a) the court may consider the past conduct of a person toward any child if that person is caring for or has access to or may care for or have access to a child who is the subject of the proceeding; and
   (b) any oral or written statement or report that the court considers relevant to the proceeding, including a transcript, exhibit or finding or the reasons for a decision in an earlier civil or criminal proceeding, is admissible into evidence.

Evidence re disposition not admissible before finding

(2) In a hearing under subsection 47 (1), evidence relating only to the disposition of the matter shall not be admitted before the court has determined that the child is in need of protection.

> **Note: Despite the proclamation of the Statutes of Ontario, 1999, chapter 2, section 12, section 50 of this Act, as it read before March 31, 2000, continues to apply with respect to any proceeding under Part III, including a status review proceeding, that was commenced before March 31, 2000. See: 1999, c. 2, ss. 37 (5), 38.**

Adjournments

51. (1) The court shall not adjourn a hearing for more than thirty days,

   (a) unless all the parties present and the person who will be caring for the child during the adjournment consent; or
   (b) if the court is aware that a party who is not present at the hearing objects to the longer adjournment.

Custody during adjournment

(2) Where a hearing is adjourned, the court shall make a temporary order for care and custody providing that the child,

(a) remain in or be returned to the care and custody of the person who had charge of the child immediately before intervention under this Part;

(b) remain in or be returned to the care and custody of the person referred to in clause (a), subject to the society's supervision and on such reasonable terms and conditions relating to the child's supervision as the court considers appropriate;

(c) be placed in the care and custody of a person other than the person referred to in clause (a), with the consent of that other person, subject to the society's supervision and on such reasonable terms and conditions relating to the child's supervision as the court considers appropriate; or

(d) remain or be placed in the care and custody of the society, but not be placed in,

(i) a place of secure custody as defined in Part IV (Young Offenders), or

(ii) a place of open temporary detention as defined in that Part that has not been designated as a place of safety.

Criteria

(3) The court shall not make an order under clause (2) (c) or (d) unless the court is satisfied that there are reasonable grounds to believe that there is a risk that the child is likely to suffer harm and that the child cannot be protected adequately by an order under clause (2) (a) or (b).

Application of s. 62

(4) Where the court makes an order under clause (2) (d), section 62 (parental consents) applies with necessary modifications.

Access

(5) An order made under clause (2) (c) or (d) may contain provisions regarding any person's right of access to the child on such terms and conditions as the court considers appropriate.

Power to vary

(6) The court may at any time vary or terminate an order made under subsection (2).

Evidence on adjournments

(7) For the purpose of this section, the court may admit and act on evidence that the court considers credible and trustworthy in the circumstances.

Note: Despite the proclamation of the Statutes of Ontario, 1999, chapter 2, section 13, section 51 of this Act, as it read before March 31, 2000, continues to apply with respect to any proceeding under Part III, including a status review proceeding, that was commenced before March 31, 2000. See: 1999, c. 2, ss. 37 (5), 38.

Delay: court to fix date

52. Where an application is made under subsection 40 (1) or a matter is brought before the court to determine whether a child is in need of protection and the determination has not been made within three months after the commencement of the proceeding, the court,

(a) shall by order fix a date for the hearing of the application, and the date may be the earliest date that is compatible with the just disposition of the application; and

(b) may give such directions and make such orders with respect to the proceeding as are just.

Reasons, etc.

53. (1) Where the court makes an order under this Part, the court shall give,

(a) a statement of any terms or conditions imposed on the order;

(b) a statement of every plan for the child's care proposed to the court;

(c) a statement of the plan for the child's care that the court is applying in its decision; and

(d) reasons for its decision, including,

(i) a brief statement of the evidence on which the court bases its decision, and

(ii) where the order has the effect of removing or keeping the child from the care of the person who had charge of the child immediately before intervention under this Part, a statement of the reasons why the child cannot be adequately protected while in the person's care.

Idem

(2) Clause (1) (b) does not require the court to identify a person with whom or a place where it is proposed that a child be placed for care and supervision.

Assessments

Order for assessment

54. (1) Where a child has been found to be in need of protection, the court may order that within a specified time,

(a) the child; or

(b) a parent or a person, except a foster parent, in whose charge the child has been or may be,

attend before and undergo an assessment by a specified person who is qualified, in the court's opinion, to perform medical, emotional, developmental, psychological, educational or social assessments and has consented to perform the assessment.

Report

(2) The person performing an assessment under subsection (1) shall make a written report of the assessment to the court within the time specified in the order, which shall not be more than thirty days unless the court is of the opinion that a longer assessment period is necessary.

Copies of report

(3) At least seven days before the court considers the report at a hearing, the court or, where the assessment was requested by a party, that party, shall provide a copy of the report to,

(a) the person assessed, subject to subsections (4) and (5);

(b) the child's solicitor or agent of record;

(c) a parent appearing at the hearing, or the parent's solicitor of record;

(d) the society caring for or supervising the child;

(e) a Director, where he or she requests a copy;

(f) where the child is an Indian or a native person, a representative chosen by the child's band or native community; and

(g) any other person who, in the opinion of the court, should receive a copy of the report for the purposes of the case.

Child under twelve

(4) Where the person assessed is a child less than twelve years of age, the child shall not receive a copy of the report unless the court considers it desirable that the child receive a copy of the report.

Child twelve or older

(5) Where the person assessed is a child twelve years of age or more, the child shall receive a copy of the report, except that where the court is satisfied that disclosure of all or part of the report to the child would cause the child emotional harm, the court may withhold all or part of the report from the child.

Conflict

(5.1) Subsections (4) and (5) prevail despite anything in the *Personal Health Information Protection Act, 2004.*

Assessment is evidence

(6) The report of an assessment ordered under subsection (1) is evidence and is part of the court record of the proceeding.

Inference from refusal

(7) The court may draw any inference it considers reasonable from a person's refusal to undergo an assessment ordered under subsection (1).

Report inadmissible

(8) The report of an assessment ordered under subsection (1) is not admissible into evidence in any other proceeding except,

(a) a proceeding under this Part, including an appeal under section 69;

(b) a proceeding referred to in section 81; or

(c) a proceeding under the *Coroners Act,*

without the consent of the person or persons assessed.

Note: Despite the proclamation of the Statutes of Ontario, 1999, chapter 2, section 14, section 54 of this Act,
as it read before March 31, 2000, continues to apply with respect to any proceeding under Part III, including a status review proceeding, that was commenced before March 31, 2000. See: 1999, c. 2, ss. 37 (5), 38.

Consent order: special requirements

55. Where a child is brought before the court on consent as described in clause 37 (2) (l), the court shall, before making an order under section 57 that would remove the child from the parent's care and custody,

(a) ask whether,

(i) the society has offered the parent and child services that would enable the child to remain with the parent, and

(ii) the parent and, where the child is twelve years of age or older, the child has consulted independent legal counsel in connection with the consent; and

(b) be satisfied that,

(i) the parent and, where the child is twelve years of age or older, the child understands the nature and consequences of the consent,

(ii) every consent is voluntary, and

(iii) the parent and, where the child is twelve years of age or older, the child consents to the order being sought.

Society's plan for child

56. The court shall, before making an order under section 57 or 65, obtain and consider a plan for the child's care prepared in writing by the society and including,

(a) a description of the services to be provided to remedy the condition or situation on the basis of which the child was found to be in need of protection;

(b) a statement of the criteria by which the society will determine when its wardship or supervision is no longer required;

(c) an estimate of the time required to achieve the purpose of the society's intervention;

(d) where the society proposes to remove or has removed the child from a person's care,

(i) an explanation of why the child cannot be adequately protected while in the person's care, and a description of any past efforts to do so, and

(ii) a statement of what efforts, if any, are planned to maintain the child's contact with the person; and

(e) where the society proposes to remove or has removed the child from a person's care permanently, a description of the arrangements made or being made for the child's long-term stable placement.

Order where child in need of protection

57. (1) Where the court finds that a child is in need of protection and is satisfied that intervention through a court order is necessary to protect the child in the future, the court shall make one of the following orders, in the child's best interests:

Supervision order
1. That the child be placed with or returned to a parent or another person, subject to the supervision of the society, for a specified period of at least three and not more than twelve months.

Society wardship
2. That the child be made a ward of the society and be placed in its care and custody for a specified period not exceeding twelve months.

Crown wardship
3. That the child be made a ward of the Crown, until the wardship is terminated under section 65 or expires under subsection 71 (1), and be placed in the care of the society.

Consecutive orders of society wardship and supervision
4. That the child be made a ward of the society under paragraph 2 for a specified period and then be returned to a parent or another person under paragraph 1, for a period or periods not exceeding an aggregate of twelve months.

Court to inquire
(2) In determining which order to make under subsection (1), the court shall ask the parties what efforts the society or another agency or person made to assist the child before intervention under this Part.

Less disruptive alternatives preferred
(3) The court shall not make an order removing the child from the care of the person who had charge of him or her immediately before intervention under this Part unless the court is satisfied that alternatives that are less disruptive to the child, including non-residential services and the assistance referred to in subsection (2), would be inadequate to protect the child.

Community placement to be considered
(4) Where the court decides that it is necessary to remove the child from the care of the person who had charge of him or her immediately before intervention under this Part, the court shall, before making an order for society or Crown wardship under paragraph 2 or 3 of subsection (1), consider whether it is possible to place the child with a relative, neighbour or other member of the child's community or extended family under paragraph 1 of subsection (1) with the consent of the relative or other person.

Idem: where child an Indian or a native person
(5) Where the child referred to in subsection (4) is an Indian or a native person, unless there is a substantial reason for placing the child elsewhere, the court shall place the child with,
   (a) a member of the child's extended family;
   (b) a member of the child's band or native community; or
   (c) another Indian or native family.
(6) REPEALED.

Idem
(7) When the court has dispensed with notice to a person under subsection 39 (7), the court shall not make an order for Crown wardship under paragraph 3 of subsection (1), or an order for society wardship under paragraph 2 of subsection (1) for a period exceeding thirty days, until a further hearing under subsection 47 (1) has been held upon notice to that person.

Terms and conditions of supervision order
(8) Where the court makes a supervision order under paragraph 1 of subsection (1), the court may impose reasonable terms and conditions relating to the child's care and supervision on,
   (a) the person with whom the child is placed or to whom the child is returned;
   (b) the supervising society;
   (c) the child; and
   (d) any other person who participated in the hearing.

Where no court order necessary
(9) Where the court finds that a child is in need of protection but is not satisfied that a court order is necessary to protect the child in the future, the court shall order that the child remain with or be returned to the person who had charge of the child immediately before intervention under this Part.

> **Note: Despite the proclamation of the Statutes of Ontario, 1999, chapter 2, section 15, section 57 of this Act, as it read before March 31, 2000, continues to apply with respect to any proceeding under Part III, including a status review proceeding, that was commenced before March 31, 2000. See: 1999, c. 2, ss. 37 (5), 38.**

Access

Access order

58. (1) The court may, in the child's best interests,
   (a) when making an order under this Part; or
   (b) upon an application under subsection (2),
make, vary or terminate an order respecting a person's access to the child or the child's access to a person, and may impose such terms and conditions on the order as the court considers appropriate.

Who may apply
(2) Where a child is in a society's care and custody or supervision,
   (a) the child;

(b)   any other person, including, where the child is an Indian or a native person, a representative chosen by the child's band or native community; or

(c)   the society,

may apply to the court at any time for an order under subsection (1).

Notice

(3)   An applicant referred to in clause (2) (b) shall give notice of the application to the society.

Idem

(4)   A society making or receiving an application under subsection (2) shall give notice of the application to,

(a)   the child, subject to subsections 39 (4) and (5) (notice to child);

(b)   the child's parent;

(c)   the person caring for the child at the time of the application; and

(d)   where the child is an Indian or a native person, a representative chosen by the child's band or native community.

Child over sixteen

(5)   No order respecting access to a person sixteen years of age or more shall be made under subsection (1) without the person's consent.

Six-month period

(6)   No application shall be made under subsection (2) by a person other than a society within six months of,

(a)   the making of an order under section 57;

(b)   the disposition of a previous application by the same person under subsection (2);

(c)   the disposition of an application under section 64 (review); or

(d)   the final disposition or abandonment of an appeal from an order referred to in clause (a), (b) or (c),

whichever is later.

No application where child placed for adoption

(7)   No person or society shall make an application under subsection (2) where the child,

(a)   is a Crown ward;

(b)   has been placed in a person's home by the society or by a Director for the purpose of adoption under Part VII (Adoption); and

(c)   still resides in that person's home.

Access: where child removed from person in charge

59. (1)   Where an order is made under paragraph 1 or 2 of subsection 57 (1) removing a child from the person who had charge of the child immediately before intervention under this Part, the court shall make an order for access by the person unless the court is satisfied that continued contact with him or her would not be in the child's best interests.

Access: Crown ward

(2)   The court shall not make or vary an access order with respect to a Crown ward under section 58 (access) or section 65 (status review) unless the court is satisfied that,

(a)   the relationship between the person and the child is beneficial and meaningful to the child; and

(b)   the ordered access will not impair the child's future opportunities for a permanent or stable placement.

Termination of access: Crown ward

(3)   The court shall terminate an access order with respect to a Crown ward if,

(a)   the order is no longer in the best interests of the child; or

(b)   the court is no longer satisfied that clauses (2) (a) and (b) apply with respect to that access.

> **Note: Despite the proclamation of the Statutes of Ontario, 1999, chapter 2, section 16, section 59 of this Act, as it read before March 31, 2000, continues to apply with respect to any proceeding under Part III, including a status review proceeding, that was commenced before March 31, 2000. See: 1999, c. 2, ss. 37 (5), 38.**

Payment Orders

Order for payment by parent

60. (1)   Where the court places a child in the care of,

(a)   a society; or

(b)   a person other than the child's parent, subject to a society's supervision,

the court may order a parent or a parent's estate to pay the society a specified amount at specified intervals for each day the child is in the society's care or supervision.

Criteria

(2)   In making an order under subsection (1), the court shall consider those of the following circumstances of the case that the court considers relevant:

1.   The assets and means of the child and of the parent or the parent's estate.

2.   The child's capacity to provide for his or her own support.

3.   The capacity of the parent or the parent's estate to provide support.

4.   The child's and the parent's age and physical and mental health.

5.   The child's mental, emotional and physical needs.

6.   Any legal obligation of the parent or the parent's estate to provide support for another person.

7.   The child's aptitude for and reasonable prospects of obtaining an education.

8.   Any legal right of the child to support from another source, other than out of public money.

Order ends at eighteen
(3) No order made under subsection (1) shall extend beyond the day on which the child attains the age of eighteen years.

Power to vary
(4) The court may vary, suspend or terminate an order made under subsection (1) where the court is satisfied that the circumstances of the child or parent have changed.

Collection by municipality
(5) The council of a municipality may enter into an agreement with the board of directors of a society providing for the collection by the municipality, on the society's behalf, of the amounts ordered to be paid by a parent under subsection (1).

Enforcement
(6) An order made against a parent under subsection (1) may be enforced as if it were an order for support made under Part III of the *Family Law Act*.

Society and Crown Wardship

Placement of wards

61. (1) This section applies where a child is made a society or Crown ward under paragraph 2 or 3 of subsection 57 (1).

Placement
(2) The society having care of a child shall choose a residential placement for the child that,
   (a) represents the least restrictive alternative for the child;
   (b) where possible, respects the religious faith, if any, in which the child is being raised;
   (c) where possible, respects the child's linguistic and cultural heritage;
   (d) where the child is an Indian or a native person, is with a member of the child's extended family, a member of the child's band or native community or another Indian or native family, if possible; and
   (e) takes into account the child's wishes, if they can be reasonably ascertained, and the wishes of any parent who is entitled to access to the child.

Education
(3) The society having care of a child shall ensure that the child receives an education that corresponds to his or her aptitudes and abilities.

Placement outside or removal from Ontario
(4) The society having care of a child shall not place the child outside Ontario or permit a person to remove the child from Ontario permanently unless a Director is satisfied that extraordinary circumstances justify the placement or removal.

Rights of child, parent and foster parent
(5) The society having care of a child shall ensure that,
   (a) the child is afforded all the rights referred to in Part V (Rights of Children); and
   (b) the wishes of any parent who is entitled to access to the child and, where the child is a Crown ward, of any foster parent with whom the child has lived continuously for two years are taken into account in the society's major decisions concerning the child.

Change of placement
(6) The society having care of a child may remove the child from a foster home or other residential placement where, in the opinion of a Director or local director, it is in the child's best interests to do so.

Rights of foster parents in certain cases
(7) Where a child is a Crown ward and has lived with a foster parent continuously for two years, the society shall not remove the child under subsection (6) without first giving the foster parent ten days notice of the proposed removal and of his or her right to a review under section 68.

Time for review
(8) Where a foster parent requests a review under section 68 within ten days of receiving a notice under subsection (7), the society shall not remove the child until the review and any further review by a Director have been completed and unless the society's board of directors or the Director, as the case may be, recommend that the child be removed.

Exception where child at risk
(9) Subsections (7) and (8) do not apply where, in the opinion of a Director or local director, there would be a risk that the child is likely to suffer harm during the time necessary for notice to the foster parent and a review under section 68.

Review of certain placements
(10) Sections 34, 35 and 36 (review by Residential Placement Advisory Committee, further review by Children's Services Review Board) of Part II (Voluntary Access to Services) apply to a residential placement made by a society.

Society wards — medical treatment and marriage

Society ward: consent to medical treatment
62. (1) Where a child is made a society ward under paragraph 2 of subsection 57 (1), the society may consent to and authorize medical treatment for the child where a parent's consent would otherwise be required, unless the court orders that the parent shall retain any right that he or she may have to give or refuse consent to medical treatment for the child.

Idem

(2) The court shall not make an order under subsection (1) where failure to consent to necessary medical treatment was a ground for finding that the child was in need of protection.

Court order

(3) Where a parent referred to in an order made under subsection (1) refuses or is unavailable or unable to consent to medical treatment for the child and the court is satisfied that the treatment would be in the child's best interests, the court may authorize the society to consent to the treatment.

Consent to child's marriage

(4) Where a child is made a society ward under paragraph 2 of subsection 57 (1), the child's parent retains any right that he or she may have under the *Marriage Act* to give or refuse consent to the child's marriage.

Custodianship of wards

Crown custodian of Crown wards

63. (1) Where a child is made a Crown ward under paragraph 3 of subsection 57 (1), the Crown has the rights and responsibilities of a parent for the purpose of the child's care, custody and control and has the right to give or refuse consent to medical treatment for the child where a parent's consent would otherwise be required, and the Crown's powers, duties and obligations in respect of the child, except those assigned to a Director by this Act or the regulations, shall be exercised and performed by the society caring for the child.

Society custodian of society wards

(2) Where a child is made a society ward under paragraph 2 of subsection 57 (1), the society has the rights and responsibilities of a parent for the purpose of the child's care, custody and control.

Review

Status review

64. (1) This section applies where a child is the subject of an order for society supervision, society wardship or Crown wardship under subsection 57 (1).

Society to seek status review

(2) The society having care, custody or supervision of a child,

    (a) may apply to the court at any time, subject to subsection (9);

    (b) where the order is for society supervision or society wardship, shall apply to the court before the expiry of the order, except under subsection 71 (1) (age of eighteen); and

    (c) where the society has removed the child from the care of a person with whom the child was placed under an order for society supervision, shall apply to the court within five days of the child's removal,

for review of the child's status.

Application of subs. (2) (a, c)

(3) Where a child is the subject of an order for society supervision under subsection 57 (1), clauses (2) (a) and (c) also apply to the society that has jurisdiction in the county or district in which the parent or other person with whom the child is placed resides.

Others may seek status review

(4) An application for review of a child's status may be made on notice to the society by,

    (a) the child, where the child is at least twelve years of age;

    (b) any parent of the child, subject to subsection (5);

    (c) the person with whom the child was placed under an order for society supervision; or

    (d) where the child is an Indian or a native person, a representative chosen by the child's band or native community.

Leave required in certain cases

(5) Where the child is a Crown ward and has lived with the same foster parent continuously during the two years immediately before the application, an application under subsection (4) shall not be made by any parent of the child without the court's leave.

Notice

(6) A society making an application under subsection (2) or receiving notice of an application under subsection (4) shall give notice of the application to,

    (a) the child, subject to subsections 39 (4) and (5) (notice to child);

    (b) the child's parent, unless the child is a Crown ward and is sixteen years of age or older;

    (c) the person with whom the child was placed under an order for society supervision;

    (d) a foster parent who has cared for the child continuously during the six months immediately before the application;

    (e) where the child is an Indian or a native person, a representative chosen by the child's band or native community; and

    (f) a Director, if the child is a Crown ward.

Six-month period

(7) No application shall be made under subsection (4) within six months of,

    (a) the making of the original order under subsection 57 (1);

    (b) the disposition of a previous application by any person under subsection (4); or

    (c) the final disposition or abandonment of an appeal from an order referred to in clause (a) or (b),

whichever is the latest.

Exception

(8) Subsection (7) does not apply where,

    (a) the child is a society ward or the subject of an order for society supervision, or the child is a Crown ward and an order for access has been made under section 58; and

    (b) the court is satisfied that a major element of the plan for the child's care that the court applied in its decision is not being carried out.

No review where child placed for adoption

(9) No person or society shall make an application under this section where the child,

    (a) is a Crown ward;

    (b) has been placed in a person's home by the society or by a Director for the purpose of adoption under Part VII; and

    (c) still resides in that person's home.

Interim care and custody

(10) Where an application is made under this section, the child shall remain in the care and custody of the person or society having charge of the child, until the application is disposed of, unless the court is satisfied that the child's best interests require a change in the child's care and custody.

Court may vary, etc.

65. (1) Where an application for review of a child's status is made under section 64, the court may, in the child's best interests,

    (a) vary or terminate the original order made under subsection 57 (1), including a term or condition or a provision for access that is part of the order;

    (b) order that the original order terminate on a specified future date; or

    (c) make a further order or orders under section 57.

Restriction

(2) Where a child has been made a Crown ward under paragraph 3 of subsection 57 (1), the court shall not make an order for society wardship under subsection (1).

(3) Repealed.

> Note: Despite the proclamation of the Statutes of Ontario, 1999, chapter 2, section 19, subsection (3) of this section, as it read before March 31, 2000, continues to apply with respect to any proceeding under Part III, including a status review proceeding, that was commenced before March 31, 2000. See: 1999, c. 2, ss. 37 (5), 38.

Director's annual review of Crown wards

66. (1) A Director or a person authorized by a Director shall, at least once during each calendar year, review the status of every child,

    (a) who is a Crown ward;

    (b) who was a Crown ward throughout the immediately preceding twenty-four months; and

    (c) whose status has not been reviewed under this section or under section 65 during that time.

Idem

(2) After a review under subsection (1), the Director may direct the society to make an application for review of the child's status under subsection 64 (2) or give any other direction that, in the Director's opinion, is in the child's best interests.

Investigation by judge

67. (1) The Minister may appoint a judge of the Court of Ontario to investigate a matter relating to a child in a society's care or the proper administration of this Part, and a judge who is appointed shall conduct the investigation and make a written report to the Minister.

Powers of judge

(2) For the purposes of an investigation under subsection (1), the judge has the powers of a commission under Part II of the *Public Inquiries Act*, and that Part applies to the investigation as if it were an inquiry under that Act.

Society review procedure

68. (1) A society shall establish a written review procedure, which shall be approved by a Director, for hearing and dealing with complaints by any person regarding services sought or received from the society, and shall make the review procedure available to any person on request.

Idem

(2) A review procedure established under subsection (1), shall include an opportunity for the person making the complaint to be heard by the society's board of directors.

Further review by Director

(3) A person who makes a complaint and is not satisfied with the response of the society's board of directors may have the matter reviewed by a Director.

Appeals

Appeal

69. (1) An appeal from a court's order under this Part may be made to the Superior Court of Justice by,

    (a) the child, if the child is entitled to participate in the proceeding under subsection 39 (6) (child's participation);

    (b) any parent of the child;

    (c) the person who had charge of the child immediately before intervention under this Part;

    (d) a Director or local director; or

    (e) where the child is an Indian or a native person, a representative chosen by the child's band or native community.

Exception

(2) Subsection (1) does not apply to an order for an assessment under section 54.

Care and custody pending appeal

(3) Where a decision regarding the care and custody of a child is appealed under subsection (1), execution of the decision shall be stayed for the ten days immediately following service of the notice of appeal on the court that made the decision, and where the child is in the society's custody at the time the decision is made, the child shall remain in the care and custody of the society until,

(a) the ten-day period of the stay has expired; or

(b) an order is made under subsection (4),

whichever is earlier.

Temporary order

(4) The Superior Court of Justice may, in the child's best interests, make a temporary order for the child's care and custody pending final disposition of the appeal, except an order placing the child in a place of secure custody as defined in Part IV (Young Offenders) or a place of secure temporary detention as defined in that Part that has not been designated as a place of safety, and the court may, on any party's motion before the final disposition of the appeal, vary or terminate the order or make a further order.

No extension where child placed for adoption

(5) No extension of the time for an appeal shall be granted where the child has been placed for adoption under Part VII (Adoption).

Further evidence

(6) The court may receive further evidence relating to events after the appealed decision.

Place of hearing

(7) An appeal under this section shall be heard in the county or district in which the order appealed from was made.

> **s. 45 applies**

(8) Section 45 (hearings private, etc.) applies with necessary modifications to an appeal under this section.

Expiry of Orders

Time limit

70. (1) Subject to subsections (3) and (4), the court shall not make an order for society wardship under this Part that results in a child being a society ward for a period exceeding,

(a) 12 months, if the child is less than 6 years of age on the day the court makes an order for society wardship; or

(b) 24 months, if the child is 6 years of age or older on the day the court makes an order for society wardship.

> **Note: For the purposes of subsection (1), as re-enacted by the Statutes of Ontario, 1999, chapter 2, subsection 21 (1), no period that a child was in a society's care and custody before March 31, 2000 shall be counted. See: 1999, c. 2, s. 37 (3).**

> **Note: Despite the proclamation of the Statutes of Ontario, 1999, chapter 2, subsection 21 (1), subsection (1) of this section, as it read before March 31, 2000, shall continue to apply with respect to a child who is in the care and custody of a society on March 31, 2000 so long as that child continues to be in the care and custody of a society. See: 1999, c. 2, ss. 37 (4), 38.**

Same

(2) In calculating the period referred to in subsection (1), time during which a child has been in a society's care and custody under,

(a) an agreement made under subsection 29 (1) or 30 (1) (temporary care or special needs agreement); or

(b) a temporary order made under clause 51 (2) (d),

shall be counted.

> **Note: For the purposes of subsection (2), as re-enacted by the Statutes of Ontario, 1999, chapter 2, subsection 21 (1), no period that a child was in a society's care and custody before March 31, 2000 shall be counted. See: 1999, c. 2, s. 37 (3).**

> **Note: Despite the proclamation of the Statutes of Ontario, 1999, chapter 2, subsection 21 (1), subsection (2) of this section, as it read before March 31, 2000, shall continue to apply with respect to a child who is in the care and custody of a society on March 31, 2000 so long as that child continues to be in the care and custody of a society. See: 1999, c. 2, ss. 37 (4), 38.**

Previous periods to be counted

(2.1) The period referred to in subsection (1) shall include any previous periods that the child was in a society's care and custody as a society ward or as described in subsection (2) other than periods that precede a continuous period of five or more years that the child was not in a society's care and custody.

> **Note: For the purposes of subsection (2.1), as enacted by the Statutes of Ontario, 1999, chapter 2, subsection 21 (1), no period that a child was in a society's care and custody before March 31, 2000 shall be counted. See: 1999, c. 2, s. 37 (3).**

Idem

(3) Where the period referred to in subsection (1) or (4) expires and,

(a) an appeal of an order made under subsection 57 (1) has been commenced and is not yet finally disposed of; or

(b) the court has adjourned a hearing under section 65 (status review), the period shall be deemed to be extended until the appeal has been finally disposed of and any new hearing ordered on appeal has been completed or an order has been made under section 65, as the case may be.

> **Note: Despite the proclamation of the Statutes of Ontario, 1999, chapter 2, subsection 21 (2), subsection (3) of this section, as it read before March 31, 2000, shall continue to apply with respect to a child who is in the care and custody of a society on March 31, 2000 so long as that child continues to be in the care and custody of a society. See: 1999, c. 2, ss. 37 (4), 38.**

Six-month extension
(4) Subject to paragraphs 2 and 4 of subsection 57 (1), the court may by order extend the period permitted under subsection (1) by a period not to exceed six months if it is in the child's best interests to do so.

Expiry of orders
71. (1) An order under this Part expires when the child who is the subject of the order,
    (a) attains the age of eighteen years; or
    (b) marries,
whichever comes first.

Crown ward: continuing care
(2) Where an order for Crown wardship expires under subsection (1), the society may, with a Director's approval, continue to provide care and maintenance for the former Crown ward in accordance with the regulations.

Duty to Report

Duty to report child in need of protection
72. (1) Despite the provisions of any other Act, if a person, including a person who performs professional or official duties with respect to children, has reasonable grounds to suspect one of the following, the person shall forthwith report the suspicion and the information on which it is based to a society:
1. The child has suffered physical harm, inflicted by the person having charge of the child or caused by or resulting from that person's,
    i. failure to adequately care for, provide for, supervise or protect the child, or
    ii. pattern of neglect in caring for, providing for, supervising or protecting the child.
2. There is a risk that the child is likely to suffer physical harm inflicted by the person having charge of the child or caused by or resulting from that person's,
    i. failure to adequately care for, provide for, supervise or protect the child, or
    ii. pattern of neglect in caring for, providing for, supervising or protecting the child.

3. The child has been sexually molested or sexually exploited, by the person having charge of the child or by another person where the person having charge of the child knows or should know of the possibility of sexual molestation or sexual exploitation and fails to protect the child.
4. There is a risk that the child is likely to be sexually molested or sexually exploited as described in paragraph 3.
5. The child requires medical treatment to cure, prevent or alleviate physical harm or suffering and the child's parent or the person having charge of the child does not provide, or refuses or is unavailable or unable to consent to, the treatment.
6. The child has suffered emotional harm, demonstrated by serious,
    i. anxiety,
    ii. depression,
    iii. withdrawal,
    iv. self-destructive or aggressive behaviour, or
    v. delayed development,
    and there are reasonable grounds to believe that the emotional harm suffered by the child results from the actions, failure to act or pattern of neglect on the part of the child's parent or the person having charge of the child.
7. The child has suffered emotional harm of the kind described in subparagraph i, ii, iii, iv or v of paragraph 6 and the child's parent or the person having charge of the child does not provide, or refuses or is unavailable or unable to consent to, services or treatment to remedy or alleviate the harm.
8. There is a risk that the child is likely to suffer emotional harm of the kind described in subparagraph i, ii, iii, iv or v of paragraph 6 resulting from the actions, failure to act or pattern of neglect on the part of the child's parent or the person having charge of the child.
9. There is a risk that the child is likely to suffer emotional harm of the kind described in subparagraph i, ii, iii, iv or v of paragraph 6 and that the child's parent or the person having charge of the child does not provide, or refuses or is unavailable or unable to consent to, services or treatment to prevent the harm.
10. The child suffers from a mental, emotional or developmental condition that, if not remedied, could seriously impair the child's development and the child's parent or the person having charge of the child does not provide, or refuses or is unavailable or unable to consent to, treatment to remedy or alleviate the condition.
11. The child has been abandoned, the child's parent has died or is unavailable to exercise his or her custodial rights over the child and has not made

adequate provision for the child's care and custody, or the child is in a residential placement and the parent refuses or is unable or unwilling to resume the child's care and custody.

12.   The child is less than 12 years old and has killed or seriously injured another person or caused serious damage to another person's property, services or treatment are necessary to prevent a recurrence and the child's parent or the person having charge of the child does not provide, or refuses or is unavailable or unable to consent to, those services or treatment.

13.   The child is less than 12 years old and has on more than one occasion injured another person or caused loss or damage to another person's property, with the encouragement of the person having charge of the child or because of that person's failure or inability to supervise the child adequately.

Ongoing duty to report

(2) A person who has additional reasonable grounds to suspect one of the matters set out in subsection (1) shall make a further report under subsection (1) even if he or she has made previous reports with respect to the same child.

Person must report directly

(3) A person who has a duty to report a matter under subsection (1) or (2) shall make the report directly to the society and shall not rely on any other person to report on his or her behalf.

Offence

(4) A person referred to in subsection (5) is guilty of an offence if,

(a)   he or she contravenes subsection (1) or (2) by not reporting a suspicion; and

(b)   the information on which it was based was obtained in the course of his or her professional or official duties.

Same

(5) Subsection (4) applies to every person who performs professional or official duties with respect to children including,

(a)   a health care professional, including a physician, nurse, dentist, pharmacist and psychologist;

(b)   a teacher, school principal, social worker, family counsellor, priest, rabbi, member of the clergy, operator or employee of a day nursery and youth and recreation worker;

(c)   a peace officer and a coroner;

(d)   a solicitor; and

(e)   a service provider and an employee of a service provider.

Same

(6) In clause (5) (b), "youth and recreation worker" does not include a volunteer.

Same

(6.1) A director, officer or employee of a corporation who authorizes, permits or concurs in a contravention of an offence under subsection (4) by an employee of the corporation is guilty of an offence.

Same

(6.2) A person convicted of an offence under subsection (4) or (6.1) is liable to a fine of not more than $1,000.

Section overrides privilege

(7) This section applies although the information reported may be confidential or privileged, and no action for making the report shall be instituted against a person who acts in accordance with this section unless the person acts maliciously or without reasonable grounds for the suspicion.

Exception: solicitor client privilege

(8) Nothing in this section abrogates any privilege that may exist between a solicitor and his or her client.

Conflict

(9) This section prevails despite anything in the *Personal Health Information Protection Act, 2004.*

Duty of society

72.1 (1) A society that obtains information that a child in its care and custody is or may be suffering or may have suffered abuse shall forthwith report the information to a Director.

Definition

(2) In this section and sections 73 and 75,

"to suffer abuse", when used in reference to a child, means to be in need of protection within the meaning of clause 37 (2) (a), (c), (e), (f), (f.1) or (h).

> **Note: On a day to be named by proclamation of the Lieutenant Governor, subsection 72.1 (2) is amended by the Statutes of Ontario, 1999, chapter 2, subsection 23 (2) by striking out "sections 73 and 75" and substituting "section 73". See: 1999, c. 2, ss. 23 (2), 38.**

Review Teams

Review team

73. (1) In this section,

"review team" means a team established by a society under subsection (2).

Same

(2) Every society shall establish a review team that includes,

(a) persons who are professionally qualified to perform medical, psychological, developmental, educational or social assessments; and

(b) at least one legally qualified medical practitioner.

Chair
(3) The members of a review team shall choose a chair from among themselves.

Duty of team
(4) Whenever a society refers the case of a child who may be suffering or may have suffered abuse to its review team, the review team or a panel of at least three of its members, designated by the chair, shall,

(a) review the case; and

(b) recommend to the society how the child may be protected.

Disclosure to team permitted
(5) Despite the provisions of any other Act, a person may disclose to a review team or to any of its members information reasonably required for a review under subsection (4).

Subsection overrides privilege
(6) Subsection (5) applies although the information disclosed may be confidential or privileged and no action for disclosing the information shall be instituted against a person who acts in accordance with subsection (5), unless the person acts maliciously or without reasonable grounds.

Where child not to be returned without review or hearing
(7) Where a society with a review team has information that a child placed in its care under subsection 51 (2) (temporary care and custody) or subsection 57 (1) (order where child in need of protection) may have suffered abuse, the society shall not return the child to the care of the person who had charge of the child at the time of the possible abuse unless,

(a) the society has,

(i) referred the case to its review team, and

(ii) obtained and considered the review team's recommendations; or

(b) the court has terminated the order placing the child in the society's care.

Court-Ordered Access to Records

Record
74. (1) In this section and sections 74.1 and 74.2,

"record" means recorded information, regardless of physical form or characteristics;

"record of personal health information" has the same meaning as in the *Mental Health Act.*

Motion or application, production of record
(2) A Director or a society may at any time make a motion or an application for an order under subsection (3) or (3.1) for the production of a record or part of a record.

Order
(3) Where the court is satisfied that a record or part of a record that is the subject of a motion referred to in subsection (2) contains information that may be relevant to a proceeding under this Part and that the person in possession or control of the record has refused to permit a Director or the society to inspect it, the court may order that the person in possession or control of the record produce it or a specified part of it for inspection and copying by the Director, by the society or by the court.

Same
(3.1) Where the court is satisfied that a record or part of a record that is the subject of an application referred to in subsection (2) may be relevant to assessing compliance with one of the following and that the person in possession or control of the record has refused to permit a Director or the society to inspect it, the court may order that the person in possession or control of the record produce it or a specified part of it for inspection and copying by the Director, by the society or by the court:

1. An order under clause 51 (2) (b) or (c) that is subject to supervision.

2. An order under clause 51 (2) (c) or (d) with respect to access.

3. A supervision order under section 57.

4. An access order under section 58.

5. An order under section 65 with respect to access or supervision.

6. A restraining order under section 80.

Court may examine record
(4) In considering whether to make an order under subsection (3) or (3.1), the court may examine the record.

Information confidential
(5) No person who obtains information by means of an order made under subsection (3) or (3.1) shall disclose the information except,

(a) as specified in the order; and

(b) in testimony in a proceeding under this Part.

Conflict
(5.1) Subsection (5) prevails despite anything in the *Personal Health Information Protection Act, 2004.*

Application: solicitor client privilege excepted
(6) Subject to subsection (7), this section applies despite any other Act, but nothing in this section abrogates any privilege that may exist between a solicitor and his or her client.

Matters to be considered by court

(7) Where a motion or an application under subsection (2) concerns a record of personal health information, subsection 35 (6) (attending physician's statement, hearing) of the *Mental Health Act* applies and the court shall give equal consideration to,

  (a) the matters to be considered under subsection 35 (7) of that Act; and

  (b) the need to protect the child.

Same

(8) Where a motion or an application under subsection (2) concerns a record that is a record of a mental disorder within the meaning of section 183, that section applies and the court shall give equal consideration to,

  (a) the matters to be considered under subsection 183 (6); and

  (b) the need to protect the child.

Warrant for access to record

74.1 (1) The court or a justice of the peace may issue a warrant for access to a record or a specified part of it if the court or justice of the peace is satisfied on the basis of information on oath from a Director or a person designated by a society that there are reasonable grounds to believe that the record or part of the record is relevant to investigate an allegation that a child is or may be in need of protection.

Authority conferred by warrant

(2) The warrant authorizes the Director or the person designated by the society to,

  (a) inspect the record specified in the warrant during normal business hours or during the hours specified in the warrant;

  (b) make copies from the record in any manner that does not damage the record; and

  (c) remove the record for the purpose of making copies.

Return of record

(3) A person who removes a record under clause (2) (c) shall promptly return it after copying it.

Admissibility of copies

(4) A copy of a record that is the subject of a warrant under this section and that is certified as being a true copy of the original by the person who made the copy is admissible in evidence to the same extent as and has the same evidentiary value as the record.

Duration of warrant

(5) The warrant is valid for seven days.

Execution

(6) The Director or the person designated by the society may call on a peace officer for assistance in executing the warrant.

Solicitor-client privilege

(7) This section applies despite any other Act, but nothing in this section abrogates any privilege that may exist between a solicitor and his or her client.

Matters to be considered

(8) If a warrant issued under this section concerns a record of personal health information and the warrant is challenged under subsection 35 (6) (attending physician's statement, hearing) of the *Mental Health Act*, equal consideration shall be given to,

  (a) the matters set out in subsection 35 (7) of that Act; and

  (b) the need to protect the child.

Same

(9) If a warrant issued under this section concerns a record of a mental disorder within the meaning of section 183 and the warrant is challenged under section 183, equal consideration shall be given to,

  (a) the matters set out in subsection 183 (6); and

  (b) the need to protect the child.

Telewarrant

74.2 (1) Where a Director or a person designated by a society believes that there are reasonable grounds for the issuance of a warrant under section 74.1 and that it would be impracticable to appear personally before the court or a justice of the peace to make application for a warrant in accordance with section 74.1, the Director or person designated by the society may submit an information on oath by telephone or other means of telecommunication to a justice designated for the purpose by the Chief Justice of the Ontario Court of Justice.

Same

(2) The information shall,

  (a) include a statement of the grounds to believe that the record or part of the record is relevant to investigate an allegation that a child is or may be in need of protection; and

  (b) set out the circumstances that make it impracticable for the Director or person designated by the society to appear personally before a court or justice of the peace.

Warrant to be issued

(3) The justice may issue a warrant for access to the record or the specified part of it if the justice is satisfied that the application discloses,

  (a) reasonable grounds to believe that the record or the part of a record is relevant to investigate an allegation that a child is or may be in need of protection; and

  (b) reasonable grounds to dispense with personal appearance for the purpose of an application under section 74.1.

Validity of warrant
(4) A warrant issued under this section is not subject to challenge by reason only that there were not reasonable grounds to dispense with personal appearance for the purpose of an application under section 74.1.

Application of provisions
(5) Subsections 74.1 (2) to (9) apply with necessary modifications with respect to a warrant issued under this section.

Definition
(6) In this section,
"justice" means justice of the peace, a judge of the Ontario Court of Justice or a judge of the Family Court of the Superior Court of Justice.

Child Abuse Register

Register
75. (1) In this section and in section 76,

"Director" means the person appointed under subsection (2);

"register" means the register maintained under subsection (5);

"registered person" means a person identified in the register, but does not include,
   (a) a person who reports to a society under subsection 72 (2) or (3) and is not the subject of the report, or
   (b) the child who is the subject of a report.

Director
(2) The Minister may appoint an employee of the Ministry as Director for the purposes of this section.

Duty of society
(3) A society that receives a report under section 72 that a child, including a child in the society's care, is or may be suffering or may have suffered abuse shall forthwith verify the reported information, or ensure that the information is verified by another society, in the manner determined by the Director, and if the information is verified, the society that verified it shall forthwith report it to the Director in the prescribed form.

Protection from liability
(4) No action or other proceeding for damages shall be instituted against an officer or employee of a society, acting in good faith, for an act done in the execution or intended execution of the duty imposed on the society by subsection (3) or for an alleged neglect or default of that duty.

Child abuse register
(5) The Director shall maintain a register in the manner prescribed by the regulations for the purpose of recording information reported to the Director under subsection (3), but the register shall not contain information that has

the effect of identifying a person who reports to a society under subsection 72 (2) or (3) and is not the subject of the report.

Register confidential
(6) Despite any other Act, no person shall inspect, remove, alter or permit the inspection, removal or alteration of information maintained in the register, or disclose or permit the disclosure of information that the person obtained from the register, except as this section authorizes.

Coroner's inquest, etc.
(7) A person who is,
   (a) a coroner, or a legally qualified medical practitioner or peace officer authorized in writing by a coroner, acting in connection with an investigation or inquest under the *Coroners Act*; or
   (b) the Children's Lawyer or the Children's Lawyer's authorized agent,
may inspect, remove and disclose information in the register in accordance with his or her authority.

Minister or Director may permit access to register
(8) The Minister or the Director may permit,
   (a) a person who is employed by,
      (i) the Ministry,
      (ii) a society, or
      (iii) a recognized child protection agency outside Ontario; or
   (b) a person who is providing or proposes to provide counselling or treatment to a registered person,
to inspect and remove information in the register and to disclose the information to a person referred to in subsection (7) or to another person referred to in this subsection, subject to such terms and conditions as the Director may impose.

Director may disclose information
(9) The Minister or the Director may disclose information in the register to a person referred to in subsection (7) or (8).

Research
(10) A person who is engaged in research may, with the Director's written approval, inspect and use the information in the register, but shall not,
   (a) use or communicate the information for any purpose except research, academic pursuits or the compilation of statistical data; or
   (b) communicate any information that may have the effect of identifying a person named in the register.

Registered person
(11) A child, a registered person or the child's or registered person's solicitor or agent may inspect only the information in the register that refers to the child or registered person.

Physician

(12) A legally qualified medical practitioner may, with the Director's written approval, inspect the information in the register that is specified by the Director.

Amendment of register

(13) The Director or an employee of the Ministry acting under the Director's authority,

(a) shall remove a name from or otherwise amend the register where the regulations require the removal or amendment; and

(b) may amend the register to correct an error.

Register inadmissible: exceptions

(14) The register shall not be admitted into evidence in a proceeding except,

(a) to prove compliance or non-compliance with this section;

(b) in a hearing or appeal under section 76;

(c) in a proceeding under the *Coroners Act*; or

(d) in a proceeding referred to in section 81 (recovery on child's behalf).

> **Note: On a day to be named by proclamation of the Lieutenant Governor, section 75 is repealed by the Statutes of Ontario, 1999, chapter 2, section 27. See: 1999, c. 2, ss. 27, 38.**

Hearing re registered person

76. (1) In this section,

"hearing" means a hearing held under clause (4) (b).

Notice to registered person

(2) Where an entry is made in the register, the Director shall forthwith give written notice to each registered person referred to in the entry indicating that,

(a) the person is identified in the register;

(b) the person or the person's solicitor or agent is entitled to inspect the information in the register that refers to or identifies the person; and

(c) the person is entitled to request that the Director remove the person's name from or otherwise amend the register.

Request to amend register

(3) A registered person who receives notice under subsection (2) may request that the Director remove the person's name from or otherwise amend the register.

Director's response

(4) On receiving a request under subsection (3), the Director may,

(a) grant the request; or

(b) hold a hearing, on ten days written notice to the parties, to determine whether to grant or refuse the request.

Delegation

(5) The Director may authorize another person to hold a hearing and exercise the Director's powers and duties under subsection (8).

Procedure

(6) The *Statutory Powers Procedure Act* applies to a hearing and a hearing shall be conducted in accordance with the prescribed practices and procedures.

Hearing

(7) The parties to a hearing are,

(a) the registered person;

(b) the society that verified the information referring to or identifying the registered person; and

(c) any other person specified by the Director.

Director's decision

(8) Where the Director determines, after holding a hearing, that the information in the register with respect to a registered person is in error or should not be in the register, the Director shall remove the registered person's name from or otherwise amend the register, and may order that the society's records be amended to reflect the Director's decision.

Appeal to Divisional Court

(9) A party to a hearing may appeal the Director's decision to the Divisional Court.

Hearing private

(10) A hearing or appeal under this section shall be held in the absence of the public and no media representative shall be permitted to attend.

Publication

(11) No person shall publish or make public information that has the effect of identifying a witness at or a participant in a hearing, or a party to a hearing other than a society.

Record inadmissible: exception

(12) The record of a hearing or appeal under this section shall not be admitted into evidence in any other proceeding except a proceeding under clause 85 (1) (d) (confidentiality of register) or clause 85 (1) (e) (amendment of society's records).

> **Note: On a day to be named by proclamation of the Lieutenant Governor, section 76 is repealed by the Statutes of Ontario, 1999, chapter 2, section 28. See: 1999, c. 2, ss. 28, 38.**

Powers of Director

Director's power to transfer

77. (1) A Director may direct, in the best interests of a child in the care or supervision of a society, that the child,

(a) be transferred to the care or supervision of another society; or

(b) be transferred from one placement to another placement designated by the Director.

Criteria

(2) In determining whether to direct a transfer under clause (1) (b), the Director shall take into account,

(a) the length of time the child has spent in the existing placement;

(b) the views of the foster parents; and

(c) the views and preferences of the child, where they are reasonably ascertainable.

Homemakers

Homemaker

78. (1) In this section,

"homemaker" means a person who is approved by a Director or local director for the purposes of this section.

Homemaker may remain on premises

(2) Where it appears to a person entering premises under section 40 or 44 that,

(a) a child who in the person's opinion is unable to care for himself or herself has been left on the premises without competent care or supervision; and

(b) no person having charge of the child is available or able to consent to the placement of a homemaker on the premises,

the person may, instead of taking the child to a place of safety,

(c) remain on the premises; or

(d) arrange with a society for the placement of a homemaker on the premises.

Homemaker's authority

(3) A homemaker who remains or is placed on premises under subsection (2) may enter and live there, carry on normal housekeeping activities that are reasonably necessary for the care of any child on the premises and exercise reasonable control and discipline over any such child.

Protection from personal liability

(4) No action shall be instituted against a homemaker who remains or is placed on premises under subsection (2) for,

(a) entering and living on the premises;

(b) anything done or omitted in connection with normal housekeeping activities on the premises;

(c) providing goods and services reasonably necessary for the care of any child on the premises; or

(d) the exercise of reasonable control and discipline over any child on the premises,

so long as the homemaker acts in good faith with reasonable care in the circumstances.

Notice to person having charge of child

(5) Where a homemaker remains or is placed on premises under subsection (2), the society shall forthwith notify or make reasonable efforts to notify the person last having charge of the child that a homemaker has been placed on the premises.

Court order, etc.

(6) Where a child with whom a homemaker has been placed under subsection (2),

(a) is found not to be in need of protection, the homemaker shall leave the premises; or

(b) is found to be in need of protection, the court may authorize the homemaker to remain on the premises until,

(i) a specified day not more than thirty days from the date of the order, or

(ii) a person who is entitled to custody of the child returns to care for the child,

whichever is sooner.

Extension

(7) Where no person returns to care for the child before the day specified in an order under clause (6) (b), the court may,

(a) extend the order; or

(b) hold a further hearing under section 47 and make an order under section 57.

Offences, Restraining Orders, Recovery on Child's Behalf

Abuse, failure to provide for reasonable care, etc.

Definition

79. (1) In this section,

"abuse" means a state or condition of being physically harmed, sexually molested or sexually exploited.

Child abuse

(2) No person having charge of a child shall,

(a) inflict abuse on the child; or

(b) by failing to care and provide for or supervise and protect the child adequately,

(i) permit the child to suffer abuse, or

(ii) permit the child to suffer from a mental, emotional or developmental condition that, if not remedied, could seriously impair the child's development.

Leaving child unattended

(3) No person having charge of a child less than sixteen years of age shall leave the child without making provision for his or her supervision and care that is reasonable in the circumstances.

Reverse onus

(4) Where a person is charged with contravening subsection (3) and the child is less than ten years of age, the

onus of establishing that the person made provision for the child's supervision and care that was reasonable in the circumstances rests with the person.

Allowing child to loiter, etc.
(5) No parent of a child less than sixteen years of age shall permit the child to,
  (a) loiter in a public place between the hours of midnight and 6 a.m.; or
  (b) be in a place of public entertainment between the hours of midnight and 6 a.m., unless the parent accompanies the child or authorizes a specified individual eighteen years of age or older to accompany the child.

Police may take child home or to place of safety
(6) Where a child who is actually or apparently less than sixteen years of age is in a place to which the public has access between the hours of midnight and 6 a.m. and is not accompanied by a person described in clause (5) (b), a peace officer may apprehend the child without a warrant and proceed as if the child had been apprehended under subsection 42 (1).

Child protection hearing
(7) The court may, in connection with a case arising under subsection (2), (3) or (5), proceed under this Part as if an application had been made under subsection 40 (1) (child protection proceeding) in respect of the child.

Restraining order
80. (1) Where the court finds that a child is in need of protection, the court may, instead of or in addition to making an order under subsection 57 (1), make an order in the child's best interests restraining or prohibiting a person's access to or contact with the child, and may include in the order such directions as the court considers appropriate for implementing the order and protecting the child.

Idem: notice
(2) An order shall not be made under subsection (1) unless notice of the proceeding has been served personally on the person to be named in the order.

Six-month maximum
(3) An order made under subsection (1) shall be in force for a specified period not exceeding six months.

Extension, variation and termination
(4) An application for the extension, variation or termination of an order made under subsection (1) may be made by,
  (a) the person who is the subject of the order;
  (b) the child;
  (c) the person having charge of the child;
  (d) a society;
  (e) a Director; or

  (f) where the child is an Indian or a native person, a representative chosen by the child's band or native community.

Idem
(5) Where an application is made under subsection (4), the court may, in the child's best interests,
  (a) extend the order for a further period or periods of six months; or
  (b) vary or terminate the order.

Child in society's care not to be returned while order in force
(6) Where a society has care of a child and an order made under subsection (1) prohibiting a person's access to the child is in force, the society shall not return the child to the care of,
  (a) the person named in the order; or
  (b) a person who may permit that person to have access to the child.

Recovery because of abuse
81. (1) In this section,

"to suffer abuse", when used in reference to a child, means to be in need of protection within the meaning of clause 37 (2) (a), (c), (e), (f), (f.1) or (h).

Recovery on child's behalf
(2) When the Children's Lawyer is of the opinion that a child has a cause of action or other claim because the child has suffered abuse, the Children's Lawyer may, if he or she considers it to be in the child's best interests, institute and conduct proceedings on the child's behalf for the recovery of damages or other compensation.

Idem: society
(3) Where a child is in a society's care and custody, subsection (2) also applies to the society with necessary modifications.

Prohibition
82. No person shall place a child in the care and custody of a society, and no society shall take a child into its care and custody, except,
  (a) in accordance with this Part; or
  (b) under an agreement made under subsection 29 (1) or 30 (1) (temporary care or special needs agreement) of Part II (Voluntary Access to Services).

Offence
83. Where a child is the subject of an order for society supervision, society wardship or Crown wardship under subsection 57 (1), no person shall,
  (a) induce or attempt to induce the child to leave the care of the person with whom the child is placed by the court or by the society, as the case may be;

(b) detain or harbour the child after the person or society referred to in clause (a) requires that the child be returned;

(c) interfere with the child or remove or attempt to remove the child from any place; or

(d) for the purpose of interfering with the child, visit or communicate with the person referred to in clause (a).

Offence

84. No person shall,

(a) knowingly give false information in an application under this Part; or

(b) obstruct, interfere with or attempt to obstruct or interfere with a child protection worker or a peace officer who is acting under section 40, 41, 42, 43 or 44.

Offences

85. (1) A person who contravenes,

(a) an order for access made under subsection 58 (1);

(b) REPEALED.

(c) subsection 74 (5) (disclosure of information obtained by court order);

(d) subsection 75 (6) or (10) (confidentiality of child abuse register);

> **Note: On a day to be named by proclamation of the Lieutenant Governor, clause (d) is repealed by the Statutes of Ontario, 1999, chapter 2, subsection 30 (2). See: 1999, c. 2, ss. 30 (2), 38.**

(e) an order made under subsection 76 (8) (amendment of society's records);

> **Note: On a day to be named by proclamation of the Lieutenant Governor, clause (e) is repealed by the Statutes of Ontario, 1999, chapter 2, subsection 30 (3). See: 1999, c. 2, ss. 30 (3), 38.**

(f) subsection 79 (3) or (5) (leaving child unattended, etc.);

(g) a restraining order made under subsection 80 (1);

(h) section 82 (unauthorized placement);

(i) any provision of section 83 (interference with child, etc.); or

(j) clause 84 (a) or (b),

and a director, officer or employee of a corporation who authorizes, permits or concurs in such a contravention by the corporation is guilty of an offence and on conviction is liable to a fine of not more than $1,000 or to imprisonment for a term of not more than one year, or to both.

Idem

(2) A person who contravenes subsection 79 (2) (child abuse), and a director, officer or employee of a corporation who authorizes, permits or concurs in such a contravention by the corporation is guilty of an offence and on

conviction is liable to a fine of not more than $2,000 or to imprisonment for a term of not more than two years, or to both.

Idem

(3) A person who contravenes subsection 45 (8) or 76 (11) (publication of identifying information) or an order prohibiting publication made under clause 45 (7) (c) or subsection 45 (9), and a director, officer or employee of a corporation who authorizes, permits or concurs in such a contravention by the corporation, is guilty of an offence and on conviction is liable to a fine of not more than $10,000 or to imprisonment for a term of not more than three years, or to both.

> **Note: On a day to be named by proclamation of the Lieutenant Governor, subsection (3) is amended by the Statutes of Ontario, 1999, chapter 2, subsection 30 (5) by striking out "or 76 (11)". See: 1999, c. 2, ss. 30 (5), 38.**

Child's Religious Faith

How child's religious faith determined

86. (1) For the purposes of this section, a child shall be deemed to have the religious faith agreed upon by the child's parent, but where there is no agreement or the court cannot readily determine what the religious faith agreed upon is or whether any religious faith is agreed upon, the court may decide what the child's religious faith is, if any, on the basis of the child's circumstances.

Child's wishes to be consulted

(2) The court shall consider the child's views and wishes, if they can be reasonably ascertained, in determining what the child's religious faith is, if any.

Religious faith of child

(3) A Protestant child shall not be committed under this Part to the care of a Roman Catholic society or institution and a Roman Catholic child shall not be committed under this Part to a Protestant society or institution, and a Protestant child shall not be placed in a foster home with a Roman Catholic family and a Roman Catholic child shall not be placed in a foster home with a Protestant family, and, where a child committed under this Part is other than Protestant or Roman Catholic, the child shall be placed where practicable with a family of his or her own religious faith, if any.

Where only one society

(4) Subsection (3) does not apply to the commitment of a child to the care of a society in a municipality in which there is only one society.

Director's discretion re foster placement

(5) Where a society,

(a)   is unable to place a child in a suitable foster home within a reasonable time because of the operation of subsection (3); and

(b)   would be able to place the child in a suitable foster home but for the operation of subsection (3),

the society may apply to a Director who may order that subsection (3) does not apply to the child in respect of the placement.

Injunctions

Injunction

87. (1) The Superior Court of Justice may grant an injunction to restrain a person from contravening section 83, on the society's application.

Variation, etc.
(2)   The court may vary or terminate an order made under subsection (1), on any person's application.

PART IV
YOUNG OFFENDERS

Definitions

88. In this Part,

"bailiff" means a bailiff appointed under clause 90 (1) (c);

"Board" means the Custody Review Board established under subsection 96 (1);

"federal Act" means the *Young Offenders Act* (Canada);

"maximum security place of custody" means a place of secure custody in which the Minister has established a maximum security custody program;

"medium security place of custody" means a place of secure custody in which the Minister has established a medium security custody program;

"place of open custody" means a place or facility designated as a place of open custody under subsection 24.1 (1) of the federal Act and operated by or for the Minister;

"place of open temporary detention" means a place of temporary detention in which the Minister has established an open detention program;

"place of secure custody" means a place or facility designated for the secure containment or restraint of young persons under subsection 24.1 (1) of the federal Act and operated by or for the Minister;

"place of secure temporary detention" means a place of temporary detention in which the Minister has established a secure detention program;

"place of temporary detention" means a place or facility designated as a place of temporary detention under sub-

section 7 (1) of the federal Act and operated by or for the Minister;

"probation officer" means a probation officer appointed under clause 90 (1) (b);

"provincial director" means a provincial director appointed under clause 90 (1) (a);

"services and programs" means,
   (a)   prevention programs,
   (b)   pre-trial detention and supervision programs,
   (c)   open and secure custody programs,
   (d)   probation services,
   (e)   programs for the administration and supervision of dispositions, and
   (f)   other related services and programs;

"young person" means a child as defined in subsection 3 (1) who is, or, in the absence of evidence to the contrary, appears to be,
   (a)   twelve years of age, or more, but
   (b)   under sixteen years of age,
and includes a person sixteen years of age or more charged with having committed an offence while he or she was twelve years of age or more but under sixteen years of age.

Programs and Officers

Services and programs

89. (1) The Minister may,
   (a)   establish, operate and maintain services and programs; and
   (b)   make agreements with persons for the provision of services and programs,
for or on behalf of young persons for the purposes of the federal Act and the *Provincial Offences Act*, and may make payments for those services and programs out of legislative appropriations.

Secure and open temporary detention programs
(2)   The Minister may establish,
   (a)   secure temporary detention programs, in which restrictions are continuously imposed on the liberty of young persons by physical barriers, close staff supervision or limited access to the community; and
   (b)   open temporary detention programs, in which restrictions that are less stringent than in a secure temporary detention program are imposed on the liberty of young persons,
in places of temporary detention.

Maximum and medium security custody programs
(3)   The Minister may establish,
   (a)   maximum security custody programs, in which restrictions are continuously imposed on the liberty of young persons by physical barriers, close staff

supervision or limited access to the community; and

(b) medium security custody programs, in which restrictions that are less stringent than in a maximum security custody program are imposed on the liberty of young persons,

in places of secure custody.

Open custody programs
(4) The Minister may establish open custody programs in places of open custody.

Where locking up permitted
(5) A place of secure custody and a place of secure temporary detention may be locked for the detention of young persons.

Appointments by Minister

90. (1) The Minister may appoint any person as,

(a) a provincial director, to perform any or all of the duties and functions of a provincial director,
(i) under the federal Act, and
(ii) under the regulations;

(b) a probation officer, to perform any or all of the duties and functions,
(i) of a youth worker under the federal Act, and
(ii) of a probation officer for the purpose of dealing with young persons under the *Provincial Offences Act*, and
(iii) of a probation officer under the regulations; and

(c) a bailiff, to perform any or all of the duties and functions of a bailiff under the regulations.

Limitations, etc., on appointments
(2) The Minister may set out in an appointment made under subsection (1) any conditions or limitations to which it is subject.

Probation officer and bailiff have powers of peace officer
(3) While performing their duties and functions, a probation officer appointed under clause (1) (b) and a bailiff appointed under clause (1) (c) have the powers of a peace officer.

Remuneration and expenses
(4) The remuneration and expenses of a person appointed under subsection (1) who is not a public servant under the *Public Service Act* shall be fixed by the Minister and shall be paid out of legislative appropriations.

Approval of provincial director for provision of services to person over sixteen

91. (1) With the approval of a provincial director, services may be provided under this Part to a person sixteen years of age or more who is a young person within the meaning of the federal Act but not within the meaning of young person as defined in section 88.

Person deemed to be young person
(2) A person who is the subject of an approval under subsection (1) shall be deemed to be a young person for the purposes of this Part.

Reports and information

92. A person in charge of a service or program provided under subsection 89 (1), a person in charge of a place of temporary detention, open custody or secure custody, a bailiff and a probation officer,

(a) shall make the prescribed reports and furnish the prescribed information to the Minister, in the prescribed form and at the prescribed intervals; and

(b) shall make a report to the Minister whenever the Minister requests it, in the form and containing the information specified by the Minister.

Temporary Detention

Open and secure detention

Open detention unless provincial director determines otherwise
93. (1) A young person who is detained under the federal Act in a place of temporary detention shall be detained in a place of open temporary detention unless a provincial director determines under subsection (2) that the young person is to be detained in a place of secure temporary detention.

Where secure detention available
(2) A provincial director may detain a young person in a place of secure temporary detention if the circumstances described in paragraph 1 or 2 apply to the young person and if the provincial director is satisfied that it is necessary to detain the young person in a place of secure temporary detention to ensure the young person's attendance in court or to protect the public interest or safety:

1. The young person is charged with an offence for which an adult would be liable to imprisonment for five years or more and,
   i. the offence includes causing or attempting to cause serious bodily harm to another person,
   ii. the young person has, at any time, failed to appear in court when required to do so under the federal Act or escaped or attempted to escape from lawful detention, or
   iii. the young person has, within the twelve months immediately preceding the offence on which the current charge is based, been convicted of an offence for which an adult would be liable to imprisonment for five years or more.

2. The young person is detained in a place of temporary detention and leaves or attempts to leave without the consent of the person in charge or is charged with having escaped or attempting to

escape from lawful custody or being unlawfully at large under the *Criminal Code* (Canada).

Idem

(3) Despite subsection (1), a young person who is apprehended because he or she has left or has not returned to a medium security or maximum security place of custody may be detained in a place of secure temporary detention until he or she is returned to the first-named place of custody.

Idem

(4) Despite subsection (1), a young person who is detained under the federal Act in a place of temporary detention may be detained in a place of secure temporary detention for a period not exceeding twenty-four hours while a provincial director makes a determination in respect of the young person under subsection (2).

Review by youth court

(5) A young person who is being detained in a place of secure temporary detention and is brought before a youth court for a review under the *Criminal Code* (Canada) may request that the youth court review the level of his or her detention, and the youth court may confirm the provincial director's decision under subsection (2) or may direct that the young person be transferred to a place of open temporary detention.

Custody

Medium and maximum security

Medium rather than maximum security custody unless provincial director determines otherwise

94. (1) A young person who is committed to secure custody under the federal Act shall be held in a medium security place of custody unless a provincial director determines under subsection (2) that the young person is to be held in a maximum security place of custody.

Where maximum security custody available

(2) A provincial director may place a young person in or transfer a young person to a maximum security place of custody if the young person is committed to secure custody under the federal Act for an offence for which an adult would be liable to imprisonment for five years or more and,

   (a) the offence for which the young person is committed to secure custody includes causing or attempting to cause serious bodily harm to another person; or

   (b) the young person has, within the twelve months immediately preceding the offence for which he or she is committed to secure custody,

      (i) been held in a maximum security place of custody, or

      (ii) been found guilty of an offence for which an adult would be liable to imprisonment for five years or more,

where the provincial director is satisfied that it would not be appropriate to hold the young person in a medium security place of custody, having regard to,

   (c) the young person's age and previous history;

   (d) the circumstances of the commission of the offence for which the young person is committed to secure custody;

   (e) the contents of a pre-disposition report;

   (f) the needs of the young person; and

   (g) the need to protect the public interest and safety.

Transfer from maximum to medium security custody

(3) A provincial director may transfer a young person from a maximum security place of custody to a medium security place of custody if the provincial director is satisfied that the transfer is justified because the young person has made sufficient progress or for some other appropriate reason.

Reasons

(4) A provincial director who makes a determination under this section shall give written reasons for the determination to the young person and to the persons in charge of the places of custody from and to which the young person is transferred.

Young persons in open custody

95. Where a young person is sentenced to a term of imprisonment for breach of probation under clause 75 (d) of the *Provincial Offences Act*, to be served in open custody as set out in section 103 of that Act,

   (a) the young person shall be held in a place of open custody specified by a provincial director; and

   (b) the provisions of section 35 (temporary release) of the federal Act apply with necessary modifications.

Custody Review Board

Custody Review Board

96. (1) The Custody Review Board is continued under the name Custody Review Board in English and Commission de révision des placements sous garde in French and shall have the powers and duties given to it by this Part and the regulations.

Chair and vice-chairs

(2) The Board shall be composed of the prescribed number of members who shall be appointed by the Lieutenant Governor in Council.

Members

(3) The Lieutenant Governor in Council may appoint a member of the Board as chair and may appoint one or more other members as vice-chairs.

Term

(4) A member of the Board shall hold office for the prescribed term.

Quorum

(5) The prescribed number of members of the Board are a quorum.

Remuneration

(6) The chair and vice-chairs and the other members of the Board shall be paid the daily allowances determined by the Lieutenant Governor in Council and are entitled to their reasonable and necessary travelling and living expenses while attending meetings or otherwise engaged in the work of the Board.

Duties of Board

(7) The Board shall conduct reviews under section 97 and perform such other duties as are assigned to it by the regulations.

Application to Board

97. (1) A young person may apply to the Board for a review of,

    (a) a provincial director's decision to hold the young person in or transfer the young person to a maximum security place of custody;

    (b) the particular place where the young person is held or to which the young person has been transferred;

    (c) a provincial director's refusal to authorize the young person's temporary release under section 35 of the federal Act; or

    (d) the young person's transfer from a place of open custody to a place of secure custody under subsection 24.2 (9) of the federal Act,

within thirty days of the decision, placement or transfer, as the case may be.

Duty of Board

(2) The Board shall conduct a review with respect to an application made under subsection (1) and may do so by holding a hearing.

Idem

(3) The Board shall advise the young person whether it intends to hold a hearing or not within ten days of receiving the young person's application.

Procedure

(4) The *Statutory Powers Procedure Act* does not apply to a hearing held under subsection (2).

Idem

(5) The Board shall complete its review and make a determination within thirty days of receiving a young person's application, unless,

    (a) the Board holds a hearing with respect to the application; and

    (b) the young person and the provincial director whose decision is being reviewed consent to a longer period for the Board's determination.

Board's recommendations

(6) After conducting a review under subsection (2), the Board may,

    (a) recommend to the provincial director,

       (i) that the young person be transferred to a medium security place of custody,

       (ii) where the Board is of the opinion that the place where the young person is held or to which he or she has been transferred is not appropriate to meet the young person's needs, that the young person be transferred to another place,

       (iii) that the young person's temporary release be authorized under section 35 of the federal Act, or

       (iv) where the young person has been transferred under subsection 24.2 (9) of the federal Act, that the young person be returned to a place of open custody; or

    (b) confirm the decision, placement or transfer.

Apprehension of Young Persons who are Absent from Custody without Permission

Apprehension

Apprehension of young person absent from place of temporary detention

98. (1) A peace officer, the person in charge of a place of temporary detention or that person's delegate, who believes on reasonable and probable grounds that a young person detained under the federal Act or the *Provincial Offences Act* in a place of temporary detention has left the place without the consent of the person in charge and fails or refuses to return there may apprehend the young person with or without a warrant and take the young person or arrange for the young person to be taken to a place of temporary detention.

Idem: place of open custody

(2) A peace officer, the person in charge of a place of open custody or that person's delegate, who believes on reasonable and probable grounds that a young person held in a place of open custody as described in section 95,

    (a) has left the place without the consent of the person in charge and fails or refuses to return there; or

    (b) fails or refuses to return to the place of open custody upon completion of a period of temporary release under clause 95 (b),

may apprehend the young person with or without a warrant and take the young person or arrange for the young person to be taken to a place of open custody or a place of temporary detention.

Young person to be returned within forty-eight hours
(3) A young person who is apprehended under this section shall be returned to the place from which he or she is absent within forty-eight hours after being apprehended unless the provincial director detains the young person in secure temporary detention under paragraph 2 of subsection 93 (2).

Warrant to apprehend young person
(4) A justice of the peace who is satisfied on the basis of a sworn information that there are reasonable and probable grounds to believe that a young person held in a place of temporary detention or open custody,

  (a) has left the place without the consent of the person in charge and fails or refuses to return there; or

  (b) fails or refuses to return to a place of open custody upon completion of a period of temporary release under clause 95 (b),

may issue a warrant authorizing a peace officer, the person in charge of the place of temporary detention or open custody or that person's delegate to apprehend the young person.

Authority to enter, etc.
(5) Where a person authorized to apprehend a young person under subsection (1) or (2) believes on reasonable and probable grounds that a young person referred to in the relevant subsection is on any premises, the person may with or without a warrant enter the premises, by force, if necessary, and search for and remove the young person.

Regulations re exercise of power of entry
(6) A person authorized to enter premises under subsection (5) shall exercise the power of entry in accordance with the regulations.

PART V
RIGHTS OF CHILDREN

Definition
99. In this Part,

"child in care" means a child who is receiving residential services from a service provider and includes,

  (a) a child who is in the care of a foster parent, and

  (b) a child who is detained in a place of temporary detention, committed to secure or open custody under the *Young Offenders Act* (Canada), or held in a place of open custody under section 95 of Part IV (Young Offenders).

Locking Up

Locking up restricted
100. (1) No service provider shall detain a child or permit a child to be detained in locked premises in the course of the provision of a service to the child, except as Part IV (Young Offenders) and Part VI (Extraordinary Measures) authorize.

Application of subs. (1)
(2) Subsection (1) does not prohibit the routine locking of premises for security at night.

Corporal Punishment

No corporal punishment
101. No service provider or foster parent shall inflict corporal punishment on a child or permit corporal punishment to be inflicted on a child in the course of the provision of a service to the child.

Office of Child and Family Service Advocacy

Office of Child and Family Service Advocacy
102. The Office of Child and Family Service Advocacy is continued under the name Office of Child and Family Service Advocacy in English and Bureau d'assistance à l'enfance et à la famille in French, to,

  (a) co-ordinate and administer a system of advocacy, except for advocacy before a court, on behalf of children and families who receive or seek approved services or services purchased by approved agencies;

  (b) advise the Minister on matters and issues concerning the interests of those children and families; and

  (c) perform any similar functions given to it by this Act or the regulations or another Act or the regulations made under another Act.

Rights of Children in Care

Rights of communication, etc.
103. (1) A child in care has a right,

  (a) to speak in private with, visit and receive visits from members of his or her family regularly, subject to subsection (2);

  (b) to speak in private with and receive visits from,
    (i) the child's solicitor,
    (ii) another person representing the child, including an advocate appointed for the child by the Office of Child and Family Service Advocacy referred to in section 102,
    (iii) the Ombudsman appointed under the *Ombudsman Act* and members of the Ombudsman's staff, and
    (iv) a member of the Legislative Assembly of Ontario or of the Parliament of Canada; and

  (c) to send and receive mail that is not read, examined or censored by another person, subject to subsection (3).

When child a Crown ward
(2) A child in care who is a Crown ward is not entitled as of right to speak with, visit or receive visits from a member of his or her family, except under an order for access made under Part III (Child Protection).

Opening, etc., of mail to child

(3) Mail to a child in care,

    (a) may be opened by the service provider or a member of the service provider's staff in the child's presence and may be inspected for articles prohibited by the service provider;

    (b) where the service provider believes on reasonable grounds that the contents of the mail may cause the child physical or emotional harm, may be examined or read by the service provider or a member of the service provider's staff in the child's presence, subject to clause (c);

    (c) shall not be examined or read by the service provider or a member of the service provider's staff if it is to or from the child's solicitor; and

    (d) shall not be censored or withheld from the child, except that articles prohibited by the service provider may be removed from the mail and withheld from the child.

Personal liberties

104. A child in care has a right,

    (a) to have reasonable privacy and possession of his or her own personal property; and

    (b) to receive the religious instruction and participate in the religious activities of his or her choice, subject to section 106.

Plan of care

105. (1) A child in care has a right to a plan of care designed to meet the child's particular needs, which shall be prepared within thirty days of the child's admission to the residential placement.

Rights to care

(2) A child in care has a right,

    (a) to participate in the development of the child's individual plan of care and in any changes made to it;

    (b) to receive meals that are well-balanced, of good quality and appropriate for the child;

    (c) to be provided with clothing that is of good quality and appropriate for the child, given the child's size and activities and prevailing weather conditions;

    (d) to receive medical and dental care, subject to section 106, at regular intervals and whenever required, in a community setting whenever possible;

    (e) to receive an education that corresponds to the child's aptitudes and abilities, in a community setting whenever possible; and

    (f) to participate in recreational and athletic activities that are appropriate for the child's aptitudes and interests, in a community setting whenever possible.

Parental consent, etc.

106. Subject to subsection 51 (4) and sections 62 and 63 (temporary order, society and Crown wards) of Part III (Child Protection), the parent of a child in care retains any right that he or she may have,

    (a) to direct the child's education and religious upbringing; and

    (b) to give or refuse consent to medical treatment for the child.

Right to be heard

107. A child in care has a right to be consulted and to express his or her views, to the extent that is practical given the child's level of understanding, whenever significant decisions concerning the child are made, including decisions with respect to medical treatment, education and religion and decisions with respect to the child's discharge from the placement or transfer to another residential placement.

Right to be informed

108. A child in care has a right to be informed, in a language suitable for the child's level of understanding, of,

    (a) the child's rights under this Part;

    (b) the internal complaints procedure established under subsection 109 (1) and the further review available under section 110;

    (c) the existence of the Office of Child and Family Service Advocacy referred to in section 102;

    (d) the review procedures available for children twelve years of age or older under sections 34, 35 and 36 of Part II (Voluntary Access to Services);

    (e) the review procedures available under section 97 of Part IV (Young Offenders), in the case of a child who is detained in a place of temporary detention, committed to secure or open custody under the *Young Offenders Act* (Canada), or held in a place of open custody under section 95 of Part IV (Young Offenders);

    (f) the child's responsibilities while in the placement; and

    (g) the rules governing day-to-day operation of the residential service, including disciplinary procedures,

upon admission to the residential placement, to the extent that is practical given the child's level of understanding.

Complaint and Review Procedures

Internal complaints procedure

109. (1) A service provider who provides residential services to children or places children in residential placements shall establish a written procedure, in accordance with the regulations, for hearing and dealing with complaints regarding alleged violations of the rights under this Part of children in care.

Idem

(2) A service provider shall conduct a review or ensure that a review is conducted, in accordance with the procedure established under subsection (1), on the complaint of,

 (a) a child in care;

 (b) the child's parent; or

 (c) another person representing the child,

and shall seek to resolve the complaint.

Further review

110. (1) Where a person referred to in subsection 109 (2) who makes a complaint and is not satisfied with the result of the review conducted under that subsection requests in writing that the Minister appoint a person to conduct a further review of the complaint, the Minister shall appoint a person who is not employed by the service provider to do so.

Idem

(2) A person appointed under subsection (1) shall review the complaint in accordance with the regulations and may, but is not required to, do so by holding a hearing.

Procedure

(3) The *Statutory Powers Procedure Act* does not apply to a hearing held under subsection (2).

Powers of appointed person

(4) A person appointed under subsection (1) has, for the purposes of the review, all the powers of a program supervisor appointed under subsection 5 (2) of Part I (Flexible Services).

Review and report within thirty days

(5) A person appointed under subsection (1) shall, within thirty days after the day of the appointment, complete the review, set out in a report his or her findings and recommendations, including the reasons for not holding a hearing if none was held, and provide copies of the report to,

 (a) the person who made the complaint;

 (b) the service provider; and

 (c) the Minister.

Minister to advise persons affected of any decision

111. (1) Where the Minister decides to take any action with respect to a complaint after receiving a report under subsection 110 (5), the Minister shall advise the person who made the complaint and the service provider of the decision.

Remedies preserved

(2) The Minister's decision referred to in subsection (1) does not affect any other remedy that may be available.

PART VI
EXTRAORDINARY MEASURES

Definitions

112. In this Part,

"administrator" means the person in charge of a secure treatment program;

"intrusive procedure" means,

 (a) a mechanical means of controlling behaviour,

 (b) an aversive stimulation technique, or

 (c) any other procedure that is prescribed as an intrusive procedure;

"mental disorder" means a substantial disorder of emotional processes, thought or cognition which grossly impairs a person's capacity to make reasoned judgments;

"psychotropic drug" means a drug or combination of drugs prescribed as a psychotropic drug;

"review team" means an interdisciplinary review team established under subsection 129 (1);

"secure isolation room" means a locked room approved under subsection 126 (1) for use for the secure isolation of children;

"secure treatment program" means a program established or approved by the Minister under subsection 113 (1).

Secure Treatment Programs

Minister may establish or approve programs

113. (1) The Minister may,

 (a) establish, operate and maintain; or

 (b) approve,

programs for the treatment of children with mental disorders, in which continuous restrictions are imposed on the liberty of the children.

Terms and conditions

(2) The Minister may impose terms and conditions on an approval given under subsection (1) and may vary or amend the terms and conditions or impose new terms and conditions at any time.

Admission of children

(3) No child shall be admitted to a secure treatment program except by a court order under section 117 (commitment to secure treatment program) or under section 124 (emergency admission).

Locking up permitted

(4) The premises of a secure treatment program may be locked for the detention of children.

Commitment to Secure Treatment

Application for order for child's commitment

114. (1) Any one of the following persons may, with the administrator's written consent, apply to the court for an order for the child's commitment to a secure treatment program:

1. Where the child is less than sixteen years of age,
   i. the child's parent,
   ii. a person other than an administrator who is caring for the child, if the child's parent consents to the application, or
   iii. a society that has custody of the child under an order made under Part III (Child Protection).
2. Where the child is sixteen years of age or more,
   i. the child,
   ii. the child's parent, if the child consents to the application,
   iii. a society that has custody of the child under an order made under Part III (Child Protection), if the child consents to the application, or
   iv. a physician.

Time for hearing
(2) Where an application is made under subsection (1), the court shall deal with the matter within ten days of the making of an order under subsection (6) (legal representation) or, where no such order is made, within ten days of the making of the application.

Adjournments
(3) The court may adjourn the hearing of an application but shall not adjourn it for more than thirty days unless the applicant and the child consent to the longer adjournment.

Interim order
(4) Where a hearing is adjourned, the court may make a temporary order for the child's commitment to a secure treatment program if the court is satisfied that the child meets the criteria for commitment set out in clauses 117 (1) (a) to (f) and, where the child is less than twelve years old, the Minister consents to the child's admission.

Evidence on adjournments
(5) For the purpose of subsection (4), the court may admit and act on evidence that the court considers credible and trustworthy in the circumstances.

Legal representation of child
(6) Where an application is made under subsection (1) in respect of a child who does not have legal representation, the court shall, as soon as practicable and in any event before the hearing of the application, direct that legal representation be provided for the child.

Hearing private
(7) A hearing under this section shall be held in the absence of the public and no media representative shall be permitted to attend.

Child entitled to be present
(8) The child who is the subject of an application under subsection (1) is entitled to be present at the hearing unless,
   (a) the court is satisfied that being present at the hearing would cause the child emotional harm; or
   (b) the child, after obtaining legal advice, consents in writing to the holding of the hearing in his or her absence.

Court may require child's presence
(9) The court may require a child who has consented to the holding of the hearing in his or her absence under clause (8) (b) to be present at all or part of the hearing.

Oral evidence

115. (1) Where an application is made under subsection 114 (1), the court shall deal with the matter by holding a hearing and shall hear oral evidence unless the child, after obtaining legal advice, consents in writing to the making of an order under subsection 117 (1) without the hearing of oral evidence, and the consent is filed with the court.

Court may hear oral evidence despite consent
(2) The court may hear oral evidence although the child has given a consent under subsection (1).

Time limitation
(3) A child's consent under subsection (1) is not effective for more than the period referred to in subsection 118 (1) (period of commitment).

Assessment

116. (1) The court may, at any time after an application is made under subsection 114 (1), order that the child attend within a specified time for an assessment before a specified person who is qualified, in the court's opinion, to perform an assessment to assist the court to determine whether the child should be committed to a secure treatment program and has consented to perform the assessment.

Report
(2) The person performing an assessment under subsection (1) shall make a written report of the assessment to the court within the time specified in the order, which shall not be more than thirty days unless the court is of the opinion that a longer assessment period is necessary.

Who may not perform assessment
(3) The court shall not order an assessment to be performed by a person who provides services in the secure treatment program to which the application relates.

Copies of report

(4) The court shall provide a copy of the report to,

(a) the applicant;

(b) the child, subject to subsection (6);

(c) the child's solicitor;

(d) a parent appearing at the hearing;

(e) a society that has custody of the child under an order made under Part III (Child Protection);

(f) the administrator of the secure treatment program; and

(g) where the child is an Indian or a native person, a representative chosen by the child's band or native community.

Idem

(5) The court may cause a copy of the report to be given to a parent who does not attend the hearing but is, in the court's opinion, actively interested in the proceedings.

Court may withhold report from child

(6) The court may withhold all or part of the report from the child where the court is satisfied that disclosure of all or part of the report to the child would cause the child emotional harm.

Commitment to secure treatment: criteria

117. (1) The court may order that a child be committed to a secure treatment program only where the court is satisfied that,

(a) the child has a mental disorder;

(b) the child has, as a result of the mental disorder, within the forty-five days immediately preceding,

(i) the application under subsection 114 (1),

(ii) the child's detention or custody under the *Young Offenders Act* (Canada) or under the *Provincial Offences Act*, or

(iii) the child's admission to a psychiatric facility under the *Mental Health Act* as an involuntary patient,

caused or attempted to cause serious bodily harm to himself, herself or another person;

(c) the child has,

(i) within the twelve months immediately preceding the application, but on another occasion than that referred to in clause (b), caused, attempted to cause or by words or conduct made a substantial threat to cause serious bodily harm to himself, herself or another person, or

(ii) in committing the act or attempt referred to in clause (b), caused or attempted to cause a person's death;

(d) the secure treatment program would be effective to prevent the child from causing or attempting to cause serious bodily harm to himself, herself or another person;

(e) treatment appropriate for the child's mental disorder is available at the place of secure treatment to which the application relates; and

(f) no less restrictive method of providing treatment appropriate for the child's mental disorder is appropriate in the circumstances.

Where child under twelve

(2) Where the child is less than twelve years old, the court shall not make an order under subsection (1) unless the Minister consents to the child's commitment.

Additional requirement where applicant is physician

(3) Where the applicant is a physician, the court shall not make an order under subsection (1) unless the court is satisfied that the applicant believes the criteria set out in that subsection are met.

Period of commitment

118. (1) The court shall specify in an order under subsection 117 (1) the period not exceeding 180 days for which the child shall be committed to the secure treatment program.

Where society is applicant

(2) Where a child is committed to a secure treatment program on a society's application and the period specified in the court's order is greater than sixty days, the child shall be released on a day sixty days after the child's admission to the secure treatment program unless before that day,

(a) the child's parent consents to the child's commitment for a longer period; or

(b) the child is made a Crown or society ward under Part III (Child Protection),

but in no case shall the child be committed to the secure treatment program for longer than the period specified under subsection (1).

How time calculated

(3) In the calculation of a child's period of commitment, time spent in the secure treatment program before an order has been made under section 117 (commitment) or pending an application under section 120 (extension) shall be counted.

Where order expires after eighteenth birthday

(4) A person who is the subject of an order made under subsection 117 (1) or 120 (5) may be kept in the secure treatment program after attaining the age of eighteen years, until the order expires.

Reasons, plans, etc.

119. (1) Where the court makes an order under subsection 117 (1) or 120 (5), the court shall give,

(a) reasons for its decision;

(b) a statement of the plan, if any, for the child's care on release from the secure treatment program; and

(c) a statement of the less restrictive alternatives considered by the court, and the reasons for rejecting them.

Plan for care on release
(2) Where no plan for the child's care on release from the secure treatment program is available at the time of the order, the administrator shall, within ninety days of the date of the order, prepare such a plan and file it with the court.

Extension of Period of Commitment

Extension
120. (1) Where a child is the subject of an order made under subsection 117 (1) (commitment) or subsection (5),
  (a) a person referred to in subsection 114 (1), with the administrator's written consent; or
  (b) the administrator, with a parent's written consent or, where the child is in a society's lawful custody, the society's consent,
may, before the expiry of the period of commitment, apply for an order extending the child's commitment to the secure treatment program.

Idem
(2) Where a person is kept in the secure treatment program under subsection 118 (4) after attaining the age of eighteen years,
  (a) the person, with the written consent of the administrator;
  (b) the person's parent, with the written consent of the person and the administrator;
  (c) a physician, with the written consent of the administrator and the person; or
  (d) the administrator, with the written consent of the person,
may, before the expiry of the period of commitment, apply for one further order extending the person's commitment to the secure treatment program.

Child may be kept in program while application pending
(3) Where an application is made under subsection (1) or (2), the child may be kept in the secure treatment program until the application is disposed of.

ss. 114 (3), (6-9), 115, 116 apply

(4) Subsections 114 (3), (6), (7), (8) and (9) (hearing) and sections 115 (child's waiver) and 116 (assessment) apply with necessary modifications to an application made under subsection (1) or (2).

Criteria for extension
(5) The court may make an order extending a child's commitment to a secure treatment program only where the court is satisfied that,
  (a) the child has a mental disorder;

  (b) the secure treatment program would be effective to prevent the child from causing or attempting to cause serious bodily harm to himself, herself or another person;
  (c) no less restrictive method of providing treatment appropriate for the child's mental disorder is appropriate in the circumstances;
  (d) the child is receiving the treatment proposed at the time of the original order under subsection 117 (1), or other appropriate treatment; and
  (e) there is an appropriate plan for the child's care on release from the secure treatment program.

Period of extension
(6) The court shall specify in an order under subsection (5) the period not exceeding 180 days for which the child shall be committed to the secure treatment program.

Release by Administrator

Release

Unconditional release by administrator
121. (1) The administrator may release a child from a secure treatment program unconditionally where the administrator,
  (a) has given the person with lawful custody of the child reasonable notice of the intention to release him or her; and
  (b) is satisfied that,
    (i) the child no longer requires the secure treatment program, and
    (ii) there is an appropriate plan for the child's care on release from the secure treatment program.

Conditional release
(2) The administrator may release a child from a secure treatment program temporarily for medical or compassionate reasons, or for a trial placement in an open setting, for such period and on such terms and conditions as the administrator determines.

Administrator may release despite court order
(3) Subsections (1) and (2) apply despite an order made under subsection 117 (1) (commitment) or 120 (5) (extension).

Review of Commitment

Review of commitment
122. (1) Any one of the following persons may apply to the court for an order terminating an order made under subsection 117 (1) (commitment) or 120 (5) (extension):
  1. The child, where the child is twelve years of age or more.
  2. The child's parent.
  3. The society having care, custody or supervision of the child.

ss. 114 (3), (6-9), 115, 116 apply

(2) Subsections 114 (3), (6), (7), (8) and (9) (hearing) and sections 115 (child's waiver) and 116 (assessment) apply with necessary modifications to an application made under subsection (1).

Termination of order
(3) The court shall make an order terminating a child's commitment unless the court is satisfied that,

(a) the child has a mental disorder;

(b) the secure treatment program would continue to be effective to prevent the child from causing or attempting to cause serious bodily harm to himself, herself or another person;

(c) no less restrictive method of providing treatment appropriate for the child's mental disorder is appropriate in the circumstances; and

(d) the child is receiving the treatment proposed at the time of the most recent order under subsection 117 (1) or 120 (5), or other appropriate treatment.

Idem
(4) In making an order under subsection (3), the court shall consider whether there is an appropriate plan for the child's care on release from the secure treatment program.

ss. 120 (3-6), 121, 122 apply

123. Subsections 120 (3), (4), (5) and (6) and sections 121 and 122 apply with necessary modifications to a person who is eighteen years of age or older and committed to a secure treatment program as if the person were a child.

Emergency Admission

Emergency admission
124. (1) Any one of the following persons may apply to the administrator for the emergency admission of a child to a secure treatment program:

1. Where the child is less than sixteen years of age,
    i.   the child's parent,
    ii. a person who is caring for the child with a parent's consent,
    iii. a child protection worker who has apprehended the child under section 40 of Part III (Child Protection), or
    iv. a society that has custody of the child under an order made under Part III.

2. Where the child is sixteen years of age or more,
    i.   the child,
    ii. the child's parent, if the child consents to the application,
    iii. a society that has custody of the child under an order made under Part III (Child Protection), if the child consents to the application, or
    iv. a physician.

Criteria for admission
(2) The administrator may admit a child to the secure treatment program on an application under subsection (1) for a period not to exceed thirty days where the administrator believes on reasonable grounds that,

(a) the child has a mental disorder;

(b) the child has, as a result of the mental disorder, caused, attempted to cause or by words or conduct made a substantial threat to cause serious bodily harm to himself, herself or another person;

(c) the secure treatment program would be effective to prevent the child from causing or attempting to cause serious bodily harm to himself, herself or another person;

(d) treatment appropriate for the child's mental disorder is available at the place of secure treatment to which the application relates; and

(e) no less restrictive method of providing treatment appropriate for the child's mental disorder is appropriate in the circumstances.

Admission on consent
(3) The administrator may admit the child under subsection (2) although the criterion set out in clause (2) (b) is not met, where,

(a) the other criteria set out in subsection (2) are met;

(b) the child, after obtaining legal advice, consents to his or her admission; and

(c) if the child is less than sixteen years of age, the child's parent or, where the child is in a society's lawful custody, the society consents to the child's admission.

Where child under twelve
(4) Where the child is less than twelve years old, the administrator shall not admit the child under subsection (2) unless the Minister consents to the child's admission.

Additional requirement where applicant is physician
(5) Where the applicant is a physician, the administrator shall not admit the child under subsection (2) unless the administrator is satisfied that the applicant believes the criteria set out in that subsection are met.

Notices required
(6) The administrator shall ensure that within twenty-four hours after a child is admitted to a secure treatment program under subsection (2),

(a) the child is given written notice of his or her right to a review under subsection (9); and

(b) the Office of Child and Family Service Advocacy and the Children's Lawyer are given notice of the child's admission.

Mandatory advice
(7) The Office of Child and Family Service Advocacy shall ensure that forthwith after the notice is received a person

who is not employed by the secure treatment facility explains to the child his or her right to a review in language suitable for the child's level of understanding.

Children's Lawyer to ensure child represented
(8) The Children's Lawyer shall represent the child at the earliest possible opportunity and in any event within five days after receiving a notice under subsection (6) unless the Children's Lawyer is satisfied that another person will provide legal representation for the child within that time.

Application for review
(9) Where a child is admitted to a secure treatment program under this section, any person, including the child, may apply to the Board for an order releasing the child from the secure treatment program.

Child may be kept in program while application pending
(10) Where an application is made under subsection (9), the child may be kept in the secure treatment program until the application is disposed of.

Procedure
(11) Subsections 114 (7), (8) and (9) (hearing) and section 115 (waive oral evidence) apply with necessary modifications to an application made under subsection (9).

Time for review
(12) Where an application is made under subsection (9), the Board shall dispose of the matter within five days of the making of the application.

Order
(13) The Board shall make an order releasing the child from the secure treatment program unless the Board is satisfied that the child meets the criteria for emergency admission set out in clauses 124 (2) (a) to (e).

Police Assistance

Powers of peace officers, period of commitment

Police may take child for secure treatment
125. (1) A peace officer may take a child to a place where there is a secure treatment program,
   (a) for emergency admission, at the request of an applicant referred to in subsection 124 (1); or
   (b) where an order for the child's commitment to the secure treatment program has been made under section 117.

Apprehension of child who leaves
(2) Where a child who has been admitted to a secure treatment program leaves the facility in which the secure treatment program is located without the consent of the administrator, a peace officer may apprehend the child with or without a warrant and return the child to the facility.

Period of commitment
(3) Where a child is returned to a facility under subsection (2), the time that the child was absent from the facility shall not be taken into account in calculating the period of commitment.

Secure Isolation

Director's approval
126. (1) A Director may approve a locked room that complies with the prescribed standards and is located in premises where an approved service or a service purchased by an approved agency is provided, for use for the secure isolation of children, on such terms and conditions as the Director determines.

Withdrawal of approval
(2) Where a Director is of the opinion that a secure isolation room is unnecessary or is being used in a manner that contravenes this Part or the regulations, the Director may withdraw the approval given under subsection (1) and shall give the affected service provider notice of the decision, with reasons.

Secure isolation
127. (1) No service provider or foster parent shall isolate in a locked place a child who is in his or her care or permit the child to be isolated in a locked place, except in accordance with this section and the regulations.

Secure treatment, secure custody and secure temporary detention
(2) Subsection (1) does not prohibit the routine locking at night of rooms in the premises of secure treatment programs or in places of secure custody and places of secure temporary detention under Part IV (Young Offenders).

Criteria for use of secure isolation
(3) A child may be placed in a secure isolation room where,
   (a) in the service provider's opinion,
      (i) the child's conduct indicates that the child is likely, in the immediate future, to cause serious property damage or to cause another person serious bodily harm, and
      (ii) no less restrictive method of restraining the child is practicable; and
   (b) where the child is less than twelve years of age, a Director gives permission for the child to be placed in a secure isolation room because of exceptional circumstances.

One hour limit
(4) A child who is placed in a secure isolation room shall be released within one hour unless the person in charge of the premises approves the child's longer isolation in writing and records the reasons for not restraining the child by a less restrictive method.

Continuous observation of child

(5) The service provider shall ensure that a child who is placed in a secure isolation room is continuously observed by a responsible person.

Review

(6) Where a child is kept in a secure isolation room for more than one hour, the person in charge of the premises shall review the child's isolation at prescribed intervals.

Release

(7) A child who is placed in a secure isolation room shall be released as soon as the person in charge is satisfied that the child is not likely to cause serious property damage or serious bodily harm in the immediate future.

Maximum periods

(8) In no event shall a child be kept in a secure isolation room for a period or periods that exceed an aggregate of eight hours in a given twenty-four hour period or an aggregate of twenty-four hours in a given week.

Review of use of secure isolation

128. A person in charge of premises containing a secure isolation room shall review,

>(a) the need for the secure isolation room; and
>
>(b) the prescribed matters,

every three months from the date on which the secure isolation room is approved under subsection 126 (1), shall make a written report of each review to a Director and shall make such additional reports as are prescribed.

Review Teams

Review team

129. (1) A service provider who is approved under subsection 130 (1) shall establish an interdisciplinary review team with the duty of reviewing and approving or refusing the proposed use of intrusive procedures.

Idem

(2) A review team shall consist of,

>(a) persons employed by the service provider; and
>
>(b) one person who is not employed by the service provider and is approved by the Minister,

and may also include a legally qualified medical practitioner.

Panel

(3) Any three members of a review team may review and approve or refuse the proposed use of an intrusive procedure.

Report to service provider

(4) A review team shall make a report to the service provider concerning every review conducted under subsection (3) and subsection 133 (1) (review of certain recommended procedures).

Report to Minister

(5) A review team shall make reports of its activities to the Minister at the prescribed intervals.

Intrusive Procedures

Approval by Minister

130. (1) The Minister may approve a service provider for the use of the intrusive procedures specified in the approval and may set out in the approval any conditions and limitations to which it is subject.

Revocation, etc., of approval

(2) The Minister may at any time revoke, suspend or amend an approval given under subsection (1) and shall give the affected service provider notice, with reasons, of the Minister's decision.

Proclamation

(3) This section shall come into force on a day to be named by proclamation of the Lieutenant Governor.

Intrusive procedures restricted

131. (1) No service provider shall use or permit the use of an intrusive procedure in respect of a child in the service provider's care, except in accordance with this section.

Exception

(2) Subsection (1) does not prohibit the use of restraints that are reasonably necessary for the secure transportation or transfer of a child who has been admitted to a secure treatment program under this Part, who is detained or has been committed to custody under the *Young Offenders Act* (Canada) or to whom section 95 of Part IV (Young Offenders) (open custody) applies.

When service provider may use or permit intrusive procedure

(3) A service provider who is approved under subsection 130 (1) may use or permit the use of an intrusive procedure in respect of a child in the service provider's care only,

>(a) if the intrusive procedure is specified in the approval;
>
>(b) in accordance with the conditions and limitations set out in the Minister's approval; and
>
>(c) with the approval, obtained in advance and not more than thirty days before the intrusive procedure is used, of the service provider's review team.

Criteria

(4) A review team shall not approve the use of an intrusive procedure in respect of a child unless,

>(a) if the child is sixteen years of age or more, the child consents to its use;
>
>(b) if the child is less than sixteen years of age, the child's parent or, where the child is in a society's lawful custody, the society consents to its use;

(c) the child's behaviour warrants its use;

(d) at least one less intrusive alternative has been attempted without success in improving the child's behaviour;

(e) no other less intrusive alternative is practicable; and

(f) there are reasonable grounds to believe that the procedure would improve the child's behaviour.

Idem

(5) A review team shall not approve the use of an intrusive procedure in respect of a child who is less than sixteen years of age or lacks capacity within the meaning of section 4 without first considering the child's views and preferences, where they can be reasonably ascertained.

Emergency

(6) Where,

(a) a service provider who is approved under subsection 130 (1) believes on reasonable grounds that delay in the use of an intrusive procedure in respect of a child in the service provider's care would cause the child or another person serious mental or physical harm;

(b) the intrusive procedure is specified in the Minister's approval;

(c) if the child is sixteen years of age or more, the child consents to the use of the intrusive procedure or apparently does not have capacity; and

(d) if the child is less than sixteen years of age, the child's parent or, where the child is in a society's lawful custody, the society,

(i) consents to the use of the intrusive procedure, or

(ii) is not immediately available,

the service provider may use or permit the use of the intrusive procedure in respect of the child, in accordance with the conditions and limitations set out in the Minister's approval, during a period not exceeding seventy-two hours, without the approval of the review team, despite clause (3) (c).

Idem

(7) Where a service provider uses or permits the use of an intrusive procedure under subsection (6), the service provider shall seek the review team's approval as soon as possible, and in any event within seventy-two hours of the first use of the intrusive procedure, and shall not continue its use or permit its continued use in respect of the child unless the review team approves it.

Proclamation

(8) This section shall come into force on a day to be named by proclamation of the Lieutenant Governor.

Psychotropic Drugs

Consents required for use of psychotropic drug

132. (1) A service provider shall not administer or permit the administration of a psychotropic drug to a child in the service provider's care without,

(a) if the child is sixteen years of age or more, the child's consent; or

(b) if the child is less than sixteen years of age, the consent of the child's parent or, where the child is in a society's lawful custody, the society's consent.

Idem

(2) A consent referred to in subsection (1) shall identify the psychotropic drug clearly and shall specify,

(a) what condition the psychotropic drug is intended to alleviate;

(b) the range of intended dosages;

(c) the risks and possible side effects associated with the psychotropic drug, and how they vary with different dosages; and

(d) the frequency with which and the period of time during which the psychotropic drug is to be administered.

Child's views and preferences

(3) A service provider shall not administer or permit the administration of a psychotropic drug to a child in the service provider's care who is less than sixteen years of age or lacks capacity within the meaning of section 4 without first considering the child's views and preferences, where they can be reasonably ascertained, except under subsection (4).

Emergency

(4) Where,

(a) a service provider believes on reasonable grounds that,

(i) delay in the administration of a psychotropic drug to a child in the service provider's care would cause the child or another person serious mental or physical harm, and

(ii) no less restrictive course of action would prevent the harm;

(b) if the child is sixteen years of age or more, the child apparently does not have capacity; and

(c) if the child is less than sixteen years of age, the child's parent or, where the child is in a society's lawful custody, the society, is not immediately available,

the service provider may administer or permit the administration of the psychotropic drug to the child during a period not exceeding seventy-two hours without the consent referred to in subsection (1).

Idem

(5) Where a service provider administers or permits the administration of a psychotropic drug under subsection

(4), the service provider shall seek the consent referred to in subsection (1) as soon as possible, and in any event within seventy-two hours of the first administration of the psychotropic drug, and shall not continue its administration or permit its continued administration to the child unless the consent is given.

Proclamation
(6) Subsections (4) and (5) shall come into force on a day to be named by proclamation of the Lieutenant Governor.

Additional Duty of Review Teams

Review of certain recommended procedures
133. (1) Where it is recommended that a child in the care of or regularly receiving services from a service provider who has established a review team undergo,

- (a) non-therapeutic medical or chemical experimentation;
- (b) psychosurgery;
- (c) non-therapeutic sterilization; or
- (d) electro-convulsive therapy,

three members of the review team shall review the matter and advise the child's parent or, where the child is in a society's lawful custody, the society, and the service provider of the review team's opinion as to the appropriateness of the recommendation.

Panel to include medical practitioner
(2) One of the members of the review team acting under subsection (1) shall be a legally qualified medical practitioner.

Prohibition
(3) No procedure referred to in subsection (1) shall be carried out in premises where an approved service or a service purchased by an approved agency is provided.

Professional Advisory Board

Professional Advisory Board
134. (1) The Minister may establish a Professional Advisory Board, composed of physicians and other professionals who,

- (a) have special knowledge in the use of intrusive procedures and psychotropic drugs;
- (b) have demonstrated an informed concern for the welfare and interests of children; and
- (c) are not employed by the Ministry.

Chair
(2) The Minister shall appoint one of the members of the Professional Advisory Board as its chair.

Duties of Board
(3) The Professional Advisory Board shall, at the Minister's request,
- (a) advise the Minister on,
  - (i) prescribing procedures as intrusive procedures, and
  - (ii) making, amending, suspending and revoking approvals under section 130;
- (b) investigate and review the use of intrusive procedures and psychotropic drugs and make recommendations to the Minister; and
- (c) review the practices and procedures of service providers with respect to,
  - (i) secure isolation,
  - (ii) intrusive procedures, and
  - (iii) psychotropic drugs,
  and make recommendations to the Minister.

Request for review
135. Any person may request that the Minister refer the matter of the use of secure isolation or an intrusive procedure in respect of a child, or the administration of a psychotropic drug to a child, to the Professional Advisory Board for investigation and review.

PART VII
ADOPTION

Interpretation
136. (1) In this Part,

"licensee" means the holder of a licence issued under Part IX (Licensing) to place children for adoption;

"relative", when used in reference to a child, means the child's grandparent, great-uncle, great-aunt, uncle or aunt, whether by blood, marriage or adoption;

"spouse" has the same meaning as in Parts I and II of the *Human Rights Code*.

Best interests of child
(2) Where a person is directed in this Part to make an order or determination in the best interests of a child, the person shall take into consideration those of the following circumstances of the case that he or she considers relevant:

1. The child's physical, mental and emotional needs, and the appropriate care or treatment to meet those needs.
2. The child's physical, mental and emotional level of development.
3. The child's cultural background.
4. The religious faith, if any, in which the child is being raised.
5. The importance for the child's development of a positive relationship with a parent and a secure place as a member of a family.
6. The child's relationships by blood or through an adoption order.

7. The importance of continuity in the child's care and the possible effect on the child of disruption of that continuity.

8. The child's views and wishes, if they can be reasonably ascertained.

9. The effects on the child of delay in the disposition of the case.

10. Any other relevant circumstance.

Where child an Indian or native person
(3) Where a person is directed in this Part to make an order or determination in the best interests of a child and the child is an Indian or native person, the person shall take into consideration the importance, in recognition of the uniqueness of Indian and native culture, heritage and traditions, of preserving the child's cultural identity.

Consent to Adoption

Consents
137. (1) In this section,

"parent", when used in reference to a child, means each of,
   (a) the child's mother,
   (b) an individual described in one of paragraphs 1 to 6 of subsection 8 (1) of the *Children's Law Reform Act*, unless it is proved on a balance of probabilities that he is not the child's natural father,
   (c) the individual having lawful custody of the child,
   (d) an individual who, during the twelve months before the child is placed for adoption under this Part, has demonstrated a settled intention to treat the child as a child of his or her family, or has acknowledged parentage of the child and provided for the child's support,
   (e) an individual who, under a written agreement or a court order, is required to provide for the child, has custody of the child or has a right of access to the child, and
   (f) an individual who has acknowledged parentage of the child in writing under section 12 of the *Children's Law Reform Act*,
but does not include a licensee or a foster parent.

Consent of parent, etc.
(2) An order for the adoption of a child who is less than sixteen years of age, or is sixteen years of age or more but has not withdrawn from parental control, shall not be made without,
   (a) the written consent of every parent; or
   (b) where the child has been made a Crown ward under Part III (Child Protection), the written consent of a Director.

Idem
(3) A consent under clause (2) (a) shall not be given before the child is seven days old.

Idem
(4) Where a child is being placed for adoption by a society or licensee, a consent under clause (2) (a) shall not be given until,
   (a) the society or licensee has advised the parent of his or her right,
      (i) to withdraw the consent under subsection (8),
      (ii) to be informed, on his or her request, whether an adoption order has been made in respect of the child, and
      (iii) to obtain non-identifying information under section 166 and to participate in the adoption disclosure register maintained under clause 163 (2) (a); and
   (b) the society or licensee has given the parent an opportunity to seek counselling and independent legal advice with respect to the consent.

Custody of child
(5) Where,
   (a) a child is being placed for adoption by a society or licensee;
   (b) every consent required under subsection (2) has been given and has not been withdrawn under subsection (8); and
   (c) the twenty-one day period referred to in subsection (8) has expired,
the rights and responsibilities of the child's parents with respect to the child's custody, care and control are transferred to the society or licensee, until the consent is withdrawn under subsection 139 (1) (late withdrawal with leave of court) or an order is made for the child's adoption under section 146.

Consent of person to be adopted
(6) An order for the adoption of a person who is seven years of age or more shall not be made without the person's written consent.

Idem
(7) A consent under subsection (6) shall not be given until the person has had an opportunity to obtain counselling and independent legal advice with respect to the consent.

Withdrawal of consent
(8) A person who gives a consent under subsection (2) or (6) may withdraw it in writing within twenty-one days after the consent is given and where that person had custody of the child immediately before giving the consent, the child shall be returned to him or her as soon as the consent is withdrawn.

Dispensing with person's consent
(9) The court may dispense with a person's consent required under subsection (6) where the court is satisfied that,

(a) obtaining the consent would cause the person emotional harm; or

(b) the person is not able to consent because of a developmental disability.

Consent of applicant's spouse

(10) An adoption order shall not be made on the application of a person who is a spouse without the written consent of the other spouse.

Consents by minors: role of Children's Lawyer

(11) Where a person who gives a consent under clause (2) (a) is less than eighteen years of age, the consent is not valid unless the Children's Lawyer is satisfied that the consent is fully informed and reflects the person's true wishes.

Affidavits of execution

(12) An affidavit of execution in the prescribed form shall be attached to a consent and a withdrawal of a consent under this section.

Form of foreign consents

(13) A consent required under this section that is given outside Ontario and whose form does not comply with the requirements of subsection (12) and the regulations is not invalid for that reason alone, if its form complies with the laws of the jurisdiction where it is given.

Dispensing with consent

138. The court may dispense with a consent required under section 137 for the adoption of a child, except the consent of the child or of a Director, where the court is satisfied that,

(a) it is in the child's best interests to do so; and

(b) the person whose consent is required has received notice of the proposed adoption and of the application to dispense with consent, or a reasonable effort to give the notice has been made.

Late withdrawal of consent

139. (1) The court may permit a person who gave a consent to the adoption of a child under section 137 to withdraw the consent after the twenty-one day period referred to in subsection 137 (8) where the court is satisfied that it is in the child's best interests to do so, and where that person had custody of the child immediately before giving the consent, the child shall be returned to him or her as soon as the consent is withdrawn.

Exception: child placed for adoption

(2) Subsection (1) does not apply where the child has been placed with a person for adoption and remains in that person's care.

Placement for Adoption

Duty of society

140. (1) A society shall make all reasonable efforts to secure the adoption of,

(a) every child who has been made a Crown ward under Part III (Child Protection) and is in the society's care and custody; and

(b) at the request of a Director or of another society, any child who has been made a Crown ward and is in that society's care and custody.

When society may place child for adoption

(2) No society shall place a child for adoption until,

(a) any outstanding order of access to the child made under subsection 58 (1) of Part III has been terminated;

(b) where the child is a Crown ward, the time for commencing an appeal of the order of Crown wardship or of an order under subsection 65 (1) of Part III (status review) has expired; or

(c) where the child is a Crown ward, any appeal of an order referred to in clause (b) has been finally disposed of or abandoned,

whichever is the latest.

Where child an Indian or native person

(3) Where a child to be placed for adoption is an Indian or a native person, the society shall give the child's band or native community thirty days written notice of its intention to place the child for adoption.

Only societies and licensees may place children, etc.

141. (1) No person except a society or licensee shall,

(a) place a child with another person for adoption; or

(b) take, send or attempt to take or send a child who is a resident of Ontario out of Ontario to be placed for adoption.

Only societies, etc., may bring children into Ontario

(2) No person except a society or a licensee whose licence contains a term permitting the licensee to act under this subsection shall bring a child who is not a resident of Ontario into Ontario to be placed for adoption.

Licensee to notify Director of placement

(3) No licensee except a licensee exempted under subsection (5) shall,

(a) place a child with another person for adoption; or

(b) take, send or attempt to take or send a child who is a resident of Ontario out of Ontario to be placed for adoption,

without first notifying a Director of the proposed placement.

Director's approval required

(4) No person shall receive a child for adoption, except from a society or from a licensee exempted under subsec-

tion (5), without first receiving a Director's approval of the placement under clause 142 (2) (a).

Designation of licensee
(5) A Director may designate a licensee that is an agency as exempt from the requirements of subsections (3) and (4).

Placements to be registered
(6) A society or licensee who places a child with another person for adoption shall register the placement in the prescribed manner within thirty days of placing the child.

Idem: Director
(7) A Director who becomes aware of any placement for adoption of a child that has not been registered under subsection (6) shall forthwith register the placement in the prescribed manner.

Exception: family adoptions
(8) Subsections (1), (2), (3), (4), (6) and (7) do not apply to,
    (a) the placement for adoption of a child with the child's relative, the child's parent or a spouse of the child's parent; or
    (b) the taking or sending of a child out of Ontario for adoption by the child's relative, the child's parent or a spouse of the child's parent.

Adoption homestudy

142. (1) A licensee who notifies a Director of a proposed placement under subsection 141 (3) shall at the same time provide the Director with a report of an adoption homestudy of the person with whom placement is proposed, prepared by a person who, in the opinion of the Director or a local director, is qualified to make an adoption homestudy.

Director's approval
(2) A Director who receives a report under subsection (1) shall consider it and, as soon as possible,
    (a) approve the proposed placement; or
    (b) refuse to approve the placement and give notice of the refusal to the licensee and the person with whom placement is proposed.

Right to hearing
(3) Where a Director gives notice under clause (2) (b), the licensee and the person with whom placement is proposed are entitled to a hearing before the Board.

Application of other sections
(3.1) Sections 197, 199, 201 and 202 of Part IX (Licensing) apply to the hearing with necessary modifications and for that purpose references to the Tribunal shall be deemed to be references to the Board.

Extension of time
(3.2) If the Board is satisfied that there are reasonable grounds for the licensee or the person with whom place-

ment is proposed to apply for an extension of the time fixed for requiring the hearing and for the Board to grant relief, it may,
    (a) extend the time either before or after the expiration of the time; and
    (b) give the directions that it considers proper as a result of extending the time.

Recording of evidence
(3.3) The evidence taken before the Board at the hearing shall be recorded.

Placement outside Canada
(4) A Director shall not approve the proposed placement of a child outside Canada unless the Director is satisfied that a prescribed special circumstance justifies the placement.

Terms and conditions
(5) A Director may approve a proposed placement under clause (2) (a) subject to any terms and conditions that the Director considers appropriate, including supervision of the placement by,
    (a) a specified society, licensee or person; or
    (b) in the case of a placement outside Ontario, a specified child protection agency recognized in the jurisdiction of the placement.

Right to hearing
(6) Where a Director imposes a term or condition on an approval under subsection (5), the licensee and the person with whom placement is proposed are entitled to a hearing before the Board.

Application of other sections
(7) Sections 198, 199, 201 and 202 of Part IX (Licensing) apply to the hearing with necessary modifications and for that purpose references to the Tribunal shall be deemed to be references to the Board.

Access orders terminate

143. (1) Where a child is placed for adoption by a society or licensee, every order respecting access to the child is terminated, except an order made under Part III (Child Protection).

No interference, etc., with child in placement
(2) Where a child has been placed for adoption by a society or licensee and no adoption order has been made, no person shall,
    (a) interfere with the child; or
    (b) for the purpose of interfering with the child, visit or communicate with the child or with the person with whom the child has been placed.

Director's Review

Review by Director

144. (1) Where,

(a) a society makes a decision refusing to place a child with a person, including a foster parent who is caring for the child, for adoption; or

(b) a society or licensee makes a decision to remove a child who has been placed with a person for adoption,

a Director may review the decision of the society or licensee and may,

(c) confirm the decision, giving written reasons for doing so; or

(d) rescind the decision and do anything further that the society or licensee may do under this Part with respect to the child's placement.

Idem

(2) A Director who reviews a decision under subsection (1) shall take into account the importance of continuity in the child's care.

Notice to Director

145. (1) Where a child has been placed for adoption under this Part, no order for the child's adoption has been made and,

(a) the person with whom the child is placed asks the society or licensee that placed the child to remove the child; or

(b) the society or licensee proposes to remove the child from the person with whom the child was placed,

the society or licensee shall notify a Director.

Idem

(2) Where no order for a child's adoption has been made and a year has expired since,

(a) the earlier of the child's placement for adoption or the giving of the most recent consent under clause 137 (2) (a); or

(b) the most recent review under subsection (3),

whichever is later, the society or licensee shall notify a Director, unless the child is a Crown ward.

Director's review

(3) A Director who receives notice under subsection (1) or (2) shall review the child's status and may, in the child's best interests,

(a) where the child is in the care of the person with whom the child was placed for adoption, confirm the child's placement or do anything the society or licensee that placed the child may do with respect to the child's placement or further placement;

(b) where the child was placed for adoption by a licensee, direct the licensee to place the child in the care and custody of a specified society;

(c) where the child is in the care, custody and control of a society, direct the society to bring the child before the court under Part III to determine whether the child is in need of protection;

(d) where the child leaves or is removed from the care of the person with whom the child was placed for adoption, do anything the society or licensee that placed the child may do with respect to the child's further placement; or

(e) where a parent who gave consent under clause 137 (2) (a) and had charge of the child at the time the consent was given agrees to resume the child's care and custody, direct the society or licensee that placed the child to return the child to the parent.

Deemed withdrawal of consent

(4) Where a Director directs a society or licensee to return a child to a parent under clause (3) (e), the parent's consent under clause 137 (2) (a) shall be deemed to be withdrawn.

Adoption Orders

Orders for adoption

Adoption of child

146. (1) The court may make an order for the adoption of a child who is less than sixteen years of age, or is sixteen years of age or more but has not withdrawn from parental control, and,

(a) has been placed for adoption by a society or licensee; or

(b) has been placed for adoption by a person other than a society or licensee and has resided with the applicant for at least two years,

in the child's best interests, on the application of the person with whom the child is placed.

Family adoption

(2) The court may make an order for the adoption of a child, in the child's best interests, on the application of,

(a) a relative of the child;

(b) the child's parent; or

(c) the spouse of the child's parent.

Adoption of adult, etc.

(3) The court may make an order for the adoption of,

(a) a person eighteen years of age or more; or

(b) a child who is sixteen years of age or more and has withdrawn from parental control,

on another person's application.

Who may apply

(4) An application under this section may only be made,

(a) by one individual; or

(b) jointly, by two individuals who are spouses of one another.

(c) Repealed.

Residency requirement

(5) The court shall not make an order under this section for the adoption of, or on the application of, a person who is not a resident of Ontario.

Where applicant a minor

147. The court shall not make an order under section 146 on the application of a person who is less than eighteen years of age unless the court is satisfied that special circumstances justify making the order.

Where order not to be made

148. Where the court has made an order,

    (a) dispensing with a consent under section 138; or

    (b) refusing to permit the late withdrawal of a consent under subsection 139 (1),

the court shall not make an order under section 146 until,

    (c) the time for commencing an appeal of the order has expired; or

    (d) any appeal of the order has been finally disposed of or abandoned,

whichever is later.

Director's statement

149. (1) Where an application is made for an order for the adoption of a child under subsection 146 (1), a Director shall, before the hearing, file a written statement with the court indicating,

    (a) that the child has resided with the applicant for at least six months or, in the case of an application under clause 146 (1) (b), for at least two years and, in the Director's opinion, it would be in the child's best interests to make the order;

    (b) in the case of an application under clause 146 (1) (a), that for specified reasons it would be in the child's best interests, in the Director's opinion, to make the order although the child has resided with the applicant for less than six months; or

    (c) that the child has resided with the applicant for at least six months or, in the case of an application under clause 146 (1) (b), for at least two years and, in the Director's opinion, it would not be in the child's best interests to make the order,

and referring to any additional circumstances that the Director wishes to bring to the court's attention.

Local director may make statement

(2) Where a child was placed by a society and has resided with the applicant for at least six months, the statement under subsection (1) may be made and filed by the local director.

Amendment of statement, etc.

(3) The Director or local director, as the case may be, may amend the statement referred to in subsection (1) at any time and may attend at the hearing and make submissions.

Where recommendation negative

(4) Where the statement under subsection (1) indicates that, in the Director's or local director's opinion, it would not be in the child's best interests to make the order, a copy of the statement shall be filed with the court and served on the applicant at least thirty days before the hearing.

Report of child's adjustment

(5) The statement under subsection (1) shall be based on a report of the child's adjustment in the applicant's home, prepared by,

    (a) the society that placed the child or has jurisdiction where the child is placed; or

    (b) a person approved by the Director or local director.

Family adoptions: court may require statement

(6) Where an application is made for an order for the adoption of a child under subsection 146 (2), the court may order that subsections (1), (3), (4) and (5) shall apply to the application.

Place of hearing

150. (1) An application for an adoption order shall be heard and dealt with in the county or district in which,

    (a) the applicant; or

    (b) the person to be adopted,

resides at the time the application is filed.

Transfer of proceeding

(2) Where the court is satisfied at any stage of an application for an adoption order that there is a preponderance of convenience in favour of conducting it in another county or district, the court may order that it be transferred to that other county or district and be continued as if it had been commenced there.

Rules re applications

Hearing in private

151. (1) An application for an adoption order shall be heard and dealt with in the absence of the public.

Court files private

(2) No person shall have access to the court file concerning an application for an adoption order, except,

    (a) the court and authorized court employees;

    (b) the parties and their solicitors and agents; and

    (c) a Director and a local director.

Stale applications

(3) Where an application for an adoption order is not heard within twelve months of the day on which the applicant signed it,

    (a) the court shall not hear the application unless the court is satisfied that it is just to do so; and

    (b) the applicant may make another application.

No right to notice

(4) No person,

  (a) who has given a consent under clause 137 (2) (a) and has not withdrawn it;

  (b) whose consent has been dispensed with under section 138; or

  (c) who is a parent of a Crown ward who is placed for adoption,

is entitled to receive notice of an application under section 146.

Power of court

152. (1) The court may, on its own initiative, summon a person to attend before it, testify and produce any document or thing, and may enforce obedience to the summons as if it had been made in a proceeding under the *Family Law Act.*

Duty of court

(2) The court shall not make an order for the adoption of a child under subsection 146 (1) or (2) unless the court is satisfied that,

  (a) every person who has given a consent under section 137 understands the nature and effect of the adoption order; and

  (b) every applicant understands and appreciates the special role of an adoptive parent.

Participation of child

(3) Where an application is made for an order for the adoption of a child under subsection 146 (1) or (2), the court shall,

  (a) inquire into the child's capacity to understand and appreciate the nature of the application; and

  (b) consider the child's views and wishes, if they can be reasonably ascertained,

and where it is practical to do so shall hear the child.

Participation of adult, etc.

(4) Where an application is made for an order for the adoption of a person under subsection 146 (3), the court shall consider the person's views and wishes and, on request, hear the person.

Change of name

153. (1) Where the court makes an order under section 146, the court may, at the request of the applicant or applicants and, where the person adopted is twelve years of age or more, with the person's written consent,

  (a) change the person's surname to a surname that the person could have been given if he or she had been born to the applicant or applicants; and

  (b) change the person's given name.

When child's consent not required

(2) A child's consent to a change of name under subsection (1) is not required where the child's consent was dispensed with under subsection 137 (9).

Interim Orders

Interim order

154. (1) Where an application is made for an order for the adoption of a child under subsection 146 (1) or (2), the court, after considering the statement made under subsection 149 (1), may postpone the determination of the matter and make an interim order in the child's best interests placing the child in the applicant's care and custody for a specified period not exceeding one year.

Terms and conditions

(2) The court may make an order under subsection (1) subject to any terms and conditions that the court considers appropriate respecting,

  (a) the child's maintenance and education;

  (b) supervision of the child; and

  (c) any other matter the court considers advisable in the child's best interests.

Not an adoption order

(3) An order under subsection (1) is not an adoption order.

Consents required

(4) Sections 137 and 138 (consents to adoption) apply to an order under subsection (1) with necessary modifications.

Departure from Ontario

(5) Where an applicant takes up residence outside Ontario after obtaining an order under subsection (1), the court may nevertheless make an adoption order under subsection 146 (1) or (2) where the statement made under subsection 149 (1) indicates that, in the Director's or local director's opinion, it would be in the child's best interests to make the order.

Successive adoption orders

155. An adoption order under subsection 146 (1) or (2) or an interim custody order under subsection 154 (1) may be made in respect of a person who is the subject of an earlier adoption order.

Appeals

Appeals

Appeal: adoption order

156. (1) An appeal from a court's order under section 146 may be made to the Superior Court of Justice by,

  (a) the applicant for the adoption order; and

  (b) the Director or local director who made the statement under subsection 149 (1).

Idem: dispensing with consent

(2) An appeal from a court's order under section 138 dispensing with a consent may be made to the Superior Court of Justice by,

  (a) the persons referred to in subsection (1); and

  (b) the person whose consent was dispensed with.

Idem: late withdrawal of consent
(3) An appeal from a court's order under subsection 139 (1) permitting the late withdrawal of a consent may be made to the Superior Court of Justice by,

    (a) the persons referred to in subsection (1); and

    (b) the person who gave the consent.

No extension of time for appeal
(4) No extension of the time for an appeal shall be granted.

Place of hearing
(5) An appeal under this section shall be heard in the county or district in which the order appealed from was made.

Hearing in private
(6) An appeal under this section shall be heard in the absence of the public.

Effect of Adoption Order

Order final
157. An adoption order under section 146 is final and irrevocable, subject only to section 156 (appeals), and shall not be questioned or reviewed in any court by way of injunction, declaratory judgment, *certiorari, mandamus*, prohibition, *habeascorpus* or application for judicial review.

Status of adopted child
158. (1) In this section,

"adopted child" means a person who was adopted in Ontario.

Same
(2) For all purposes of law, as of the date of the making of an adoption order,

    (a) the adopted child becomes the child of the adoptive parent and the adoptive parent becomes the parent of the adopted child; and

    (b) the adopted child ceases to be the child of the person who was his or her parent before the adoption order was made and that person ceases to be the parent of the adopted child, except where the person is the spouse of the adoptive parent,

as if the adopted child had been born to the adoptive parent.

How relationships determined
(3) The relationship to one another of all persons, including the adopted child, the adoptive parent, the kindred of the adoptive parent, the parent before the adoption order was made and the kindred of that former parent shall for all purposes be determined in accordance with subsection (2).

Reference in will or other document
(4) In any will or other document made at any time before or after the 1st day of November, 1985, and whether the maker of the will or document is alive on that day or not, a reference to a person or group or class of persons described in terms of relationship by blood or marriage to another person shall be deemed to refer to or include, as the case may be, a person who comes within the description as a result of an adoption, unless the contrary is expressed.

Application of section
(5) This section applies and shall be deemed always to have applied with respect to any adoption made under any Act heretofore in force, but not so as to affect,

    (a) any interest in property or right of the adopted child that has indefeasibly vested before the date of the making of an adoption order; and

    (b) any interest in property or right that has indefeasibly vested before the 1st day of November, 1985.

Exception
(6) Subsections (2) and (3) do not apply for the purposes of the laws relating to incest and the prohibited degrees of marriage to remove a person from a relationship that would have existed but for those subsections.

Effect of foreign adoption
159. An adoption effected according to the law of another jurisdiction, before or after the 1st day of November, 1985, has the same effect in Ontario as an adoption under this Part.

No order for access by birth parent, etc.
160. (1) Where an order for the adoption of a child has been made under this Part, no court shall make an order under this Part for access to the child by,

    (a) a birth parent; or

    (b) a member of a birth parent's family.

Definition
(2) In this section,

"birth parent" has the same meaning as in section 166.

Records, Confidentiality and Disclosure

Parent to be informed on request
161. At the request of a person whose consent to an adoption was required under clause 137 (2) (a) or a predecessor of that provision and was given or was dispensed with, any society or the licensee that placed the child for adoption shall inform the person whether an order has been made for the child's adoption.

Court papers
162. (1) In this section,

"court" includes the Superior Court of Justice.

Papers to be sealed up

(2) Subject to subsections (3) and 167 (6), the documents used upon an application for an adoption order under this Part or a predecessor of this Part shall be sealed up together with a certified copy of the original order and filed in the office of the court by the proper officer of the court, and shall not be open for inspection except upon an order of the court or the written direction of the Registrar of Adoption Information appointed under subsection 163 (1).

Transmission of order

(3) Within thirty days after an adoption order is made under this Part, the proper officer of the court shall cause a sufficient number of certified copies of it to be made, under the seal of the proper certifying authority, and shall transmit,

(a) the original order to the adoptive parent;

(b) one certified copy to the Registrar of Adoption Information;

(c) one certified copy to the Registrar General under the *Vital Statistics Act*, or, if the adopted child was born outside Ontario, two certified copies;

(d) if the adopted child is an Indian, one certified copy to the Registrar under the *Indian Act* (Canada).

Registrar of Adoption Information

Registrar of Adoption Information

163. (1) The Minister may appoint an employee of the Ministry as Registrar of Adoption Information for the purposes of this section and sections 164 to 174.

Duties of Registrar

(2) The Registrar shall,

(a) maintain a register for the purposes of section 167;

(b) ensure that counselling is provided to persons who receive identifying information from the Registrar;

(c) ensure that counselling is made available to persons who receive non-identifying information from the Registrar, who are or may wish to be named in the register, or who are concerned that they may be affected by the disclosure of identifying information;

(d) have searches conducted in accordance with subsection 169 (3).

Delegation of Registrar's powers and duties

(3) The Registrar may, in writing, authorize other employees of the Ministry to exercise any or all of the Registrar's powers and perform any or all of the Registrar's duties.

Counselling

(4) The counselling referred to in this section and in sections 166 (disclosure of non-identifying information), 167 (adoption disclosure register) and 170 (persons adopted outside Ontario) shall be provided by persons who are, in

the opinion of the Registrar or a local director, qualified to do so.

Confidentiality rules apply

164. Sections 165 to 174 apply regardless of when the adoption order was made.

Confidentiality of Adoption Records

Adoption information confidential

165. (1) Despite any other Act, after an adoption order is made, no person shall inspect, remove, alter or permit the inspection, removal or alteration of information that relates to the adoption and is kept,

(a) by the Ministry;

(b) by a society or licensee; or

(c) in the adoption disclosure register maintained under clause 163 (2) (a),

or disclose or permit the disclosure of such information that the person obtained from the records of the Ministry, including the register, or from the records of a society or licensee.

Exceptions

(2) Subsection (1) does not apply to,

(a) the disclosure of information by a person who obtained it before the adoption order was made, if the information was obtained in accordance with this Act and the regulations or with the consent of the person to whom the information relates;

(b) the disclosure of non-identifying information in accordance with section 166 or 170 (persons adopted outside Ontario);

(c) the disclosure of identifying information in accordance with section 167 (adoption disclosure register) or 170;

(d) the disclosure of identifying or non-identifying information in accordance with section 168 (disclosure to protect health, safety or welfare);

(e) the disclosure of information in accordance with an order of the Board under subsection 172 (10);

(f) the routine maintenance and updating of records by the Ministry or a society or licensee;

(g) the release by the Registrar of Adoption Information of a copy of an adoption order to,

(i) the adoptive parent,

(ii) the adopted person or any other person if, in the Registrar's opinion, it is desirable that he or she receive a copy of the adoption order, or

(iii) a governmental authority that requires the copy to issue a birth certificate, passport or visa;

(h) the inspection, by a person named in subsection (3), of information kept by the Ministry or a society or licensee, or the disclosure of such information to such a person;

(i)   the disclosure of information to a person who is engaged in research, in accordance with subsection (4).

Persons entitled to share information
(3) Clause (2) (h) applies in respect of:
1. The Minister.
2. The Registrar of Adoption Information.
3. A Director, or an employee of the Ministry who has a Director's written authority.
4. A local director, or an employee of a society who has the local director's written authority.
5. A licensee who is an individual, a director of a licensee that is a corporation, or an employee of a licensee who has the licensee's written authority.
6. A child protection or child placement agency that is recognized in another jurisdiction.

Research
(4) A person who is engaged in research may, with the written approval of the Registrar of Adoption Information or, in the case of information kept by a society, with the local director's written approval, inspect and use information that relates to adoptions, but shall not,
(a) use or communicate the information for any purpose except research, academic pursuits or the compilation of statistical data; or
(b) communicate any identifying information.

Privacy
(5) The *Freedom of Information and Protection of Privacy Act* does not apply to information that relates to an adoption.

Disclosure of Non-Identifying Information

Interpretation, information

Definition
166. (1) In this section and in sections 167 to 174,

"Registrar" means the Registrar of Adoption Information appointed under subsection 163 (1).

Idem
(2) In this section and in sections 163, 165 and 167 to 174,

"identifying information" means information whose disclosure, alone or in combination with other information, will in the circumstances reveal the identity of the person to whom it relates;

"non-identifying information" means information that is not identifying information.

Idem
(3) In this section and in sections 167, 168 and 169,

"adopted person" means a person who was adopted in Ontario;

"birth grandparent" means any parent of a birth parent;

"birth parent" means an adopted person's biological mother or father, and includes a person whose consent to another person's adoption was required under clause 137 (2) (a) or a predecessor of that provision and was given or was dispensed with;

"birth sibling" means a child of the same birth parent as an adopted person, and includes the birth parent's adopted child and a person whom the birth parent has demonstrated a settled intention to treat as a child of his or her family;

"register" means the register maintained under clause 163 (2) (a).

Who may request information
(4) Each of the following persons may make a request to the Registrar for non-identifying information that relates to an adoption:
1. The adopted person, if he or she has attained the age of eighteen years or has the written consent of an adoptive parent.
2. An adoptive parent.
3. A birth parent or birth grandparent.
4. A birth sibling who has attained the age of eighteen years.
5. A person who is a member of a prescribed class, if the person has the written consent of the adopted person and the adopted person would be entitled to make the request or, if not, the written consent of an adoptive parent.
6. Any other person if, in the Registrar's opinion, it is desirable that the person be able to request non-identifying information as if he or she were a birth parent.

Disclosure of information
(5) When a person makes a request under subsection (4), the Registrar shall do one of the following:
1. Disclose to the person all the relevant non-identifying information in the Ministry's possession that relates to the adoption.
2. Forward that information to a society or licensee for disclosure to the person in accordance with subsection (7).
3. If the person lives outside Ontario, disclose that information to a child protection or child placement agency that is recognized in the jurisdiction where the person lives, or to an individual in that jurisdiction who, in the Registrar's opinion, is qualified to provide counselling.
4. Refer the person's request to a society or licensee that has the relevant information.

Counselling

(6) When the Registrar discloses information under subsection (5), he or she shall also ensure that counselling is made available to the person receiving the information.

Information forwarded to society or licensee

(7) When the Registrar forwards information to a society or licensee under subsection (5), the society or licensee shall disclose it to the person who requested it and shall also make counselling available to him or her.

Societies and licensees

(8) Subsections (4), (5), (6) and (7) also apply with necessary modifications to societies and licensees.

Further disclosure

(9) A person who receives information under subsection (5) or (7) may disclose it to any person.

Adoption Disclosure Register

Disclosure of identifying information

167. (1) After an adoption order is made in Ontario, identifying information that relates to the adoption may be disclosed in accordance with this section or section 168 (disclosure to protect health, safety or welfare).

Who may apply to be named in register

(2) Each of the following persons may apply to a society or to the Registrar to be named in the register:

1. An adopted person who has attained the age of eighteen years.
2. The birth parent or birth grandparent of an adopted person.
3. The birth sibling of an adopted person, if the birth sibling has attained the age of eighteen years.
4. Any other person if, in the Registrar's opinion, it is desirable that the person be named in the register as if he or she were a birth parent.

Society to forward application

(3) A society that receives an application shall promptly send it to the Registrar.

Entry in register, etc.

(4) On receiving an application, the Registrar shall enter the applicant's name in the register and then make a search to determine whether the adopted person and his or her birth parent, birth grandparent or birth sibling or a person described in paragraph 4 of subsection (2) are both named in the register.

Further consents

(5) If the Registrar determines that an adopted person and his or her birth parent, birth grandparent or birth sibling or a person described in paragraph 4 of subsection (2) are both named in the register, the Registrar shall, after ensuring that each of them receives counselling, give both persons an opportunity to consent in writing to the disclosure of information in accordance with subsections (8) and (9).

Registrar to compile relevant material

(6) If both persons give the further consent referred to in subsection (5), the Registrar shall compile the material described in paragraphs 1, 2 and 3:

1. All relevant identifying information from the records of the Ministry and of societies and licensees.
2. If the adopted person requests it, copies of the documents referred to in subsection 162 (2) (court file).
3. If the adopted person requests it, an extract of information from his or her original birth registration kept by the Registrar General under the *Vital Statistics Act*.

Idem

(7) The compiled material shall include only information that pertains to the adopted person or the other person named in the register and shall not include a copy of the adopted person's original birth registration.

Disclosure by Registrar

(8) The Registrar shall ensure that the compiled material is promptly disclosed to the adopted person and also to the other person named in the register, separately and in accordance with one or more of the methods described in subsection (9).

Idem

(9) The Registrar may,

(a) make the compiled material available to the adopted person or the other person named in the register, or to both, first ensuring that each person to whom the material is made available receives counselling;

(b) forward the compiled material to a society that he or she considers appropriate to undertake disclosure to the adopted person or the other person named in the register, or to both;

(c) if the adopted person or the other person named in the register lives outside Ontario, forward the compiled material to a child protection or child placement agency that is recognized in the jurisdiction where the person lives, or to an individual in that jurisdiction, but only if the Registrar is satisfied that the person will receive appropriate counselling.

Exception: further consent

(10) If a person whose further consent to disclosure would be required is named in the register but has died, cannot be found despite a discreet and reasonable search that has continued for at least six months, or appears to lack capacity as defined in subsection 4 (1), the Registrar may disclose information to the other person named in

the register in accordance with subsection (9) without the first-named person's further consent.

Duty of society

(11) A society that receives compiled material under clause (9) (b) shall promptly make it available to the adopted person or the other person named in the register, or both, as the case may be, first ensuring that each person to whom the material is made available receives counselling.

Additional information

(12) If the society's records contain identifying information that pertains to the adopted person or the other person named in the register and that is not included in the compiled material, the society shall disclose the information in the same manner as the compiled material.

Duty of society

(13) A society shall provide counselling to persons who receive identifying information from the society, and shall make counselling available to persons who are named or may wish to be named in the register or who are concerned that they may be affected by the disclosure of identifying information.

Further disclosure

(14) A person who is named in the register and receives information under subsection (9), (10), (11) or (12) may disclose it to any person.

Disclosure to Protect Health, Safety or Welfare

Disclosure to protect health, safety or welfare

168. (1) The Registrar may disclose identifying or non-identifying information that relates to an adoption to any person if, in the Registrar's opinion, the health, safety or welfare of that person or of any other person requires the disclosure.

Application of subs. (1)

(2) Subsection (1) applies whether the adoption order was made in Ontario or elsewhere.

Further disclosure

(3) A person who receives information under this section in the course of his or her professional or official duties may disclose it further only for the purpose of protecting a person's health, safety or welfare.

Idem

(4) A person who receives information under this section otherwise than as described in subsection (3) may disclose it to any person.

Searches

Request for search by Registrar

169. (1) An adopted person who has attained the age of eighteen years may ask the Registrar to search on his

or her behalf for a specific person in one of the following categories:

1. A person whose consent to the adoption was required under clause 137 (2) (a) or a predecessor of that provision and was given or was dispensed with.
2. A person who has acknowledged that he is the adopted person's biological father.
3. A parent of a person described in paragraph 1 or 2.
4. A birth sibling of the adopted person who has also attained the age of eighteen years.

Idem, member of prescribed class

(2) A person who is a member of a prescribed class may ask the Registrar to search on his or her behalf for a specific adopted person who has attained the age of eighteen years.

Duty of Registrar

(3) The Registrar shall have a discreet and reasonable search made for the person mentioned in the request, and shall seek to ascertain whether that person wishes to be named in the register.

Exception re disclosure

(4) If the Registrar discovers that the person mentioned in the request has died or appears to lack capacity as defined in subsection 4 (1), or if the person cannot be found despite a discreet and reasonable search that has continued for at least six months, the Registrar may disclose information to the person who made the request, in accordance with section 167, as if both persons were named in the register.

Persons Adopted Outside Ontario

Out of province adoption information

170. (1) In this section,

"adopted person" means a person who was adopted outside Ontario;

"birth parent" means an adopted person's biological mother or father, or a person whose consent to another person's adoption was given or dispensed with;

"birth grandparent" means any parent of a birth parent;

"birth sibling" means a child of the same birth parent as an adopted person, and includes the birth parent's adopted child and a person whom the birth parent has demonstrated a settled intention to treat as a child of his or her family;

"out of province adoption" means an adoption where the adoption order was made outside Ontario.

Who may request non-identifying information

(2) Each of the following persons may make a request to the Registrar for non-identifying information that relates to an out of province adoption:

1. The adopted person, if he or she has attained the age of eighteen years or has the written consent of an adoptive parent.
2. An adoptive parent.
3. A birth parent or birth grandparent.
4. A birth sibling who has attained the age of eighteen years.
5. Any other person if, in the opinion of the Registrar or local director, it is desirable that the person receive non-identifying information as if he or she were a birth parent.

Disclosure of information
(3) When a person makes a request under subsection (2), the Registrar shall disclose to the person all the relevant non-identifying information in the Ministry's possession that relates to the adoption.

Counselling
(4) When the Registrar discloses information under subsection (3), he or she shall also ensure that counselling is made available to the person receiving the information, to the extent that it is feasible to do so.

Societies and licensees
(5) Subsections (2), (3) and (4) also apply with necessary modifications to societies and licensees.

Disclosure of identifying information
to agency outside Ontario
(6) If identifying information that relates to an out of province adoption is kept by the Ministry or by a society, the Registrar may provide the information to a child protection or child placement agency that is recognized in another jurisdiction, for disclosure in accordance with the laws of that jurisdiction.

Further disclosure
(7) A person who receives information under this section may disclose it to any person.

Refusal of Information

Refusal to disclose information

Refusal to disclose non-identifying information
171. (1) The disclosure of non-identifying information that a person would otherwise be entitled to receive under section 166 or 170 may be refused,
   (a) by the Registrar if, in his or her opinion, the disclosure might result in serious physical or emotional harm to any person;
   (b) by a society if, in the local director's opinion, the disclosure might result in serious physical or emotional harm to any person;
   (c) by a licensee if, in the Registrar's opinion, the disclosure might result in serious physical or emotional harm to any person.

Refusal to disclose identifying information
(2) The disclosure of identifying information that a person would otherwise be entitled to receive under section 167 may be refused by the Registrar or by a society if, in the Registrar's opinion, the disclosure might result in serious physical or emotional harm to any person.

Notice of refusal
(3) When the disclosure of information is refused under this section, the Registrar or local director, as the case may be, shall promptly give the person seeking the information notice of the refusal, the reason for it and the person's right to a review under section 172.

Review

Review by Child and Family Services Review Board

172. (1) A person who is refused information in accordance with section 171 may, within twenty days of receiving notice of the decision, request that the Board review the matter.

Duty of Board
(2) The Board shall conduct a review with respect to the request, following the prescribed procedures.

Hearings
(3) Unless the parties to a review agree otherwise, the Board shall hold a hearing.

Parties
(4) The parties to a review are,
   (a) the person who requested the review;
   (b) the person who gave notice of the decision to withhold the information.

Registrar to be added
(5) At any stage in a review, the Board shall add the Registrar as a party on his or her request.

Information need not be disclosed in course of review
(6) The Board may examine the information without disclosing it to the person who requested the review.

Idem, evidence and submissions
(7) The Board may receive any evidence and submissions without disclosing them to the person who requested the review, and when the Board holds a hearing it may hear any part of the evidence and submissions in that person's absence.

Lawyer or agent not to be excluded
(8) When the Board acts under subsection (6) or (7), the lawyer or agent of the person who requested the review is nevertheless entitled to examine the information and to be present, to cross-examine witnesses and to make submissions, or to examine the evidence and submissions and respond to them, as the case may be, on condition that the lawyer or agent undertakes not to reveal the information, evidence and submissions to his or her client.

Time for decision
(9) The Board shall complete its review and make a decision within ninety days of receiving notice of the request, unless the parties consent to a longer period.

Board's decision
(10) After conducting a review, the Board may make an order requiring the Registrar, society or licensee, as the case may be, to disclose all or part of the information to the person, or may make an order confirming the refusal.

Conditions
(11) The Board may include conditions in its order.

Written decision with reasons
(12) Whether the Board holds a hearing or not, it shall give its decision in writing, with reasons.

Information in Court File

Information in court file
173. (1) This section applies to court proceedings that relate to decisions made by the Board under section 172 or by the Registrar, local directors or licensees under sections 165, 166, 167, 168, 169, 170 and 171.

Examination of identifying information in court file
(2) Unless the court orders otherwise, only the court may examine identifying information that is in the court file and comes from the records of the Ministry or of a society or licensee.

Disclosure of information
(3) No person shall, without the court's permission, disclose identifying information described in subsection (2) that he or she obtained from the court file.

Fees and Expenses

Fees and expenses
174. The Registrar, societies and licensees may charge the prescribed fees for services provided under clause 165 (2) (g) and sections 166, 167, 169 and 170, and may charge up to the prescribed amounts for expenses incurred in providing services under sections 166, 167, 169 and 170.

Offences

No payments for adoption
175. No person, whether before or after a child's birth, shall give, receive or agree to give or receive a payment or reward of any kind in connection with,
  (a) the child's adoption or placement for adoption;
  (b) a consent under section 137 to the child's adoption; or
  (c) negotiations or arrangements with a view to the child's adoption,
except for,

  (d) the prescribed expenses of a licensee, or such greater expenses as are approved by a Director;
  (e) proper legal fees and disbursements; and
  (f) a subsidy paid by an approved agency or by the Minister to an adoptive parent or to a person with whom a child is placed for adoption.

Offence
176. (1) A person who contravenes subsection 141 (1), (2) or (3) (placement for adoption) and a director, officer or employee of a corporation who authorizes, permits or concurs in such a contravention by the corporation is guilty of an offence, whether an order is subsequently made for the child's adoption or not, and on conviction is liable to a fine of not more than $2,000 or to imprisonment for a term of not more than two years, or to both.

Idem
(2) A person who contravenes subsection 141 (4) (receiving child) is guilty of an offence and on conviction is liable to a fine of not more than $2,000 or to imprisonment for a term of not more than two years, or to both.

Idem
(3) A person who contravenes subsection 143 (2) (interference with child) is guilty of an offence and on conviction is liable to a fine of not more than $1,000 or to imprisonment for a term of not more than one year, or to both.

Idem
(4) A person who contravenes section 175 and a director, officer or employee of a corporation who authorizes, permits or concurs in such a contravention by the corporation is guilty of an offence and on conviction is liable to a fine of not more than $25,000 or to imprisonment for a term of not more than three years, or to both.

Limitation period
(5) A proceeding under subsection (1), (2) or (4) shall not be commenced after the expiration of two years after the date on which the offence was, or is alleged to have been, committed.

Injunction

Injunction
177. (1) The Superior Court of Justice may grant an injunction to restrain a person from contravening subsection 143 (2), on the society's or licensee's application.

Variation, etc.
(2) The Court may vary or terminate an order made under subsection (1), on any person's application.

PART VIII
CONFIDENTIALITY OF AND
ACCESS TO RECORDS

Definitions

178. (1) In this Part,

"family", when used in reference to a person, means,

    (a) the person's parents and children, and

    (b) the person's spouse within the meaning of Part III of the *Family Law Act*;

"record", when used in reference to a person, means all recorded information, regardless of physical form or characteristics, that,

    (a) relates to the person,

    (b) is recorded in connection with the provision of an approved service, or a service purchased by an approved agency, to the person or a member of the person's family, and

    (c) is under the control of a service provider.

Proclamation

(2) This section shall come into force on a day to be named by proclamation of the Lieutenant Governor.

Exceptions

Exception: information in existing records

179. (1) This Part does not apply to information recorded before the day this Part comes into force.

Exception: certain kinds of records

(2) This Part does not apply to a record,

    (a) obtained by means of an order made under subsection 74 (3) of Part III (child abuse investigation);

> **Note: On a day to be named by proclamation of the Lieutenant Governor, clause (a) is repealed by the Statutes of Ontario, 1999, chapter 2, section 31 and the following substituted:**

    (a) obtained by means of an order made under subsection 74 (3) or (3.1) or a warrant obtained under section 74.1 or 74.2;

> **See: 1999, c. 2, ss. 31, 38.**

    (b) in the register maintained under subsection 75 (5) of Part III (child abuse register);

> **Note: On a day to be named by proclamation of the Lieutenant Governor, clause (b) is repealed by the Statutes of Ontario, 1999, chapter 2, section 31. See: 1999, c. 2, ss. 31, 38.**

    (c) that relates to the adoption of a child under Part VII;

    (d) in the adoption disclosure register maintained under clause 163 (2) (a) of Part VII;

    (e) that relates to a patient and whose disclosure without the patient's consent would contravene a regulation made under the *Health Disciplines Act*;

    (f) that is a record of personal health information within the meaning of "record of personal health information" in the *Mental Health Act*;

    (g) that is a medical record kept by a hospital that is approved under the *Public Hospitals Act*.

Proclamation

(3) Subsection (1) and clauses (2) (a), (b), (c), (e), (f) and (g) shall come into force on a day to be named by proclamation of the Lieutenant Governor.

Disclosure of Records

Prohibition

180. (1) No service provider or employee of a service provider shall disclose a person's record to any person, except in accordance with section 181 (disclosure with consent), 182 (disclosure without consent) or 183 (access by subject and parents) or subsection 188 (4) (review by Board).

Exception

(2) Subsection (1) does not prevent the disclosure of a person's record that is,

    (a) required or permitted by,

        (i) another Act or a regulation made under another Act, or

        (ii) an order of a court; or

    (b) permitted by the *Young Offenders Act* (Canada).

Proclamation

(3) This section shall come into force on a day to be named by proclamation of the Lieutenant Governor.

Consent to disclosure: child under sixteen

181. (1) A service provider may disclose the record of a child under the age of sixteen years, with the written consent of the child's parent or, where the child is in a society's lawful custody, the society's written consent.

Exception: child's counselling records

(2) Subsection (1) does not apply to a record created in connection with the provision of counselling services to a child under section 28 of Part II (Voluntary Access to Services), which may be disclosed only with the child's written consent.

Consent to disclosure: person over sixteen

(3) A service provider may disclose the record of a person who is sixteen years of age or older with that person's written consent.

Requirements for consent

(4) A consent given under subsection (1), (2) or (3) to the disclosure of a person's record shall specify,

    (a) what information is to be disclosed;

    (b) the purpose of the disclosure;

    (c) to whom the record is to be disclosed;

(d) whether the consent authorizes the further disclosure of the record by the person referred to in clause (c), and, if so, to whom and for what purposes; and

(e) the period of time during which the consent remains effective, unless revoked.

When revocation of consent effective
(5) The revocation of a consent given under subsection (1), (2) or (3) is effective when it is delivered to the service provider in writing or the service provider otherwise obtains actual notice of it.

Proclamation
(6) This section shall come into force on a day to be named by proclamation of the Lieutenant Governor.

Disclosure without consent
182. (1) A service provider may disclose a person's record without any consent referred to in section 181,

(a) to persons who provide approved services as employees or agents of the service provider;

(b) to a foster parent, if the person is a child who is in the foster parent's care;

(c) to employees, officers and professional advisors of the service provider who require access to the person's record for the performance of their duties;

(d) to a society, if the person is a child who is in the society's care under,

(i) an order made under Part III (Child Protection), or

(ii) a temporary care agreement or special needs agreement made under Part II (Voluntary Access to Services), unless the agreement provides otherwise;

(e) to a peace officer, if the service provider believes on reasonable grounds that,

(i) failure to disclose the person's record is likely to cause the person or another person physical or emotional harm, and

(ii) the need for disclosure is urgent;

(f) to a person who is providing medical treatment to the person whose record is concerned, if the service provider believes on reasonable grounds that,

(i) failure to disclose the record is likely to cause the person whose record is concerned physical or emotional harm, and

(ii) the need for disclosure is urgent; or

(g) to a review team for the purposes of section 73 of Part III (Child Protection).

Idem: research
(2) A service provider may, with a Director's written approval obtained in accordance with the regulations, disclose a person's record to a person engaged in research, but that person shall not,

(a) use or communicate information from the record for any purpose except research, academic pursuits or the compilation of statistical data; or

(b) communicate any information that may have the effect of identifying a person whose record is disclosed.

Mandatory disclosure
(3) A service provider shall disclose a person's record without any consent referred to in section 181,

(a) to a program supervisor; or

(b) to a Director,

who requests its disclosure.

Prohibition
(4) A program supervisor or Director shall not use or communicate information from a person's record obtained under subsection (3) for any purpose outside the scope of his or her duties.

Notice of disclosure without consent
(5) A service provider who discloses a person's record under clause (1) (e) or (f) shall promptly give written notice of the disclosure to the person whose record was disclosed.

Proclamation
(6) This section shall come into force on a day to be named by proclamation of the Lieutenant Governor.

Disclosure of records of mental disorders
183. (1) In this section,

"record of a mental disorder" means a record or a part of a record made about a person concerning a substantial disorder of emotional processes, thought or cognition of the person which grossly impairs the person's capacity to make reasoned judgments.

Disclosure pursuant to summons
(2) A service provider shall disclose, transmit or permit the examination of a record of a mental disorder pursuant to a summons, order, direction, notice or similar requirement in respect of a matter in issue or that may be in issue in a court of competent jurisdiction or under any Act unless a physician states in writing that he or she believes that to do so,

(a) is likely to result in harm to the treatment or recovery of the person to whom the record relates; or

(b) is likely to result in,

(i) injury to the mental condition of another person, or

(ii) bodily harm to another person.

Hearing to be held
(3) The court before which a matter described in subsection (2) is in issue on motion or, where a disclosure, transmittal or examination is not required by a court, the Divisional Court on motion shall determine whether the

record referred to in the physician's statement should be disclosed, transmitted or examined.

Idem

(4) A motion under subsection (3) shall be on notice to the physician and shall be held in the absence of the public.

Consideration of court

(5) In a motion under subsection (3), the court shall consider whether or not the disclosure, transmittal or examination of the record referred to in the physician's statement is likely to have a result described in clause (2) (a) or (b) and for the purpose the court may examine the record.

Order of court

(6) The court shall not order that the record referred to in the physician's statement be disclosed, transmitted or examined if the court is satisfied that a result described in clause (2) (a) or (b) is likely unless satisfied that to do so is essential in the interests of justice.

Conflict

(6.1) Subsections (2) to (6) prevail despite anything in the *Personal Health Information Protection Act, 2004.*

Return of record to service provider

(7) Where a record of a mental disorder is required under this section, the clerk of the court or body in which it is admitted in evidence or, if not so admitted, the person to whom the record is transmitted shall return the record to the service provider forthwith after the determination of the matter in issue in respect of which the record was required.

Access to Records

Right of access to personal records

184. (1) Subject to subsection (2) and section 185, a person who is twelve years of age or older has a right to and shall on request be given access to,

    (a) his or her own records;

    (b) the records of his or her child who is under the age of sixteen years; and

    (c) the records of a child who is in his or her lawful custody or charge and is under the age of sixteen years.

Exception: child's counselling records

(2) Clauses (1) (b) and (c) do not apply to a record created in connection with the provision of counselling services to a child under section 28 of Part II (Voluntary Access to Services), which may be disclosed to the child's parent only with the child's written consent.

Restriction by parent, etc.

(3) Any parent of a child, if the child is under the age of sixteen years, may designate specific information that is contained in the child's record and relates to the parent as

information that shall not be disclosed to the child, and the service provider shall not disclose the designated information to the child.

Child's access to own records

(4) The consent of a child's parent is not required for the child's access to a record under subsection (1).

Proclamation

(5) This section shall come into force on a day to be named by proclamation of the Lieutenant Governor.

Where access may be refused

185. (1) A service provider may refuse to give a person referred to in subsection 184 (1) access to all or part of his or her record where the person is a child under the age of sixteen years and the service provider is of the opinion that access to all or part of the record would cause the child physical or emotional harm.

Information that may be withheld

(2) A service provider may withhold from a person referred to in subsection 184 (1) the name of another person and other information relating to that other person where the service provider is of the opinion that disclosure is likely to result in physical or emotional harm to that other person.

Idem: informants

(3) A service provider may withhold from a person referred to in subsection 184 (1) the name of an individual who has provided information in the person's record but is not engaged in providing services.

Idem: assessments

(4) A service provider may withhold from a person referred to in subsection 184 (1) the contents of a medical, emotional, developmental, psychological, educational or social assessment performed by a person who is not employed by the service provider, but may not withhold that person's name.

Proclamation

(5) This section shall come into force on a day to be named by proclamation of the Lieutenant Governor.

Duty of service provider

186. (1) Where a person referred to in subsection 184 (1) requests access to a record, the service provider shall, within thirty days of receiving the request,

    (a) give the person access to the record;

    (b) notify the person that the service provider refuses to give him or her access to part of the record, stating the reasons for the refusal, and give the person access to the rest of the record;

    (c) notify the person that the service provider refuses to give him or her access to the record, stating the reasons for the refusal; or

(d) notify the person that this Part does not apply to the record or that the record does not exist, if that is the case.

Notice of right of review
(2) A notice of a refusal of access under clause (1) (b) or (c) shall contain a statement of the person's right to request a review of the matter under subsection 188 (1).

Proclamation
(3) This section shall come into force on a day to be named by proclamation of the Lieutenant Governor.

Right to have record corrected

187. (1) A person who has a right to access to a record under subsection 184 (1) also has a right to have errors or omissions in the record corrected.

Duty of service provider
(2) Where a person referred to in subsection (1) requests that a service provider correct an error or omission in a record, the service provider shall, within thirty days of receiving the request,
(a) make the correction as requested, and give notice of the correction to every person to whom the service provider has disclosed the record;
(b) notify the person that the service provider refuses to make the correction as requested, stating the reasons for the refusal, and note the request and response on the record; or
(c) notify the person that this Part does not apply to the record or that the record does not exist, if that is the case.

Notice of right of review
(3) A notice of a refusal to make a correction under clause (2) (b) shall contain a statement of the person's right to request a review of the matter under subsection 188 (1).

Proclamation
(4) This section shall come into force on a day to be named by proclamation of the Lieutenant Governor.

Review

Right to review: refusal of access or correction

188. (1) A person referred to in subsection 184 (1) or 187 (1) whose request for access to or correction of a record is refused in whole or in part may, within twenty days of receiving notice of the refusal, request that the Board review the matter.

Idem: unauthorized disclosure
(2) A person who believes that a service provider may have disclosed his or her record without authority may, within twenty days of becoming aware of the possible unauthorized disclosure, request that the Board review the matter.

Duty of Board
(3) Where the Board receives notice of a request for review under subsection (1) or (2), it shall review the matter, following the prescribed procedures, and may do so by holding a hearing.

Board may examine record
(4) In conducting a review requested under subsection (1) or (2), the Board may examine the record in question.

Decision of Board
(5) On completing a review requested under subsection (1), the Board may,
(a) order the service provider to give the person access to all or part of the record;
(b) order the service provider to make a correction to the record and give the notice referred to in clause 187 (2) (a); or
(c) if it is satisfied that the refusal appealed from is justified, confirm the refusal,
and shall provide a copy of its decision to the person who requested the review, the service provider and the Minister.

Idem
(6) On completing a review requested under subsection (2), the Board,
(a) shall, unless it is satisfied that no disclosure or no unauthorized disclosure of the person's record took place, declare that the disclosure was unauthorized;
(b) may order the service provider to change its procedures for the maintenance and disclosure of persons' records, or to desist from a particular disclosure practice; and
(c) where it is satisfied that an unauthorized disclosure took place, may recommend to the Minister that the service provider's approval under Part I (Flexible Services), if any, be revoked or, where the service provider is a licensee, that the licence be revoked under Part IX (Licensing),
and shall provide a copy of its decision to the person who requested the review, the service provider and the Minister.

Proclamation
(7) This section shall come into force on a day to be named by proclamation of the Lieutenant Governor.

General

Access, etc., to be noted on record

189. (1) Every disclosure of all or part of a person's record and every correction to a person's record shall be noted on and forms part of the record.

Exception
(2) Subsection (1) does not apply to routine use of a person's record by a service provider and the service provider's

employees or, where the service provider is the Minister, the Minister's employees engaged in providing services.

Proclamation

(3) This section shall come into force on a day to be named by proclamation of the Lieutenant Governor.

Protection from liability for disclosure

190. (1) Where a service provider discloses a person's record in accordance with this Part, no action or other proceeding shall be instituted against the service provider or anyone acting under the service provider's authority,

(a) if this Part requires the disclosure; or

(b) if this Part permits the disclosure and the service provider has reasonable grounds to believe the information contained in the record to be accurate.

Proclamation

(2) This section shall come into force on a day to be named by proclamation of the Lieutenant Governor.

Code of record-keeping procedures

191. (1) Every service provider shall establish and follow a written code of procedure for the creation, maintenance and disclosure of persons' records.

Idem

(2) A code of procedure referred to in subsection (1) shall contain,

(a) a description of the types of information that may be recorded and the purposes for which information may be recorded;

(b) a requirement that information, wherever possible, be collected from or confirmed by the person to whom it relates;

(c) a requirement that no more information be recorded than is actually necessary for the provision of the service in question; and

(d) the prescribed provisions.

Retention, storage and destruction schedules

(3) Every service provider shall retain, store and destroy persons' records in accordance with the prescribed schedules.

Proclamation

(4) This section shall come into force on a day to be named by proclamation of the Lieutenant Governor.

PART IX
LICENSING

Definitions

192. In this Part,

"children's residence" means,

(a) a parent model residence where five or more children not of common parentage, or

(b) a staff model residence where three or more children not of common parentage,

live and receive residential care, and includes a foster home or other home or institution that is supervised or operated by a society, but does not include,

(c) a house licensed under the *Private Hospitals Act*,

(d) a day nursery as defined in the *Day Nurseries Act*,

(e) a recreational camp under the *Health Protection and Promotion Act*,

(f) a home for special care under the *Homes for Special Care Act*,

(g) a school or private school as defined in the *Education Act*,

(h) a hostel intended for short term accommodation,

(i) a hospital that receives financial aid from the Government of Ontario, or

(j) a group home or similar facility that receives financial assistance from the Minister of Correctional Services but receives no financial assistance from the Minister under this Act;

"non-profit agency" means a corporation without share capital that has objects of a charitable nature and,

(a) to which Part III of the *Corporations Act* applies, or

(b) that is incorporated by or under a general or special Act of the Parliament of Canada;

"parent model residence" means a building, group of buildings or part of a building where not more than two adult persons live and provide care for children on a continuous basis;

"staff model residence" means a building, group of buildings or part of a building where adult persons are employed to provide care for children on the basis of scheduled periods of duty.

Where Licence Required

Licences

Licence required to operate children's residence, etc.

193. (1) No person shall,

(a) establish, operate or maintain a children's residence; or

(b) provide, directly or indirectly, residential care for three or more children not of common parentage in places that are not children's residences,

except under the authority of a licence issued by a Director under this Part.

Idem: placement for adoption

(2) No person other than a society shall place a child for adoption, except under the authority of a licence issued by a Director under this Part.

Issuing licence

(3) Subject to section 195, a person who applies for a licence in accordance with this Part and the regulations and

pays the prescribed fee is entitled to be issued a licence by a Director, subject to any terms and conditions imposed by the Director.

Idem
(4) Despite subsection (3),
    (a) a licence shall not be issued to a partnership or association of persons; and
    (b) a licence to place a child for adoption shall only be issued to an individual or a non-profit agency.

Renewal of licence
(5) Subject to section 196, a licensee who applies for renewal of the licence in accordance with this Part and the regulations and pays the prescribed fee is entitled to have the licence renewed by a Director, subject to any terms and conditions imposed by the Director.

Provisional licence or renewal
(6) Where an applicant for a licence or renewal of a licence does not meet all the requirements for the issuing or renewal of the licence and requires time to meet them, a Director may, subject to such terms and conditions as the Director may prescribe, issue a provisional licence for the period that the Director considers necessary to give the applicant time to meet the requirements.

Not transferable
(7) A licence is not transferable.

Placements must be in accord with Act and regulations
(8) No licensee shall place a child in a residential placement except in accordance with this Act and the regulations.

Powers of Program Supervisor

Powers of program supervisor
194. (1) For the purpose of ensuring compliance with this Act and the regulations a program supervisor may, at all reasonable times, upon producing proper identification, enter,
    (a) the premises of a licensee;
    (b) a children's residence; or
    (c) a place where a child receives residential care,
and may inspect the facilities, the services provided, the books of account and the records relating to the services, and make copies of those books and records or remove them from the premises to copy them as may be reasonably required.

Offence
(2) No person shall hinder, obstruct or attempt to hinder or obstruct a program supervisor in the performance of the program supervisor's duties or knowingly give false information about the premises or services to a program supervisor.

Idem
(3) No licensee or person in charge of premises referred to in clause (1) (a), (b) or (c) shall refuse to give a program supervisor access to the books and records referred to in subsection (1) or refuse to give a program supervisor information about the premises or services that the program supervisor reasonably requires.

Regulations re exercise of power of entry
(4) A program supervisor shall exercise the power of entry set out in subsection (1) in accordance with the regulations.

Refusal and Revocation

Grounds for refusal
195. A Director may refuse to issue a licence where, in the Director's opinion,
    (a) the applicant or an employee of the applicant, or, where the applicant is a corporation, an officer or director of the corporation is not competent to carry on the activity for which the licence is required in a responsible manner in accordance with this Act and the regulations;
    (b) the past conduct of the applicant or an employee of the applicant or, where the applicant is a corporation, of an officer or director of the corporation, affords reasonable grounds for belief that the activity for which the licence is required will not be carried on in a responsible manner in accordance with this Act and the regulations; or
    (c) the premises in which the applicant proposes to establish, operate and maintain a children's residence or to provide residential care, as the case may be, do not comply with the requirements of this Part and the regulations.

Refusal to renew; revocation
196. A Director may refuse to renew or may revoke a licence where, in the Director's opinion,
    (a) the licensee or an employee of the licensee, or where the licensee is a corporation, an officer or director of the corporation has contravened or has knowingly permitted a person under his or her control or direction or associated with him or her to contravene,
        (i) this Act or the regulations,
        (ii) another Act, or the regulations made under another Act, that applies to the activity for which the licence is required, or
        (iii) a term or condition of the licence;
    (b) the premises where the children's residence is located or the residential care is provided do not comply with the requirements of this Part and the regulations;

(c) the activity for which the licence is required is carried on in a manner that is prejudicial to the children's health, safety or welfare;

(d) a person has made a false statement in the application for the licence or for its renewal, or in a report or document required to be furnished by this Act or the regulations, or by another Act or the regulations made under another Act that applies to the activity for which the licence is required; or

(e) a change has occurred in the employees, officers or directors of the applicant that would, if the applicant were applying for the licence in the first instance, afford grounds under clause 195 (b) for refusing to issue the licence.

Hearing by Tribunal

Hearings arising out of s. 195 or 196

Notice of proposal

197. (1) Where a Director proposes to refuse to issue a licence under section 195 or to refuse to renew or to revoke a licence under section 196, the Director shall cause notice of the proposal, together with written reasons, to be served on the applicant or licensee, who may require a hearing.

Request for hearing

(2) A notice under subsection (1) shall inform the applicant or licensee that the applicant or licensee is entitled to a hearing by the Tribunal if he, she or it mails or delivers to the Director and to the Tribunal, within ten days after the notice under subsection (1) is served, a written request for a hearing.

Note: Despite the amendment made by the Statutes of Ontario, 1999, chapter 12, Schedule G, subsection 16 (4), members of the Child and Family Services Review Board immediately before April 1, 2000 shall be members of the Licence Appeal Tribunal for the purpose of performing the duties of the Tribunal with respect to proceedings before the Board that were commenced before April 1, 2000. See: 1999, c. 12, Sched. G, s. 16 (5).

Powers of Director where no hearing required

(3) Where an applicant or licensee does not require a hearing under subsection (2), the Director may carry out the proposal.

Powers of Tribunal where hearing required

(4) Where an applicant or licensee requires a hearing under subsection (2), the Tribunal shall appoint a time for and hold a hearing and may, on hearing the matter,

(a) order the Director to carry out the proposal; or

(b) order the Director to take such other action as the Tribunal considers appropriate, in accordance with this Part and the regulations,

and the Tribunal may substitute its opinion for that of the Director.

Note: Despite the amendment made by the Statutes of Ontario, 1999, chapter 12, Schedule G, subsection 16 (4), members of the Child and Family Services Review Board immediately before April 1, 2000 shall be members of the Licence Appeal Tribunal for the purpose of performing the duties of the Tribunal with respect to proceedings before the Board that were commenced before April 1, 2000. See: 1999, c. 12, Sched. G, s. 16 (5).

Review of terms of licence by Tribunal

198. (1) A licensee who is dissatisfied with the terms and conditions prescribed by a Director under subsection 193 (3), (5) or (6) is entitled to a hearing by the Tribunal if the licensee mails or delivers to the Director and to the Tribunal, within fifteen days after receiving the licence, a written request for a hearing.

Note: Despite the amendment made by the Statutes of Ontario, 1999, chapter 12, Schedule G, subsection 16 (4), members of the Child and Family Services Review Board immediately before April 1, 2000 shall be members of the Licence Appeal Tribunal for the purpose of performing the duties of the Tribunal with respect to proceedings before the Board that were commenced before April 1, 2000. See: 1999, c. 12, Sched. G, s. 16 (5).

Powers of Tribunal

(2) Where a licensee requires a hearing under subsection (1), the Tribunal shall appoint a time for and hold a hearing and may, on hearing the matter,

(a) confirm any or all of the terms and conditions;

(b) strike out any or all of the terms and conditions; or

(c) impose such other terms and conditions as the Tribunal considers appropriate.

Note: Despite the amendment made by the Statutes of Ontario, 1999, chapter 12, Schedule G, subsection 16 (4), members of the Child and Family Services Review Board immediately before April 1, 2000 shall be members of the Licence Appeal Tribunal for the purpose of performing the duties of the Tribunal with respect to proceedings before the Board that were commenced before April 1, 2000. See: 1999, c. 12, Sched. G, s. 16 (5).

Receipt of licence

(3) For the purposes of subsection (1), a licensee shall be deemed to receive the licence on the tenth day after the day of its mailing, unless the licensee establishes that he, she or it did not receive it or did not, through absence, accident,

illness or another cause beyond the licensee's control, acting in good faith, receive the licence until a later date.

Continuation of licence

199. (1) REPEALED.

Continuation of licence pending renewal
(2) Subject to section 200, where a licensee has applied for renewal of the licence and paid the prescribed fee within the prescribed time or, if no time is prescribed, before the licence expires, the licence shall be deemed to continue,

    (a) until the renewal is granted; or

    (b) where the licensee is served with notice that the Director proposes to refuse to grant the renewal, until the time for requiring a hearing has expired and, where a hearing is required, until the Tribunal has made its decision.

Provisional suspension of licence

200. (1) A Director may, by causing notice to be served on a licensee, provisionally and without a hearing suspend the licence where, in the Director's opinion, the manner in which the children's residence is operated, residential care is provided or children are placed for adoption, as the case may be, is an immediate threat to the health, safety or welfare of the children.

Contents of notice
(2) A notice served under subsection (1) shall contain a statement of the grounds for suspending the licence.

When suspension takes effect
(3) A provisional suspension takes effect on the date that the licensee receives the notice.

s. 197 (2-4) apply

(4) Where a notice is served under subsection (1), subsections 197 (2), (3) and (4) apply with necessary modifications.

Rules re proceedings

Parties
201. (1) The Director, the applicant or licensee who requires the hearing and any other persons that the Tribunal specifies are parties to a proceeding under this Part.

Members with prior involvement
(2) A member of the Tribunal who has taken part before a hearing in any investigation or consideration of its subject matter, including a review under section 188 of Part VIII (Confidentiality of and Access to Records) that relates to the applicant or licensee, shall not take part in the hearing.

Discussion of subject matter of hearing
(3) A member of the Tribunal who takes part in a hearing shall not communicate with any person, except another member, a solicitor who is not the solicitor of any party, or an employee of the Tribunal, about the subject matter of the hearing, unless all parties are notified and given an opportunity to participate.

When Tribunal seeks independent legal advice
(4) The Tribunal may seek independent legal advice about the subject matter of a hearing and, if it does so, shall disclose the nature of the advice to the parties to enable them to respond.

Examination of documentary evidence
(5) A party to a proceeding under this Part shall be given an opportunity, before the hearing, to examine any written or documentary evidence that will be produced and any report whose contents will be given in evidence at the hearing.

(6) REPEALED.

Only members at hearing to participate in decision, etc.
(7) No member of the Tribunal shall participate in a decision of the Tribunal under this Part unless he or she was present throughout the hearing and heard the evidence and argument of the parties and, unless the parties consent, the Tribunal shall not make a decision under this Part unless all the members who were present at the hearing participate in the decision.

Final decision of Tribunal within ninety days
(8) Despite section 21 of the *Statutory Powers Procedure Act*, the Tribunal shall make a final decision and notify the parties of it within ninety days from the day the Tribunal receives the applicant's or licensee's request for a hearing under subsection 197 (2) or 198 (1).

Appeal

Appeal

202. (1) An appeal lies to the Divisional Court from the Tribunal's decision under this Part.

Record to be filed in the court-
(2) Where notice of an appeal is served under this section, the Tribunal shall forthwith file with the court the record of the proceeding in which the decision appealed from was made.

Minister entitled to be heard
(3) The Minister is entitled to be heard, by counsel or otherwise, on the argument of an appeal under this section.

Delivery of Licence and Records

Records and licence, removal of children

Records and licence to be handed over to Minister
203. (1) A licensee whose licence is revoked or who ceases to carry on the activity for which the licence is required shall deliver up to the Minister the licence and all the records in the licensee's possession or control that relate to the children to whom services were being provided.

Removal of children

(2) Where a licence to operate a children's residence or to provide residential care is suspended or revoked, the parent of every child in the children's residence or other place where residential care is provided shall arrange for the child's removal from the residence or other place as soon as is practicable, having regard to the child's best interests, and the Minister may assist in finding an alternative placement for the child.

Occupation by Minister

Order for Minister's occupation

204. (1) The Minister may, where a Director's proposal to revoke or not to renew a licence under subsection 197 (1) or notice of provisional suspension under subsection 198 (1) has been served on a licensee who operates a children's residence or provides residential care and the matter has not yet been finally disposed of, apply without notice to the Superior Court of Justice for an order,

(a) authorizing the Minister to occupy and operate the children's residence or the premises where the residential care is provided, pending the outcome of the proceeding until alternative accommodation may be found for the children who are being cared for; and

(b) directing the sheriff to assist the Minister as may be necessary in occupying the premises.

Where court may make order

(2) The court may make an order referred to subsection (1) where it is satisfied that the health, safety or welfare of the children being cared for require it.

Interim management

(3) Where an order has been made under subsection (2), the Minister may, despite sections 25 and 39 of the *Expropriations Act*, immediately occupy and operate or arrange for the occupation and operation of the premises for a period not exceeding six months.

Injunctions

Injunction

205. (1) A Director may apply to the Superior Court of Justice for an order enjoining any person from,

(a) contravening subsection 193 (1) (licence requirement); or

(b) carrying on an activity for which a licence is required while the licence is provisionally suspended under section 200.

Idem

(2) Any person may apply to the court for an order varying or discharging an order made under subsection (1).

Offences

Offence

206. (1) Every person who,

(a) contravenes subsection 193 (1);

(b) contravenes a term or condition of a licence relating to the maximum number of children to be cared for in a children's residence or other place where residential care is provided under the authority of a licence;

(c) causes a child to be cared for in a children's residence operated by a person who is not licensed under this Part, or in another place where residential care is provided by a person who is required to be but is not licensed to provide residential care under this Part; or

(d) is a child's parent or a person under a legal duty to provide for the child and permits the child to be cared for in a children's residence or other place referred to in clause (c),

and every director, officer or employee of a corporation who authorizes, permits or concurs in such an act by the corporation is guilty of an offence and on conviction is liable to a fine of not more than $1,000 for each day on which the offence continues or to imprisonment for a term of not more than one year, or to both.

Idem

(2) Every person who,

(a) knowingly contravenes subsection 194 (2) or (3) (obstructing program supervisor, etc.);

(b) knowingly furnishes false information in an application under this Part or in a statement, report or return required to be furnished under this Part or the regulations; or

(c) fails to comply with an order or direction made by a court under this Part,

and every director, officer or employee of a corporation who authorizes, permits or concurs in such a contravention, furnishing or failure by the corporation is guilty of an offence and on conviction is liable to a fine of not more than $2,000.

Child and Family Services Review Board

Child and Family Services Review Board

207. (1) The Child and Family Services Review Board is continued under the name Child and Family Services Review Board in English and Commission de révision des services à l'enfance et à la famille in French.

Idem

(2) The Board is composed of the prescribed number of members appointed by the Lieutenant Governor in Council and has the powers and duties given to it by this Act and the regulations.

Chair and vice-chairs

(3) The Lieutenant Governor in Council may appoint a member of the Board as chair and may appoint one or more other members as vice-chairs.

Term

(4) A member of the Board shall hold office for the prescribed term.

Quorum

(5) The prescribed number of members of the Board are a quorum.

Remuneration

(6) The chair and vice-chairs and the other members of the Board shall be paid the daily allowances determined by the Lieutenant Governor in Council and are entitled to their reasonable and necessary travelling and living expenses while attending meetings or otherwise engaged in the work of the Board.

PART X
INDIAN AND NATIVE CHILD
AND FAMILY SERVICES

Definition

208. In this Part,

"customary care" means the care and supervision of an Indian or native child by a person who is not the child's parent, according to the custom of the child's band or native community.

Designation of native communities

209. The Minister may designate a community, with the consent of its representatives, as a native community for the purposes of this Act.

Agreements with bands and native communities

210. The Minister may make agreements with bands and native communities, and any other parties whom the bands or native communities choose to involve, for the provision of services.

Designation of child and family service authority

211. (1) A band or native community may designate a body as an Indian or native child and family service authority.

Agreements, etc.

(2) Where a band or native community has designated an Indian or native child and family service authority, the Minister,

    (a) shall, at the band's or native community's request, enter into negotiations for the provision of services by the child and family service authority;

    (b) may enter into agreements with the child and family service authority and, if the band or native com-

munity agrees, any other person, for the provision of services; and

    (c) may designate the child and family service authority, with its consent and if it is an approved agency, as a society under subsection 15 (2) of Part I (Flexible Services).

Subsidy for customary care

212. Where a band or native community declares that an Indian or native child is being cared for under customary care, a society or agency may grant a subsidy to the person caring for the child.

Consultation with bands and native communities

213. A society or agency that provides services or exercises powers under this Act with respect to Indian or native children shall regularly consult with their bands or native communities about the provision of the services or the exercise of the powers and about matters affecting the children, including,

    (a) the apprehension of children and the placement of children in residential care;

    (b) the placement of homemakers and the provision of other family support services;

    (c) the preparation of plans for the care of children;

    (d) status reviews under Part III (Child Protection);

    (e) temporary care and special needs agreements under Part II (Voluntary Access to Services);

    (f) adoption placements;

    (g) the establishment of emergency houses; and

    (h) any other matter that is prescribed.

PART XI
REGULATIONS

Regulations: Part I (Flexible Services)

214. (1) The Lieutenant Governor in Council may make regulations for the purposes of Part I,

1. prescribing additional powers and duties of Directors and program supervisors;

2. prescribing reports to be made and information to be furnished under subsection 5 (5), their form and the intervals at which they are to be made or furnished;

3. governing the exercise of the power of entry set out in subsection 6 (1);

4. governing the management and operation of approved agencies or any class of them;

5. governing the provision of approved services or any class of them;

6. exempting designated approved agencies or approved services or any class of them from any provision of this Act or the regulations for a specified period or periods;

6.1 respecting the composition of boards of approved agencies or classes of approved agencies, requiring board members to undertake training programs and prescribing those programs;

7.   governing the accommodation, facilities and equipment to be provided,
   i.   in buildings in which approved services are provided, and
   ii. in the course of the provision of approved services;

8.   further defining "service", "child development service", "child treatment service", "child welfare service", "community support service" and "young offenders service";

9.   defining "prevention service";

10. governing the establishment, management, operation, location, construction, alteration and renovation of buildings, or any class of them, in which approved services are provided;

11. prescribing procedures and conditions of eligibility for the admission of children and other persons to and their discharge from places where approved services are provided;

12. prescribing the qualifications, powers and duties of persons employed in providing approved services or any class of approved services;

12.1 prescribing classes of persons employed or to be employed in providing approved services or any class of approved services who must undertake training, prescribing that training and prescribing the circumstances under which that training must be undertaken;

13. governing the residential placement of children and prescribing procedures for placements, discharge, assessments and case management;

14. requiring and prescribing medical and other related or ancillary services for the care and treatment of children and other persons in places where services or any class of them are provided;

15. governing applications by agencies for approval under subsections 8 (1) and 9 (1) and establishing criteria for approval;

16. governing applications by approved agencies for payments under this Part, prescribing the method, time, manner, terms and conditions of payments and providing for the suspension and withholding of payments and for the making of deductions from payments;

17. prescribing the manner of computing the amount of financial assistance for the purposes of sections 8 and 9, prescribing classes of payments for the purposes of those sections and determining the amounts of payments;

18. governing the transfer and assignment of the assets of approved agencies acquired with financial assistance from the Province of Ontario, or of any class of such assets, for the purposes of subsection 10 (3), and prescribing classes of such assets;

19. requiring approved agencies to provide the prescribed information to the prescribed persons, and prescribing the information and the persons;

20. prescribing the accounts and records to be kept by approved agencies, the claims, returns and reports to be made and budgets to be submitted to the Minister and the methods, time and manner in which they shall be made or submitted;

21. requiring service providers, or any class of service providers, to keep records, and prescribing the form and content of those records;

22. providing for the recovery, by an approved agency or by the Minister, from the person or persons in whose charge a child is or has been or from the estate of that person or persons of amounts paid by the agency for the child's care and maintenance, and prescribing the circumstances and the manner in which such a recovery may be made;

23. providing for the recovery of payments made to approved agencies under this Part and the regulations;

24. prescribing provisions to be included in the by-laws of approved agencies, or any class of them, for the purpose of subsection 13 (2);

25. prescribing the number of band or native community representatives on the boards of directors of agencies or any class of them, the manner of their appointment and their terms, for the purpose of subsection 13 (3);

26. prescribing forms and providing for their use;

27. prescribing fees or classes of fees that may be charged for services and the terms and conditions under which a fee may be charged;

28. REPEALED.

29. providing for an executive committee of the board of directors of a society, its composition, quorum, powers and duties;

30. prescribing a system for determining,
   i.   the amounts of payments under subsection 19 (2) (payments by Minister), and
   ii. a society's estimated expenditures;

31. REPEALED.

32. governing the construction, alteration, renovation, extension, furnishing and equipping of homes operated or supervised by societies, other than children's residences as defined in Part IX (Licensing), where residential care is provided to children.

Same

(2) A regulation made under paragraph 6.1, 12.1, 18, 24 or 25 of subsection (1) (boards of approved agencies, training of persons providing approved services, transfer of assets, prescribed provisions in agency by-laws, band or native community representatives) may be general or specific in its application.

Same

(3) A regulation made under paragraph 17 or 30 of subsection (1) (financial assistance for the purposes of sections 8 and 9, amounts of payments to societies) is, if it so provides, effective with reference to a period before it is filed.

Idem

(4) The Minister shall prescribe,

    (a) standards of services; and

    (b) procedures and practices to be followed by societies,

for the purposes of subsection 15 (4).

Regulations: Part II (Voluntary Access to Services)

215. The Lieutenant Governor in Council may make regulations for the purposes of Part II,

    (a) defining "counselling";

    (b) prescribing provisions to be contained in agreements made under section 29 (temporary care agreements) and sections 30 and 31 (special needs agreements);

    (c) requiring that residential placements with or by service providers be made in accordance with written agreements, and prescribing their form and contents;

    (d) prescribing practices, procedures and further duties for advisory committees;

    (e) further defining "special need" and "developmental disability".

Regulations: Part III (Child Protection)

216. The Lieutenant Governor in Council may make regulations for the purposes of Part III,

    (a) governing the exercise of the powers of entry set out in subsections 40 (6) and (11) and section 44;

    (b) assigning to a Director any powers, duties or obligations of the Crown with respect to Crown wards;

    (c) prescribing the care and maintenance that may be provided to a former Crown ward under subsection 71 (2), and the terms and conditions on which the care and maintenance may be provided;

    (c.1) respecting the format of warrants under sections 74.1 and 74.2 and the procedures to be followed in applying for, issuing, receiving and filing warrants of different formats;

    (c.2) prescribing manners of applying for a warrant under section 74.2, including a manner other than submitting an information on oath, setting out the circumstances under which those manners may be used and providing for any additional requirements that must be met if those manners are used;

    (d) prescribing the form in which reports are to be made under subsection 75 (3);

Note: On a day to be named by proclamation of the Lieutenant Governor, clause (d) is repealed by the Statutes of Ontario, 1999, chapter 2, subsection 33 (2). See: 1999, c. 2, ss. 33 (2), 38.

    (e) respecting the manner in which the register referred to in subsection 75 (5) is to be kept;

Note: On a day to be named by proclamation of the Lieutenant Governor, clause (e) is repealed by the Statutes of Ontario, 1999, chapter 2, subsection 33 (2). See: 1999, c. 2, ss. 33 (2), 38.

    (f) requiring the removal of a name from the register referred to in subsection 75 (5), or the amendment of the register, under specified circumstances, and specifying those circumstances;

Note: On a day to be named by proclamation of the Lieutenant Governor, clause (f) is repealed by the Statutes of Ontario, 1999, chapter 2, subsection 33 (2). See: 1999, c. 2, ss. 33 (2), 38.

    (g) prescribing practices and procedures for hearings held under clause 76 (4) (b) (amendment of register);

Note: On a day to be named by proclamation of the Lieutenant Governor, clause (g) is repealed by the Statutes of Ontario, 1999, chapter 2, subsection 33 (2). See: 1999, c. 2, ss. 33 (2), 38.

    (h) prescribing forms and providing for their use.

Regulations: Part IV (Young Offenders)

217. (1) The Lieutenant Governor in Council may make regulations for the purposes of Part IV,

    (a) governing the establishment, operation, maintenance, management and use of places of temporary detention, open custody and secure custody and other services and programs provided under subsection 89 (1);

    (b) governing the establishment and operation of and the accommodation, equipment and services to be provided in any premises or class of premises established, operated, maintained or designated for the purposes of the federal Act or for providing services or programs under subsection 89 (1);

    (c) prescribing additional duties and functions of,

        (i) probation officers, and

        (ii) provincial directors;

    (d) prescribing the duties and functions of bailiffs;

    (e) prescribing the qualifications of probation officers;

    (f) prescribing additional duties and functions of persons in charge of places of temporary detention, open custody and secure custody;

    (g) prescribing reports to be made and information to be furnished under section 92, their form and the intervals at which they are to be made or furnished;

(h) governing the conduct, discipline, rights and privileges of young persons in places of temporary detention, open custody or secure custody or any class of them or in a service or program provided under subsection 89 (1);

(i) prescribing procedures for the admission of young persons to and their discharge from places of temporary detention, open custody or secure custody or any class of them or premises in which a service or program is provided under subsection 89 (1);

(j) prescribing classes of payment by way of provincial aid for the establishment, operation or maintenance of places of temporary detention, open custody or secure custody, the methods of determining the payments, the manner and time of making them, the terms and conditions of such payments and the circumstances under which such payments may be suspended or withheld or deductions may be made from them;

(k) prescribing the number of members of the Board, their terms of office and the number of members that is a quorum;

(l) prescribing additional powers, duties and procedures of the Board;

(m) governing the exercise of the power of entry given under subsection 98 (5);

(n) respecting any matter considered necessary or advisable to carry out effectively the intent and purpose of Part IV.

Idem

(2) A regulation made under clause (1) (j) (classes of payment by way of provincial aid) is, if it so provides, effective with reference to a period before it is filed.

Regulations: Part V (Rights of Children)

218. The Lieutenant Governor in Council may make regulations for the purposes of Part V,

(a) governing internal complaints procedures to be established under section 109;

(b) establishing procedures for reviews under section 110;

(c) prescribing additional functions of the Office of Child and Family Service Advocacy.

Regulations: Part VI (Extraordinary Measures)

219. The Lieutenant Governor in Council may make regulations for the purposes of Part VI,

(a) prescribing procedures for the admission of persons to and their discharge from secure treatment programs;

(b) prescribing standards for secure treatment programs;

(c) prescribing standards for secure isolation rooms;

(d) prescribing procedures to be followed when a child is placed in or released from a secure isolation room;

(e) prescribing the frequency of reviews under subsection 127 (6);

(f) prescribing matters to be reviewed and prescribing additional reports under section 128;

(g) prescribing procedures as intrusive procedures;

(h) prescribing the intervals at which reports are to be made by review teams under subsection 129 (5);

(i) prescribing drugs, combinations of drugs or classes of drugs as psychotropic drugs;

(j) prescribing forms and requiring their use.

Regulations: Part VII (Adoption)

220. (1) The Lieutenant Governor in Council may make regulations for the purposes of Part VII,

(a) prescribing the form of an affidavit of execution for the purposes of subsection 137 (12);

(b) prescribing the manner in which placements are to be registered under subsection 141 (6);

(c) prescribing special circumstances for the purposes of subsection 142 (4) (placement outside Canada);

(d) prescribing forms and providing for their use;

(e) further defining "identifying information" and "non-identifying information" for the purposes of sections 163 to 174;

(f) prescribing classes of persons for the purposes of paragraph 5 of subsection 166 (4) (persons who may request non-identifying information);

(g) prescribing classes of persons for the purposes of subsection 169 (2) (search by Registrar);

(h) prescribing additional powers, duties and procedures for the Board under section 172;

(i) prescribing fees and amounts for the purposes of section 174;

(j) prescribing expenses that may be charged under clause 175 (d), classes of such expenses and the terms and conditions under which such expenses or classes of expenses may be charged.

Idem

(2) Regulations made under clause (1) (i) may prescribe different fees and amounts for the Registrar, for societies and for licensees.

Regulations: Part VIII (Confidentiality of and Access to Records)

221. The Lieutenant Governor in Council may make regulations for the purposes of Part VIII,

(a) prescribing the manner in which a Director's approval is to be obtained under subsection 182 (2) (disclosure for research);

(b) prescribing review procedures for the Board under subsection 188 (3);

(c) prescribing provisions for the purposes of subsection 191 (2) (service providers' codes of procedure);

(d) prescribing retention, storage and destruction schedules for the purposes of subsection 191 (3).

Regulations: Part IX (Licensing)

222. The Lieutenant Governor in Council may make regulations for the purposes of Part IX,

(a) governing the establishment, management, operation and use of children's residences, and other premises where residential care is provided under the authority of a licence;

(b) defining "common parentage" for the purposes of the definition of "children's residence" in section 192 and clause 193 (1) (b);

(c) governing the issuing, renewal and expiry of licences and prescribing fees payable by an applicant for a licence or its renewal;

(d) governing the exercise of the power of entry set out in subsection 194 (1);

(e) governing the establishment of and the accommodation, facilities, equipment and services to be provided in,
  (i) children's residences, and
  (ii) other premises where residential care is provided under the authority of a licence,
  or any class of them;

(f) exempting designated,
  (i) children's residences,
  (ii) other premises where residential care is provided under the authority of a licence, or
  (iii) persons placing children for adoption,
  or any class of them, from any provision of this Part or the regulations for a prescribed period, and prescribing the period;

(g) prescribing the accounts and records to be kept by licensees;

(h) prescribing the qualifications, powers and duties of persons supervising children in,
  (i) children's residences, or
  (ii) other premises where residential care is provided under the authority of a licence,
  or any class of them;

(i) governing procedures for the admission to and discharge of children from,
  (i) children's residences, or
  (ii) other premises where residential care is provided under the authority of a licence,
  or any class of them;

(j) requiring the operators of children's residences or persons who provide residential care or place children for adoption under the authority of a licence to provide the prescribed information and to make the prescribed returns and reports, and prescribing the information, returns and reports;

(k) prescribing the number of members of the Board, their terms of office and the number of members that is a quorum;

(l) prescribing additional powers, duties and procedures of the Board;

(m) governing the placement of children for adoption;

(n) prescribing rules and standards governing the placement of children by licensees for adoption;

(o) providing for the inspection of the records of persons licensed to place children for adoption;

(p) governing the qualifications of persons or classes of persons employed by persons licensed to place children for adoption;

(q) requiring persons licensed to place children for adoption to be bonded or to submit letters of credit in the prescribed form and terms and with the prescribed collateral security, prescribing the form, terms and collateral security and providing for the forfeiture of bonds and letters of credit and the disposition of the proceeds;

(r) prescribing forms and providing for their use.

Regulations: Part X (Indian and Native Child and Family Services)

223. The Lieutenant Governor in Council may make regulations for the purposes of Part X,

(a) exempting an Indian or native child and family service authority, a band or native community or specified persons or classes of persons, including persons caring for children under customary care, from any provision of this Act or the regulations;

(b) prescribing matters requiring consultation between societies or agencies and bands or native communities for the purposes of clause 213 (h).

PART XII
MISCELLANEOUS

Review of Act

224. (1) The Minister shall periodically conduct a review of this Act or those provisions of it specified by the Minister.

Beginning of review
(2) The Minister shall inform the public when a review under this section begins and what provisions of this Act are included in the review.

Written report
(3) The Minister shall prepare a written report respecting the review and shall make that report available to the public.

Period for review
(4) The first review shall be completed and the report made available to the public within five years after the day this section comes into force.

Same
(5) Each subsequent review shall be completed and the report made available to the public within five years after the day the report on the previous review has been made available to the public.

Glossary of Key Terms

access in the family law context, a child and her non-custodial parent's opportunity to visit with each other, and the right to this opportunity

actus reus Latin for "guilty act"; the objective element of an offence, which may be an act, an omission, or a state of being

administrative tribunal a decision maker or panel of decision makers who decide contentious issues that arise within a particular administrative framework — for example, the Ontario Labour Relations Board

affidavit a witness's written and sworn account of his or her own evidence. Sworn means the witness has promised, before a person who has taken the account, that the contents are true

age of majority the age at which a young person is given full adult rights or responsibilities with respect to a particular subject matter (the age varies depending on the subject-matter)

applicant a person who files an application for legal relief with a court or an administrative tribunal

apprehension in the child protection context, the taking into protective custody of a child

assault under the *Criminal Code*, any unwanted touching; under the common law, a threat of injury with no touching can be an assault

autism a condition in which the sufferer's reaction to stimuli is impaired, often causing learning or behavioural problems

best interests of the child a legal principle, embraced by several statutes and areas of the common law, as a basis for decision-making

bodily harm usually, an injury to the body that has some degree of persistence — that is, it takes time to heal and limits activity

bylaw a rule, policy, law, or regulation, chosen by the organization's members, that governs the operations of a private organization

child of the marriage any child conceived or adopted after a marriage and before a divorce

children of tender years children whose limited development makes them incapable of intending harm in the legal sense, or who require a particular level of, often maternal, care

Children's Lawyer a government office, headed by an individual lawyer, which provides legal assistance to unrepresented child litigants in certain kinds of cases or by order of a court

common law a legal rule or a body of legal principles, established through judicial decisions, that deal with a particular legal issue or subject area

consent order in the context of child protection services, an agreement arrived at voluntarily by two parties that is given legal status as an order by the court

consent the informed, voluntary, and demonstrated approval by one party of the actions of another

convention usually, a traditional rule of law or policy that has persuasive value and tends to be applied by formal decision makers

coroner's inquest a court-like hearing, conducted by the coroner's office, designed to investigate a suspicious death and, often, to provide recommendations for avoiding similar incidents in the future

costs the granting by a court, as a form of legal relief, of a sum, payable by one litigant (usually the unsuccessful one) to the other, to pay for (some) of the costs of the litigation

Criminal Code the statute that describes the legislative component of Canada's criminal law

criminal law laws designed to prevent behaviour harmful to society by punishing those who demonstrate it and by deterring others who might contemplate it

criminal responsibility the condition of being liable to criminal sanctions because one has the capacity to understand the moral wrongness or illegality of one's actions

Crown ward a child or young person who, having been taken into protective custody of a children's aid society, will not be returned to the care of his or her parents and may be made available for adoption

custody (in sentencing context) in the criminal law context, residence in a corrections facility.

custody legal arrangement governing the care of a child; in the child protection context, being kept in a place of safety under the care of a children's aid society.

customary care in the context of the *Child and Family Services Act*, "the care and supervision of an Indian or native child by a person who is not the child's parent, according to the custom of the child's band or native community"

damages monetary compensation for a legal wrong

defendant the accused in a criminal case; or, in a civil case, the person against whom a lawsuit is filed

deterrence in the criminal context, the use of sanctions against convicted offenders to discourage similar offending by those who might contemplate it

differential response a system for distinguishing between serious cases and less serious cases

duty of care in negligence law, an obligation on the part of one person to take into account the effect of his or her actions on another person. The duty usually arises based on a recognized relationship.

enhanced duty to report a duty to report that, if ignored, can lead to the laying of charges

extraordinary measures under the *Child and Family Services Act*, severe measures used to control the symptoms or behaviour of a child with mental health or behavioural problems — for example, the use of physical restraints or the administration of psychotropic drugs

fiduciary duty an enhanced duty of care that arises in a fiduciary relationship

fiduciary somebody who is entrusted with the care of another person based on a relationship of service and/or dependence

foster family a family authorized by a children's aid society to provide residential care for children in need of protective services

guardian a person who, though not the parent of a child, has assumed or is charged with responsibility for his or her care

hybrid offence a crime that allows the prosecution to proceed by way of either summary conviction or indictment

in loco parentis Latin for "in place of a parent"

in need of protection in the context of child protection, a court's finding that action must be taken to protect a child

indictable offence a serious crime that is subject to stiff penalties and that is prosecuted using the more formal of two possible sets of criminal procedures

joint legal custody an arrangement under which both parents of a child have the legal right to make decisions with respect to his or her care, and in which the child lives with one parent most of the time

jurisdictions areas over which the legal authority of a particular statute or court extends

justice of the peace an officer of the court who makes administrative decisions — for example, issuing warrants

lawsuit a formal request, by one party, for the court's assistance in obtaining, through its processes, compensation or relief as against another party

legal capacity the ability of a person, based on his or her personal characteristics (for example, age of majority), to take actions with legal effects (for example, bring a lawsuit)

legislation law passed by a parliament and codified in writing

litigation guardian a person with legal capacity who pursues legal relief on behalf of a person who lacks legal capacity

litigation legal action, usually with a court component — for example, a lawsuit

matrimonial home defined under the *Family Law Act* as a property the value of which, due to its use as a primary residence during a marriage or common law union, must be divided equally between the divorcing spouses upon dissolution of the union

mens rea Latin for "guilty mind"; the subjective element of an offence that describes the state of mind or required intention of the accused

necessaries of life under the criminal law, a fairly narrowly defined list including food, shelter, clothing, and necessary medical treatment

negligence the failure of a person to respect or carry out a duty of care owed to another

parent-model residence a children's residence that is structured like a family home, with one or two adult caregivers and a small number of children

party an individual or corporation with an interest in — who will be affected by — legal proceedings

peace officer a term that is usually broader than "police officer," that can be assigned to an individual (usually a government employee), and that is the basis for that individual's authority to take law enforcement or victim protection action

place of safety under the *Child and Family Services Act*, a hospital, foster home, or other residential facility or place designated as a place of safety under section 17

plaintiff a person who commences a lawsuit

plan of care a personalized statement of a child's needs and the strategies that will be undertaken to meet those needs that is generally prepared by a child protection agency and approved by a court

preliminary inquiry a judicial hearing where the prosecution must prove that it has enough evidence to prove, if uncontested and accepted by the trier of fact, that the accused is guilty of the charges against him or her; also called a charge screening device

prescriptive standards standards that prescribe (require) specific action

private guardian an individual who has assumed responsibility for a child (as distinguished from an agent of the province)

procedural fairness fairness that flows from the observance of procedures designed to promote the protection of individual rights

proscriptive standards standards that prohibit particular actions

provincial school attendance counsellor an agent of the Ministry of Education charged with confirming compliance with compulsory school attendance legislation

question of fact something that can only be determined by the court after an examination of the specific circumstances of the case

real property land and/or buildings

recidivism the tendency to revert to criminality and commit further offences

regulation a legal instrument that is subservient to a statute and created to provide guidance for the administration of the statute

restitution the act of putting someone back into the (usually economic) position that he or she enjoyed before a culpable event intervened

restraining order a court order that imposes restrictions on the person to whom it applies — for example, restrictions on movement

sanctions punishments imposed as a consequence for breaking a law

secular not religious in nature

sex offender registry a government database in which indentifying information about people who have committed sexual offences in the past is collected

shared custody (usually used to describe physical custody) an arrangement under which a child resides for part of the time with each of two or more parents

society wardship term that describes the status of a child in care who is considered to be under the temporary care of a society and who will eventually be returned to his or her parent(s)

sole custody an arrangement under which one parent is charged with almost all child care responsibilities and in which the child resides full-time with that parent

staff-model residence a children's residence in which care is provided by staff to a number of children not related to the staff or to each other

standard of care the standard by which discharge of a duty of care is measured, which depends on the relationship between the parties and the circumstances under which the duty arises

standing the status of being recognized by a court as a legitimate party to a legal proceeding

status immigrant an immigrant who has been granted rights attendant with citizenship — for example, the right to work

statute a written law passed by a parliament

summary conviction offence a less serious crime than an indictable offence that carries a light penalty; the accused may be tried in Provincial Court without the benefit of a jury or a preliminary hearing

supervised access access that is subject to supervision, usually by a social worker, to ensure the safety of the child

supervision order an order by the court that provides that certain activities (for example, a child's residence in the family home after a period of society care) will be monitored by a third party (usually a government employee)

temporary care agreement under the *Child and Family Services Act*, a voluntary agreement between a society and a child's parent(s) or guardian that provides for residential care of the child on a temporary basis

trust a legal relationship under which one person (the trustee) holds and manages assets for the benefit of another person (the beneficiary), often until the beneficiary is able to manage the assets for himself or herself

trustee a person who holds property in trust for another

warrant a document (or occasionally, oral statement) providing court authorization for certain described action (such as the apprehension of a child)

youth justice court a special court created by the *Youth Criminal Justice Act* for handling criminal cases where the accused was between the ages of 12 and 17 at the time of the alleged offence

Index

Acknowledgments

American Academy of Pediatrics Theo Solomon, "History and Demography of Child Abuse" (1973), 51:4 *Pediatrics* 773-76. Volumes 1-112, copyright © 1948-2003 by the American Academy of Pediatrics. All rights reserved.

Canadian Council on Social Development David P. Ross, "Rethinking Child Poverty" (1999), 23:1 *Perception Magazine*. http://www.ccsd.ca.

Jessie's Centre for Teenagers Jessie's Centre for Teenagers, *Jessie's Volunteer Child Abuse and Neglect Reporting Policies and Procedures* (unpublished) (Toronto: Jessie's Centre for Teenagers, 2005), at 7.

Ontario Association of Children's Aid Societies Ontario Association of Children's Aid Societies, Toronto, 2005, http://www.oacas.org.

Public Works and Government Services Canada Health Canada, *Language Barriers in Access to Health Care* (Ottawa: Minister of Public Works and Government Services Canada, 2001). Reproduced with the permission of the Minister of Public Works and Government Services Canada, 2005.